HINDU SCRIPTURES

HINDU SCRIPTURES

Edited with new translations by
DOMINIC GOODALL
Wolfson College, University of Oxford
Based on an anthology by
R. C. ZAEHNER

University of California
Berkeley Los Angeles

University of California Press
Berkeley and Los Angeles, California

Published by arrangement with J. M. Dent,
a division of The Orion Publishing Group

Cataloguing-in-Publication Data on file with the Library of Congress.
ISBN 0-520-20782-3; 0-520-20778-5 (pbk.)

Printed in the United Kingdom
9 8 7 6 5 4 3 2 1

CONTENTS

NOTE ON THE EDITOR

DOMINIC GOODALL was educated at Ampleforth College and at Pembroke College, Oxford, where he read Sanskrit. After two years at the University of Hamburg (as a Hanseatic scholar of the Stiftung Freiherr von Stein) and doctoral studies at Wolfson College, Oxford, he is now attached to the Institut Français de Pondichéry in South India and is working with the manuscript collection there.

INTRODUCTION

Two anthologies entitled *Hindu Scriptures* have previously appeared in the Everyman series alone, that of Nicol MacNicol in 1938 and that of Professor R. C. Zaehner in 1966. Now that I come to add a third it is perhaps not inappropriate, paraphrasing P. G. Wodehouse, to express the modest hope that it will be considered worthy of inclusion in the list of the Hundred Best Books of that title.[1]

The texts in the anthology are arranged in chronological order and this Introduction explains the reasons for their inclusion, sets them in context, and briefly characterizes their contents. Much of the last anthology has been retained unchanged, but cuts have had to be made to accommodate portions of three previously unrepresented works: the *Yājñavalkya-Smṛti*, the *Kiraṇa-Tantra*, and the *Bhāgavata-Purāṇa*. With this new selection the principal aim has been to broaden the book's scope. Most would hesitate to define what is and what is not Hindu scripture, and many may quibble with what I have presumed to include, but a good case can be made for including more than just the *Bhagavad-Gītā* and the Vedic corpus, to which the selections of both previous editors were restricted.

Apart from the new translations one or two extra portions from works that featured in the previous selections have also been added in an attempt to make the selections from the earliest material more representative of what they contain. Professor Zaehner perhaps tended to exclude from the early Upanishads passages that conflicted with his reading of them as centred on a *philosophia perennis*, and some of these have been restored. From among the Vedic hymns, he has included only ones which point forward to later developments, and this weakness has been remedied by supplementing his selection with three more hymns from the *Ṛg-Veda*. The bias in his selection is explained when we know his understandable, but by no means universally held views on the Vedic corpus (p. v):

it is generally agreed that only a relatively small portion of it is of abiding importance and interest; and this portion is the latest in time, – what is called the *Vedānta* or 'End of the Veda', which means those speculative treatises in prose and verse known as the *Upanishads.*

The Vedic corpus

Veda is a Sanskrit word meaning 'knowledge' and is commonly used either to refer to the entire Vedic corpus of literature or to one of the four collections with its dependent prose literature: the *Ṛg-Veda*, the Veda of hymns; the *Yajur-Veda*, that of sacrificial formulas; the *Sāma-Veda*, that of chants; and the *Atharva-Veda*, most of whose hymns are magical spells and incantations. The latter is the latest collection and is often, even in later times, not included among them (hence its separate enumeration in *Yājña-valkya-Smṛti* 1:101 and omission in *Bhagavad-Gītā* IX.17 and 20). The earliest parts of these collections, the hymns, were remarkably faithfully preserved for centuries by oral transmission even long after scripts developed for writing Sanskrit. This feat was achieved not just by pupils learning by rote and repeatedly reciting the texts as composed, but also by their learning and reciting texts with the words rearranged in the repetitive patterns. The most complicated of these devices, intended to secure the textual transmission from all error, is called the *ghanapāṭha* ('dense text') in which the order of words is ab, ba, abc, cba, abc, bc, cb, bcd, etc.

Numerous recensions of each collection of the Vedic corpus developed, many of which have now been partially or entirely lost. Each collection was divided into the following four groups of material: Saṃhitā, Brāhmaṇa, Āraṇyaka and Upanishad. The Saṃhitā of each collection contains its hymns or mantras, which form the earliest stratum of Vedic literature.[2] (The term Veda has in recent times been incorrectly used to refer to this part of each collection alone.) The Brāhmaṇas, which are perhaps the earliest examples of sustained prose writing in an Indo-European language, are attached treatises that enjoin and describe rituals and relate aetiological myths about them. Forming the end of the Brāhmaṇas are the Āraṇyakas ('Forest Books'), probably so called because their material was too secret and too dangerous to be taught except in the forest. The oldest of the Upanishads are embedded in the Āraṇyakas and usually form their concluding portion.[3] The *Bṛhadāraṇyaka* Upanishad, 'the big forest-book-Upanishad', is both an Āraṇyaka and an Upanishad and forms the last part of the *Śatapatha-Brāhmaṇa*, a Brāhmaṇa of the White *Yajur-Veda*; the *Chāndogya Upanishad* forms the concluding part of the *Chāndogya Brāhmaṇa* belonging to the *Sāma-Veda*.

The earliest entries in this anthology are hymns from the one surviving recension of the Saṃhitā of the *Ṛg-Veda*, universally acknowledged to be the oldest collection of Vedic hymns. The dates of composition of the hymns of the Vedas, the dates of their organization, whether their composers were recently arrived in North India or long-settled nomadic tribals of Indo-European origin or mixed descendants of such Āryan settlers and indigenous peoples – all these issues are hotly debated, and the attendant problems of interpreting linguistic and archaeological evidence are far from solved. An influential traditional view of these questions is that of the Mīmāṃsakas, adherents of the orthodox atheist school of thought that was devoted to the exegesis of Vedic scripture. These held that the Veda was eternal and without author. They disregarded the pointers in the Vedas to human authorship and to strata of composition, and they justified their position with the help of a fourfold categorization of scripture: injunctions to perform Vedic ritual (*vidhi*); mantras, the use of which necessarily accompanies ritual; names (*nāmadheya*); and *arthavāda*, praise of ritual comprising explanatory material, exhortations to perform it, and aetiological myths. Whatever they classified in this last category they were not obliged to understand to be literally true. The views of recent Indological scholarship are various; but a consensus shared by many[4] is that an Āryan invasion took place in the second millennium BC; that the oldest hymns, those of the *Ṛg-Veda*, were composed between 1300 and 1000 BC; that the Brāhmaṇas and early prose Upanishads were composed between 800 and 500 BC; and the verse Upanishads, between 500 and 200 BC.

The religion of the earliest poets of the *Ṛg-Veda* was polytheistic – like that of other Indo-European peoples – and it contains hymns to a large number of deities, most of whom are powers of nature: Agni (fire), Parjanya (rain), Vāyu (wind), Uṣas (dawn), etc. These powers are partially personified in the hymns; that is to say the attributes of the forces or things that they are or represent are often mixed up in the immediate context with anthropomorphic attributes. The most completely anthropomorphic and the most lauded deity of the *Ṛg-Veda* is Indra, to whom about a quarter of its 1028 hymns are addressed. He is a warrior hero associated with storms and praised for his destruction of semi-anthropomorphic demons. The legends about these demons, indeed all mythology in the *Ṛg-Veda*, can be gleaned only from often obscure allusions and are never related. (This may have to do with the structure of the hymns, in which each stanza can stand by itself as an independent unit of sense.) After Indra the most prominent deity is Agni, the god of fire, and this reflects the importance in the religion of the Vedic hymns of sacrifice, in which Agni is the messenger and mediator between gods and men. By the time of the Brāhmaṇa literature the sacrifice was conceived of as indispensable for sustaining the cosmos. Another crucial deity of the sacrifice is Soma. Soma is a liquid pressed in bowls and passed through a woollen filter from a plant that may have been Ephedra, but whose identity has been debated from the beginnings of Vedic research. (In Classical India, long after the Vedic age, other substances were used as substitutes of Soma in the rituals.) It is the favourite drink of the immortals, particularly of the valorous Indra, and is often identified with the moon, which, when full, is said to be brimming with the ambrosial liquid. Hymns to Indra, Agni and Soma did not feature in the previous selection and translations by Edgerton and by Wendy Doniger have been supplied here.

In what are assumed to be later hymns we can observe the tendency to attribute ever greater qualities to the particular deity being addressed. If this were isolated, then it might have been supposed to be incipient monotheism; but different gods are praised for disproportionate and overlapping powers. It is a logical impossibility that each should be as powerful as claimed. This modified polytheism has been called henotheism. Professor Edgerton[5] distinguished two kinds of henotheistic hymn: that in which other deities are identified with, and so absorbed into, the deity being addressed (*Ṛg-Veda* II, i); and that in which such a plethora of attributes or attributes of such a kind are ascribed as could belong only to a single all-powerful deity (*Ṛg-Veda* II, xii).

Professor Zaehner's selection from the *Ṛg-Veda* predominantly contained hymns that point forward to later developments. Thus he includes the hymn to Rudra (II, xxxiii), a minor storm deity at the time of the composition of the hymns, but subsequently of vast importance as Śiva, the central deity of monotheistic sects such as the Śaiva Siddhānta (a sect represented in this anthology with the *Kiraṇa-Tantra*) and a popular focus of devotion outside them too, and a hymn to Viṣṇu (I, cliv), whose importance also grew enormously after the Vedic period and who reappears in this anthology in his incarnation as Kṛṣṇa, both in the *Bhagavad-Gītā* and in the *Bhāgavata-Purāṇa*. He also included a number of cosmogonic hymns from the tenth and last section (*maṇḍala*) of the *Ṛg-Veda*, which, though it contains some old material, is agreed by many to be the latest part of the Saṃhitā. Instead of composing paeans to the older deities of the pantheon, in whom they have perhaps lost faith, the authors of these hymns speculated about the origins of the universe and addressed their praises to functional deities responsible for its creation. Hymns of this kind are those to Viśvakarman, 'creator of all' (X, lxxxi and lxxxii); to Puruṣa, 'primal man' (X, xc); and to Prajāpati, 'lord of offspring' (X, cxxi).

From the *Atharva-Veda* Professor Zaehner included further examples of such speculative gropings towards a first principle of the universe. Magical charms, imprecations, amulets, pleas for self-protection and for the destruction of enemies in fact make up the bulk of that collection. This combination of magical spells for small personal goals with speculation about cosmogony might at first seem odd; but Edgerton has asserted that it is a natural corollary of the view of the authors about the nature of knowledge and of their motivation for seeking it: he suggests that the quest for knowledge is not motivated by interest in it for its own sake, but by a desire for attaining power. Knowledge of a thing is conceived of as a means of gaining magical power over it and this, he suggests, underlies the mystical identifications that we also find in the literature of the Brāhmaṇa period:

> We want to control, let us say, the breath of life, in ourselves or someone else (perhaps an enemy); so we earnestly and insistently identify it with something that we *can* control, and the trick is turned.[6]

The hymns of the *Yajur-Veda* and *Sāma-Veda*, sometimes referred to as liturgical collections, are not represented in this anthology. Those of the *Sāma-Veda* are almost all taken from the

Ṛg-Veda – distinctive of the *Sāma-Veda* is that its hymns are sung with elaborate chants. A large number of the hymns of the *Yajur-Veda* are also from the *Ṛg-Veda*, but there they are organized from the point of view of their relevance to sacrifice.

The Upanishads

Of the thirteen Upanishads included in the last Everyman edition only six have been retained here: the two early prose Upanishads, the *Bṛhadāraṇyaka* and the *Chāndogya*, which belong to the last phase of Brāhmaṇa literature, and four slightly later verse Upanishads, the *Īśā*, the *Kaṭha*, the *Māṇḍūkya*, and the *Śvetāśvatara*. Some of the archaic passages – omitted from the *Bṛhadāraṇyaka* by Zaehner – that are more typical of an earlier phase of Brāhmaṇa literature have been restored. This means that the present selection of Upanishads is similar to that of Nicol Macnicol's Everyman edition of 1938 (he included the first five of these in toto). Having to oust the Upanishads that Professor Zaehner added is indeed regrettable but space is thereby made for representatives of other, later genres of scripture.

As an admirer of the Upanishads, Professor Zaehner admits to finding certain archaic passages embarrassing and has not hesitated to remove them. In Professor Edgerton's felicitous words, 'the dry bones of the Vedic ritual cult frequently rattle about in them in quite a noisy fashion and seriously strain our patience and our charity';[7] nevertheless it is important that they are represented, because they go some way towards explaining the context from which the mystical ideas of the Upanishads grow. The first such passage is the very first section of the *Bṛhadāraṇyaka*: here parts of the world are identified, on grounds that are not obviously discernible, with parts of the horse destined for sacrifice. Such identifications are characteristic of an earlier phase of Brāhmaṇa literature, in which all manner of deliberations about sacrifice are gathered together. At first sight groundless, they make sense – when understood in the light of Edgerton's above-quoted remarks about knowledge being conceived of as a means of gaining power – as a rationale of how the immensely prestigious horse sacrifice brings the universe under the control of the sacrificer. The quest for knowledge of the universe that characterizes the Upanishads, may be understood in a similar light:

> The Upanishads . . . seek to know the real truth about the universe, not for its own sake; not for the mere joy of knowledge; not as an abstract speculation; but simply because they conceive such knowledge as a short-cut to the control of every cosmic power.[8]

It should be emphasized that this is by no means the only way of looking at the Upanishads: Professor Zaehner quotes from *Chāndogya* VII, xxv

> This [Infinite] is below, it is above, it is to the west, to the east, to the south, to the north. Truly it is this whole universe.
>
> Next the teaching concerning the ego.
>
> I am below, I am above, I am to the west, to the east, to the south, to the north. Truly I am this whole universe.
>
> Next the teaching concerning the Self. The Self is below, the Self is above, the Self is to the west, to the east, to the south, to the north. Truly the Self is this whole universe.

and he has this to say about it (p. viii–ix):

> Now this may not sound particularly sensible to the modern mind, but it does express what so-called 'nature mystics' experience and try to describe. The barrier between subject and object seems magically to melt away, and experiencer, experience and the thing experienced seem to merge into one single whole: the One indwelling the human spirit realizes its own identity with the same One which is the unchanging ground of the phenomenal world outside. This is the lesson tirelessly rammed home in the Upanishads: it is an expression of something that cannot be logically formulated, but can only be hinted at in paradox . . .

Nonetheless Edgerton's view that the quest for knowledge is a quest for power is a convincing attempt to explain what motivated the thinkers of the early Upanishads – it accounts for the oft-repeated assertions of the power that knowledge brings:

> Whoso thus knows that he is Brahman, becomes this whole [universe]. Even the gods have not the power to cause him to un-Be, for he becomes their own self. (*Bṛhadāraṇyaka* I, iv.10)

> It has been said: 'Since men think that by knowing Brahman they will become the All', what was it that Brahman knew by which he became the All? (*Bṛhadāraṇyaka* I, iv.9)

> This sacrifice is fivefold; cattle are fivefold; man is fivefold; this whole universe is fivefold, – everything that exists. Whoso thus knows wins this whole universe. (*Bṛhadāraṇyaka* I, iv.17)

> In whatever family there is a man who has this knowledge, the family is called after him; but whoever sets himself up in rivalry with him, withers away; and after withering away, he finally dies. (*Bṛhadāraṇyaka* I, v.21)

> He who knows this great and strange being (*yakṣa*), the first-born, [who is] the truth and Brahman, overcomes these worlds.
> 'Could he be overcome who thus knows that this great and strange being, the first-born, is the truth and Brahman?'
> '[No,] for Brahman is Truth.' (*Bṛhadāraṇyaka* V, iv)

> Just as [a clod of earth] would be smashed to pieces on striking a solid stone, so too would anyone who bears ill-will towards one who knows this or who does him harm, be smashed to pieces, for he is a solid stone. (*Chāndogya* I, ii.8)

> But whoever thus knows these five fires is not defiled by evil ... Pure and clean, he reaches the world of the good and pure (*puṇya*), – whoever thus knows, whoever thus knows. (*Chāndogya* V, x.10)

Further assertions of the corresponding impotence of ignorance could be similarly listed:

> '... he is the "Person" of the Upanishads about whom I question you. If you do not tell me who he is, your head will fall off.'
> But Śākalya did not know him, and so his head did fall off. And robbers made away with his bones, thinking they were something else. (*Bṛhadāraṇyaka* III, ix.26)

Furthermore, Professor Edgerton's analysis makes logically cohesive what other writers assume to be disparate and jarring:

> There is much in the *Upanishads* which belongs to their own time. This has a historical interest, but not the spiritual value that belongs to all times.[9]

and more pointedly

> In a few passages the Upanishads are sublime in their conception of the Infinite and of God, but more often they are puerile and groveling in trivialities and superstitions.[10]

The salient characteristic of the early Upanishads is the quest for a basis for the world. This is found in brahman – a word which in the language of the Ṛg-Vedic hymns seems to have meant 'sacred knowledge' or that in which sacred knowledge is expressed, 'sacred hymn'; but brahman shifts in meaning so that it becomes identified with the origin of the universe (*Bṛhadāraṇyaka* I, iv.10–11), with all the gods (*Bṛhadāraṇyaka* III, ix.1–9), with everything in the universe (*Bṛhadāraṇyaka* I, iv.10), with the soul of the universe (*Bṛhadāraṇyaka* II, v), and with the soul of the individual as the universe in microcosm (*Bṛhadāraṇyaka* III, iv.1). In spite of its being in everything, it is beyond understanding:

> This Self – [what can one say of it but] 'No, no!' It is impalpable, for it cannot be grasped; indestructible, for it cannot be destroyed; free from attachment, for it is not attached [to anything], not bound. It does not quaver nor can it be hurt. (*Bṛhadāraṇyaka* III, ix.26)

But in sleep this absolute is attained:

> When a man is properly (*nāma*) asleep (*svapiti*), then, dear boy, is he suffused in Being – he will have returned to his own (*svam apīta*). That is why it is said of him '*svapiti*, he is asleep'; for he will have returned to his own (*svam apīto bhavati*). (*Chāndogya* VI, viii.1)

and it is attained in moments of intense experience:

> Just as a man, closely embraced by his loving wife, knows nothing without, nothing within, so does this 'person', closely embraced by the Self that consists of wisdom (*prājña*), know nothing without, nothing within. That is his [true] form in which [all] his desires are fulfilled, in which Self [alone] is his desire, in which he has no desire, no sorrow. (*Bṛhadāraṇyaka* IV, iii.21)

It is on the ground of such and other assertions from this latest phase of Vedic literature (the Vedānta) that the philosophers of the monist school of Advaita Vedānta defended their position that the universe is one and that the plurality of the empirical world is illusory. The most famous writer to apply in his exegesis of scriptures the monist tenets of this school was Śaṅkara (fl. c. 700 AD[11]). By these thinkers the empirical world came to be called such names as *avidyā*, 'nescience', and *māyā*, 'cosmic illusion'.[12]

But the Upanishads do not always support monism, because they are not systematic treatises expounding and defending a single world view. There are points on which they contradict both each other and themselves. Thus, in spite of its clearly monistic passages, the *Chāndogya* also has this to say of liberation (VIII, xii.1–3):

> For sure this body is mortal, held in the grip of death. Yet it is the dwelling-place of the immortal, incorporeal Self. [And this Self,] while still in the body, is held in the grip of pleasure and pain; and so long as it remains in the body there is no means of ridding it of pleasure and pain. But once it is freed from the body, pleasure and pain cannot [so much as] touch it.
>
> The wind has no body. Clouds, thunder and lightning, – these too have no body. So, just as these arise from [the broad expanse of] space up there and plunge into the highest light, revealing themselves each in its own form, so too does this deep serenity arise out of this body and plunge into the highest light, revealing itself in its own form. Such a one is a superman (*uttara puruṣa*); and there he roves around, laughing, playing, taking his pleasure with women, chariots, or friends and remembering no more that excrescence [which was] his body.

Furthermore, some of the later Upanishads, such as the *Śvetāśvatara* and the *Kaṭha*, introduce ideas that are characteristic of Sāṅkhya thinkers. These dualists held that souls and matter are radically different, that souls become involved in the evolutes of matter, mistakenly identify with their bodies that are made up of those evolutes and are then trapped in earthly existence. They enumerated twenty-three evolutes of matter: the intellect (*buddhi*); the sense of self-identity responsible for the mistaken identification of the self with what is material (*ahaṅkāra*); the mind; the ten faculties of sense and action; the five subtle elements (*tanmātra*); and the five gross elements. These, together with souls (*puruṣa*) and matter itself, were known as the twenty-five principles (*tattva*). In *Kaṭha* III.10–11 a number of these are listed, admittedly not exactly as they are in the mature school, and in *Śvetāśvatara* I.4 numerology appears that has often been claimed to be distinctive of Sāṅkhya thinkers.[13] Some assert that certain key ideas of the Sāṅkhyas appear in embryo in the earliest Upanishads: thus seventeen of the principles might be said to be discernible in *Bṛhadāraṇyaka* II, iv.11; and *Chāndogya* VI, iv is said to describe what became the three *guṇas*, the strands of light/good (*sattva*), passion/activity/redness (*rajas*), and darkness/delusion (*tamas*) –

strands which, according to the Sāṅkhyas, pervade the entire material world.

Another important feature of these two Upanishads is their theism. In the case of the *Śvetāśvatara*, this is focused on the minor Vedic deity Rudra/Śiva (IV.12–22). The *Śvetāśvatara* in fact bears signs characteristic of a particular theistic cult, that of the Pāśupatas. This ascetic cult of Paśupati (Śiva as lord of animals or bound souls) was open to Brahmin males who had had Vedic initiation; but those who joined it were referred to as *atyāśramin*, 'beyond the orthodox walks of life' (for which see *Yājñavalkya-Smṛti* 1:1 and note ad loc.), because they withdrew from ordinary life and imitated Rudra, by such practices as bathing in ash. *Śvetāśvatara* VI.21 proclaims that it is the teaching of the sage Śvetāśvatara to *atyāśramins* (which Zaehner, following Śaṅkara's obfuscating gloss, translates 'those who had gone furthest on the ascetic path'). They held that only Rudra could rescue souls from the fetters of worldly existence. The *Śvetāśvatara* repeatedly mentions fetters (I.8, I.11, IV.15, IV.16, V.13, VI.13) and the image of the net (*jāla*) (V.3, III.1), which is a Pāśupata synonym for primal matter. The term *māyā* also occurs in this sense (IV.9 and 10) – a usage transmitted to the cult of the Śaiva Siddhānta whose tenets are described below in the section on the *Kiraṇa-Tantra*. The Pāśupatas' life of asceticism culminated in withdrawal to a cremation ground to meditate on five Vedic mantras and to achieve thereby uninterrupted consciousness of Rudra. They held that the qualities of Śiva would pass into them at death. It is a moot point whether the *Śvetāśvatara* represents an early stage of development of what eventually became Pāśupatism or whether it is a work that draws on and modifies the ideas of an already developed Pāśupata cult.

It remains to draw attention to one more nexus of ideas, one that has appeared since the period of the Vedic hymns but has already become well established by the time of the redaction of the Upanishads and is deeply rooted in all subsequent Indian thought, including the religious systems of the heterodox Jains and Buddhists – the belief in a cycle of rebirth determined by previous actions.

The earliest term that presupposes such a cycle is *punarmṛtyu*, 're-death'. This occurs in Brāhmaṇa literature and is still in use in the *Bṛhadāraṇyaka* (I, ii.7; I, v.2; III, ii.10; III, iii.2). The *Chāndogya* (V, x) gives a fascinating early account of the supposed mechanics of metempsychosis, and both early Upanishads make clear the causal link between good and bad action and good and bad rebirth (*Chāndogya* V, x.10 and *Bṛhadāraṇyaka* IV, iv.4–5). In subsequent Indian thought the virtually unquestioned belief is that humans are tied to what might, unless corrected, be an unending series of rebirths, and this was invariably perceived as an evil. All subsequent heterodox and orthodox soteriologies, however they defined their final goal – proximity to Viṣṇu in his heavenly abode, Vaikuṇṭha; identity to Śiva in powers of knowledge and action; disjunction of the spirit from the material – conceived of it as a liberation from this painful and potentially endless round of birth and death. The commonest term for this transmigration, *saṃsāra*, is first attested in this sense in the verse Upanishads (*Kaṭha* III:7; *Śvetāśvatara* VI.16).

The Categories of śruti *and* smṛti

We have so far discussed what is accepted by the orthodox to be part of the fundamental canon of 'Hindu Scripture', the Veda. This corpus is often referred to as *śruti*, 'hearing'. *Smṛti*, 'remembering', designates scripture of a lower order that, from an orthodox perspective, is authoritative only where it does not contradict *śruti*. *Śruti* is accorded vast respect and is of enormous intrinsic interest. But the veneration in which it has been held by subsequent Indian thinkers has not meant that all the ideas expounded therein were believed, studied, or even understood as intended by its authors and redactors. Many of those who asserted the absolute authority of the Veda – such as the Mīmāṃsakas, mentioned above – denied even that it had author or beginning. For some, it might even be argued, the significance of the content of scripture was in inverse proportion to the reverence they accorded it. No apology then need be made for widening the scope of the selection to include more works of *smṛti*. The previous editors included one work of this category, the *Bhagavad-Gītā*; and this Zaehner was at pains to stress had almost the status of *śruti*, indeed the colophons of many of its manuscripts call it an Upanishad.

The boundaries of *śruti* are clearly defined, for it refers to the Vedic corpus and no more; but *smṛti* is an elastic category in which different thinkers included different texts. The commentator Vijñāneśvara (ad *Yājñavalkya-Smṛti* 1:7) would have it include only treatises on moral law (*dharmaśāstra*); but the text of the *Yājñavalkya-Smṛti* itself probably intends to define *smṛti* with its enumeration of authorities in 1:3 (the first member of the list comprises *śruti*):

> The Vedas, together with the Purāṇas, the [system of logic and natural philosophy called] Nyāya, the [exegetical school of] Mīmāṃsā, treatises on moral duty (*dharmaśāstra*), and the [six classes of work that are] necessary auxiliaries (*aṅga*) [to the Veda, namely pronunciation, prosody, grammar, word-derivation, astronomy and ritual (*kalpa*)] are the fourteen bases of knowledge and moral duty (*vidyānāṃ dharmasya ca*).

Even in this relatively full list the epics of the *Mahābhārata* and the *Rāmāyaṇa*, which many would without hesitation include, are not mentioned, and it is left to a commentator, Viśvarūpa, to explain that they are to be understood under Purāṇas. Prosody, grammar and the like serve to perpetuate the accurate transmission of the Veda; the inclusion of treatises on such subjects that relate only indirectly to the core agenda of scripture – theology, soteriology, and morality – demonstrates that renderings of the term *smṛti*, such as 'secondary scriptural revelation', are not wholly satisfactory. In this anthology three works of *smṛti*, are represented: the *Bhagavad-Gītā*, the *Yājñavalkya-Smṛti*, and the *Bhāgavata-Purāṇa*.

The Bhagavad-Gītā

The *Bhagavad-Gītā* (hereafter *Gītā*) is a tiny portion of the vast epic, the *Mahābhārata*, 'the great history of the descendants of Bharata'. Two sides of a family, the Pāṇḍavas and the Kauravas, are drawn up ready for war over their disputed kingdom after a failed attempt made by Kṛṣṇa, who is Viṣṇu incarnate, to sue for peace. The *Gītā* consists of a discourse between Arjuna, the third of the Pāṇḍava brothers, and Kṛṣṇa, who is acting as his charioteer. The dialogue is relayed by the minister Sañjaya to the blind king of the Kauravas, Dhṛtarāṣṭra. Standing on his chariot between the warring factions arrayed for battle, Arjuna loses conviction in the war that is about to begin, and Kṛṣṇa persuades him that he must fight.

Some scholars have suggested that the whole *Gītā* is an early interpolation, others – on grounds of its length being inappropriate to the dramatic context or of philosophical inconsistencies – suggest that only parts of it have been interpolated. The *Mahābhārata*, in which it is embedded, is a text of many layers transmitted in a number of regional recensions, and it is often impossible to assert with certainty what is early and what is late in it. These speculative doubts are not considered here and the *Gītā* is treated as a unitary composition of the last half of the first millennium BC.

After the scene has been set in the first chapter, Kṛṣṇa argues that Arjuna should not shy away from battle, that killing is not really killing, because souls are indestructible:

Who thinks that he can be a slayer,
Who thinks that he is slain,
Both these have no [right] knowledge:
He slays not, is not slain.

Never is he born nor dies;
Never did he come to be, nor will he ever come to be again:
Unborn, eternal, everlasting he – primeval:
He is not slain when the body is slain. (II.19–20, cf. *Kaṭha* II.19)

He reminds Arjuna (II.31–7) that it is his duty (*svadharma*) as a Kṣatriya, a man of the estate of warriors and kings, to fight. (For the occupations of the estates see *Yājñavalkya-Smṛti* 1:119–20.) He impresses upon Arjuna that he must act in accordance with the duties of his estate, but with utter disregard for the fruits of his actions (II.47). This ideal of dispassionate performance of enjoined action is taken to a logical extreme:

Better one's own duty (*dharma*) [to perform], though void of merit,
Than to do another's well:
Better to die within [the sphere of] one's own duty:
Perilous is the duty of other men. (III.35)

After this direct treatment of Arjuna's dilemma about whether to fight, Kṛṣṇa embarks on a number of theological and soteriological digressions, in the course of which he grants Arjuna a vision of himself as supreme God (Chapter XI).

In the Upanishads there is no sign of the emerging prominence of Kṛṣṇa/Viṣṇu (he is addressed as Viṣṇu in XI.24 and 30), and his unprecedented appearance in the *Gītā* as omnipotent all-pervading God is mysterious. It might in part be accounted for by the fact that the highest of the 'footsteps' of the minor Vedic solar deity, Viṣṇu, (for which see *Ṛg-Veda* I, cliv) was conceived of as the highest point in the universe and thus a goal in the after life.[14] Viṣṇu later came to be identified with numerous mythical figures (commonly ten incarnations (*avatāra*), including that as the Buddha) of whom Kṛṣṇa and Rāma are the best known, and the *Gītā* contains verses that enable later theologians to accommodate these:

> For whenever the law of righteousness (*dharma*)
> Withers away, and lawlessness (*adharma*)
> Raises its head
> Then do I generate Myself [on earth]. (IV.7)

As in the *Kaṭha* and the *Śvetāśvatara* Upanishads, much of the speculation in the *Gītā* about the universe is in terms that are characteristic of the school of the Sāṅkhyas (XIII.5 lists the bottom twenty-four principles of the Sāṅkhyas in random order, III.43 lists some of them in the standard hierarchy, and many passages (e.g. Chapter XIV) deal with the three strands (*guṇa*) that pervade the material world), but the *Gītā* does not give a reasoned and consistent presentation of the Sāṅkhya cosmos as described in the works of the mature school. This is not just because the *Gītā* is not a systematic work. The strict dualism between souls and matter and the absence of a personal god, both defining features of the classical school of the Sāṅkhyas, are not characteristics of the *Kaṭha* and *Śvetāśvatara* Upanishads either – and those are among the earliest sources in which categories associated with the Sāṅkhyas appear – and so we should not expect to find them in the *Gītā*.

According to the Sāṅkhyas, as we have seen above, souls, which are by definition sentient and inactive (V.8–9), become (unaccountably) involved with insentient, active matter (III.28) and mistakenly identify themselves with it. Souls are passive observers of the transformation of matter that is the universe (XIII.29); it is their involvement in this transformation that condemns them to a potentially endless cycle of death and rebirth in the material world (XIII.21); and they attain release (*brahman*) by knowing their essential difference from matter (XIII.23 and 30). In the classical school of the Sāṅkhyas souls are numerically distinct both in the world and in release from worldly existence. In the *Gītā* this is not the case: Brahman, the world-absolute of the Upanishads, is identified (V.24–6) with *nirvāṇa*, a term for liberation shared with Buddhism, and Brahman and *nirvāṇa* are said to be in or on Kṛṣṇa (VI.15, VI.30, XIV.27), who is that of which there is nothing higher (VII.7), and who is the father who inseminates Brahman, the womb (XIV.4). Although Kṛṣṇa *is* everything (VII.19), the *Gītā* does not assert, as, for instance, does the *Chāndogya*, (VI, viii–xvi), that the individual self *is* the universe, but that

> In the region of the heart of all
> Contingent beings dwells the Lord,
> Twirling them hither and thither by his uncanny power (*māyā*)
> [Like puppets] fixed in a machine. (XVIII.61)

and

> In the world of living things a [minute] part of Me,
> Eternal [still], becomes a living [self],
> Drawing to itself the five senses and the mind,
> Which have their roots in Nature. (XV.7)

Furthermore, the state of ultimate release is not consistently described: in VI.15 and XIV.26–7 it is said to be *nirvāṇa* or Brahman, which is in Kṛṣṇa; in XVIII.68 *Kṛṣṇa* speaks of souls coming to himself; in XVIII.55 and XI.54 of them entering himself; but in XIV.1–2 he states

> . . . On knowing this all sages, when they passed on hence,
> Attained the highest prize.
>
> With this wisdom as their bulwark
> They reached a rank [in the order of existence] equivalent to (*sādharmya*) my own;
> And even when [the universe is once again] engendered, they are not born [again] . . .

Kṛṣṇa teaches (III.3) two ways to attain liberation: that of the means of knowledge (*jñānayoga*), which is accompanied by the renunciation of action, and the means of dispassionate action (*karmayoga*), in which people perform what is enjoined for them without any interest in the fruit that it brings them. Knowledge of the truth of the doctrines discussed above is salvific (as we saw in XIII.23), and so too is the course of dispassion in action that Kṛṣṇa commended to Arjuna when he first started to persuade him to act. This is because there is no binding force in the power of actions themselves; it is attachment to the fruits of actions that makes those actions bind men to future rebirths. Although the *Gītā* acknowledges that knowledge is salvific and, in places, commends ascetic withdrawal from the world and restraint of the faculties to achieve this knowledge (VI.10–14), Kṛṣṇa is much more emphatic in his recommendation of dispassionate action. Asceticism, renunciation of all action, and the path of gnosis are highly respected ideals in India; but the *Gītā*'s message is that people can remain active in the world and yet be detached and reap the rewards of renunciation:

> Not by leaving works undone
> Does a man win freedom from the [bond of] work,
> Nor by renunciation alone
> Can he win perfection['s prize].
>
> Not for a moment can a man
> Stand still and do no work;
> For every man is powerless and forced to work
> By the 'constituents' born of Nature.
>
> Whoso controls his limbs through which he acts
> But sits remembering in his mind
> Sense-objects, deludes himself:
> He's called a hypocrite.
>
> How much more excellent he all unattached,
> Who with his mind controls [those] limbs,
> And through those limbs [themselves] by which he acts
> Embarks on the Yogic exercise (*yoga*) of works!
>
> Do thou the work that is prescribed for thee . . . (III.4–8)

Some remarks are called for on what yoga is and the man who practises it, the yogin. The terms are very variously translated, because they can convey a number of related ideas. Yoga became the name of a classical system of exercises of control and asceticism intended to culminate in liberation or in some supernatural goal. (It is developments from this that may be familiar to many from evening classes.) In the *Gītā* yoga is frequently used to mean 'way, means' (e.g. III.3) or 'exertion, effort'. When it stands on its own (not in compound) it is commonly an ellipsis for *karmayoga*, the way of dispassionate action (e.g. II.48 and VI.2). There is a common core to these meanings: yoga is a sustained, disciplined effort that leads to the attainment of something.

In addition to these means of knowledge and action, and transcending them, Kṛṣṇa preaches devotion (*bhakti*) to himself. As Hardy has pointed out,[15] the word *bhakti* in demonstrably early texts means no more than a mild predilection for material things, such as places and sweetmeats; but in the closing verse of the *Śvetāśvatara*, as in the *Gītā*, the word is used of an individual's feeling towards God. Hardy further argues that *bhakti* in the *Gītā* has an 'intellectual tenor' and is dependent on the concentration of the mind in yoga. In other words, it cannot be argued that the use of the word *bhakti* in the *Gītā* reflects the existence of the sort of passionate, emotional devotionalism that pervades the chapters of the *Bhāgavata-Purāṇa* (at the end of this anthology) and that has come to be implied by the term *bhakti*. Nevertheless, some sort of *bhakti* (which might in this context be cautiously rendered 'loyal devotion') has attained importance: it is repeatedly commended (VI.47, IX.13–15 and 30) and the work closes with a final affirmation that it is salvific:

> And now again give ear to this my all-highest Word,
> Of all the most mysterious:
> 'I love thee well.'
> Therefore will I tell thee thy salvation (*hita*).
>
> Bear Me in mind, love Me and worship Me
> (*bhakta*),
> Sacrifice, prostrate thyself to Me:
> So shalt thou come to Me, I promise thee
> Truly, for thou art dear to Me.
>
> Give up all things of law (*dharma*),
> Turn to Me, thine only refuge,
> [For] I will deliver thee
> From all evils; have no care. (XVIII.64–6)

The Law Book of Yājñavalkya

Treatises on law and duty (*dharmaśāstra*) are the fundamental texts of the scriptural category of *smṛti*, indeed for some (such as *Vijñāneśvara* ad *Yājñavalkya-Smṛti* 1:7 cited above) the only ones. The most prestigious and widely authoritative is that of the first man, Manu; but the genre is here represented by what is the next most prestigious, and perhaps more often actually followed authority, the *Yājñavalkya-Smṛti*. The principal reason for its selection here is that it is a concise work and one that is more systematically ordered by theme. It is divided into three large sections: 1) that on conduct (*ācāra*), which outlines the social order, describes the essential life-cycle rites, and gives the modern reader an impression of daily concerns and occupations; 2) that on legal proceedings; and 3) that on penitential rites of reparation. This last section also covers rules about impurity, acceptable infringements of rules during times of emergency, and rules for forest ascetics (*vānaprastha*) (who still maintain sacrificial fires) and for renunciates who have internalized the fires (*yati* or *sannyāsin*). It seemed preferable to give large, unbroken, coherent units of text from the first and third sections of the less prestigious *Yājñavalkya-Smṛti* than to attempt to anthologize the *Manusmṛti*, the law book of Manu, in which the themes here represented are often more diffusely treated and scattered through the work. Furthermore, good English translations of Manu's law book are widely available; but of the *Yājñavalkya-Smṛti* the only complete and reliable translation is that of Adolf Friedrich Stenzler into German, published in 1849.

Dating the *Yājñavalkya-Smṛti* is problematic: it is not intended to be an original work – much of it is a concise and reordered presentation of the material of the law book of Manu – and its claim (3:110) that it was taught by the sage Yājñavalkya of Books 3 and 4 of the *Bṛhadāraṇyaka* is a pious fiction. It is probably to be placed in the first two centuries of the Christian era.[16]

Most of the works included in this anthology have been selected in order to trace the emergence and development of doctrines of theology, soteriology and cosmogony. The *Yājñavalkya-Smṛti* has no bearing on these, but it addresses another side of Indian religiosity. It is with justice frequently asserted that orthopraxy (correct behaviour), rather than orthodoxy (correct opinion), is often of greater significance as a criterion for determining religious allegiance in India. Definitions of Hindu orthodoxy are necessarily minimal, because such a plethora of beliefs are possible: about the most that can be said is that orthodoxy requires lip-service to the authoritativeness of the Veda. Orthopraxy, however, is exhaustively codified in the many treatises on law (*dharma*) and in their commentaries. These too are not unanimous: what people practise is defined by their caste, family, adherence to a particular Vedic school, etc.; but they are perhaps more unitary than the plethora of soteriologies that are contained within Hinduism, and so might be more usefully employed in attempted definitions of what Hinduism is.

It should be stressed that the treatises on *dharma* do not give a timeless representation of the way things were and are; they give an ideal model – a model that in part describes the way things are and in part prescribes the way they should be. Many of the prescriptions of the *Yājñavalkya-Smṛti* have long not been followed. Keeping the Vedic fires, for instance, and performing the sacrifices that that entailed, was extremely expensive and time-consuming. Today almost no one keeps them and there are indications that it was not common even at the time of the redaction of the *Yājñavalkya-Smṛti*.[17]

An Indian technical treatise typically begins with a proclamation of the topic, the aim of studying the treatise, how this is achieved (*sambandha*), and, equally importantly, who is entitled to study it (*adhikārin*). In Indian religion this notion of *adhikāra*, both the right and the duty to perform something, is crucial. Kṛṣṇa's teachings in the *Gītā* made clear that sanctioned behaviour is not defined by absolute moral laws, nor general principles modified to suit differing situations, but that it is particular to each person, their status and their position: Arjuna is a slighted warrior and therefore he must fight. Much religious practice was not conceived of as a matter of free choice, personal conviction or conscience, but was determined by status, wealth, birth. It might be said that the same is true of all religion, that high-church Anglicans, for instance, tend to be born to their religion; but, even if this is conceded, it is true in a much stronger sense in Indian religions. Conversion to Christianity and Islam are open to all; but studying the Veda and keeping Vedic fires is possible only for those of the three highest estates, and is in practice the preserve of Brahmins. It is this fact that is the basis of the entire brahminical social order.

> *Śruti* is eternally true and infallible. It tells men what to do. Since it is the prerogative of brahmins to learn and interpret it, all authority (on ultimate matters) rests with them. At an early stage, brahmins made the easy transition from saying that the Vedas are authoritative to saying that whatever is authoritative is in the Veda . . . Nor is it necessary – or even plausible – to posit a brahmin conspiracy to

account for this change: it was a transition which occurred as an unintended consequence of constantly invoking the authority of a very large and only partially intelligible body of texts, to which in any case very few people had access.[18]

The *Yājñavalkya-Smṛti* explains some of the fundamental divisions of the brahminical social order and codifies the behaviour of those in these divisions. Few of Yājñavalkya's pronouncements are moral laws of universal application (a rare example would be 1:122); they are precepts for particular persons in particular positions. These are what the assembled sages ask to hear in the first verse of the work. The injunctions are most frequently third-person singular optatives: 'he should perform this'. When, as is usually the case, the subject is not made explicit, the injunction is generally directed at the male Brahmin who is the head of his own household. In addition to following such social religion, determined by position, individuals might also practise other observances and have a personal devotion to a particular deity.

It has been stated that sanctioned behaviour is conceived of as specific to people and not universal, and that the *Yājñavalkya-Smṛti* is a terse work, the redactors of which attempted to treat what is handled in the comparatively prolix and haphazardly organized law book of Manu, but systematically and concisely. Its concision means that it cannot list all the injunctions governing all people of every part of India and of every family, and that it must be imprecise. But this imprecision is probably not just motivated by considerations of space; to an extent it may be deliberately cultivated in order that the text accommodate a range of possibilities and thus remain broadly authoritative. Thus of the rite of tonsure (1:12) Yājñavalkya says nothing but that it 'should be performed according to family [practice]', leaving entirely open the details of how the hair should be cut, whether one, two, three or five tufts are to be left, and in what year of the child's life it should be performed.

Details of behaviour specific to castes and families are too much for a broadly authoritative text such as the *Yājñavalkya-Smṛti* to take into consideration. For such details, and for accurate descriptions of the performance of rituals, the reader would have to turn to commentaries, to works describing rituals specific to particular Vedic schools of transmission and to ritual manuals of lesser or more localized authority. Accordingly the translation relies heavily on the commentators, and their suggestions frequently appear in the notes, even where they may appear to be at variance with the intentions of the redactor(s). It is evident, for instance from their conflicting identifications of animals and plants in the discussion of food that may and may not be eaten (1:172–8), that they were far removed in time and place from the redaction of the *Yājñavalkya-Smṛti*; but they are closer than the modern reader. It is evident too that they have sometimes distorted the text and made it yield meanings that are most unlikely to have been intended (see for instance 1:52–3 and the notes thereon); but even there their interpretations are valuable, because they show how the text was adapted to new needs and made consistent with itself and with other sources. To call it distortion suggests that such exegesis is a conscious and deliberate perversion of the intended meaning of the text; but the commentators' inventive interpretations may often proceed from the belief that the text is authoritative, and so where it appears inconsistent with itself, with other authorities or with facts, this inconsistency can only be apparent and must be shown to be so by correct interpretation. In this commentators are assisted by the fact that the language of technical treatises in Sanskrit can be far removed from natural idiom.

It was as interpreted by its commentators that the *Yājñavalkya-Smṛti* came to be applied to litigation and to daily life. Its high status and widely accepted authoritativeness have been further secured by one particular commentary, the *Mitākṣarā*, 'of measured syllables' (the work is not metrical; what is meant is that it is not prolix), by Vijñāneśvara, who wrote between c. 1100 and c. 1120 AD.[19] Quite apart from other arguments for the indispensability of commentaries, Vijñāneśvara's commentary deserves attention because it came to be regarded as a high authority in its own right, particularly for its interpretation of the legal section of the text. For this reason I have almost invariably accepted Vijñāneśvara's readings, frequently adopted his interpretations, and, except where the notes specify otherwise, I have followed the text of an edition of his commentary.[20] This has obviated many text-critical difficulties. Commentaries are invaluable to an editor, because they show the works they explain frozen at a particular place and time in their transmission. Thus those of Aparārka and Viśvarūpa (also consulted for this translation) frequently comment on a substantially different text of the *Yājñavalkya-Smṛti* from that known to Vijñāneśvara.[21]

The Kiraṇa-Tantra

One text has been chosen that cannot be included either in the category of *śruti* or in that of *smṛti*, and that is the *Kiraṇa-Tantra*. Although it preaches a heterodox and heteropractic cult, there are good reasons for its inclusion. The main currents of Indian religion are often said to be Buddhism, Jainism and Hinduism (or Brāhmanism); but listings from within the Indian tradition differ widely: the first two categories they would include, perhaps further subdivided, but they would not recognize the last. In its place various soteriologies and schools of thought might be enumerated, but three streams are commonly separated out: Vedic orthodoxy, and those of the heterodox Vaiṣṇavas, and Śaivas.[22]

The terms Vaiṣṇava and Śaiva refer here to those initiated into sects whose scriptures claim the authorship of Viṣṇu and Śiva, and not simply to uninitiated devotees of Viṣṇu and Śiva. (Such devotees are perhaps more commonly referred to in primary Indian sources respectively as Bhāgavata and Māheśvara.) From the perspective of an orthodox Mīmāṃsaka (see p. xi), both Vaiṣṇavas and Śaivas, and not just Buddhists and Jains, were heterodox (*vedabāhya*) and to be shunned by the law-abiding (see *Yājñavalkya-Smṛti* 1:130). But there is good reason for including them in Hinduism, for while the Jains and Buddhists rejected the authority of the Veda outright, the Śaivas and Vaiṣṇavas did recognize the Veda, albeit as lower scriptural revelation. Both Śaivas and Vaiṣṇavas (and most particularly the latter) increasingly asserted that their tradition was congruent with, though it transcended, orthodox Vedism; but in early scriptures, such as the *Kiraṇa-Tantra*, no concession is made to Vedism. Both outwardly observed the requirements of Vedic social religion, even though they held them to be soteriologically irrelevant. Thus a frequently quoted[23] Śaiva scriptural passage proclaims:

> Thus he should not transgress even in thought the [rules of] conduct appropriate to his estate and walk of life. Once he has attained the initiation that is [becoming identical to] Śiva, he remains in whichever walk of life he was, and should protect the Śaiva teachings (*śivadharmam*) [there].

Furthermore they used the Vedic ritual framework as a paradigm for their own; many tantric rites had elements calqued upon Vedic ones, in which the efficient parts of the ritual, i.e. the mantras, were taken from tantric scriptures instead of from the Vedic corpus; tantric versions of the Gāyatrī and tantric life-cycle rites beyond that of initiation were devised; and the Vedic syllabus could be supplanted with a tantric one at times when recitation was enjoined. Unlike the Vedic corpus, that of the Śaiva Siddhānta was accessible also to those outside the three highest estates (*Kiraṇa-Tantra* 1:10 and note ad loc.). Tantric initiation was what qualified and bound followers to its study.

The term tantra is popularly supposed to refer to the magical acquisition of supernatural powers and pleasures by means of transgressive rites involving sexual intercourse and the consumption of meat and alcohol. The word need carry no such connotations. It is used of works that are not religious (e.g. the *Pañcatantra*, a compendium of didactic fables) and appears also in the titles of orthodox treatises (such as Kumārila's *Mīmāṃsātantravārttika*). In this anthology tantra refers to a body of non-Vedic scriptures which preach initiation into a cult and post-initiatory rituals using non-Vedic mantras. The magical acquisition of supernatural powers by means of elaborate rites with tantric mantras is also a characteristic of tantric sects; but in the Śaiva Siddhānta, to which the *Kiraṇa-Tantra* belongs, such magical power-mongering has been largely sublimated by the striving for salvation.

There is a huge variety of such sectarian scriptures and, had there been more space, more might have been selected to represent that variety. In this edition the first seven chapters of the *Kiraṇa-Tantra*, a tantra of the Śaiva Siddhānta, are given. The Śaiva Siddhānta is a label that is commonly applied both to a pan-Indian dualist Śaiva school, whose scriptures and exegetical treatises are exclusively in Sanskrit, and to a later South Indian school, much of whose authoritative literature is in Tamil. The South Indian school developed from the pan-Indian one and differs from it in that it compromised the tenets of early scriptures of the Śaiva Siddhānta by succumbing increasingly to conformity with Vedism (in particular to the influence of the orthodox school of Advaita Vedānta), and by laying increasing stress on the importance of devotion to God. The term is used here to refer exclusively to the old pan-Indian Śaiva Siddhānta.

The old Śaiva Siddhānta has, in the past, mistakenly been subsumed within the later one and called South Indian, and its scriptures (called variously *tantra*, *āgama* or *siddhānta*) have often been wrongly distinguished from tantras. Both these misconceptions can be refuted: among the principal exegetes of the original Śaiva Siddhānta are Kashmirians (from the far North); manuscripts of the scriptures have been transmitted in Nepal and Kashmir as well as in South India; their colophons in manuscripts both in the South and in the North almost invariably refer to them as tantras; and they are also cited as authorities by exegetes of transgressive Śaiva tantras, such as Abhinavagupta, who clearly regarded them as a branch – admittedly an exoteric and therefore relatively inferior one – of the authoritative canon of Śaiva tantra. Their doctrine is in fact closely related to that of the tantra which Abhinavagupta regarded as the highest revelation of the entire Śaiva canon, the *Mālinīvijayottaratantra*.[24]

It was remarked above that the Śaiva Siddhānta has often been said to be South Indian. The pan-Indian character of the early sect has been obscured, because almost all the extant works that bear the names of the twenty-eight principal scriptures of the Śaiva Siddhānta have been substantially altered or entirely rewritten in South India.[25] This took place either later than, or beyond the knowledge of, the latest Kashmirian exegetes of the sect, Bhaṭṭa Nārāyaṇakaṇṭha and his son, Bhaṭṭa Rāmakaṇṭha (tenth century AD).[26] The *Kiraṇa-Tantra* is however one of the very few extant tantras that are demonstrably early, because it has been transmitted both in Nepal and in South India, and because its earliest extant commentary is by the Kashmirian Bhaṭṭa Rāmakaṇṭha, mentioned above. The *Kiraṇa-Tantra* cannot be precisely dated, but it was probably composed between the fifth and the eighth centuries AD.

One of the reasons for the selection of the *Kiraṇa-Tantra* is that its essential doctrines are gathered together and set forth succinctly in its first few chapters. The whole work consists of a dialogue between Garuḍa, the mythical bird on whom Viṣṇu travels, and Śiva, his teacher. Compared with interlocutors in other tantras Garuḍa asks searching questions that probe genuine problems. Only the first seven chapters are translated here – the remaining fifty-seven have been omitted. The excluded chapters deal with cosmology, ritual, architecture, religious observance, yoga, and all that relates to the sect's religious practice and behaviour.[27] Unlike the preceding texts in this anthology, the *Kiraṇa-Tantra* attempts in succinct, sometimes cryptic language to present and defend a systematic theology and soteriology. Often it is too compressed and the modern reader is obliged to rely heavily on the commentators.

Technical treatises in Sanskrit are extremely terse and the train of thought is often difficult to follow. Sometimes they are no more than concatenations of elliptically expressed key ideas whose real purpose is mnemonic: that is to say they are intended to be read with the assistance of a learned teacher or, failing that, commentary, whose exegesis is afterwards remembered whenever the brief statements of the original work are called to mind. The *Kiraṇa-Tantra* is not such a skeletal treatise, but parts of it are written in the style characteristic of such treatises and so I have been liberal with square brackets, basing most of my insertions on the interpretations offered by Rāmakaṇṭha, Tryambakaśambhu and Siṃharāja, commentators on the *Kiraṇa-Tantra*. But their suggestions have sometimes been ignored, because they distort the text, obscuring the most natural interpretations of certain verses in order to obviate perceived inconsistencies.

Composed by Śiva the *Kiraṇa-Tantra* must be cogent, consistent with itself (and with the body of other scriptures of the Śaiva Siddhānta) and replete with meaning. This last consideration inspires a good commentator like Rāmakaṇṭha to read significance into every syllable. In 1:11 Śiva is described with the phrase 'the diadem of his crescent moon quivering'. Such a phrase is commonplace in descriptions of Śiva, but Rāmakaṇṭha explains that it indicates that Śiva's head shook with surprise at the ignorance of his questioner, Garuḍa, whom Rāmakaṇṭha has shown by similarly ingenious strategies to be a Śaiva initiate.

As will be clear from the above, a fine commentary such as Rāmakaṇṭha's is much more than an exposition of the primary meaning of a text: it fills out the frequent ellipses that are characteristic of the compressed 'telegraphic' style of Sanskrit technical treatises; and it makes every phrase of the work resonate with meaning.

The Śaiva Siddhānta inherits from the Sāṅkhyas the notion of a universe fundamentally divided into sentient souls and insentient matter. All souls are potentially omnipotent and omniscient, just as Śiva is, but they are bound by three physical bonds: innate impurity (*mala*), primal matter (*māyā*) and past actions. Primal matter is goaded into action, at Śiva's instigation, to generate all the principles (*tattva*) that make up the material universe and the bodies into which souls transmigrate. Once embodied, the souls reap the rewards of past actions and commit further actions that bind them to further births in the material universe (1:19–20). Like the beginningless sequence of the chicken and the egg, this process has no original cause – past actions are beginningless (3:7–8). Śiva alone is beginninglessly free of bonds (2:3–5). It is out of compassion alone that he instigates the periodic creation of the universe out of primal matter, because souls can only use up the rewards of their past actions by experience in the material universe (4:26–8).

At a full initiation into the Śaiva Siddhānta the soul of the initiand is ritually removed from his body by means of mantras and made to experience immediately the rewards of all his past actions that would accrue to him in different embodiments in various worlds (7:25–7).[28] It is only the past actions that sustain him in his present life whose rewards are not instantly destroyed (6:19). Śiva himself, although all-pervading, does not directly involve himself with primal matter, and so it is through deputies, the chief of whom is called Ananta, that he creates, administers and resorbs the universe. These deputies are souls along the path to the realization of their own innate omnipotence. Other Hindu deities are conceived of as such souls invested with office by Śiva. Mantras, through which initiation is achieved, are also souls invested with office, so too is the particular Śiva who teaches the *Kiraṇa-Tantra* to Garuḍa.[29]

The following excursus upon lists of constitutive principles of the universe may seem unnecessary and unnecessarily complex; but some explanation is required and, although impatient readers may skip over it now, they may be grateful for it when they come to grapple with the opaquely incomplete treatment of the structure of the universe in the text. The Śaiva Siddhānta inherited the structure of its dualist ontology from Sāṅkhya thinkers. These held the soul to be the topmost principle, fundamentally different from that of matter (*prakṛti*) and all the principles derived from matter. Those derived principles were the intellect (*buddhi*); the principle of self-identity (*ahaṃkāra*); the eleven faculties of sense and action (the mind, the ears, skin, eyes, tongue, nose, mouth, hand, anus, reproductive organs and feet); the five subtle elements (sound, touch, form, taste and smell); and the five gross elements (ether, air, fire, water and earth). The tantras of the Śaiva Siddhānta modified this structure in two ways: they added principles to the top, demonstrating that the Sāṅkhyas had correctly grasped the nature of only the inferior levels of the universe, and they attempted to place worlds inherited from older Śaiva scriptures on the levels of these various principles (*tattva*). The latter change meant that the *tattvas*, in some contexts, approximate to levels or strata of reality in which various worlds are placed, rather than to elements or constitutive principles of the universe. Once again, the scriptures of the Śaiva Siddhānta differ widely in their allocations of worlds to principles, and in some cases no allocation is made at all.[30]

In the post-scriptural Śaiva Siddhānta of the commentators a consensus was reached that there were altogether thirty-six principles (*tattva*). Five of them – Śiva, his power (*śakti*), his two aspects of Sadāśiva and Īśvara, and pure knowledge – constitute the pure universe above primal matter. The remaining thirty-one principles make up the impure universe. The latter, in order of their evolution from the first, primal matter, are: limited power to act (*kalā*), limited power of knowledge (*vidyā*), passion (*rāga*), time, binding fate (*niyati*), and then all the principles of the mature Sāṅkhya listed above, but with two modifications: firstly, the Sāṅkhyas' top category, the soul, became that of the bound soul (because the Śaiva Siddhānta holds the free soul to be equivalent to Śiva), and secondly, that of matter (*prakṛti*) became a redundant lower duplication of primal matter (*māyā*).

No demonstrably early extant scripture of the Śaiva Siddhānta has exactly this list of principles. In Chapter 8 of the *Kiraṇa-Tantra* (in which the world systems of the Śaiva cosmos are distributed among the different principles) not only are no worlds allocated to the principles of the five subtle elements and of the eleven faculties – in fact no tantra places worlds in these – but no principles intervene between that of ether and the sense of self-identity (*ahaṃkāra*).[31]

Following the eighth chapter, the sequence of the *Kiraṇa-Tantra* is as follows: the formless (*niṣkala*), Sadāśiva, Īśvara, pure knowledge, primal matter, limited power to act (*kalā*), time, binding fate (*niyati*), limited power of knowledge, passion (*rāga*), secondary matter (*prakṛti*), the principle of the constitutive strands of the material world (*guṇa*), intellect (*buddhi*), the principle of self-identity, and the five gross elements. This yields a total of nineteen; but there are later (22:51) declared to be thirty-six. We can reach this number by adding the eleven faculties and five subtle elements (mentioned in 4:23) and either the bound soul (8:125) or Śiva's power (8:139).

What the above demonstrates is that there is no consensus in the scriptures about: 1) how many *tattvas* there are; 2) what their order is; 3) exactly what they are – in some cases they are better rendered 'principle', in others 'reality level'[32] (in the case of the *tattva* of the bound soul and the uppermost *tattvas* of the pure universe neither of these translations is adequate); and 4) which worlds belong in which *tattvas*.

The first chapter of the *Kiraṇa-Tantra* begins with a eulogy of Śiva, enumerating a number of his mythical deeds. This opening is unusual given that the Śaiva Siddhānta held such mythology to be of no importance, and the commentators claim these myths are metaphors for the ways in which Śiva brings about salvation. Thereafter the first chapter explains the sequence in which an ordinary soul is linked to the evolutes of primal matter that make up the psycho-physical entity capable of worldly experience. The second chapter is devoted to explaining the different functions of impurity and primal matter, that they are quite separate things, and why it is that impurity is not counted among the evolutes of primal matter. Chapter 3 begins with a discussion of what the bonds of the soul bring about and an assertion of their beginninglessness; it concludes with a discussion of the unknowability of Śiva as he is at the highest level of reality.

In spite of being all-pervasive, Śiva is unapproachable, because he is formless. This is why he manifests himself in the relatively coarse forms that give their names to the upper principles of the universe. The fourth chapter explains the role of Śiva's chief deputy, Ananta, in stimulating primal matter to generate the universe. Chapter 5 explains the prerequisites for the performance of salvific initiation. According to the *Kiraṇa-Tantra*, two equally powerful past actions that ripen simultaneously and are thus ready to produce their rewards can cause a blockage of experience and prevent an individual from consuming the fruits of his past actions. Śiva then releases a shaft of his power to remove the blockage. Only when this has occurred should a person be initiated. That it has taken place can be inferred from an initiand's devotion to Śiva. Chapter 6 explains that the Śaiva Siddhānta preaches different codes for those initiates incapable of following all that is enjoined for normal initiates. It concludes with an explanation of the effects of initiation. The seventh chapter discusses mantras and expounds the position that some of them are Śiva, some are his power, and some are individual souls which he has invested with power and office.

The text of Vivanti's edition[33] has been followed, but modified on the basis of twenty other manuscripts and of two extra commentaries unknown to her. These modifications have been listed at the end of the *Kiraṇa-Tantra*.

The Bhāgavata-Purāṇa

The Purāṇas are large compendia, mainly mythological, and written for the most part in simple narrative metre (*anuṣṭubh*, the metre also of the *Yājñavalkya-Smṛti*, the *Kiraṇa-Tantra* and of most of the *Gītā*), and in straightforward, sometimes slightly debased, Sanskrit. They are a genre of scripture to which women and those of the lowest of the four estates of Hindu society (Śūdras) were not denied access, and they give a portrait of popular religiosity through the ages. They belong to the category of *smṛti* (*Yājñavalkya-Smṛti* 1:3); but, with notable exceptions, scholars long ignored them, partly because of their popular character, partly because of text-critical problems, and perhaps partly because they disapproved of them:

> Of all false religions that of the Purans is perhaps the most monstrous in its absurdities – a stupendous memorial to the easy credulity of an imbecile race.[34]

> It [Puranism] is a long chain of gross fables, disjointed and indefinite, huge, wild, and fragmentary, having no distinct and tangible object to fulfil, and totally at variance in its several parts. Every detached story may have a deep, hidden, and even moral meaning if you please; but all the fables together make a discordant system, unintelligible and bewildering, for which it is impossible to entertain any but a mean and contemptible opinion. The instructions which it professes to give are useless, where they are not scandalous and criminal. The only things clearly to be understood, are the profane songs, the obscene ceremonies, and the other indecencies connected with the prescribed festivals.[35]

The chroniclers of British India turned to the Purāṇas, in the absence of other materials, as defective historical sources, and they too were were eloquent about their shortcomings:

> Doubtless the original Puranas contained much valuable historical matter; but, at present, it is difficult to separate a little pure metal from the base alloy of ignorant expounders and interpolators.
>
> . . . in the East, in the moral decrepitude of ancient Asia, with no judge to condemn, no public to praise, each priestly expounder may revel in an unfettered imagination, and reckon his admirers in proportion to the mixture of the marvellous. Plain historical truths have long ceased to interest this artificially fed people.[36]

It is commonly asserted that a Purāṇa must treat of the following five topics: creation of the world; recreation (after periodic destruction); the genealogies of gods and heroes (*vaṃśa*); the periods named after particular progenitors called Manus (*manvantara*); the deeds of the gods and heroes (*vaṃśyanucarita*). Many Purāṇas do not follow such an agenda. (The *Bhāgavata-Purāṇa* (in II.10:1 and XII.7.9) gives two different, but overlapping, lists of ten topics.) They do predominantly contain mythology and cosmology; but many also fill the role of popular encyclopaedias and have amassed a wealth of material from technical treatises on all manner of subjects. The *Agni* and *Garuḍa Purāṇas*, for example, duplicate much of the legal material from the *Yājñavalkya-Smṛti*. The Purāṇas are also a vehicle for sectarian religion. They often have much in common with sectarian tantras, but with the important difference that the religious practices they teach remain *vaidika*, 'congruent with orthodox Vedism'. This means that they do not preach initiation into tantric cults and that their rites use *vaidika* mantras – that is to say ones not actually drawn from the Vedic corpus (*śrauta*), but not drawn from tantras either.[37] Much of what they contain may have been written by those with sectarian tendencies who wished to give some respectability to heterodox ideas, while still remaining within the fold of Vedic orthodoxy.

Although they contain early material, it is often impossible to date a Purāṇa, or even to place within it material that is relatively late or relatively early. Printed versions of the same Purāṇa often diverge widely. In certain cases it seems that originally independent Purāṇic works came to be called books or sub-sections of other well-known ones, and thus, although transmitted quite separately, they have come to be printed as parts of the Purāṇas to which they ascribe themselves, or have even come to supplant them. A clear case is that of the *Skandapurāṇa*.[38] As with tantras of the

Śaiva Siddhānta, the title was used as a locus of attribution for suitable material while the original work was forgotten. Because Purāṇas contain such a mixture of material from different periods, and because manuscripts and printed versions diverge so widely, it is sometimes asserted[39] that they are oral or epic literature in a perpetual state of flux and that it is therefore not only impossible but methodologically incorrect to try to make definitive editions of them. As they are always undergoing composition in transmission, it is argued, 'they do not belong in books'.[40]

The same has been said of the *Bhāgavata-Purāṇa*; but most admit that this work is a South Indian creation and that it possesses, more perhaps than any other Purāṇa, a distinctive and extremely literary style – features of which are its archaizing language, metrical variety, and its alliterative and assonantal word-play – and that that is consistently maintained throughout the work. This homogeneity, and the relative paucity of substantial variations in its textual transmission, suggest that it was composed at one place and time. Rocher – presumably as a corollary of his view that all Purāṇas undergo composition in transmission – does not approve any of the suggested datings of the *Bhāgavata-Purāṇa*, but presents a table of them that ranges from 1200 BC to 1300 AD. But, following Hardy,[41] (who demonstrates that the *Bhāgavata-Purāṇa* drew on South Indian devotional poetry in Tamil composed by singer-saints called the Ālvārs), we may assign the *Bhāgavata-Purāṇa* to the ninth or tenth century AD.

The *Bhāgavata-Purāṇa* has been selected for this anthology not only to represent the Purāṇa genre (of which – because of its homogeneity, relatively late date, and poetic diction – it is not entirely typical): it also illustrates a much more developed form of devotionalism than that found in the *Gītā*. In the latter devotion to Kṛṣṇa is of an intellectual kind; in the *Bhāgavata-Purāṇa* however, the devotion described is intense and emotional. Here the cowherd women are by turns racked by the insupportable pain of separation from Kṛṣṇa, and overpowered by the bliss of union with him, and the descriptions of their emotions are characterized by a heady sensuality quite alien to the *Gītā*. The passionate devotionalism of the *Bhāgavata-Purāṇa* had an incalculable impact on religiosity across the entire subcontinent. It found expression in personal devotional poetry by singer-saints in the vernacular tongues of every part of India, and their poems are still revered and sung by devotees today.

The *Bhāgavata-Purāṇa*, like the *Bhagavad-Gītā* and the Upanishads, is not a systematic work of soteriology: much of the work has an unmistakably non-dualist tenor; and yet it contains passages devoted to expounding the Sāṅkhya system, and others, (such as the section translated here), which emphasize above all else the salvific grace of God and the transcendent importance of devotion to him. It is a mark of the *Bhāgavata-Purāṇa*'s great popularity and importance that thinkers of very different persuasions have commented upon it, and thereby drawn it over into their own camp.[42]

The chapters translated are not the earliest account of Kṛṣṇa's dallying with the cowherd women, the Gopīs, but they are the most famous, and they have been the subject of a great deal of discussion by later theologians. Some were troubled by the moral problems that they throw up; others relished their emotional intensity and poetry and regarded them as a focal scripture for their theology of devotion and aesthetic delight. The *Bhāgavata-Purāṇa* declares from the outset (I.1:3) that it is intended to be relished:

> Aesthetes, you who love the flavour of poetry! Ah, drink again and again at this vessel of juice that is the Bhāgavata, this fruit that has fallen to earth from the mouth of Śuka,[43] full of liquid nectar, from the wish-fulfilling tree of the Vedas.'

Of all the translation in this volume, this may be the least successful, because it is impossible to capture and convey in English the beauty of the original. The Sanskrit verses are replete with alliterative and assonantal textures and all manner of word-play, and are composed in a variety of elaborate metres. With more time and skill I might have attempted a metrical translation; but this prose translation serves, I hope, to convey the story and some flavour of the original.

The story that frames the bulk of the *Bhāgavata-Purāṇa* is that of the death of King Parīkṣit. Parīkṣit is cursed to die within seven days by Śṛṅgī, the son of a sage called Śamīka. He withdraws to the Ganges to fast to death and there meets the learned sage Śuka, the son of Vyāsa, and takes the opportunity to question him. What Śuka teaches Parīkṣit constitutes the main body of the Purāṇa, and that is why the chapters translated here take the form of a conversation between Śuka and the king. The text consists of twelve books (*skandha*), the tenth and most popular of which narrates the life of Kṛṣṇa. In the *Mahābhārata* we learn of Kṛṣṇa only as an adult; the *Bhāgavata-Purāṇa* narrates also the episodes of Kṛṣṇa's early life.

Kṛṣṇa was born to Vasudeva and Devakī, but he did not grow up with them. Vasudeva, the son of a king of Mathurā called Śūrasena, turned to cattle-tending, and at his father's death the throne passed to Ugrasena, a man of the same clan. Ugrasena was ousted and imprisoned by his violent son, Kaṃsa, the brother of Devakī. At the marriage of Kṛṣṇa's parents Kaṃsa heard a disembodied voice warning him that he would be killed by Devakī's eighth son. Kaṃsa imprisoned the couple and murdered their offspring as they were born. Their seventh son, however, was miraculously transplanted into the womb of Rohiṇī, another wife of Vasudeva's, and that son was Kṛṣṇa's elder brother, Balarāma. When their eighth son was born, Vasudeva was able to escape miraculously, swap the baby for a female child born to the cowherd woman Yaśodā, and return to the prison. Thus Kṛṣṇa also came to be known as the son of Nanda and Yaśodā, who brought him up in Gokula among the cowherds of Vraja. When he discovered the deception, Kaṃsa sent many demons to dispatch Kṛṣṇa, but, to the astonishment of Gokula, each was vanquished. Throughout a childhood packed with incident Kṛṣṇa's pranks, his butter-thieving, and his beauty maddened and delighted the cowherd women, the Gopīs.

When all other means to kill Kṛṣṇa had failed, Kaṃsa invited him to a festival in Mathurā. A wrestling contest was arranged, from which Balarāma and Kṛṣṇa emerged victorious, and Kṛṣṇa then killed the enraged Kaṃsa and became the ruler of Mathurā. Thereafter he was kept busy with affairs of state and never returned to Gokula. Before he left for the court, he spent the nights of an autumn moon singing, dancing and making love to the captivated beauties of Vraja. Their impassioned pleas for his return during every day of his absence fill many verses here and later in the book:

> Each second seems an aeon, when you wander the forest by day and we do not see you, and when [in the evening at your return] our eyes look up at your beauteous face with its curling locks, how stupid [the creator seems,] who gave us lids over our eyes. (X.31:15)

More than the bliss of union, it is the agony of separation from God that is at the heart of the devotionalism of the *Bhāgavata-*

Purāṇa, and it will be clear from the following summary that the Gopīs are given frequent opportunity to express this agony: In X.29 Kṛṣṇa decides to make love to the Gopīs and calls them with music. When they arrive he sends them back to their families. They plead not to have to leave and all go together to the banks of the Yamunā, where Kṛṣṇa disappears. In X.30 the Gopīs wander the forest searching for him, asking the trees where he has gone and imitating him. One Gopī Kṛṣṇa took away with him to another part of the forest; but she grew conceited at this high favour and Kṛṣṇa again disappeared. In X.31 the Gopīs sing Kṛṣṇa's praises and beg for his return. In X.32 Kṛṣṇa reappears; they go to the bank of the Yamunā, and the Gopīs reproach him for not loving them in return for their love. In X.33 Kṛṣṇa multiplies himself and they dance the dance called the Rāsa.

DOMINIC GOODALL

References

1 P. G. Wodehouse in his preface to *Summer Lightning* (Herbert Jenkins, 1929).

2 This paradigm does not apply to all the Vedas: the *Taittirīya* subrecension of the Black *Yajur-Veda* in fact contains mantras and Brāhmaṇa portions in its Saṃhitā, its Brāhmaṇa and in its Āraṇyaka.

3 There are many later works calling themselves Upanishads, often assigned to the *Atharva-Veda*, which do not properly belong to the Vedic corpus.

4 See e.g. Jan Gonda, *Vedic Literature (Saṃhitās and Brāhmaṇas)*, (Harassowitz, 1975), pp. 20–5.

5 Franklin Edgerton, *The Beginnings of Indian Philosophy* (Allen and Unwin, 1965), p. 18.

6 ibid. p. 22.

7 ibid. p. 28.

8 ibid.

9 Juan Mascaró, *The Upanishads* (Penguin, 1965), p. 45.

10 Robert Ernest Hume, *The Thirteen Principal Upanishads Translated from the Sanskrit* (Oxford University Press, 1934), p. 70.

11 Thus A. J. Alston, *Śaṅkara on the Absolute* (London: Shanti Sadan, 1980), pp. 42–3.

12 *Māyā* in the Upanishads (and in *Bhāgavata-Purāṇa* 29:1) actually means something more like 'supernatural power', and occasionally (*Śvetāśvatara* IV.10) 'primal matter', foreshadowing the use of the term in the Śaiva Siddhānta.

13 In fact many of the numbers there are still a riddle. Some identifications were suggested by E. H. Johnston, 'Some Sāṃkhya and Yoga conceptions of the *Śvetāśvatara Upanishad*' in *Journal of the Royal Asiatic Society*, 1930, pp. 855–78.

14 Thus Franklin Edgerton, *The Bhagavad Gītā* (Harvard University Press, 1972), pp. 133–4.

15 Friedhelm Hardy, *Viraha-Bhakti: The early history of Kṛṣṇa devotion in South India* (Oxford University Press, 1983), pp. 25–8.

16 This conclusion is reached after a review of the evidence by P. V. Kane, *History of Dharmaśāstra* Volume I, Part I of the revised and enlarged second edition (Poona: Bhandarkar Oriental Research Institute, 1968), pp. 442–7.

17 Verse 2 of Chapter 3, for instance, speaks of cremation being performed with the household fire, as though that were the norm, and only afterwards makes clear that those who kept the Vedic fires were to be burnt with those instead.

18 Richard Gombrich, *Theravada Buddhism: a social history from ancient Benares to modern Colombo* (Routledge and Kegan Paul, 1988), pp. 33–4.

19 Thus P. V. Kane, *History of Dharmaśāstra* (Volume I, Part II of the revised and enlarged second edition; Poona: Bhandarkar Oriental Research Institute, 1975), pp. 607–9.

20 Narayan Ram Acharya (ed.), *Yājñavalkyasmṛti of Yogīśvara Yājñavalkya with the Commentary Mitākṣarā of Vijñāneśvara* (Bombay: Nirnaya Sagar Press, 1949). Other editions consulted for their commentaries were: *Yājñavalkyasmṛti* with the commentary of Aparārka edited by the Pundits of the Ānandāśrama and published by Hari Nārāyaṇa Āpaṭe (Poona: Ānandāśrama Sanskrit Series, 1903); T. Ganapati Sastri (ed.) *The Yājñavalkyasmṛti With the Commentary of Viśvarūpācārya* (Trivandrum, 1921–2, and reprinted Delhi: Munshiram Manoharlal, 1982); Nārāyaṇa Śāstrī Khiste and Jagannātha Śāstrī Hośiṅga (ed.) *The Yājñavalkya Smṛti With the Commentary of Mitra Miśra's Vīramitrodaya and Vijñāneśvara's Mitākṣara* (Benares: Chowkhamba Sanskrit Series, 1930).

21 As with almost all literature in Sanskrit, the understanding of the text of the *Yājñavalkya-Smṛti* could be much improved by a full collation of the manuscripts of the work and of its commentaries. A compari-

son with the sections of the *Agni* and *Garuḍa Purāṇas*, which have incorporated large portions of the *Yājñavalkya-Smṛti* at an early stage in the work's transmission, must also prove fruitful.

22 The observations in this paragraph were made by Professor Sanderson in a course of lectures at All Souls' College, Oxford in 1992–3.

23 e.g. ad *Tattvasaṅgraha* 38 and 57 and ad *Mokṣakārikā* 146 and 151 in Vrajavallabha Dvivedī (ed.) *Aṣṭaprakaraṇam* (Varanasi: Sampurnananda Sanskrit University, 1988).

24 See Alexis Sanderson, 'The Doctrine of the Mālinīvijayottaratantra', pp. 281–312 in Teun Goudrian (ed.) *Ritual and Speculation in Early Tantrism: studies in honor of André Padoux* (State University of New York, 1992).

25 The case for the relative lateness of most extant *siddhāntas* is argued in Hélène Brunner's 'Jñāna and Kriyā: Relation between Theory and Practice in the Śaivāgamas', in Teun Goudrian (ed.) *Ritual and Speculation in Early Tantrism: studies in honor of André Padoux* (State University of New York, 1992), pp. 1–59.

26 Professor Sanderson has pointed out to me that a passage from Bhaṭṭa Rāmakaṇṭha's commentary on the *Mataṅgapārameśvaratantra* (the summary verses ad 23:85) is cited in Abhinavagupta's *Tantrāloka* 8:428–34b. This means that he can tentatively be dated between c. 950 and 1000 AD. For the terminus post quem see Alexis Sanderson's review of N. R. Bhatt, *Mataṅgapārameśvarāgama (Kriyāpāda, Yogapāda et Caryāpāda), avec le commentaire de Bhaṭṭa Rāmakaṇṭha. Édition Critique* (Pondicherry, 1982) in *Bulletin of the School of Oriental and African Studies*, 48 (London, 1985).

27 For a detailed summary see Hélène Brunner, 'Analyse du Kiraṇāgama' pp. 309–29 in *Journal Asiatique*, CCLIII (Paris, 1965).

28 The worlds are conceived of as plateaux of existence (like our own world) in which souls become embodied and are thus capable of the experience that alone consumes the fruits of their past actions.

29 According to Rāmakaṇṭha he is the lord of a world in the upper crust of the egg that englobes this and other worlds in the principle of earth, which is the lowest of the principles evolved from primal matter. Other Hindu cosmologies describe nothing beyond the worlds inside this egg.

30 The *Rauravasūtrasaṅgraha* demonstrates its antiquity because it has not attempted any such correlation and because it lists (10:98–101) only thirty rather than the canonical thirty-six principles – the work is printed as the *vidyā pāda* of the *Rauravāgama*, edited by N. R. Bhatt. (Pondicherry: Publications de l'Institut Français d'Indologie,

1961). The structure of the cosmos can affect the mode of initiation, because the soul's stockpile of actions must be purified through initiation in all the worlds and in all the principles in which those stored actions are to bear fruit.

31 These sixteen principles are also singled out in certain early sources of Sāṅkhya thought as non-productive modifications (*vikṛti*) of the other eight material principles (*prakṛti*), e.g. *Mahābhārata* 12.294.27–9 and 12.298.10–15 (Edgerton, 1965 pp. 310 and 323).

32 Both these translations are those of Professor Sanderson, who is attempting a stratigraphy of early Śaiva scriptures partly on the basis of their discrepant lists of principles and world-systems.

33 Maria Pia Vivanti (ed. and trans.), *Il Kiraṇāgama* (Naples: Istituto Orientale di Napoli, 1975).

34 Anonymous, 'Puranism; or the popular religion of India', *Calcutta Review*, 24, 1855, p. 223; quoted in Ludo Rocher, *The Purāṇas* (Wiesbaden: Harassowitz, 1986), p. 8.

35 Anonymous, art. cit., pp. 229–230.

36 James Tod, *Annals and Antiquities of Rajasthan* (originally published 1829–32), edited by William Crooke (London, 1920; reprinted, Delhi: Motilal Banarsidass, 1971), p. 30.

37 Such Paurāṇic mantras often take the form of the name of a deity in the dative preceded by the sacred syllable *oṃ* and followed by the word *namaḥ*, 'homage'.

38 Early Nepalese manuscripts (one dated to the ninth century AD) of the original *Skandapurāṇa* have been identified, an entirely different work from what has hitherto been printed under the title of *Skandapurāṇa*. See R. Adriaensen, H. T. Bakker and H. Isaacson, 'Towards a Critical Edition of the *Skandapurāṇa*', in *Indo-Iranian Journal*, 37 (Kluwer Academic Publishers, 1994) pp. 325–31.

39 See, for example, Ludo Rocher, op. cit., pp. 49–67.

40 ibid. p. 53

41 op. cit. pp. 486–8.

42 Except where stated the text translated is that of Jagadīś Lāl Śāstrī (ed.), *Bhāgavata Purāṇa of Kṛṣṇa Dvaipāyana Vyāsa with Sanskrit Commentary Bhāvārthabodhinī of Śrīdhara Svāmin* (Delhi: Motilal Banarsidass, 1983). The other commentaries consulted and referred to here are the fourteenth-century *Bhāgavatacandrikā*, 'moonlight upon the *Bhāgavata-Purāṇa*' of Vīrarāghava (edited by A. V. and T. C. Narasiṃhācārya, Madras: Ānanda Press, 1910); the *Padaratnāvalī* (fifteenth century) of Vijayadhvaja, (edited by Bhāvācārya Aṣṭaputra, Bombay: Gaṇapatakṛṣṇājī Press, 1868); the

Toṣaṇīsāra of Kāśīnāthopādhyāya (Bombay: Nirnaya Sagar Press, 1895); the *Subodhinī*, 'which makes easy to understand' of Vallabhācārya (1479–1531). The last is printed as an appendix to James D. Redington, *Vallabhācārya on the Love Games of Kṛṣṇa* (Delhi: Motilal Banarsidass, 1983). For the dates of the commentators I have followed Ganesh Vasudeo Tagare, *The Bhāgavata-Purāṇa*, Part I (Delhi: Motilal Banarsidass), pp. lxvi–lxviii.

43 Śuka is both the narrator of the bulk of the *Bhāgavata-Purāṇa* and a word for a parakeet. As the commentator Śrīdhara points out, a fruit that has been tasted by a parakeet is 'as sweet as nectar'.

NOTE ON THE TEXTS AND TRANSLATIONS

Any selection from the vast and diverse corpus of literature revered by Hindus is bound to be arbitrary. This selection includes nothing that is not in Sanskrit, although devotional poetry of the Ālvārs and Nāyanmārs in Tamil, and of singer-saints in many of the other languages of India, certainly deserve attention; it ignores modern developments, and includes nothing composed later than c. 1000 AD. It contains nothing to represent the widespread devotion that has long existed towards Rāma and to the Goddess; it contains no late Śākta tantras that prescribe transgressive rituals involving the consumption of wine and meat, and ritual intercourse with a consecrated partner, or that prescribe the wearing of ornaments of human bone and other accoutrements from the cremation ground; and it virtually ignores the works of philosophers and theologians.

Some of these omissions were premeditated: it was decided to exclude works that are avowedly composed by historical human authors, unless, as is the case with certain hymns of the *Ṛg-Veda*, they are not regarded in this way by subsequent Indian tradition. This ruled out the treatises of influential philosophers and theologians – even though many might be argued to have become as authoritative as scriptures – and the poems of devotion in the vernaculars, part of whose message is that they are the testament of faith of a particular saint – they therefore contain signature lines marked with the poet's own name or with the epithet of the deity used exclusively by that poet. (This might be thought to rule out also the *Bhagavad-Gītā*, the *Yājñavalkya-Smṛti*, and the *Bhāgavata-Purāṇa*; but I have chosen to regard Vyāsa (who dictated the *Mahābhārata*, in which the *Gītā* is embedded, to Gaṇeśa), Yājñavalkya and Śuka as legendary figures.) Other regrettable omissions have been impossible to avoid because of considerations of space.

Having listed all the things this volume cannot cover, it is worth reiterating what the texts added to Zaehner's selection do represent. From the *Yājñavalkya-Smṛti* some notion can be gained of daily religion, of how moral duty was conceived, of how society was structured; from the *Kiraṇa-Tantra* the reader has an impression of early theistic tantras that are heterodox but 'Hindu', of the dependence of such tantras on the system of the Sāṅkhyas, and of the compressed, telegraphic style of Indian technical treatises; the *Bhāgavata-Purāṇa* exposes the reader to the genre of the Purāṇas, to popular religion that is congruent with Vedism, and to the emotional devotionalism that characterizes many Indian theistic writings.

The items in this anthology are the work of various translators: Hymns II, i and II, xii of the *Ṛg-Veda* were translated and annotated by Franklin Edgerton and IX, lxxiv by Wendy Doniger O'Flaherty; I, i; I, iii; I, v.1–16; II, ii; III, ii–iii; and VI, i.1–6 of the *Bṛhadāraṇyaka* have been supplied again with the translator's annotations from the translation by Robert Ernest Hume;[1] and the portions from the *Yājñavalkya-Smṛti*, the *Kiraṇa-Tantra* and the *Bhāgavata-Purāṇa*, by Dominic Goodall. The rest of the anthology is the work of R. C. Zaehner. He has this to say about his translations (pp. xxi–xxii):

> I have not tried to render key Sanskrit words by one single English equivalent, as this seems to me quite unrealistic. Very occasionally I leave the Sanskrit word untranslated if, in my opinion, there simply is no adequate English equivalent. The most obvious example of this is the word *brahman* itself. I could have adopted this rather unsatisfactory procedure for other key concepts such as *purusha*, *ātman*, *yoga*, *bhakti* and *dharma*, but I have not done so, preferring to add the word in brackets after the individual translation. *Purusha* I sometimes translate as 'man', but when it refers to the supreme Being I have usually retained 'Person', since Christian readers will already be familiar with the 'Persons' of the Holy Trinity.
>
> *Yoga* has a vast number of meanings, and in chapters V and VI of the Gītā particularly these meanings and all the nuances between them are most skilfully played on, as are the meanings of *yukta*, the

1 It may seem regrettable that the styles of two translators are juxtaposed in a single work. The intention was to retain Zaehner's translation, which I admire, but to include passages he omitted. The result is, I hope, not too unsatisfactorily bitty. One or two small portions of Zaehner's translation have been replaced with those of Hume's so that the changes between one style and the other are less frequent.

past participle of the same root. Thus *yoga* can mean 'practice, spiritual exercise, integration, moderation, method, power', to quote only the most obvious meanings. In each case I have tried to choose the appropriate one. *Bhakti* too has a wide variety of meanings, prominent among which are 'loyalty, devotion, worship, love'. Frequently I have combined two of these words to render the idea, and I have followed this practice (occasionally) with other words too. *Ātman* I have nearly always translated as 'self' or 'Self' depending on context, or when it is simply a reflexive pronoun, as '[him]self', the square brackets being used to distinguish it from other reflexive pronouns which do not have the theological and philosophic connotations possessed by the word *ātman*.

Ātman, then, appears as 'self', not as 'soul', and this is because there is another key concept that corresponds fairly exactly to our word 'soul', and that is *buddhi*. For this most translators use such words as 'intellect' or 'intelligence', and this, of course, is what it often means; but the concept seems to be broader than this, for in *Bhagavad-Gītā* II.41 we read that the essence of *buddhi* is will. *Buddhi*, then, is the combination of intellect and will, and this is almost exactly what Catholic Christianity understands by 'soul'; and this is how I translate it in the later Upanishads and the Gītā. For in our Western tradition it is the soul that is the responsible and perduring element in man: it is the soul that is saved or damned. This is equally true of *buddhi*; it is man's highest faculty and ultimately responsible for whether a man continues to be reborn or is finally released. It is not the 'self', or *ātman*, which has no responsibilities and is a mere onlooker at the drama of 'works' enacted in this world. *Buddhi* and *ātman* are nevertheless closely interconnected, and in the Upanishads and Gītā it is never quite certain whether the *ātman* is wholly dissociated from *buddhi* even when it attains liberation. For *buddhi*, then, I have stuck to 'soul', for *ātman* to 'self'. The reader must firmly bear this distinction in mind.

Two conventions followed in my translations require comment: square brackets have been used to supply material not actually in the Sanskrit, but which is necessary for the text to make sense and to read smoothly in English, and which can reasonably be assumed to be understood from context by someone reading the original who is familiar with its ideas. I have also tried to ensure that the text still yields sensed if the reader ignores the material supplied in square brackets. Round brackets contain Sanskrit expressions from the text. These have usually been added for concepts for which it may be useful to know the original Sanskrit terms and in (often overlapping) cases where the words might bear different translations or interpretations. Rather than give the bibliographical details of all the Vedic works referred to in the *Yājñavalkya-Smṛti* and elsewhere in the anthology, I refer the reader to the editions used by Maurice Bloomfield in *A Vedic Concordance* (Harvard University Press, 1906; reprinted Delhi, 1964).

GUIDE TO PRONUNCIATION

a as in b*u*tter.
ā as in b*a*th.
i as in *I*ndia.
ī as in mach*i*ne.
u as in p*u*t.
ū as in r*u*le.
ṛ as in *ri*ver.
e as in s*ay*.
o as in b*o*wl.
c as in *ch*urch.

ṭ, ḍ and ṇ are retroflex – pronounced with the tongue curled back towards the roof of the mouth.

t, d and n are dental – pronounced with the tip of the tongue touching the front teeth.

ś and ṣ as in *sh*ow.

Aspirated consonants, such as th, gh and bh, can be reproduced in English when two words, such as ho*t h*ouse, big *h*eart and da*b h*and, are run together.

The letters k, ṭ, t and p are usually produced wtih slight aspiration by a native speaker of English. In Sanskrit they should be without any aspiration.

From the

ṚG-VEDA

FROM THE ṚG-VEDA

III, lxii 10: THE 'GĀYATRĪ' (THE BRĀHMAN'S DAILY PRAYER)

We meditate on the lovely light of the god, Savitṛ:[1]
   May it stimulate our thoughts!

I, xxiv : TO VARUṆA AND OTHERS
[Strophes 1–5 are omitted]

6. None hath attained to thy sovereignty and power,
None to thine undaunted spirit – [none –]
Nor swift-winged bird, nor restless-moving water,
Nor [mountain] curbing wind's impulsive might.

7. In the bottomless [abyss] king Varuṇa
By the power of his pure will upholds aloft
The [cosmic] tree's high crown. There stand below
[The branches], and above the roots. Within us
May the banners of his light be firmly set!

8. For the sun hath king Varuṇa prepared
A broad path that he may roam along it:
For the footless he made feet that he might move:
And he it is who the stricken of heart absolves.

9. A hundred and a thousand men of healing
Hast thou, O king: how wide, profound thy grace (*sumati*)!
Ward off and drive away unjust decay (*nirṛti*):
From the sin (*enas*) we have incurred deliver (*pramuc-*) us.

10. The stars of the Bear at night are set on high
[For all] to see; by day where do they go?
Of the laws of Varuṇa there's no deceiving:
At night the moon rides forth, herself displaying.

1 A sun-god.

11. Praising thee with holy prayer (*brahman*), I beg thee –
The sacrificer by his oblation begs thee:
O Varuṇa, be not enraged – thy words
Are widely heard, so rob us not of life.

12. By night, by day they tell me, as tells me too
This longing of my heart: 'Whom Śunaḥsepa
Called upon, bound [and captive as he was],
Varuṇa, the king, may he release (*muc*-) us!'

13. For Śunaḥsepa, captive, manacled
To three stakes, called upon the son of Aditi,
Varuṇa, the king, that he might free him:
May the wise one, undeceived, all fetters loose!

14. With obeisance, sacrifice, oblations we
Would pray away thine anger, Varuṇa:
Wise sovereign (*asura*), king, make loose our sins –
For thou hast powers – [the sins] we have incurred.

15. Make loose our fetters – [loose] the uppermost,
[Loose] the nethermost, and [loose] the midmost:
Then, son of Aditi, [firm] in thy covenant (*vrata*)
Will we sinless stand before [thy mother] Aditi!

I, cliv : TO VIṢṆU

1. I will now proclaim the manly powers of Viṣṇu
Who measured out earth's broad expanses,
Propped up the highest place of meeting:
Three steps he paced, the widely striding!

2. For [this], his manly power is Viṣṇu praised.
Like a dread beast he wanders where he will,
Haunting the mountains: in his three wide paces
All worlds and beings (*bhuvana*) dwell.

3. May [this] my hymn attain to Viṣṇu and inspire him,
Dwelling in the mountains, widely striding Bull,
Who, one and alone, with but three steps this long
And far-flung place of meeting measured out.

4. The marks of his three steps are filled with honey;
Unfailing they rejoice each in its own way.[2]
Though one, in threefold wise he has propped up
Heaven and earth, all beings [and all worlds].

5. Fain would I reach that well-loved home
Where god-devoted men are steeped in joy,
For that is kith and kin of the Wide-strider, –
The honey's source in Viṣṇu's highest footstep!

6. To the dwellings of you two we fain would go
Where there are cattle, many-horned and nimble(?).
There indeed the widely striding Bull's
Highest footstep, copious, downward shines.

II, i : TO AGNI

3. You, O Agni [Fire], are Indra, the bull [strongest] of all that exist; you are the wide-striding Viṣṇu, worthy of reverence; you, O Lord of the Holy Word (*Brahmaṇaspati*), are the chief priest who finds riches [for the sacrificer]; you, O distributer, are associated with munificence.

4. You, O Agni, are King Varuṇa, whose laws are firm; you are Mitra, the wonderworker to be revered; you are Aryaman, the reliable lord, of whom I would get enjoyment; O god, you are [god] Aṃśa ['Sharer'], the generous giver on the sacrificial ground.

5. You, O Agni, as Tvaṣṭar give heroic sons to the worshipper; O you who are attended by [divine] women, who have the might of Mitra, yours is relationship [with divine women? with Mitra? or both?]; as you incite swift horses [to race], you bestow good horses; you, with your abundant wealth, are the strength of men.

6. You, O Agni, are Rudra, the Asura of lofty heaven; as the troop of Maruts, you control sustenance; you travel by the ruddy winds[3] [of the dawn], bringing weal to households; as [god] Pūṣan you protect by your person the worshippers.

7. You, O Agni, give wealth to him who serves you; as god Savitṛ you are bestower of property; as [god] Bhaga ['Portioner'],

2 Following Geldner.
3 Implied is identity of Agni with the wind-god Vāta.

O king, you control riches; you are a protector in the house of him who has revered you.

II, xii : TO INDRA

1. Who as soon as born, first possessor of thought, the god, strengthened the gods by his magic [intellectual] power; of whose fury the two firmaments were afraid because of the greatness of his manliness, he, O folk, is Indra.

2. Who made firm the shaking earth, who brought to rest the mountains when they were disturbed, who measured out the wide atmosphere, who fixed the heaven, he, O folk, is Indra.

3. Who slew the dragon and made the seven streams to flow, who drove out the cows [of light] by disclosing Vala [the demon of darkness], who created the fire between two stones, winner of booty in battle, he, O folk, is Indra.

4. By whom all these shatterings were made, who put down the *dāsa* [non-Aryan] race in darkness, who takes the wealth of the enemy as a clever gambler takes the stake when he has won, he, O folk, is Indra.

5. The terrible one, of whom they ask, Where is he? and they even say of him, He is not at all; he diminishes the wealth of the enemy like gambling-stakes. Believe in him! He, O folk, is Indra.

6. Who encourages the humble, the feeble, the hard-pressed priest and poet; the one with lips effective [for drinking], who aids the soma-presser that employs the pressing-stones, he, O folk, is Indra.

7. In whose control are horses, cattle, villages, and all chariots; who created the sun, the dawn, and who guides the waters, he, O folk, is Indra.

8. Whom the two battle-lines invoke as they meet each other, both groups of foes on this side and on that; drawing near to his self-same chariot they call on him severally; he, O folk, is Indra.

9. Without whom people do not conquer, whom they invoke for aid while they fight, who has become a match for all, who shakes the unshaken, he, O folk, is Indra.

10. Who slays with his bolt, before they know it, all those that have committed great sin; who does not forgive the insolent his insolence, who slays the *dasyu* [non-Aryan], he, O folk, is Indra.

11. Who in the fortieth autumn found out [the demon] Śambara who was lurking in the mountains; who slew the might-exerting dragon, Dānu as he lay, he, O folk, is Indra.

12. The mighty bull of [requiring for control] seven reins, who let loose the seven streams to flow, who, club in arm, kicked down [presumptuous] Rauhiṇa, as he was scaling heaven, he, O folk, is Indra.

13. Even heaven and earth bow before him; of his fury even the mountains are afraid; who is recognized as soma-drinker, club in arm, club in hand, he, O folks, is Indra.

14. Who helps by his aid him that presses [soma] and cooks [sacrificial food], that chants [hymns] and is busily occupied [with sacrifice]; of whom holy utterance is a strengthening, and the soma and this gift [to officiating priests], he, O folk, is Indra.

15. You who with furious energy cause sustenance to burst forth for the one that presses and cooks, verily you are reliable. May we, O Indra, be ever dear to you. Having heroic sons, may we address the place of sacrifice.

II, xxxiii : TO RUDRA (ŚIVA)

1. Father of the Maruts! May thy grace (*sumna*) come [down]:
Do not withhold from us the vision of the sun!
May our warriors on horseback remain unscathed:[4]
Rudra, may we bring forth progeny abounding!

2. Most healing are the remedies thou givest;
By these for a hundred years I'd live!

4 Following Geldner.

Hatred, distress, disease drive far away,
Rudra, dispel them – away, on every side!

3. Most glorious in glory, in strength most strong art thou
Of all that's born, O Rudra, wielder of the bolt!
Ferry us in safety to the shore beyond distress;
Fend off [from us] all assaults of injury [and disease].

4. May we not, Bull Rudra, provoke thy wrath
By bowing down to thee,
By praising thee ineptly,
By invoking thee with others.
Raise up our men with healing remedies,
Best of physicians – so do I hear of thee.

5. To him are offered up
Oblations – invocations:
Him would I appease,
Rudra, with songs of praise.

Compassionate is he,
Easy to invoke;
Tawny [his body],
Lovely his lips:
May he not deliver us
Up to his fearful wrath!

6. With tough, compelling force
The Bull, the Maruts' lord
Hath cheered my suppliant's heart.
As shade in torrid heat,
Would I, unhurt, [My Lord] attain,
Win Rudra's [saving] grace (*sumna*).

7. O Rudra, where is thy caressing hand,
[The hand] that heals, [the hand] that cools,
[The hand] that bears away god-given hurt?
[Great] Bull, forbear with me!

8. The tawny Bull with white beflecked – for him,
The great – great, goodly praise I offer.
I will bow down – deep is my prostration –
To radiant (?) Rudra: his awful name we praise.

9. Right firm his limbs, manifold his forms;
Tawny and strong, he hath bedecked himself
With ornaments of lustrous gold.

Lord of this far-flung world is he:
Rudra [is his name].
May never celestial sovereignty (*asurya*)
Part company with him!

10. How fit it is that thou shouldst bear
Arrows and bow:
How fit [that thou shouldst bear]
A many-coloured necklace, adored [of men]:
How fit it is that thou shouldst so dispose
Of all this shattering power:
None is there, Rudra, more vast in strength than thou!

11. Praise him, the stripling widely famed,
Enthroned in his chariot – like unto a beast,
Fearful and strong, all ready for the kill(?).
Praised by the singer, Rudra, show him mercy;
Let thine armies lay another low – not us!

12. As a son bows down to a father who esteems him,
So, Rudra, [bow I] to thee as thou draw'st nigh:
[Thee,] giver of much, the lord of truth I praise –
And praised, thou givest us thy healing remedies.

13. Pure are your remedies, ye Marut-bulls;
Healing they bring, gladness they inspire:
Our father, Manu, chose them; these do I desire
With health and Rudra's blessing.

14. May Rudra's arrow pass us by;
May the great ill-will of the awful one pass on!
For our patrons' sake slacken thy taut [bow-string]:
O rich in grace (*mīḷvat*), have mercy on our children!

15. O God, O tawny Bull, who knowest all(?),
Let thy fury be restrained, do us no hurt!
Hearken thou here to this our invocation:
Rich in warriors, loud would we speak out
In [this] assembly [devoted to thy worship]!

IX, lxxiv : SOMA PRESSED IN THE BOWLS

1. Like a new-born child he bellows in the wood[5] the tawny racehorse straining to win the sun. He unites with the sky's seed that grows great with milk.[6] With kind thoughts we pray to him for far-reaching shelter.

2. He who is the pillar of the sky, the well-adorned support, the full stalk that encircles all around, he is the one who by tradition sacrifices to these two great world-halves. The poet[7] holds together the conjoined pair, and the refreshing foods.

3. The honey of Soma is a great feast; the wide pasture of Aditi is for the man who follows the right way. Child of dawn, the bull who rules over the rain here, leader of the waters, worthy of hymns, he is the one who brings help here.

4. Butter and milk are milked from the living cloud; the navel of Order, the ambrosia is born. Together those who bring fine gifts satisfy him; the swollen men[8] piss down the fluid set in motion.

5. The stalk roared as it united with the wave;[9] for man he swells the skin that attracts the gods. He places in the lap of Aditi the seed by which we win sons and grandsons.

6. Relentlessly they[10] flow down into the filter of a thousand streams; let them have offspring in the third realm of the world. Four hidden springs pouring forth butter carry down from the sky the ambrosia that is the oblation.

7. He takes on a white colour when he strains to win; Soma, the generous Asura, knows the whole world. He clings to inspired thought and ritual action as he goes forth; let him hurl down from the sky the cask full of water.

5 Soma as a new-born calf or horse wanders in the 'forest' of the wooden pressing-bowls.

6 The seed of heaven is the rain that mixes with the milk of the clouds, as Soma mixes with the milk in the bowls.

7 Soma is identified with the sun, who is called a poet, propping apart and holding together the pair of sky and earth, his parents.

8 The Maruts are the swollen men (clouds) who urinate the Soma (a male image) after it has been milked from the clouds (a female image). Soma is the living, androgynous cloud from which milk and rain are pressed.

9 Soma is the stalk; the wave is the water that mixes with it. The skin of the plant swells like the leather water-skin likened to the rain-clouds (cf I, lxxxv.5, V, lxxxiii.7) or the overturned cask (V, vii), both attributes of Parjanya.

10 The streams of Soma likened to rains are to have their 'offspring' in the third realm, for the floods of rain renew themselves in heaven. Cf. I, clxiv.

8. Now he has gone to the white pot coated by cows; the racehorse has reached the winning line and has won a hundred cows for Kakṣīvat, the man of a hundred winters.[11] Longing for the gods in their heart, they[12] hasten forth.

9. Clarifying Soma, when you are sated with waters your juice runs through the sieve made of wool. Polished by the poets, Soma who brings supreme ecstasy, be sweet for Indra to drink.

X, lxxxi : TO VIŚVAKARMAN (THE 'ALL-MAKER')

1. The seer, our father, sacrificing all these worlds,
Sat on the high priest's throne:
Pursuing wealth by [offering] prayer, he made away
With what came first, entering into the latter things.

2. What was the primal matter (*adhiṣṭhāna*)? What the beginning?
How and what manner of thing was that from which
The Maker of All, see-er of all, brought forth
The earth, and by his might the heavens unfolded?

3. His eyes on every side, on every side his face,
On every side his arms, his feet on every side –
With arms and wings he together forges
Heaven and earth, begetting them, God, the One!

4. What was the wood? What was the tree
From which heaven and earth were fashioned forth?
Ask, ask, ye wise in heart, on what did he rely
That he should [thus] support [these] worlds?

5. Teach us thy highest dwelling-places (*dhāma*), thy lowest too;
[Teach us] these, thy midmost, Maker of All:
Teach thy friends at the oblation, O thou, self-strong;
Offer sacrifice thyself to make thy body grow!

6. Maker of All, grown strong by the oblation,
Offer heaven and earth in sacrifice thyself!

11 Kakṣīvat, said to have been saved by the Aśvins (I, cxvi.7) may have regained his youth, as did many others helped by the Aśvins.

12 The Soma juices, or the priests.

Let others hither and thither, distracted, stray,
But for us let there be a bounteous patron here.

7. Let us today invoke the Lord of Speech,
Maker of All, inspirer of the mind,
To help us at the [time of] sacrifice.
Let him take pleasure in all our invocations,
Bring us all blessing, working good to help us!

X, lxxxii : TO VIŚVAKARMAN

1. The father of the eye – for wise of mind is he –
Begat these twain[13] like sacrificial ghee,
And they bowed to him [in worship].
Not till the ancient[14] bounds were firmly fixed
Were heaven and earth extended.

2. Maker of All, exceeding wise, exceeding strong,
Disposer,[15] Ordainer, highest Exemplar (*saṁdṛś*):
Their sacrifices[16] exult in nourishment
There where, they say, the One is – beyond the Seven Seers.[17]

3. He is our father, he begat us,
[He] the Ordainer: [he all] dwellings (*dhāma*) knows,
All worlds [he knows]: the gods he named,
[Himself] One only: other beings go to question him.

4. As [now our] singers [give] of their abundance.
So did the ancient seers together offer him wealth:
After the sunless and the sunlit spaces
Had been set down, together they made these beings.

5. Beyond the heavens, beyond this earth,
Beyond the gods, beyond the Asuras,
What was the first embryo the waters bore
To which all the gods bore witness?

13 i.e. heaven and earth.
14 Or, 'eastern'.
15 Or, 'Creator'.
16 Or 'wishes'.
17 i.e. the Great Bear.

6. He[18] was the first embryo the waters bore
In whom all gods together came,
The One implanted in the Unborn's navel
In which all the worlds abode.

7. You will not find him who [all] these begat:
Some other thing has stepped between you.
Blinded by fog and [ritual] mutterings
Wander the hymn-reciters, robbers of life!

X, xc : THE SACRIFICE OF PRIMAL MAN
(*puruṣa* = 'male person')

1. A thousand heads had [primal] Man,
A thousand eyes, a thousand feet:
Encompassing the earth on every side,
He exceeded it by ten fingers' [breadth].

2. [That] Man is this whole universe –
What was and what is yet to be,
The Lord of immortality
Which he outgrows by [eating] food.

3. This is the measure of his greatness,
But greater yet is [primal] Man:
All beings form a quarter of him,
Three-quarters are the immortal in heaven.

4. With three-quarters Man rose up on high,
A quarter of him came to be again [down] here:
From this he spread in all directions,
Into all that eats and does not eat.

5. From him was Virāj born,
From Virāj Man again:
Once born – behind, before,
He reached beyond the earth.

6. When with Man as their oblation
The gods performed the sacrifice,
Spring was the melted butter,
Summer the fuel, and autumn the oblation.

18 i.e. Viśvakarman.

7. Him they besprinkled on the sacrificial strew –
[Primeval] Man, born in the beginning:
With him [their victim], gods, Sādhyas, seers
Performed the sacrifice.

8. From this sacrifice completely offered
The clotted ghee was gathered up:
From this he fashioned beasts and birds,
Creatures of the woods and creatures of the village.

9. From this sacrifice completely offered
Where born the *Ṛg-* and *Sāma-Vedas*;
From this were born the metres,
From this was the *Yajur-Veda* born.

10. From this were horses born, all creatures
That have teeth in either jaw:
From this were cattle born,
From this sprang goats and sheep.

11. When they divided [primal] Man,
Into how many parts did they divide him?
What was his mouth? What his arms?
What are his thighs called? What his feet?

12. The Brāhman was his mouth,
The arms were made the Prince,
His thighs the common people,
And from his feet the serf was born.

13. From his mind the moon was born,
And from his eye the sun,
From his mouth Indra and the fire,
From his breath the wind was born.

14. From his navel arose the atmosphere,
From his head the sky evolved,
From his feet the earth, and from his ear
The cardinal points of the compass:
So did they fashion forth these worlds.

15. Seven were his enclosing sticks,
Thrice seven were made his fuel-sticks,
When the gods, performing sacrifice,
Bound Man, [their sacrificial] beast.

16. With sacrifice the gods
Made sacrifice to sacrifice:
These were the first religious rites (*dharma*),
To the firmament these powers went up
Where dwell the ancient Sādhya gods.

X, cxxi : PRAJĀPATI (THE 'GOLDEN EMBRYO')

1. In the beginning the Golden Embryo
[Stirred and] evolved:
Once born he was the one Lord of [every] being;
This heaven and earth did he sustain. . . .
What god shall we revere with the oblation?

2. Giver of life (*ātman*), giver of strength,
Whose behests all [must] obey,
Whose [behests] the gods [obey],
Whose shadow is immortality,
Whose [shadow] death. . . .
What god shall we revere with the oblation?

3. Who by his might has ever been the One
King of all that breathes and blinks the eye,
Who rules all creatures that have two feet or four. . . .
What god shall we revere with the oblation?

4. By whose might the snowy peaks,
By whose [might], they say, the sea
With Rasā, [the earth-encircling stream,]
By whose [might] the cardinal directions
Which are his arms, [exist] . . .
What god shall we revere with the oblation?

5. By whom strong heaven and earth are held in place,
By whom the sun is given a firm support,
By whom the firmament, by whom the ether (*rajas*)
Is measured out within the atmosphere. . . .
What god shall we revere with the oblation?

6. To whom opposing armies, strengthened by his help,
Look up, though trembling in their hearts,
By whom the risen sun sheds forth its light. . . .
What god shall we revere with the oblation?

7. When the mighty waters moved, conceived the All
As an embryo, giving birth to fire,
Then did he evolve, the One life-force (*asu*) of the gods. . . .
What god shall we revere with the oblation?

8. Who looked upon the waters, [looked on them] with power,
As they conceived insight,[19] brought forth the sacrifice;
Who, among the gods, was the One God above. . . .
What god shall we revere with the oblation?

9. May he not harm us, father of the earth,
Who generated heaven, for truth is his law,
Who gave birth to the waters – shimmering, strong. . . .
What god shall we revere with the oblation?

10. Prajāpati! None other than thou hath comprehended
All these [creatures] brought to birth.
Whatever desires be ours in offering up
The oblation to thee, may that be ours!
May we be lords of riches!

X, cxxix : 'IN THE BEGINNING . . .'

1. Then neither Being nor Not-being was,
Nor atmosphere, nor firmament, nor what is beyond.
What did it encompass? Where? In whose protection?
What was the water, the deep, unfathomable?

2. Neither death nor immortality was there then,
No sign of night or day.
That One breathed, windless, by its own energy (*svadhā*):
Nought else existed then.

3. In the beginning was darkness swathed in darkness;
All this was but unmanifested water.
Whatever was, that One, coming into being,
Hidden by the Void,
Was generated by the power of heat (*tapas*).

4. In the beginning this [One] evolved,
Became desire, first seed of mind.

19 Or 'strength', or a proper name (*Dakṣa*).

Wise seers, searching within their hearts,
Found the bond of Being in Not-being.

5. Their cord was extended athwart:
Was there a below? Was there an above?
Casters of seed there were, and powers;
Beneath was energy, above was impulse.

6. Who knows truly? Who can here declare it?
Whence it was born, whence is this emanation.
By the emanation of this the gods
Only later [came to be].
Who then knows whence it has arisen?

7. Whence this emanation hath arisen,
Whether [God] disposed it, or whether he did not, –[20]
Only he who is its overseer in highest heaven knows.
[He only knows,] or perhaps he does not know!

20 Or 'created'.

From the

ATHARVA-VEDA

FROM THE ATHARVA-VEDA

X, ii : PRIMAL MAN[1]

1. Who formed the heels of Man (*puruṣa*)?
Who formed his flesh, his ankles?
Who his well-formed fingers?
Who [opened up his] apertures?
Who [formed] the testicles (??) in his middle part?
Who [gave him] a firm basis?

2. Of what were made the ankles down below,
And the knee-caps of Man above them?
[Whence] were the shanks produced [and where] inserted?
Where were the knee-joints? Who can understand it?

3. [To the body] four [arms and legs] are joined
With ends welded thereinto.
Above the knees the flabby trunk;
The buttocks and the thighs, – who then produced them,
By which the trunk was firmly propped?

4. How many gods and which were they
Who built the breast and neck of Man?
How many arranged the breasts? Who [made] the nipples(?)?
How many [built] the shoulder-blades?
How many built the ribs?

5. Who brought together his two arms
That he might do manly deeds?
What god attached the shoulders to his trunk?

6. Who bored the seven apertures in the head –
These ears, the nostrils, eyes and mouth?

1 Cf. p. 13.

By mastering which with power four-footed and two-footed
beasts
Pursue their several ways in many a direction.

7. For he placed the many-sided tongue between the jaws,
And made to dwell therein the mighty [power of] speech.
Within the worlds he roves abroad, dwelling in the waters:
Who can understand it?

8. Who [fashioned] first the brain of Man,
His forehead, nape and skull, and built
What had to be built between the jaws,
Then heavenward ascended. Which god is that?

9. By whom (or what) does mighty Man endure
So much that's pleasing, so much displeasing,
Dream, affliction, weariness,
Joys and satisfactions?

10. Whence [comes] to Man distress, depression and decay,
And mindlessness; and whence [comes] affluence,
Success, prosperity, thought and exaltations?

11. Who arranged in Man the waters, flowing variously,
Wide-flowing, born to course in streams,
Pungent, brown, red and the colour of smoky copper,
Upward, down, athwart?

12. Who gave Man form, who gave him name and stature?
Who [gave him] gait, consciousness and legs?

13. Who wove in Man his breathing-in, who his breathing-out,
His breath 'diffused', his 'concentrated' breath?
What god made them dwell within him?

14. What single (*eka*) God put sacrifice in Man?
Who [planted] truth, untruth within him?
[And] whence is death, whence immortality?

15. Who wrapped him round with clothing? Who devised his
life (*āyu*)?
Who gave him strength? Who made him fleet of foot?

16. Through whom[2] did he spread the waters out?
Through whom did he make the day to shine?

2 Or 'what'. So too in the following lines and stanzas.

Through whom did he kindle the [light of] dawn?
Through whom did he grant the gift of eventide?

17. Who planted the semen in him
That his thread might be further spun?
Who brought him wisdom? Who in him put music, dance?

18. Through whom did he bedeck this earth?
Through whom the heavens encompass?
Through what power[3] does Man surpass the mountains?
Through whom are his works (*karma*) [performed]?

19. Through whom does he seek the rain-filled cloud (*parjanya*)?
Through whom the Soma, wise?
Through whom [does he seek] sacrifice and faith?
By whom was mind installed within him?

20. Through whom does he acquire one learned in the scriptures?
Through whom [does he win] the highest Lord?
Through whom does Man [acquire] this fire?
Through whom did he measure out the year?

21. Brahman [it is who] acquires one learned in the scriptures;
Brahman [wins] the highest Lord:
Brahman [as] Man [acquires] this fire;
Brahman [it is who] measured out the year.

22. Through whom does he dwell beside the gods?
Through whom beside the common people (*viś*) among the gods?
Through whom beside this other [class], not princely?
By whom is the princely [class] called Being (*sat*)?

23. Brahman [it is who] dwells beside the gods;
Brahman beside the common people among the gods;
Brahman beside this other [class], not princely;
Brahman is called Being, the princely [class].

24. By whom was this earth established?
By whom were the heavens fixed on high?
By whom was this atmosphere, this wide expanse,
Established above, athwart?

3 Or, 'through whom in greatness'.

25. By Brahman was this earth established;
Brahman the heavens fixed on high;
Brahman this atmosphere, this wide expanse,
Established above, athwart.

26. Atharvan sewed up his head and heart:
A wind, rising above the brain, expelled [it] from the head.

27. Atharvan's head assuredly
Is a casket of the gods, close sealed:
This head the bread of life (*prāṇa*) protects;
So too do food and mind.

28. Brought forth above, brought forth athwart,
All cardinal points did Man pervade –
[Yes, Man] who Brahman's city (*pur*) knows,
By which he is called 'Man' (*puruṣa*).

29. Whoso that city of Brahman truly (*vai*) knows
As swathed in immortality,
To him do Brahman and the Brāhmans give
Sight, life (*prāṇa*), and progeny.

30. Neither sight nor life desert the man
Before old age sets in,
Who the city of Brahman knows
By which he is called 'Man'.

31. The city of the gods which none lays low in battle
Has circles eight and portals nine:
In it is a golden treasure-chest –
Celestial, suffused with light.

32. In this golden treasure-chest, three-spoked and thrice supported –
In this there is a being strange (*yakṣa*) possessed of self (*ātmanvat*):
That is what knowers of Brahman know.

33. Into this radiant [city], – yellow, gold,
Compassed with glory round about,
The city unsubdued
Brahmā has entered in!

X, vii : SKAMBHA (THE SUPPORT)

1. In which of his limbs does fervour (*tapas*) dwell?
In which of his limbs is the law (*ṛta*) set down?
Where is the ordinance? Where in him does faith abide?
In which of his limbs is truth established?

2. From which of his limbs does the fire blaze forth?
From which of his limbs does Mātariśvan (the wind) blow?
From which of his limbs does the moon measure out –
Measuring a limb of mighty Skambha?

3. In which of his limbs does the earth abide?
In which of his limbs does the atmosphere dwell?
In which of his limbs are the heavens set and so abide?
In which of his limbs does the higher than heaven dwell?

4. Yearning for whom[4] does the fire blaze up on high?
Yearning for whom does Mātariśvan blow? –
Yearning for whom their courses(?) go towards him:
Tell forth that Skambha: which and what is he?

5. Whither go the half-months, whither go the months
In mutual understanding with the year? –
To where the seasons go, to where the seasons' fruits(?):
Tell forth that Skambha: which and what is he?

6. Yearning for whom do those maidens of differing form,
Day and night, run forth in mutual understanding? –
Yearning for whom the waters forward flow:
Tell forth that Skambha: which and what is he?

7. On whom Prajāpati propped up the worlds
And sustained them all [thereby]?
Tell forth that Skambha: which and what is he?

8. That which Prajāpati brought forth in every form
Above, below, and in between –
With how much [of himself] did Skambha enter in?
What he did not enter, how much was that?

9. With how much [of himself] did Skambha enter the past?
How much of him extends into the future?

4 Or, 'what'; and so in the following stanzas.

That one limb which he made a thousand-fold –
With how much [of himself] did Skambha enter in?

10. Wherein, men know, are worlds and what contains them (*kośa*),
The waters and Brahman in which are Being and Not-being:
Tell forth that Skambha: which and what is he?

11. Wherein ascetic fervour, striding forth, upholds the highest ordinance,
Wherein are law (*ṛta*) and faith, the waters and Brahman set together:
Tell forth that Skambha: which and what is he?

12. In whom are earth and atmosphere,
In whom the heavens are set, wherein the sun and moon
And fire and wind are fixed and so abide:
Tell forth that Skambha: who and what is he?

13. In a limb of whom all three and thirty gods are welded,
Tell forth that Skambha: who and what is he?

14. Wherein are the first-born seers,
The Vedas [three], Ṛg-, Sāma-, and great Yajus,
In whom the Single Seer is fixed:
Tell forth that Skambha: which and what is he?

15. Wherein, in Man (*puruṣa*), immortality and death are held together,
To whom belongs the ocean, the veins together held in Man:
Tell forth that Skambha: which and what is he?

16. Of whom the four cardinal directions are the swelling veins,
Wherein the sacrifice has mightily strode forth:
Tell forth that Skambha: which and what is he?

17. Whoso in Man knows Brahman, knows the highest Lord (*parameṣṭhin*),
Whoso knows the highest Lord, whoso Prajāpati,
Whoso knows that the Brahman-power (*brāhmaṇa*) is best,
Knows Skambha by analogy (*anu-*).

18. Whose head is the universal fire,
Whose eye the Aṅgirases became,

Whose limbs are sorcerers (*yātu*):
Tell forth that Skambha: which and what is he?

19. Whose mouth, they say, is Brahman,
Whose tongue the honeyed whip,
Whose udder is Virāj:
Tell forth that Skambha: which and what is he?

20. From whom the *Ṛg-Veda* was carved out,
From whom the *Yajur-Veda* was drawn forth,
Whose hairs the *Sāma-Veda* is, whose mouth
The *Atharva-Veda* and [the songs of] the Aṅgirases:
Tell forth that Skambha: which and what is he?

21. A branch of Not-being, jutting out, men take to be the highest.
Inferior men who this thy branch revere,
Think that it is Being too.

22. Wherein Ādityas, Rudras, Vasus are together held,
Wherein is what was and what is yet to be,
[Wherein] are all the worlds established:
Tell forth that Skambha: which and what is he?

23. Whose treasure-trove the three and thirty gods forever guard:
Today, ye gods, who knows that treasure-trove ye guard?

24. Whereas the gods who Brahman know
Revere Brahman as the highest, best,
Whoso thus knows them face to face
Is a Brahman-priest (*brahmā*) who knows.

25. Great indeed are the gods
Who from Not-being came to birth.
Men say that that Not-being is but one limb
Of Skambha: beyond [is he].

26. When Skambha generated and evolved the Ancient One,
Men knew then by analogy that this Ancient One
Is but one limb of Skambha.

27. Whereas in [that one] limb of his the three and thirty gods
Parcelled out legs [between themselves],

Some knowers of Brahman [came to] know
Those three and thirty gods.

28. Men [think they] know the Golden Embryo[5]
As the unutterable, supreme:
[No,] in the beginning Skambha poured it forth,
[Pure] gold within the world.

29. In Skambha are the worlds, in Skambha ascetic fervour,
In Skambha is the law (*ṛta*) set down:
I know thee, Skambha, face to face
In Indra wholly concentrated!

30. In Indra are the worlds, in Indra ascetic fervour,
In Indra is the law set down:
I know thee, Indra, face to face,
On Skambha wholly founded!

31. Again and again name after name a man invokes
Before [the rising of] the sun, before the dawn.
When the Unborn first grew and came to birth (*sambhū-*),
Forth did he stride to sovereignty:
No other being is higher than he!

32. Whose measure is the earth, whose belly the atmosphere,
Who made the sky his head – to him be homage – Brahman, best!

33. Whose eye is the sun, and the moon forever new,
Who made the fire his mouth – to him be homage – Brahman, best!

34. Whose breathing in and breathing out are wind,
Whose eye the Aṅgirases became,
Who made the cardinal points his wisdom,
To him be homage – Brahman, best!

35. Firmly did Skambha hold in place heaven and earth, – both these,
Firmly did Skambha hold in place the far-flung atmosphere,
Firmly did Skambha hold in place the six wide-spread directions:
Into this whole world hath Skambha entered in.

36. Who came to birth by fervour, toil,
Who mastered all the worlds,

5 See pp. 5–16.

Who made the Soma all his own (*kevala*) –
To him be homaged – Brahman, best!

37. How [is it that] the wind doth never come to rest?
How [is it that] the mind doth never cease from thinking?
How [is it that] the waters, yearning for the truth,
Are never, never still?

38. A being great and strange (*yakṣa*) in the middle of the world
Strode forth in holy fervour on the waters' crest:
In it whatever gods there be found refuge
Like branches clustered around the tree-trunk.

39. To whom with hands and feet, with voice and ear and eye
The gods forever offer up a measureless sacrifice
In a [place of sacrifice well] measured out:
Tell forth that Skambha: who and what is he?

40. From him is darkness far removed: untouched by evil he:
In him are all the lights – in Prajāpati but three.

41. Whoso doth know the golden reed standing in the waters,
He is indeed Prajāpati, though hidden.

42. Two single maidens of differing form
Weave a web on six pegs set,
Approaching it in turn:
The one draws forth the threads,
The other sets them in their place.
They do not break them off:
[Their labour] has no end.

43. They seem to dance around, and I cannot distinguish
Which of them came first. A male [now] weaves it, ties it up:
A male hath borne it [up] unto the firmament.

44. These pegs prop up the sky: the chants were made the shuttle for the weaving.

X, viii : SKAMBHA AGAIN

1. Who supervises all that was and that is yet to be,
To whom the sun alone belongs – to him be homage – Brahman, best!

2. By Skambha are these two held apart –
Heaven and earth – and so they stand:
In Skambha [dwells] this whole universe, possessed of self (*ātmanvat*); –
What breathes and blinks the eye.

3. Three generations have passed away and gone;
Others have entered in around the [sacrificial] fire.[6]
Great [is the sun which] stood [there], measuring out the firmament:
The golden-yellow male has entered the golden-yellow females.[7]

4. Twelve fellies, a single wheel, three naves:
Who can understand it?
Three hundred pegs have there been hammered in,
And sixty nails which none can move.

5. This, Savitṛ, do thou understand:
Six twins there are, another born alone:
In him among their number who alone was born
They crave association.

6. Though manifest, it is yet hidden, secret:
The 'ageing' is its name, a mighty mode of being (*pada*).[8]
Therein is this universe [firm] fixed;
Therein is [all] that moves and breathes established.

7. With a single wheel it turns, with a single felly,
With a thousand syllables, up to the east, down to the west:
With a half [of itself] it brought the whole world forth:
Its [other] half, oh, what has that become?

8. In front of these the five-horsed [chariot] moves on:
Trace-horses yoked to it help to draw it.
The path it has not traversed some have seen;
What it has traversed none.
The nearer [sees it] high above,
The further down below.

9. A bowl there is, a hole [pierced] in its side, its bottom upward turned;

6 Or 'sun' or 'praise'.
7 i.e. the plants?
8 Or, 'place'.

In it is glory stored, [glory] in all its forms:
Thereon together sit the Seven Seers
Who became this mighty one's protectors.

10. [The Ṛg-Vedic verse] which is yoked in front,
That [yoked] behind, that yoked on every side,
And that on all sides [yoked], by which
The sacrifice is forward stretched – of that
I ask thee: which of [those] verses is that?

11. What moves, what falls, what stands, what breathes,
What does not breathe, what blinks, becomes,
This keeps the world in being – many are its forms –
This, growing together, becomes just One.

12. The infinite is extended out in many places:
Infinite and finite [meet] at a common edge.
The guardian of the firmament moves – discriminates between them –
Knowing what of it was and what is yet to be.

13. The Lord of Creatures (*prajāpati*) stirs within the womb:
Unseen he comes to birth in many forms and places:
With a half [of himself] he brought the whole world forth:
His [other] half, oh, what is the mark of that?

14. Like a woman bearing water in her pitcher
He bears the water up:
All see him with the eye; not all know him with the mind.

15. Far off he dwells with what is full,
Far off he lacks what is deficient,
A being great and strange (*yakṣa*) in the middle of the world:
To him do kings bring tribute.

16. From which the sun arises,
In which [the sun] doth set;
That, I think, is the highest, best:
There is none that can surpass it.

17. When recently, or in the middle past, or long ago
Men speak about the man who knows the Veda,
It is the sun of which they one and all do speak,
Of fire as second and of the threefold swan.

18. For a thousand-day journey the wings of the yellow swan
Are spread abroad as heavenward it flies:
Gathering all the gods into its bosom, it
Flies on, surveying all the worlds.

19. By truth he gives heat on high,
By Brahman he looks below:
He breathes obliquely by the breath
In which the Best has found a home.

20. Who knows the fire-sticks from which, by rubbing, wealth is won,
He, knowing, ponders on the highest, best:
He knows the mighty Brahman-power.

21. In the beginning he, footless, came to be;
In the beginning he bore the heavenly light:
He acquired four feet and became of use;
All enjoyment took he for himself.

22. Whoso reveres the eternal God who reigns on high
[Himself] becomes of use, an eater of much food.

23. Eternal do they call him, and yet e'en now
Is he ever again renewed.
Day and night are each from the other born
Each in its different form.

24. A hundred, a thousand, a myriad, a hundred million –
What is his own, what has entered him, how can it be counted?
All that is his they slay as he looks on:
On this account this god approves it!

25. The One is finer than a hair:
The One, it seems, cannot be seen.
Hence is that deity so dear to me,
Most fit to be embraced.

26. In the house of mortal man there is [a maiden,]
Fair, unageing and immortal.
He for whom she was made lies flat;
He who made her has grown old.

27. Thou art woman, thou art man,
Thou art the lad and the maiden too,

Thou art the old man tottering on his staff:
Once born thou comest to be, thy face turned every way!

28. He is their father, he their son,
He their eldest brother and their youngest:
The One God, entering the mind,
Is the first-born; [yet] he is in the womb.

29. From the full the full he raises up;
With the full is the full besprinkled:
Would that today we knew from whence
That [full] is sprinkled round about.

30. She, the eternal, was born in right olden times;
She, the primeval, all things encompassed:
The great goddess, lighting up the dawn,
Looks out from each single thing that blinks the eye.

31. The deity whose name is 'Helpful' sits
Encompassed by the law (*ṛta*):
Because its hue is such, these trees
Are green, and green their garlands.

32. Near though he is, one cannot leave him;
Near though he is, one cannot see him.
Behold the god's wise artistry!
He does not die, he grows not old.

33. Words uttered by him than whom there's nothing earlier
Speak of things as they really are:
The place to which they, speaking, go
Men call the mighty Brahman-power (*brāhmaṇa*).

34. That wherein gods and men were set
As spokes within the hub,
Wherein the waters' flower by some uncanny power (*māyā*)
Was laid, of that I ask thee.

35. [The gods] by whom impelled the wind blows forth,
Who cause the five points of the compass to converge,
These gods who the oblations spurned,
Guides to the waters – which were they?

36. Of these one clothes himself in this [our] earth,
And one encompasseth the atmosphere;

One of them, the Disposer, gives the sky,
Others protect all the cardinal directions.

37. Who knows the thread extended
On which these creatures are spun;
Who knows the thread of the thread,
Would know the mighty Brahman-power.

38. I know the thread extended
On which these creatures are spun;
I know the thread of the thread,
Hence the mighty Brahman-power.

39. When between heaven and earth the fire
Rushed onward, burning, everything consuming,
To where the wives of but one husband stood far off,
Where was Mātariśvan then?

40. Into the waters had Mātariśvan entered,
Into the waters the gods had entered.
Great [is the sun which] stood [there], measuring out the spaces:
The cleansing [Soma][9] has entered the golden-yellow females.[10]

41. Higher, it seems, than the Gāyatrī[11]
He strode forth in immortality:
Who chant with chant together know –
[Can they know] where the Unborn saw it?

42. The bringer of rest, hoarder of wealth,
Whose law (*dharma*), like the god Savitṛ, is true,
Like Indra in the war for riches stood.

43. A lotus with nine gates[12] enveloped by three strands (*guṇa*) –
In it is a being strange (*yakṣa*), possessed of self (*ātmanvat*):
That [it is that] knowers of Brahman know.

44. Free from desire, immortal, wise and self-existent,
With [its own] savour satisfied, and nothing lacking –
Whoso knows him, the Self – wise, ageless, [ever] young –
Of death will have no fear.

9 Or, '[wind]'.
10 i.e. the plants?
11 See p. 3.
12 i.e. the body.

XI, iv : TO THE BREATH OF LIFE ('PRĀṆA')

1. Homage to the Breath of Life, for this whole universe obeys it,
Which has become the Lord of all, on which all things are based.

2. Homage to thee, O Breath of Life, [homage] to thy crashing;
Homage to thee, the thunder; homage to thee, the lightning;
Homage to thee, O Breath of Life, when thou pourest rain.

3. When upon the plants the Breath of Life in thunder roars,
They [then] conceive and form the embryo;
Then manifold are they born.

4. When upon the plants the Breath of Life, the season come, roars loud,
All things soever upon [this] earth rejoice with great rejoicing.

5. When the Breath of Life [this] mighty earth with rain bedews,
Then do the cattle [too] rejoice: 'Great [strength] will be our portion.'

6. Rained upon by the Breath of Life, the plants gave voice:
'Thou hast prolonged for us our life; fragrance hast thou given.'

7. Homage to thee, O Breath of Life, when thou comest, when thou goest:
Homage to thee when standing still; homage to thee when sitting!

8. Homage to thee, O Breath of Life, when breathing in,
Homage when breathing out:
Homage to thee when thou turnest aside, homage to thee when thou facest [us] !
To all of thee, [yea, all,] is this [our] homage [due].

9. O Breath of Life, that form of thine so dear [to us],
O Breath of Life, that [form] which is yet dearer,
And then that healing which [too] is thine
Place it in us that we may live.

10. The Breath of Life takes [living] creatures as its garment,
As father [takes] his beloved son.
The Breath of Life is the Lord of all,
Of whatever breathes and what does not.

11. The Breath of Life is death, is fever;
The Breath of Life the gods revere.
In the highest world hath the Breath of Life
Set the man who speaks the truth.

12. The Breath of Life is Virāj, the Breath of Life is guide,
The Breath of Life all things revere.
The Breath of Life is sun and moon;
The Breath of Life they call Prajāpati.

13. The breathing in and the breathing out are rice and barley:
Draught-ox [too] is [this] breath called:
The breathing in is placed in barley,
The breathing out is surnamed rice.

14. Within the womb a man (*puruṣa*) breathes in and out:
When, Breath of Life, thou quickenest him,
Then is he born again.

15. The Breath of Life some call the wind (*mātariśvan*);
Again it's called the breeze (*vāta*).
In the Breath of Life is what is past and what is yet to be;
On the Breath of Life all things are based.

16. Atharvan plants, Aṅgiras [plants, plants] derived from gods or men,
O Breath of Life, are born when thou dost quicken them.

17. When the Breath of Life [this] mighty earth with rain bedews,
The plants are born – whatever herbs there are.

18. Who this of thee knows, O Breath of Life,
And what it is that forms thy base,
To him all [men] shall tribute bring
In yonder highest world.

19. As all these creatures here, O Breath of Life,
Bring tribute unto thee,
So too shall they to him bring tribute
Who hears thee – thou, so good to hear.

20. As an embryo he stirs within the deities;
He comes to be, has been, is born again.

What was,[13] what is and what is yet to be
Hath he entered with his powers, as father [enters] son.

21. [Like] a swan from the ocean he rises up,
Withdrawing not his single foot:
Should he withdraw it, there would not be
Todays, tomorrows, nights or days;
It would never dawn again.

22. With eight wheels he turns, with a single felly,
With a thousand syllables, up to the east, down to the west.
With half [of himself] he gave birth to the whole world:
His [other] half, O, what is the mark of that?

23. To him who rules all births, all moving things,
To him whose bow is swift among the rest,
To him, to thee, O Breath of Life, be homage!

24. May he who rules all births, all moving things,
Unwearied, wise by Brahman, the Breath of Life, stand by me!

25. Erect, he stays awake when others sleep,
He never falls down prone:
That he should sleep while others sleep,
None has ever heard.

26. O Breath of Life, turn not thy back on me:
None other than I shalt thou be.
As an embryo in the waters, so I within myself
Bind thee, that I may live!

13 Reading *bhūtam*.

From the

UPANISHADS

BṚHADĀRAṆYAKA UPANISHAD[1]

Book One

I, i[2]

[*The world as a sacrificial horse*[3]]

1. Oṁ. Verily, the dawn is the head of the sacrificial horse; the sun, his eye; the wind, his breath; universal fire (*Agni Vaiśvānara*), his open mouth. The year is the body (*ātman*) of the sacrificial horse; the sky, his back; the atmosphere, his belly; the earth, the under part of his belly; the quarters, his flanks; the intermediate quarters, his ribs; the seasons, his limbs; the months and half-months, his joints; days and nights, his feet; the stars, his bones; the clouds, his flesh. Sand is the food in his stomach; rivers are his entrails. His liver and lungs are the mountains; plants and trees, his hair. The orient is his fore part; the occident, his hind part. When he yawns, then it lightens. When he shakes himself, then it thunders. When he urinates, then it rains. Voice, indeed, is his voice.

2. Verily, the day arose for the horse as the sacrificial vessel which stands before. Its place is the eastern sea.

Verily, the night arose for him as the sacrificial vessel which stands behind. Its place is the western sea. Verily, these two arose on both sides of the horse as the two sacrificial vessels.[4]

1 The *Kāṇva* text is followed throughout.

2 This Brāhmaṇa occurs also as *Śatapatha-Brāhmaṇa* 10. 6. 4.

3 The *Aśva-medha*, 'Horse-sacrifice', the most elaborate and important of the animal sacrifices in ancient India (described at length in *Śatapatha-Brāhmaṇa* 13. 1–5), is interpreted, in this and the following Brāhmaṇa, as of cosmic significance – a miniature reproduction of the world-order. In the liturgy for the Horse-sacrifice (contained in *Vājasaneyi Saṃhitā* 22–5) there is a similar apportionment of the parts of the animal to the various parts of the world. Compare also a similar elaborate cosmic correlation of the ox at *Atharva-Veda* IX; vii.

4 The vessels used to hold the libations at the *Aśva-medha*. Here they are symbolized cosmically by the Bay of Bengal and the Indian Ocean.

Becoming a steed, he carried the gods; a stallion, the Gandharvas; a courser, the demons; a horse, men.[5] The sea, indeed, is his relative. The sea is his place.

I, ii

1. In the beginning nothing at all existed here. This [whole world] was enveloped by Death, – by Hunger. For what is death but hunger? And [Death] bethought himself: 'Would that I had a self!' He roamed around, offering praise; and from him, as he offered praise, water was born. And he said [to himself]: 'Yes, it was a joy (*ka*) to me to offer praise (*arc*-).' And this is what makes fire (*arka*) fire. And joy is the lot of him who understands that this is what makes fire fire.

2. Water too is *arka*. And the froth of the water was churned together and became the earth. And on this [earth] he wore himself out. And the heat (*tejas*) and sap [generated] by him, worn out and consumed by fierce penances (*tapta*) as he was, turned into fire.

3. He divided [him]self (*ātman*) into three parts: [one third was fire,] one third the sun, one third the wind. He too is the breath of life (*prāṇa*) threefold divided.

The east is his head. The north-east and south-east[6] are his two arms. The west is his tail. The north-west and south-west are his two buttocks. The south and north are his flanks. The sky is his back, the atmosphere his belly, this [earth] his chest. Firmly is he based on the waters; and firmly is that man based who thus knows, wherever he may go.

4. [Then] he longed that a second self might be born to him; [and so he who is] Hunger and Death copulated with Speech by means of mind. What was the seed became the year; for there was no year before that. For so long did he bear him [within himself], – for a whole year; and after so long a time did he bring him forth. When he was born, [Death] opened his mouth [as if to swallow him]. 'Bhān', said he, and that became speech.

5. He considered [within himself]: 'If I should try to take his life, I should make less food for myself.' By this word, by this self, he brought forth this whole universe, – everything that exists, –

5 Different names for, and aspects of, this cosmic carrier.

6 So Sáṅkara: the text has simply 'that and that'.

Ṛg-Veda, *Yajur-Veda*, *Sāma-Veda*, metres, sacrifices, men and beasts.

And whatever he brought forth he began to eat: for he eats up everything. And that is what makes Aditi Aditi (*ad-* = 'to eat'). Whoso thus knows what makes Aditi Aditi becomes an eater of everything here: everything is his food.

6. He longed to sacrifice with a yet greater sacrifice. He wore himself out, performing fierce penances. And from him, worn out and consumed by fierce penances, glory and strength issued forth. Glory and strength are the vital breaths. And as these vital breaths issued forth, the body began to swell; and the mind was in his body.

7. He longed for his [body] to become fit for sacrifice and that thereby he might come to possess a self. And from this [longing of his] a horse (*aśva*) came to be because he had swelled (*aśvat*). 'Now it has become fit for sacrifice,' thought he. That is what makes the horse-sacrifice the horse-sacrifice. Whoso knows him thus, knows the horse-sacrifice.

Without penning the [horse] in, he kept it in mind and after a year he sacrificed it to [him]self (*ātman*). The [other] animals he distributed among the deities. That is why the victim besprinkled and offered up to Prajāpati is [really] sacrificed to all the gods.

This horse-sacrifice is the same as the burning [sun]; and the year is its self.

This fire [here] is *arka*, the sacrificial fire. These worlds are its selves.

Two they are – the sacrificial fire and the horse-sacrifice. Yet he is only one deity – Death. He [who knows this] overcomes the second death (*punarmṛtyu*); death cannot touch him; death becomes his [very] self: he becomes one of these deities.

I, iii

[*The superiority of breath among the bodily functions*]

1. The gods (*deva*) and the devils (*asura*) were the twofold offspring of Prajāpati. Of these the gods were the younger, the devils the older. They were struggling with each other for these worlds.

The gods said: 'Come, let us overcome the devils at the sacrifice with the Udgītha.'[7]

7 The important Loud Chant in the ritual.

2. They said to Speech: 'Sing for us the Udgītha.'

'So be it', said Speech, and sang for them. Whatever pleasure there is in speech, that it sang for the gods; whatever good one speaks, that for itself.

They [i.e. the devils] knew: 'Verily, by this singer they will overcome us.' They rushed upon it and pierced it with evil. That evil was the improper thing that one speaks. That was the evil.

3. Then they [i.e. the gods] said to the In-breath (*prāṇa*) 'Sing for us the Udgītha.'

'So be it', said the In-breath, and sang for them. Whatever pleasure there is in the in-breath, that it sang for the gods; whatever good one breathes in, that for itself.

They [i.e. the devils] knew: 'Verily, by this singer they will overcome us.' They rushed upon it and pierced it with evil. That evil was the improper thing that one breathes in. This, truly, was that evil.

4. Then they [i.e. the gods] said to the Eye: 'Sing for us the Udgītha.'

'So be it', said the Eye, and sang for them. Whatever pleasure there is in the eye, that it sang for the gods; whatever good one sees, that for itself.

They [i.e. the devils] knew: 'Verily, by this singer they will overcome us.' They rushed upon it and pierced it with evil. That evil was the improper thing that one sees. This, truly, was that evil.

5. Then they [i.e. the gods] said to the Ear: 'Sing for us the Udgītha.'

'So be it', said the Ear, and sang for them. Whatever pleasure there is in the ear, that it sang for the gods; whatever good one hears, that for itself.

They [i.e the devils] knew: 'Verily, by this singer they will overcome us.' They rushed upon it and pierced it with evil. That evil was the improper thing that one hears. This, truly, was that evil.

6. Then they [i.e. the gods] said to the Mind: 'Sing for us the Udgītha.'

'So be it', said the Mind, and sang for them. Whatever pleasure there is in the mind, that it sang for the gods; whatever good one imagines, that for itself.

They [i.e. the devils] knew: 'Verily, by this singer they will overcome us.' They rushed upon him and pierced him with evil.

That evil was the improper thing that one imagines. This, truly, was that evil.

And thus they let out upon these divinities with evil, they pierced them with evil.

7. Then they [i.e. the gods] said to this Breath in the mouth: 'Sing for us the Udgītha.'

'So be it', said this Breath, and sang for them.

They [i.e. the devils] knew: 'Verily, by this singer they will overcome us.' They rushed upon him and desired to pierce him with evil. As a clod of earth would be scattered by striking on a stone, even so they were scattered in all directions and perished. Therefore the gods increased, the demons became inferior. He increases with himself, a hateful enemy becomes inferior for him who knows this.

8. Then they said, 'What, pray, has become of him who stuck to us thus?' 'This one here (*ayam*) is within the mouth (*āsya*)!' He is called Ayāsya Āṅgirasa, for he is the essence (*rasa*) of the limbs (*aṅga*).

9. Verily, that divinity is Dūr by name, for death is far (*dūram*) from it. From him who knows this, death is far.

10. Verily, that divinity having struck off the evil of these divinities, even death, made this go to where is the end of the quarters of heaven. There it set down their evils. Therefore one should not go to [foreign] people, one should not go to the end [of the earth], lest he fall in with evil, with death.

11. Verily, that divinity by striking off the evil, the death, of those divinities carried them beyond death.

12. Verily, it carried Speech over as the first. When that was freed from death, it became fire. This fire, when it has crossed beyond death, shines forth.

13. Likewise it carried Smell across. When that was freed from death, it became wind. This wind, when it has crossed beyond death, purifies.

14. Likewise it carried the Eye across. When that was freed from death, it became the sun. That sun, when it has crossed beyond death, glows.

15. Likewise it carried the Ear across. When that was freed from death, it became the quarters of heaven. These quarters of heaven have crossed beyond death.

16. Likewise it carried the Mind across. When that was freed

from death, it became the moon. That moon, when it has crossed beyond death, shines.

Thus, verily, that divinity carries beyond death him who knows best.

17. Then it [i.e. breath] sang out food for itself, for whatever food is eaten is eaten by it. Hereon one is established.

18. Those gods said: 'Of such extent, verily, is this universe as food. You have sung it into your own possession. Give us an after-share in this food.'

'As such, verily, do ye enter into me.'

'So be it.' They entered into him from all sides. Therefore whatever food one eats by this breath, these are satisfied by it. Thus, verily, his people come to him, he becomes the supporter of his people, their chief, foremost leader, an eater of food, an overlord – he who knows this. And whoever among his people desires to be the equal of him who has this knowledge suffices not for his dependants. But whoever follows him and whoever, following after him, desires to support his dependants, he truly suffices for his dependants.

19. He is Ayāsya Āṅgirasa, for he is the essence (*rasa*) of the limbs (*aṅga*). Verily, breath is the essence of the limbs, for verily breath is the essence of the limbs. Therefore from whatever limb the breath departs, that indeed dries up, for it is verily the essence of the limbs.

20. And it is also Bṛhaspati. The Bṛhatī[8] is speech. He is her lord (*pati*), and is therefore Bṛhaspati.

21. And it is also Brahmaṇaspati. Prayer (*brahman*),[9] verily, is speech. He is her lord (*pati*), and is therefore Brahmaṇaspati.

[*A glorification of the Chant as breath*]

22. And it is also the *Sāma-Veda*. The Chant (*sāman*), verily, is speech. it is *sā* (she) and *ama* (he). That is the origin of the word *sāman*.

Or because it is equal (*sama*) to a gnat, equal to a fly, equal to an elephant, equal to these three worlds, equal to this universe, therefore, indeed, it is the *Sāma-Veda*. He obtains intimate union with the Sāman, he wins its world who knows thus that Sāman.

8 Name of a metre used in the *Ṛg-Veda*. Here it signifies the *Ṛg-Veda* itself.
9 Here referring particularly to the *Yajur-Veda*.

23. And it is also the Udgītha. The breath verily is up (*ut*), for by breath this whole world is upheld (*ut-tabdha*). Song (*gītha*), verily, is speech; *ut* and *gītha* – that is Udgītha.

24. As also Brahmadatta Caikitāneya, while partaking of King [Soma]ob, said: 'Let this king cause this man's[10] head to fall off, if Ayāsya Āṅgirasa sang the Udgītha with any other means than that, for', said he, 'only with speech and with breath did he sing the Udgītha.'

25. He who knows the property of that Sāman has that property. Its property, truly, is tone. Therefore let him who is about to perform the duties of an Ṛtvij priest desire a good tone in his voice. Being possessed of such a voice, let him perform the duties of the Ṛtvij priest. Therefore people desire to see at the sacrifice one who has a good tone, as being one who has a possession. He has a possession who knows thus the property of the Sāman.

26. He who knows the gold of that Sāman comes to have gold. The tone (*svara*), verily, is its gold. He comes to have gold who knows thus that gold of the Sāman.

27. He who knows the support of that Sāman is indeed supported. Voice, verily, is its support, for when supported on voice the breath sings. But some say it is supported on food.

[*Prayers to accompany an intelligent performance of the Chant*]

28. Now next, the praying of the purificatory formulas (*pavamāna*):

The Prastotṛ priest [Praiser], verily, begins to praise with the Chant (*sāman*). When he begins to praise, then let [the sacrificer] mutter the following:

> 'From the unreal (*asat*) lead me to the real (*sat*)!
> From darkness lead me to light!
> From death lead me to immortality!'

When he says 'From the unreal lead me to the real', the unreal, verily, is death, the real is immortality. 'From death lead me to immortality. Make me immortal' – that is what he says.

'From darkness lead me to light' – the darkness, verily, is death,

10 That is, 'my'. – Com.

the light is immortality. 'From death lead me to immortality. Make me immortal' – that is what he says.

'From death lead me to immortality' – there is nothing there that seems obscure.

Now whatever other verses there are of a hymn of praise (*stotra*), in them one may win food for himself by singing. And, therefore, in them he should choose a boon, whatever desire he may desire. That Udgātṛ priest who knows this – whatever desire he desires, either for himself or for the sacrificer, that he obtains by singing. This, indeed, is world-conquering. There is no prospect of his being without a world who knows thus this Sāman.

I, iv

1. In the beginning this [universe] was the Self alone, – in the likeness of a man (*puruṣa*). Looking around, he saw nothing other than [him]self. First of all he said: 'This is I.' Hence the name 'I' came to be. So, even now when a man is addressed, he says first, 'This is I,' and then speaks out any other name he may have. And because he had first (*pūrva*) burnt up (*uṣ-*) all evils from this whole universe, he is [called] 'man' (*puruṣa*). So too does the man who thus knows burn up anyone who tries to get the better of him.

2. He was afraid. So, [even now] a man who is all alone is afraid.

He took thought and said [to himself]: 'Since nothing exists other than I, of whom (or what) am I afraid?' And this fear then departed [from him]; for of whom (or what) should he have been afraid? It is of a second that one is afraid.

3. He found no pleasure at all. So, [even now] a man who is all alone finds no pleasure. He longed for a second.

Now he was of the size of a man and a woman in close embrace. He split (*pat-*) this Self in two: and from this arose husband (*pati*) and wife (*patnī*). Hence we say, 'Oneself (*sva*) is like half a potsherd', as indeed Yājñavalkya used to say. That is why space is filled up with woman. He copulated with her, and thence were human beings born.

4. She took thought and said [to herself]: 'How is it that he copulates with me, although he generated me from his very Self? Very well, I will disappear.'

She became a cow: he a bull. He copulated with her, and thence were cattle born.

She became a mare: he a stallion. She [became] a she-ass: he a he-ass. He copulated with her, and thence were single-hoofed animals born.

She became a she-goat: he a he-goat. She [became] a ewe: he a ram. He copulated with her, and thence were goats and sheep born.

So did he bring forth all couples that exist, even down to the ants: [so did he bring forth] this whole universe.

5. He knew that he was [the whole of] creation,[11] for he had brought it all forth. Hence he became [all] creation. Whoso thus knows comes to be in that creation of his.

6. Then he rubbed [backwards and forwards], – like this, – and with his hands and from his mouth [as] from the womb[12] he brought forth fire. That is why both [hands and mouth] are hairless on the inside; for the womb [too] is hairless on the inside.

Now, when people say, 'Sacrifice to this [god], sacrifice to that [god]' – one god after another, they mean this creation of his; for he himself *is* all the gods.

Now, whatever is moist, he brought forth from semen, and that is Soma. The whole extent of this universe is nothing but food and what eats food. Soma is food: fire eats it.

This is the super-emanation of Brahman,[13] namely, that he brought forth the gods, his betters; so too, though he [himself] was mortal, he brought forth immortals. That is why it is [called] a super-emanation. Whoso thus knows comes to be in that super-emanation of his.

7. Now, at that time this [world] was undifferentiated. What introduces differentiation is name and form (individuality), so that we can say: 'A man has this name; he has this form.' For even now it is name and form that introduce differentiation, so that we can say: 'A man has this name, he has this form.'

He entered in here (into the body), right up to the finger-tips just as a razor fits into a razor-case or fire into a brazier. [Yet] he cannot be seen, for he is incomplete. When breathing, his name is breath; when speaking, voice; when seeing, the eye; when hearing,

11 *Sṛṣṭi*: more accurately 'emanation'.
12 Or, 'fire-hole'.
13 Or, 'Brahmā'.

the ear; when thinking, the mind. These are the names of his [various] works (*karma*). The man who reveres any of these individually has no [right] knowledge: for he is incomplete in any of these individually.

Let a man revere Him rather as the 'Self', for therein do all these [works] become one. The Self is [as it were] a trace of all this, for it is by It that one knows all this [universe]. And just as a man can find [another] by his footprints, so does the man who thus knows find good fame and praise.

8. This [Self] is dearer than a son, dearer than wealth, dearer than all else, for the Self is what is most inward. Were one to speak of a man who says that there is some other thing dearer than the Self, [and say]: 'He will weep for what he holds dear', he would very likely do so. So, let a man revere the Self as dear. For one who reveres the Self alone as dear, what he holds dear will never perish.

9. It has been said: 'Since men think that by knowing Brahman they will become the All', what was it that Brahman knew by which he became the All?

10. In the beginning this [universe] was Brahman alone, and He truly knew [him]self (*ātman*), saying: 'I am Brahman.' And so he became the All. Whichever of the gods became aware of this, also became that [All]: so too with seers (*ṛṣi*) and men. Seeing this, Vāmadeva, the seer, realized [this, saying]:

'I became Manu and the sun!'

This is true even now. Whoso thus knows that he is Brahman, becomes this whole [universe]. Even the gods have not the power to cause him to un-Be, for he becomes their own self.

So, whoever reveres any other deity, thinking: 'He is one, and I am another', does not [rightly] understand. He is like a [sacrificial] animal for the gods; and just as many animals are of use to man, so is each single man of use to the gods. To be robbed of even a single animal is disagreeable. How much more to be robbed of many! And so the [gods] are not at all pleased that men should know this.

11. In the beginning this [universe] was Brahman, – One only. Being One only, he had not the power to develop. By a supreme effort (*ati*) he brought forth a form of the Good (*śreyo-rūpa*), [namely], princely power (*kṣatra*) – that is to say, those princely powers among the gods called Indra, Varuṇa, Soma, Rudra, Parjanya, Yama, Death and Īśāna (the Lord). Hence there is

nothing higher than princely power, and so the Brāhman [priest] sits below the prince at the ceremonial anointing of a king, thereby conferring glory on the princely office. Brahman (the quality that makes a Brāhman a Brāhman) is the womb and source of princely power. Hence, even though the king enjoys supremacy, in the end he must return to Brahman, which is his [mother's] womb. And so whoever injures a [Brāhman] does violence to his [mother's] womb. He becomes more evil in that he has injured one who is better [than himself].

12. He had no power to develop further. He brought forth the common people (*viś*), that is, those types of gods which are referred to in groups – the Vasus, the Rudras, the Ādityas, the All-gods and the Maruts.

13. He had no power to develop further. He brought forth the class[14] of serfs – Pūṣan. Pūṣan is this [earth], for the [earth] nourishes everything that exists.

14. He had no power to develop further. By a supreme effort (*ati*) he brought forth a form of the Good – right and law *(dharma)*. This is the princely power of the princely class, namely, right and law. Hence there is nothing higher than right and law. And so it is that a weaker man lords it over a stronger one by means of right and law, as by a king. Right and law are the same as truth. And so, of the man who speaks the truth it is [also] said that he speaks right, and of the man who speaks right it is said that he speaks the truth; for both of these are the same thing.

15. This Brahman, [then], is [at the same time] the princely power and class, the common people, and the serfs.[15]

Among the gods this Brahman appeared (*abhavat*) as fire, among men as the Brāhman. He is a prince [too] through the princely power [inherent in him], a member of the common people through the virtue of the common people [inherent in him], and a serf through the quality of serf [inherent in him]. And so people wish for a state of being (*loka*) among the gods through[16] the [sacrificial] fire, among men through a Brāhman. For it was in these two forms that Brahman appeared (*abhavat*).

Now whoever departs this world without having caught a

14 Lit. 'colour'.

15 Or, 'There are, [then,] this Brahman, the princely power and class, the common people, and the serfs.'

16 Lit, 'in'.

glimpse of the state of being appropriate to himself will have no part in it because it will have no knowledge of him, – just like the Veda if it is not recited, or any other work (*karma*) left undone.

Yes, even if a man were to perform a great and holy work (*karma*) without knowing this – this, in the end, would be lost for him indeed.

Let a man revere the Self only as a state of being [appropriate to himself]. Whoso reveres the Self only as a state of being [appropriate to himself], his deeds are not lost for him, for out of this very Self he brings forth whatever he desires.

16. Now this Self is the state of being (*loka*) of all contingent beings. In so far as a man pours libations and offers sacrifice, he is the sphere (*loka*) of the gods; in so far as he recites [the Veda], he is [the sphere] of the seers; in so far as he offers cakes and water to the ancestors, desiring offspring the while, he is [the sphere] of the ancestors; in so far as he gives food and lodging to men, he is [the sphere] of men; in so far as he finds grass and water for domestic animals, he is [the sphere] of domestic animals; in so far as wild beasts and birds, even down to the ants, find something to live on in his house, he is their sphere. For just as one would wish for security in one's own sphere [of activity] (*loka*), so do all contingent beings desire the security of the man who has this knowledge. This indeed is well known and has been [thoroughly] investigated.

17. In the beginning this [universe] was the Self alone – One only. He longed to have a wife so that he might procreate, win wealth for himself and perform [good] works.[17] This was the extent of [his] desire. Not even by longing for it would a man obtain more than that. And so even today a man who is all alone longs to have a wife so that he may procreate, win wealth for himself and perform [good] works. In so far as he does not obtain any one of these, he considers himself incomplete. Now, his wholeness [lies in this]: mind is his very self; the voice his wife; breath his offspring; the eye his worldly wealth, for it is by the eye that one finds it; the ear his heavenly [wealth], for by the ear does one hear it. Self[18] is his work (*karma*), for it is through the self that a man performs works.

17 Or, 'perform sacrificial acts'.
18 Meaning 'the body'?

This sacrifice is fivefold; cattle are fivefold; man is fivefold; this whole universe is fivefold – everything that exists. Whoso thus knows wins this whole universe.

I, v

[*The threefold production of the world by Prajāpati as food for himself*]

1. When the Father produced by intellect
And austerity seven kinds of food,
One of his [foods] was common to all,
Of two he let the gods partake,
Three he made for himself,
One he bestowed upon the animals.
On this [food] everything depends,
Both what breathes and what does not.
How is it that these do not perish
When they are being eaten all the time?
He who knows this imperishableness –
He eats food with his mouth (*pratīka*),
He goes to the gods,
He lives on strength.

Thus the verses.

2. 'When the Father produced by intellect and austerity seven kinds of food' – truly by intellect and austerity the Father did produce them.

'One of his [foods] was common to all.' That of his which is common to all is the food that is eaten here. He who worships that, is not turned from evil, for it is mixed [i.e. common, not selected].

'Of two he let the gods partake.' They are the *huta* (fire-sacrifice) and the *prahuta* (offering). For this reason one sacrifices and offers to the gods. People also say that these two are the new-moon and the full-moon sacrifices. Therefore one should not offer sacrifice [merely] to secure a wish.

'One he bestowed upon the animals' – that is milk, for at first both men and animals live upon milk. Therefore they either make a new-born babe lick butter or put it to the breast. Likewise they call a new-born calf 'one that does not eat grass'.

'On this [food] everything depends, both what breathes and

what does not' – for upon milk everything depends, both what breathes and what does not. This that people say, 'By offering with milk for a year one escapes repeated death (*punarmṛtyu*)' – one should know that this is not so, since on the very day that he makes the offering he who knows escapes repeated death, for he offers all his food to the gods.

'How is it that these do not perish when they are being eaten all the time?' Verily, the Person is imperishableness, for he produces this food again and again.

'He who knows this imperishableness' – verily, a person is imperishableness, for by continuous meditation he produces this food as his work. Should he not do this, all the food would perish.

'He eats food with his mouth (*pratīka*).' The *pratīka* is the mouth. So he eats food with his mouth.

'He goes to the gods, he lives on strength' – this is praise.

3. 'Three he made for himself.' Mind, speech, breath – these he made for himself.

People say: 'My mind was elsewhere; I did not see. My mind was elsewhere; I did not hear.' It is with the mind, truly, that one sees. It is with the mind that one hears. Desire, imagination, doubt, faith, lack of faith, steadfastness, lack of steadfastness, shame, meditation, fear – all this is truly mind.[19] Therefore even if one is touched on his back, he discerns it with the mind.

Whatever sound there is, it is just speech. Verily, it comes to an end [as human speech]; verily, it does not [as the heavenly voice].

The in-breath, the out-breath, the diffused breath, the up-breath, the middle-breath – all this is just breath.

Verily, the self (*ātman*) consists of speech, mind and breath.

4. These same are the three worlds. This [terrestrial] world is Speech. The middle [atmospheric] world is Mind. That [celestial] world is Breath.

5. These same are the three Vedas. The *Ṛg-Veda* is Speech. The *Yajur-Veda* is Mind. The *Sāma-Veda* is Breath.

6. The same are the gods, Manes, and men. The gods are Speech. The Manes are Mind. Men are Breath.

7. These same are father, mother, and offspring. The father is Mind. The mother is Speech. The offspring is Breath.

8. These same are what is known, what is to be known, and what is unknown.

19 This and the two preceding sentences are quoted at *Maitrī Upanishad* 6. 30.

Whatever is known is a form of Speech, for Speech is known. Speech, having become this, helps him [i.e. man].

9. Whatever is to be known is a form of Mind, for mind is to be known. Mind, having become this, helps him.

10. Whatever is unknown is a form of Breath, for Breath is unknown. Breath, having become this, helps him.

11. Of this Speech the earth is the body. Its light-form is this [terrestrial] fire. As far as Speech extends, so far extends the earth, so far this fire.

12. Likewise of that Mind the sky is the body. Its light-form is yon sun. As far as Mind extends, so far extends the sky, so far yon sun.

These two [the fire and the sun] entered sexual union. Therefrom was born Breath. He is Indra. He is without a rival. Verily, a second person is a rival. He who knows this has no rival.

13. Likewise of that Breath, water is the body. Its light-form is yon moon. As far as Breath extends, so far extends water, so far yon moon.

These are all alike, all infinite. Verily he who worships them as finite wins a finite world. Likewise he who worships them as infinite wins an infinite world.

[*One's self identified with the sixteenfold Prajāpati*]

14. That Prajāpati is the year. He is composed of sixteen parts. His nights, truly, are fifteen parts. His sixteenth part is steadfast. He is increased and diminished by his nights alone. Having, on the new-moon night, entered with that sixteenth part into everything here that has breath, he is born thence on the following morning [as the new moon]. Therefore on that night one should not cut off the breath of any breathing thing, not even of a lizard, in honour of that divinity.

15. Verily, the person here who knows this, is himself that Prajāpati with the sixteen parts who is the year. The fifteen parts are his wealth. The sixteenth part is his self (*ātman*). In wealth alone [not in self] is one increased and diminished.

That which is the self (*ātman*) is a hub; wealth, a felly.[20] Therefore even if one is overcome by the loss of everything,

20 In the analogy of a wheel.

provided he himself lives, people say merely: 'He has come off with the loss of a felly!'

[*The three worlds and how to win them*]

16. Now, there are of a truth three worlds – the world of men, the world of the fathers, and the world of the gods. This world of men is to be obtained by a son only, by no other means; the world of the fathers, by sacrifice; the world of the gods, by knowledge. The world of the gods is verily the best of worlds. Therefore they praise knowledge.

17. Now next [comes] the handing over.

When a man thinks he is on the point of death, he says to his son: 'You are Brahman (the Veda, handed from father to son), you are the sacrifice, you are the world.' The son answers: 'I am Brahman, I am the sacrifice, I am the world.'

Whatever has been learnt (from the Veda) is summed up in the one word, 'Brahman'. Whatever sacrifices [have been offered] are summed up in the one word, 'sacrifice'. Whatever worlds (or states of being) there are, are summed up in the one word, 'world'. Such is the extent of this whole universe.

[Then the father thinks:] 'Since he is this whole universe, let him help me on my way from this world.' That is why a well-instructed son is called *lokya*, 'experienced in the world'. It is for this that he is instructed.

When [a father] who has this knowledge departs this world, he enters into his son with [all] these faculties (*prāṇa*). Whatever wrong he may have done, his son frees him from it all. Hence he is called a 'son'. It is through his son that a father is firmly established in this world. Then those divine, immortal faculties enter him (the father).

18. From earth and fire a divine voice enters into him. This is the divine voice by which whatever he says comes true.

19. From sky and sun a divine mind enters into him. This is the divine mind by which he experiences bliss and knows no sorrow.

20. From water and moon a divine spirit (breath) enters into him. This is the divine breath which, whether moving or at rest, neither quavers nor is hurt.

The man who possesses this knowledge becomes the Self of all contingent beings. As is that deity, so too is he. As all contingent beings contribute to that deity, so too do all contingent beings contribute to the man who has this knowledge. Whatever sorrows these creatures endure remain with them; only good (*puṇya*) follows after him, for evil cannot reach the gods.

21. Next [comes] the investigation of observances (*vrata*).

Prajāpati brought forth the faculties (*karma*). Once they had been brought forth, they entered into competition. 'I shall speak', the voice began. 'I shall see', said the eye. 'I shall hear', said the ear. And so said [all] the other faculties each in accordance with the work [that is proper to it].

Death in the form of exhaustion laid hold of them and took possession of them. Death, on taking possession of them, penned them in. And so the voice becomes exhausted, the eye becomes exhausted and the ear becomes exhausted. But of that one known as the 'middle breath' he could not take possession. These [other faculties] began to understand it.

'This one indeed is the best of us,' [they thought,] 'for, whether moving or at rest it neither quavers nor is hurt. Come, let us all become a form of it.'

And they did all become a form of it. That is why they are called 'vital breaths' after it. In whatever family there is a man who has this knowledge, the family is called after him; but whoever sets himself up in rivalry with him, withers away; and after withering away, he finally dies. So much with regard to the self.

22. Now with regard to natural phenomena (*adhidaivata*).

'I shall blaze up', began the fire. 'I shall generate heat', said the sun. 'I shall shine', said the moon. And so said [all] the other natural phenomena each in accordance with its nature.

Just as breath holds the midmost position among the human faculties (*prāṇa*), so does the wind among natural phenomena; for the other natural phenomena fade away; not so the wind. The natural phenomena known as wind never sets [as does the sun].

23. On this there is the following verse:

> From whence the sun arises
> To whither it goes down –

This means that it rises out of the breath of life and sets in the breath of life.

> Him the gods made right and law (*dharma*):
> He is today, tomorrow too!

What those [faculties] started in olden times they still do today. So a man should follow but one observance. He should breathe in and breathe out, saying: 'May not the evil one, may not Death take possession of me!' And whatever [observance] he follows, he should want to see it through to the end. Thereby will he win union (*sāyujya*) with that natural phenomenon and will share in its state of being (*salokatā*).

I, vi

1. This [universe] is a triad – name, form and work (*karma*).

Among names the voice is the hymn of praise (*uk-tha*), for all names arise (*ut-thā-*) out of it. It is their chant (*sāman*), for it is the same (*sama*) as all names. It is their *brahman* (sacred utterance), for it bears (*bhṛ-*) all names.

2. Again, among forms the eye is the hymn of praise, for all forms arise out of it. It is their chant, for it is the same as all forms. It is their Brahman, for it bears all forms.

3. Again, among works the self is the hymn of praise, for all works arise out of it. It is their chant, for it is the same as all works. It is their Brahman, for it bears all works.

This, though a triad, is yet one – the self. The self, though one, is yet a triad. That is the immortal hidden in the real (*satya*). The breath of life is the immortal, name and form are the real. By them is the breath of life hidden.

Book Two

II, i

1. Dṛptabālāki was a learned member of the Gārgya clan. He said to Ajātaśatru, [king] of Benares: 'Shall I tell you about Brahman?' And Ajātaśatru said: 'I will give you a thousand [cows] for your teaching. In fact people do come running [to this place] saying, "A [second] Janaka[21] is here."'

2. The Gārgya said: 'It is the Person in the sun whom I revere as Brahman.'

Ajātaśatru said: 'Do not speak to me about him in this way. I

21 A king renowned for his generosity.

revere him as sovereign Lord, the head and king of all contingent beings. Whoso reveres him thus [himself] becomes a sovereign Lord, the head and king of all contingent beings.'

3. The Gārgya said: 'It is the Person in the moon whom I revere as Brahman.'

Ajātaśatru said: 'Do not speak to me about him in this way. I revere him as the great king Soma, robed in white. Whoso reveres him thus, for him is the Soma-juice pressed out day after day: he never lacks for food.'

4. The Gārgya said: 'It is the Person in the lightning whom I revere as Brahman.'

Ajātaśatru said: 'Do not speak to me about him in this way. I revere him as the effulgent. Whoso reveres him thus [himself] becomes effulgent, and effulgent is his offspring.'

5. The Gārgya said: 'It is the Person in space whom I revere as Brahman.'

Ajātaśatru said: 'Do not speak to me about him in this way. I revere him as the full – inactive, undeveloping (*apravartin*). Whoso reveres him thus is full filled with offspring and cattle; nor does his offspring die out from this world.'

6. The Gārgya said: 'It is the Person in the wind whom I revere as Brahman.'

Ajātaśatru said: 'Do not speak to me about him in this way. I revere him as invincible Indra, an unconquerable army. Whoso reveres him thus [himself] becomes a conqueror, unconquered, conqueror of others.'

7. The Gārgya said: 'It is the Person in fire whom I revere as Brahman.'

Ajātaśatru said: 'Do not speak to me about him in this way. I revere him as the all-powerful (? *viśāsahin*). Whoso reveres him thus [himself] becomes all-powerful, and all-powerful is his offspring.'

8. The Gārgya said: 'It is the Person in the water whom I revere as Brahman.'

Ajātaśatru said: 'Do not speak to me about him in this way. I revere him as the reflection [in the water]. Whoso reveres him thus is attended by what reflects [his own nature], not by what does not; and offspring reflecting [his own nature] are born to him.'

9. The Gārgya said: 'It is the Person in a mirror whom I revere as Brahman.'

Ajātaśatru said: 'Do not speak to me about him in this way. I revere him as the brilliant. Whoso reveres him thus [himself] becomes brilliant, and brilliant is his offspring. Moreover, he outshines all with whom he comes into contact.'

10. The Gārgya said: 'It is the sound that follows after a man as he walks that I revere as Brahman.'

Ajātaśatru said: 'Do not speak to me about him in this way. I revere him as life (*asu*). Whoso reveres him thus, to him does all the life-force (*āyu*) in the world accrue, nor does the breath of life leave him before his time.'

11. The Gārgya said: 'It is the Person in the points of the compass whom I revere as Brahman.'

Ajātaśatru said: 'Do not speak to me about him in this way. I revere him as the second that is inseparable [from the One]. Whoso reveres him thus acquires a "second"; plurality (*gaṇa*) is not cut away from him.'

12. The Gārgya said: 'It is the Person that consists of shadow whom I worship as Brahman.'

Ajātaśatru said: 'Do not speak to me about him in this way. I revere him as death. Whoso reveres him thus – to him does all the life-force in the world accrue, nor does death approach him before his time.'

13. The Gārgya said: 'It is the Person in the self whom I revere as Brahman.'

Ajātaśatru said: 'Do not speak to me about him in this way. I revere him as one who possesses a self (*ātmanvin*). Whoso reveres him thus will [himself] come to possess a self, as will his offspring.' And the Gārgya held his peace.

14. Ajātaśatru said: 'Is that all?'

'That is all.'

'That is not enough for knowing [Brahman].'

'Then may I come to you as a pupil?' said the Gārgya.

15. Ajātaśatru said: 'It goes against the grain that a Brāhman should come to a prince and ask him to discourse on Brahman. Even so, I shall bring you to know [him] clearly.'

He took him by the hand and stood up; and the two of them went up to a man who was asleep and addressed him in these words: 'O great King Soma, robed in white!' But he did not get up. Then Ajātaśatru rubbed him with his hand and woke him up. He stood up.

16. Ajātaśatru said: 'When this man was asleep, where was the

"person" who consists of consciousness (*vijñāna*) then? And from where did he return?' But the Gārgya did not know.

17. Ajātaśatru said: 'When this man was asleep, the "person" who consists of consciousness, with consciousness [as its instrument], took hold of the consciousness of the senses (*prāṇa*) and lay down in the space which is within the heart. When he takes hold of them [in this way], that means that the man is asleep. Then is the breath his captive – captive too the voice, the eye and ear and mind.

18. 'When he moves around in dream the worlds [of dream] are his. It seems to him that he has become a great king or a great Brāhman; regions high and low he seems to visit. As a great king, taking his people with him, might move at will within his kingdom, so does [this "person"] take the senses with him and rove at will throughout his own body.

19. 'But when he has fallen into a deep sleep and is conscious (*vid-*) of nothing at all, then does he slip out [from the heart] into the pericardium, [passing] through the seventy-two thousand channels called *hitā* which lead from the heart to the pericardium, and there he lies. Just as a youth or a great king or a great Brāhman might lie down on reaching the highest peak of bliss, so does he lie.

20. 'As a spider emerges [from itself] by [spinning] threads [out of its own body], as small sparks rise up from a fire, so too from this Self do all the life-breaths, all the worlds, all the gods, and all contingent beings rise up in all directions. The hidden meaning (*upaniṣad*) of this is the "Real of the real". The life-breaths are the real, and He is their Real.'

II, ii

[*The embodiment of Breath in a person*]

1. Verily, he who knows the new-born infant with his housing, his covering, his post, and his rope, keeps off seven hostile relatives.

Verily, this infant is Breath (*prāṇa*) in the middle. Its housing is this [body]. Its covering is this [head]. Its post is breath (*prāṇa*). Its rope is food.

2. Seven imperishable beings stand near to serve him. Thus there are these red streaks in the eye. By them Rudra is united with

him. Then there is the water in the eye. By it Parjanya is united with him. There is the pupil of the eye. By it the sun is united with him. By the black of the eye, Agni; by the white of the eye, Indra; by the lower eyelash, Earth is united with him; by the upper eyelash, Heaven. He who knows this – his food does not fail.

3. In connection herewith there is this verse:

> There is a cup with its mouth below and its bottom up.
> In it is placed every form of glory.
> On its rim sit seven seers.
> Voice as an eighth is united with prayer (*brahman*).[22]

'There is a cup having its mouth below and its bottom up' – this is the head, for that is a cup having its mouth below and its bottom up. 'In it is placed every form of glory' – breaths, verily, are the 'every form of glory' placed in it; thus he says breaths (*prāṇa*). 'On its rim sit seven seers' – verily, the breaths are the seers. Thus he says breaths. 'Voice as an eighth is united with prayer' – for voice as an eighth is united with prayer.

4. These two [sense-organs] here [i.e. the ears] are Gotama and Bharadvāja. This is Gotama and this is Bharadvāja. These two here [i.e. the eyes] are Viśvāmitra and Jamadagni. This is Viśvāmitra. This is Jamadagni. These two here [i.e. the nostrils] are Vasiṣṭha and Kaśyapa. This is Vasiṣṭha. This is Kaśyapa. The voice is Atri, for by the voice food is eaten (*ad*). Verily, eating (*atti*) is the same as the name Atri. He who knows this becomes the eater of everything; everything becomes his food.

II, iii

1. Assuredly there are two forms of Brahman, the formed and the unformed, the mortal and the immortal, the static and the moving, the actual (*sat*) and the beyond (*tya*).

2. What is called the 'formed' is [all] that is other than the wind and atmosphere. This is the mortal, the static, the actual. The essence of this formed, mortal, static, actual [Brahman] is [the sun] which gives out heat; for this is the essence of the actual.

3. Now, the unformed is the wind and atmosphere. This is the immortal, the moving, the beyond. The essence of this unformed, immortal, moving [Brahman] beyond is the Person in the disc [of

22 A very similar stanza is found at *Atharva-Veda* X, viii. 9.

the sun]; for this is the essence of the beyond. So much with regard to natural phenomena.

4. Now with regard to the self.

The formed is what is other than the breath of life and the space within the self. This is the mortal, the static, the actual. The essence of this formed, mortal, static, actual [Brahman] is the eye; for this is the essence of the actual.

5. Now the unformed is the breath of life and the space within the self. This is the immortal, the moving, the beyond. The essence of this unformed, immortal, moving [Brahman] beyond is the Person in the right eye; for this is the essence of the beyond.

6. The form of this Person is like a saffron-coloured robe, or like white wool, or an *indragopa* beetle, or a flame of fire, or a white lotus, or a sudden flash of lightning. Like a sudden flash of lightning too is the good fortune of the man who thus knows.

From this follows the teaching [summed up in the words]: 'No, no!' For there is nothing higher than this 'No'. Or again it can be named the 'Real of the real'. The life-breaths are the real and He is their Real.

II, iv

1. 'Maitreyī,' said Yājñavalkya, 'I am about to give up my status [as a householder]. Well then, let me make a settlement for you and [your co-wife] Kātyāyanī.'

2. But Maitreyī said: 'If, sir, this whole earth, filled as it is with riches, were to belong to me, would I be immortal thereby?'

'No', said Yājñavalkya. 'As is the life of the rich, so would your life be. For there is no hope of immortality in riches.'

3. And Maitreyī said: 'What should I do with something that does not bring me immortality? Tell me, good sir, what you know.'

4. And Yājñavalkya said: 'Dearly do I love you – oh, that is certain, – and lovely are the words you speak. Come, sit down, and I will explain it to you; and as I am discoursing, ponder on it well.'

5. [Thus] did he discourse:

'Mark well, it is not for the love (*kāma*) of a husband that a husband is dearly loved (*priya*). Rather it is for the love of the Self that a husband is dearly loved.

'Mark well, it is not for the love of a wife that a wife is dearly loved. Rather it is for the love of the Self that a wife is dearly loved.

'Mark well, it is not for the love of sons that sons are dearly loved. Rather it is for the love of the Self that sons are dearly loved.

'Mark well, it is not for the love of riches that riches are dearly loved. Rather it is for the love of the Self that riches are dearly loved.

'Mark well, it is not for the love of the Brāhman class (*brahman*) that the Brāhman class is dearly loved. Rather it is for the love of the Self that the Brāhman class is dearly loved.

'Mark well, it is not for the love of the princely class that the princely class is dearly loved. Rather it is for the love of the Self that the princely class is dearly loved.

'Mark well, it is not for the love of the worlds that the worlds are dearly loved. Rather it is for the love of the Self that the worlds are dearly loved.

'Mark well, it is not for the love of the gods that the gods are dearly loved. Rather it is for the love of the Self that the gods are dearly loved.

'Mark well, it is not for the love of contingent beings that contingent beings are dearly loved. Rather it is for the love of the Self that contingent beings are dearly loved.

'Mark well, it is not for the love of the All that the All is dearly loved. Rather it is for the love of the Self that the All is dearly loved.

'Mark well, it is the Self that should be seen, [the Self] that should be heard, [the Self] that should be thought on and deeply pondered, Maitreyī.

'Mark well, by seeing the Self and hearing It, by thinking of It and knowing It, this whole [universe] is known.

6. 'A Brāhman's high estate (*brahman*) forsakes the man who thinks of a Brāhman's high estate as other than the Self.

'A prince's high estate forsakes the man who thinks of a prince's high estate as other than the Self.

'The worlds forsake the man who thinks of the worlds as other than the Self.

'The gods forsake the man who thinks of the gods as other than the Self.

'Contingent beings forsake the man who thinks of contingent beings as other than the Self.

'The All forsakes the man who thinks of the All as other than the Self.

'The high estate of Brāhmans, the high estate of princes, these worlds, these gods, these contingent beings, this All are nothing but the Self!

7. 'As, when a drum is beaten, you cannot grasp the sounds that issue from it; only by grasping the drum [itself] or the drummer can you grasp the sound:

8. 'As, when a conch is blown, you cannot grasp the sounds that issue from it; only by grasping the conch [itself] or the blower of the conch can you grasp the sound:

9. 'As, when a lute is played, you cannot grasp the sounds that issue from it; only by grasping the lute or the player of the lute can you grasp the sound:

10. 'As clouds of smoke surge up in all directions from a fire kindled from damp fuel, so too, I say, was this [whole universe] breathed forth from that great Being (*bhūta*) – *Ṛg-Veda*, *Yajur-Veda*, *Sāma-Veda*, the *Atharva-Veda*, [the hymns of] the Aṅgirases, the collections of stories, the ancient tales, wisdom (*vidyā*), the secret doctrines (*upaniṣad*), the verses, aphorisms, commentaries and commentaries on commentaries – all these were breathed forth from It.

11. 'As all the waters meet in one place only – in the sea; as all sensations meet in one place only – in the skin; as all scents meet in one place only – in the nose; as all tastes meet in one place only – in the tongue; as all forms meet in one place only – in the eye; as all sounds meet in one place only – in the ear; as all concepts meet in one place only – in the mind; as all wisdom meets in one place only – in the heart; as all actions (*karma*) meet in one place only – in the hands; as all ecstasies (*ānanda*) meet in one place only – in the phallus; as all excretions meet in one place only – in the anus; as all paths meet in one place only – in the feet; as all the Vedas meet in one place only – in the voice:

12. 'As a lump of salt dropped into water dissolves in it and cannot be picked out [again], yet from whatever part of the water you draw, there is still salt there, so too, I say, is this great Being – infinite, boundless, a mass of understanding (*vijñāna*). Out of these elements (*bhūta*) do [all contingent beings] arise and along with them are they destroyed. After death there is no consciousness (*saṁjñā*): this is what I say.' Thus spake Yājñavalkya.

13. But Maitreyī said: 'In this, good sir, you have thrown me into confusion in that you say that after death there is no consciousness.'

And Yājñavalkya said: 'There is nothing confusing in what I say. This is surely as much as you can understand now.

14. 'For where there is any semblance of duality, then does one smell another, then does one see another, then does one hear another, then does one speak to another, then does one think of another, then does one understand another. But when all has become one's very (*eva*) Self, then with what should one smell whom? With what should one see whom? With what should one hear whom? With what should one speak to whom? With what should one think of whom? With what should one understand whom? With what should one understand Him by whom one understands this whole universe? With what indeed should one understand the Understander?'

II, v

1. This earth is the honey of all beings (*bhūta*), and all beings are honey for this earth. That radiant, immortal Person who indwells this earth and, in the case of the [human] self, that radiant, immortal Person who consists of the body, is indeed that very Self: this is the Immortal, this Brahman, this the All.

2. The waters are the honey of all beings and all beings are honey for the waters. That radiant, immortal Person who indwells these waters and, in the case of the [human] self, that radiant, immortal Person who consists of semen, is indeed that very Self: this is the Immortal, this Brahman, this the All.

3. Fire is the honey of all beings and all beings are honey for fire. That radiant, immortal Person who indwells this fire and, in the case of the [human] self, that radiant, immortal Person who consists of the voice, is indeed that very Self: this is the Immortal, this Brahman, this the All.

4. The wind is the honey of all beings and all beings are honey for the wind. That radiant, immortal Person who indwells this wind and, in the case of the [human] self, that radiant, immortal Person who is breath, is indeed that very Self: this is the Immortal, this Brahman, this the All.

5. The sun is the honey of all beings and all beings are honey for the sun. That radiant, immortal Person who indwells that sun

and, in the case of the [human] self, that radiant, immortal Person who consists of sight, is indeed that very Self: this is the Immortal, this Brahman, this the All.

6. The points of the compass are the honey of all beings and all beings are honey for the points of the compass. That radiant, immortal Person who indwells these points of the compass and, in the case of the [human] self, that radiant, immortal Person who consists of hearing and echo, is indeed that very Self: this is the Immortal, this Brahman, this the All.

7. The moon is the honey of all beings and all beings are honey for the moon. That radiant, immortal Person who indwells that moon and, in the case of the [human] self, that radiant, immortal Person who consists of mind, is indeed that very Self: this is the Immortal, this Brahman, this the All.

8. Lightning is the honey of all beings and all beings are honey for the lightning. That radiant, immortal Person who indwells this lightning and, in the case of the [human] self, that radiant, immortal Person who consists of radiance (*tejas*) [itself], is indeed that very Self: this is the Immortal, this Brahman, this the All.

9. Thunder is the honey of all beings and all beings are honey for the thunder. That radiant, immortal Person who indwells this thunder and, in the case of the [human] self, that radiant immortal Person who consists of sound and tone, is indeed that very Self: this is the Immortal, this Brahman, this the All.

10. Space is the honey of all beings and all beings are honey for space. That radiant, immortal Person who indwells this space and, in the case of the [human] self, that radiant, immortal Person who is the space within the heart, is indeed that very Self: this is the Immortal, this Brahman, this the All.

11. [Cosmic] law (*dhārma*) is the honey of all beings and all beings are honey for the law. That radiant, immortal Person who indwells this law and, in the case of the [human] self, that radiant, immortal Person who consists of duty (*dhārma*), is indeed that very Self: this is the Immortal, this Brahman, this the All.

12. Truth is the honey of all beings and all beings are honey for truth. That radiant, immortal Person who indwells this truth and, in the case of the [human] self, that radiant, immortal Person who consists of truthfulness (*sātya*), is indeed that very Self: this is the Immortal, this Brahman, this the All.

13. Humanity is the honey of all beings and all beings are honey for humanity. That radiant, immortal Person who indwells

humanity and, in the case of the [human] self, that radiant, immortal Person who consists of humanity, is indeed that very Self: this is the Immortal, this Brahman, this the All.

14. The Self is the honey of all beings and all beings are honey for the Self. That radiant, immortal Person who indwells the Self and that radiant, immortal Person who *is* the Self, – he is that very Self indeed: this is the Immortal, this Brahman, this the All.

15. This Self is indeed the Lord of all contingent beings, king of all beings. Just as the spokes of a wheel are together fixed on to the hub and felly, so are all contingent beings, all gods, all worlds, all vital breaths and all these selves together fixed in this Self.

[Verses 16–19*a*, which are purely mythological, are omitted.]

19b. Seeing this, a seer has said:

> He conformed himself to every form:
> This is [one] form of him [for all] to see.
> By his uncanny powers (*māyā*) does Indra
> Rove round in many a form:
> Yoked are his thousand steeds!

This [Self] is [those] steeds indeed. It is tens and thousands, many and infinite. This is Brahman – without an earlier or a later, without inside or outside. This Self is Brahman – all-experiencing (*anubhū-*). Such is the teaching.

[Chapter vi, which gives the chain of the teachers of this doctrine, is omitted.]

Book Three

III, i

1. Janaka, [king] of Videha, was offering a sacrifice at which the fees [paid to the officiating Brāhmans] were to be copious. There Brāhmans of the Kurupañcālas had assembled.

Janaka, [king] of Videha, was curious to know which of [all] these Brāhmans was the most learned in scripture. So he penned in a thousand cows, to the horns of each of which ten *pādas* [of gold] were attached.

2. He said to them: 'Venerable Brāhmans, let whichever of you

is the most conversant with Brahman (*brahmiṣṭha*) drive away these cows.'

Not one of these Brāhmans dared to. But Yājñavalkya said to his pupil: 'Sāmaśravas, my dear, drive them away.' So he drove them away.

The [other] Brāhmans were greatly vexed. 'How dare he claim to be the most conversant with Brahman among us?' said they.

At that time [one] Aśvala was the officiating priest of Janaka, [king] of Videha. He questioned Yājñavalkya and said: 'So you are the most conversant with Brahman, are you?'

'Let us do homage to whoever is the most conversant with Brahman', said he. 'But surely [all] of us would like to have the cows.' Then Aśvala, the officiating priest, began to question him.

[Verses 3 to end, which deal with magic correspondences between various classes of priest, natural phenomena and human faculties, are omitted.]

III, ii

[*The fettered soul, and its fate at death*]

1. Then Jāratkārava Ārtabhāga questioned him. 'Yājñavalkya,' said he, 'how many apprehenders are there? How many over-apprehenders?'

'Eight apprehenders. Eight over-apprehenders.'

'Those eight apprehenders and eight over-apprehenders – which are they?'

2. 'Breath (*prāṇa*), verily, is an apprehender. It is seized by the out-breath (*apāna*) as an over-apprehender, for by the out-breath one smells an odour.

3. 'Speech, verily, is an apprehender. It is seized by name as an over-apprehender, for by speech one speaks names.

4. 'The tongue, verily, is an apprehender. It is seized by taste as an over-apprehender, for by the tongue one knows tastes.

5. 'The eye, verily, is an apprehender. It is seized by appearance as an over-apprehender, for by the eye one sees appearances.

6. 'The ear, verily, is an apprehender. It is seized by sound as an over-apprehender, for by the ear one hears sounds.

7. 'The mind, verily, is an apprehender. It is seized by desire as an over-apprehender, for by the mind one desires desires.

8. 'The hands, verily, are an apprehender. It is seized by action as an over-apprehender, for by the hands one performs action.

9. 'The skin, verily, is an apprehender. It is seized by touch as an over-apprehender, for by the skin one is made to know touches.'

10. 'Yājñavalkya,' said he, 'since everything here is food for death, who, pray, is that divinity for whom death is food?'

'Death, verily, is a fire. It is the food of water (*āpas*). He wards off (*apa-jayati*) repeated death [who knows this].'[23]

11. 'Yājñavalkya,' said he, 'when a man dies, do the breaths go out of him, or no?'

'No', said Yājñavalkya. 'They are gathered together right there. He swells up. He is inflated. The dead man lies inflated.'

12. 'Yājñavalkya,' said he, 'when a man dies, what does not leave him?'

'The name. Endless, verily, is the name. Endless are the All-gods. An endless world he wins thereby.'

13. 'Yājñavalkya,' said he, 'when the voice of a dead man goes into fire, his breath into wind, his eye into the sun, his mind into the moon, his hearing into the quarters of heaven, his body into the earth, his soul (*ātman*) into space, the hairs of his head into plants, the hairs of his body into trees, and his blood and semen are placed in water, what then becomes of this person (*puruṣa*)?'

'Ārtabhāga, my dear, take my hand. We two only will know of this. This is not for us two [to speak of] in public.'

The two went away and deliberated. What they said was *karma* [action]. What they praised was *karma*. Verily, one becomes good by good action, bad by bad action.

Thereupon Jāratkārava Ārtabhāga held his peace.

III, iii

[*Where the offerers of the horse-sacrifice go*]

1. Then Bhujyu Lāhyāyani questioned him. 'Yājñavalkya,' said he, 'we were travelling around as wanderers among the Madras. As such we came to the house of Patañjala Kāpya. He had a daughter who was possessed by a Gandharva. We asked him: "Who are you?" He said: "I am Sudhanvan, a descendant of Aṅgiras." When we were asking him about the ends of the earth,

23 Supplying *ya evaṁ veda*, as in III, iii. 2 and I, ii. 7.

we said to him: "What has become of the Pārikṣitas? What has become of the Pārikṣitas?" – I now ask you, Yājñavalkya. What has become of the Pārikṣitas?'

2. He said: 'That one doubtless said, "They have, in truth, gone whither the offerers of the horse-sacrifice go."'

'Where, pray, do the offerers of the horse-sacrifice go?'

'This inhabited world, of a truth, is as broad as thirty-two days [i.e. days' journeys] of the sun-god's chariot. The earth, which is twice as wide, surrounds it on all sides. The ocean, which is twice as wide, surrounds the earth on all sides. Then there is an interspace as broad as the edge of a razor or the wing of a mosquito. Indra, taking the form of a bird, delivered them (i.e. the Pārikṣitas] to Wind. Wind, placing them in himself, led them where the offerers of the horse-sacrifice were. Somewhat thus he [i.e. Sudhanvan] praised Wind. Therefore Wind alone is individuality (*vyaṣṭi*). Wind is totality (*samaṣṭi*). He who knows this wards off repeated death.'

Thereupon Bhujyu Lāhyāyani held his peace.

III, iv

1. Then Uṣasta Cākrāyaṇa questioned him, saying: 'Yājñavalkya, explain to me that Brahman which is evident and not obscure, the Self that indwells all things.'

'This Self that indwells all things is within you (*te*).'

'[But] which one [is it], Yājñavalkya, [that] indwells all things?'

'Who breathes in with the in-breath, he is the Self within you that indwells all things; who breathes out with the out-breath, he is the Self within you that indwells all things; who breathes along with your "diffused breath" (*vyāna*), he is the Self within you that indwells all things; who breathes along with your "upper breath" (*udāna*), he is the Self within you that indwells all things: he is the Self within you that indwells all things.'

2. Uṣasta Cākrāyaṇa said: 'Your teaching on this subject is exactly like [that of] a man who says: "That is a cow, and that is a horse." Explain to me that Brahman which is really (*eva*) evident and not obscure, the Self that indwells all things.'

'This Self that indwells all things is within you.'

'[But] which one [is it], Yājñavalkya, [that] indwells all things?'

'How should you see the seer of seeing? How should you hear the hearer of hearing? How should you think on the thinker of thought? How should you understand (*vijñā-*) the understander of understanding? This Self that indwells all things is within you. What is other than It suffers (*ārta*).' Then Uṣasta Cākrāyaṇa held his peace.

III, v

Then Kahola Kauṣītakeya questioned him, saying: 'Yājñavalkya, explain to me that Brahman which is evident and not obscure, the Self that indwells all things.'

'The Self that indwells all things is within you (*te*).'

'[But] which one [is it], Yājñavalkya, [that] indwells all things?'

'He who transcends hunger and thirst, sorrow, confusion, old age and death. Once Brāhmans have come to know this Self, they rise above their desire for sons, their desire for riches, their desire for [exalted] states of being (*loka*), and wander forth to lead a beggar's life. For there is no difference between a desire for sons and a desire for riches; and there is no difference between a desire for riches and a desire for [exalted] states of being: all of them are nothing more than desire.

'So let a Brāhman put away learning with disgust and lead a childlike life. Let him then put away both the childlike life and learning with disgust, and [become] a silent sage (*muni*). Let him then put away both silence and its opposite with disgust, and [become a true] Brāhman (a man who really knows Brahman).'

'And what is it that makes him a Brāhman?'

'Whatever really makes him such. What is other than [the Self] suffers (*ārta*).' Then Kahola Kauṣītakeya held his peace.

III, vi

Then Gārgī Vācaknavī questioned him, saying: 'Yājñavalkya, since this whole universe is woven, warp and woof, on water, what is it on which water is woven, warp and woof?'

'On the wind, Gārgī', said he.

'What is it, then, on which the wind is woven, warp and woof?'

'On the worlds of the atmosphere, Gārgī.'

'What is it, then, on which the worlds of the atmosphere are woven, warp and woof?'

'On the worlds of the Gandharvas, Gārgī.'

'What is it, then, on which the worlds of the Gandharvas are woven, warp and woof?'

'On the worlds of the sun, Gārgī.'

'What is it, then, on which the worlds of the sun are woven, warp and woof?'

'On the worlds of the moon, Gārgī.'

'What is it, then, on which the worlds of the moon are woven, warp and woof?'

'On the worlds of the stars, Gārgī.'

'What is it, then, on which the worlds of the stars are woven, warp and woof?'

'On the worlds of the gods, Gārgī.'

'What is it, then, on which the worlds of the gods are woven, warp and woof?'

'On the worlds of Indra, Gārgī.'

'What is it, then, on which the worlds of Indra are woven, warp and woof?'

'On the worlds of Prajāpati, Gārgī.'

'What is it, then, on which the worlds of Prajāpati are woven, warp and woof?'

'On the worlds of Brahman, Gārgī.'

'What is it, then, on which the worlds of Brahman are woven, warp and woof?'

'Gārgī,' he said, 'do not question overmuch lest your head should fall off. You are asking too many questions about a deity about which too many questions should not be asked. Do not question overmuch.' Then Gārgī Vācaknavī held her peace.

III, vii

1. Then Uddālaka Āruṇi questioned him, saying: 'Yājñavalkya, we were living among the Madras in the house of Patañjala Kāpya, studying the sacrifice. His wife was possessed of a spirit (*gandharva*), and we asked him who he was. He answered that he was Kabandha Ātharvaṇa, and, addressing Patañjala Kāpya and the students of the sacrifice, he said: "Kāpya, do you know that thread by which this world and the next world and all beings (*bhūta*) are strung together?"

'Patañjala Kāpya said: "No, sir, I do not."

'Addressing Patañjala Kāpya and the students of the sacrifice [again], he said: "Kāpya, do you know the Inner Controller who controls this world and the next world and all beings from within?"

'Patañjala Kāpya said: "No, sir, I do not."

'Addressing Patañjala Kāpya and the students of the sacrifice [again], he said: "Kāpya, whoever knows that thread and that Inner Controller, will [also] know Brahman, [all] worlds, gods, Vedas, contingent beings, the Self – everything." So did he speak to them.

'Now I do know this. If you, Yājñavalkya, drive away the Brahman-cows without knowing the thread and the Inner Controller, your head will fall off.'

'Certainly, Gautama, I know that thread and that Inner Controller.'

'Anyone might say, "I know, I know." Tell me *what* you know.'

2. 'Wind, Gautama, is that thread', said he. 'By this thread which is the wind, this world and the next world and all beings are strung together. So it is, Gautama, that it is said of a dead man that his limbs are unstrung, for they are strung together, Gautama, by the wind as by a thread.'

'Very true, Yājñavalkya: [now] tell [us] about the Inner Controller.'

3. 'He who, abiding in the earth, is other than the earth, whom the earth does not know, whose body is the earth, who controls the earth from within – he is the Self within you (*te*), the Inner Controller, the Immortal.

4. 'He who, abiding in water, is other than water, whom water does not know, whose body is water, who controls the water from within – he is the Self within you, the Inner Controller, the Immortal.

5. 'He who, abiding in fire, is other than fire, whom fire does not know, whose body is fire, who controls fire from within – he is the Self within you, the Inner Controller, the Immortal.

6. He who, abiding in the atmosphere, is other than the atmosphere, whom the atmosphere does not know, whose body is the atmosphere, who controls the atmosphere from within – he is the Self within you, the Inner Controller, the Immortal.

7. 'He who, abiding in the wind, is other than the wind, whom the wind does not know, whose body is the wind, who controls the wind from within – he is the Self within you, the Inner Controller, the Immortal.

8. 'He who, abiding in the sky, is other than the sky, whom the sky does not know, whose body is the sky, who controls the sky

from within – he is the Self within you, the Inner Controller, the Immortal.

9. 'He who, abiding in the sun, is other than the sun, whom the sun does not know, whose body is the sun, who controls the sun from within – he is the Self within you, the Inner Controller, the Immortal.

10. 'He who, abiding in the points of the compass, is other than the points of the compass, whom the points of the compass do not know, whose body is the points of the compass, who controls the points of the compass from within – he is the Self within you, the Inner Controller, the Immortal.

11. 'He who, abiding in the moon and stars, is other than the moon and stars, whom the moon and stars do not know, whose body is the moon and stars, who controls the moon and stars from within – he is the Self within you, the Inner Controller, the Immortal.

12. 'He who, abiding in space, is other than space, whom space does not know, whose body is space, who controls space from within – he is the Self within you, the Inner Controller, the Immortal.

13. 'He who, abiding in darkness, is other than darkness, whom darkness does not know, whose body is darkness, who controls darkness from within – he is the Self within you, the Inner Controller, the Immortal.

14. 'He who, abiding in light (*tejas*), is other than light, whom light does not know, whose body is light, who controls light from within – he is the Self within you, the Inner Controller, the Immortal.

'So much with regard to natural phenomena (*adhidaivata*). Now with regard to contingent beings (*adhibhūta*).

15. 'He who, abiding in all contingent beings, is other than all contingent beings, whom all contingent beings do not know, whose body is all contingent beings, who controls all contingent beings from within – he is the Self within you, the Inner Controller, the Immortal.

'So much with regard to contingent beings. Now with regard to the self.

16. 'He who, abiding in breath, is other than breath, whom breath does not know, whose body is breath, who controls breath from within – he is the Self within you, the Inner Controller, the Immortal.

17. 'He who, abiding in the voice, is other than the voice, whom the voice does not know, whose body is the voice, who controls the voice from within – he is the Self within you, the Inner Controller, the Immortal.

18. 'He who, abiding in the eye, is other than the eye, whom the eye does not know, whose body is the eye, who controls the eye from within – he is the Self within you, the Inner Controller, the Immortal.

19. 'He who, abiding in the ear, is other than the ear, whom the ear does not know, whose body is the ear, who controls the ears from within – he is the Self within you, the Inner Controller, the Immortal.

20. 'He who, abiding in the mind, is other than the mind, whom the mind does not know, whose body is the mind, who controls the mind from within – he is the Self within you, the Inner Controller, the Immortal.

21. 'He who, abiding in the skin, is other than the skin, whom the skin does not know, whose body is the skin, who controls the skin from within – he is the Self within you, the Inner Controller, the Immortal.

22. 'He who, abiding in the understanding (*vijñāna*), is other than the understanding, whom the understanding does not know, whose body is the understanding, who controls the understanding from within – he is the Self within you, the Inner Controller, the Immortal.

23. 'He who, abiding in semen, is other than semen, whom semen does not know, whose body is semen, who controls semen from within – he is the Self within you, the Inner Controller, the Immortal.

'He is the unseen seer, the unheard hearer, the unthought thinker, the ununderstood understander. No other seer than He is there, no other hearer than He, no other thinker than He, no other understander than He: He is the Self within you, the Inner Controller, the Immortal. What is other than He suffers.'

Then Uddālaka Āruṇi held his peace.

III, viii

1. Then [Gārgī] Vācaknavī said: 'Venerable Brāhmans, look, I will ask him two questions. If he answers them for me, then not one of you will defeat him in argument about Brahman.'

'Ask on, Gārgī', said he.

2. She said: 'Yājñavalkya, like a young hero from the Kāsyas or the Videhas who, having strung his unstrung bow and grasped in his hand two arrows, murderous to his foe, advances [against his enemy], so too do I advance against you with two questions. Answer them for me.'

'Ask on, Gārgī', said he.

3. She said: 'Yājñavalkya, that which is above the sky, which is below the earth, which is between sky and earth, – that which men speak of as past, present and future: on what is *that* woven, warp and woof?'

4. He said: 'Gārgī, that which is above the sky, which is below the earth, which is between sky and earth, – that which men speak of as past, present and future: that is woven on space, warp and woof.'

5. She said: 'All honour to you, Yājñavalkya, in that you have solved this [question] for me. Hold yourself ready for another.'

'Ask on, Gārgī', said he.

6. She said: 'Yājñavalkya, that which is above the sky, which is below the earth, which is between sky and earth – that which men speak of as past, present and future: on what is *that* woven, warp and woof?'

7. He said: 'Gārgī, that which is above the sky, which is below the earth, which is between sky and earth – that which men speak of as past, present and future: that is woven on space, warp and woof.'

'On what, then, is space woven, warp and woof?' said she.

8. He said: 'Gārgī, that is what Brāhmans call the "Imperishable".

'It is not coarse nor fine; not short nor long; not red (like fire) nor adhesive (like water). It casts no shadow, is not[24] darkness. It is not wind nor is it space. It is not attached to anything. It is not taste or smell; it is not eye or ear; it is not voice or mind; it is not light (*tejas*) or life (*prāṇa*); it has no face[25] or measure; it has no "within", no "without". Nothing does It consume nor is It consumed by anyone at all.

24 'Not' can here equally be translated 'without'.

25 Or 'mouth'. One recension adds here: 'It has no personal or family name: it does not age or die; it is free from fear, immortal, immaculate: it is not revealed nor hidden.'

9. 'At the behest of this Imperishable, Gārgī, sun and moon are held apart and so abide. At the behest of this Imperishable, Gārgī, sky and earth are held apart and so abide. At the behest of this Imperishable, Gārgī, seconds and minutes, days and nights, fortnights and months, seasons and years are held apart and so abide. At the behest of this Imperishable, Gārgī, some rivers flow from the [snow-]white mountains to the east, others to the west, each pursuing its [appointed] course. At the behest of this Imperishable, Gārgī, men praise the open-handed, gods depend upon the sacrificer and the ancestors on the rites offered for the dead.

10. 'Whatever oblations a man may offer up in this world, Gārgī, whatever sacrifice he may perform, whatever penances he may impose upon himself [even though they last] for many thousands of years, all this must have an end unless he knows this Imperishable.

'Gārgī, whoso departs this world without knowing this Imperishable, pitiable is he! But, Gārgī, whoso departs this world, knowing this Imperishable, he is a Brāhman [indeed] (for he thereby knows Brahman).

11. 'Gārgī, this same Imperishable [it is who] is the unseen seer, the unheard hearer, the unthought thinker, the ununderstood understander. No other seer than It is there, no other hearer than It, no other thinker than It, no other understander than It. In this Imperishable, indeed, Gārgī, is space woven, warp and woof.'

12. [And Gārgī] said: 'Venerable Brāhmans, you should count yourselves lucky if you manage to rid yourselves of this man [simply] by paying him homage, for not one of you will defeat him in argument about Brahman.' Then [Gārgī] Vācaknavī held her peace.

III, ix

1. Then Vidagdha Śākalya questioned him, saying: 'How many gods are there, Yājñavalkya?'

He answered by [reciting] this invocatory formula:

'As many as are mentioned in the invocatory formula in the hymn to the All-gods – three hundred and three and three thousand and three (= 3306).'

'Yes (*oṁ*),' said he, 'but how many gods are there really (*eva*), Yājñavalkya?'

'Thirty-three.'

'Yes,' he said, 'but how many gods are there really, Yājñavalkya?'

'Six.'

'Yes,' he said, 'but how many gods are there really, Yājñavalkya?'

'Three.'

'Yes,' he said, 'but how many gods are there really, Yājñavalkya?'

'Two.'

'Yes,' he said, 'but how many gods are there really, Yājñavalkya?'

'One and a half.'

'Yes,' he said, 'but how many gods are there really, Yājñavalkya?'

'One.'

'Yes,' he said, 'but which are those three hundred and three and those three thousand and three?'

2. [Yājñavalkya] said: 'These are only their attributes of majesty (*mahiman*). There are only thirty-three gods.'

'Which are those thirty-three?'

'The eight Vasus, the eleven Rudras, the twelve Ādityas. That makes thirty-one. [Add] Indra and Prajāpati, [and that] makes thirty-three.'

3. 'Which are the Vasus?'

'Fire, earth, wind, atmosphere, sun, sky, moon and stars. These are the Vasus. For to these all wealth (*vasu*) is entrusted. That is why they are [called] Vasus.'

4. 'Which are the Rudras?'

'The ten breaths in man (*puruṣa*), and the eleventh is the self. When they depart this mortal body, they make [men] weep; and because they make them weep (*rud-*), they are [called] Rudras.'

5. Which are the Ādityas?'

'The twelve months of the year are the Ādityas, for they carry off everything,[26] though going on [themselves]; and because they carry off (*ādā-*) everything, though going on (*yanti*) [themselves], they are [called] Ādityas.'

6. 'Which is Indra? Which Prajāpati?'

'Indra is thunder, Prajāpati the sacrifice.'

26 Or, 'this whole universe'.

'Which is thunder?'

'The thunderbolt.'

'Which is the sacrifice?'

'Cattle.'

7. 'Which are the six?'

'Fire, earth, wind, atmosphere, sun and sky. These are the six. These six are everything.'

8. 'Which are the three gods?'

'These three worlds, for all these gods are in them.'

'Which are the two gods?'

'Food and the breath of life.'

'Which is the one and a half?'

'The purifying[27] [wind].'

9. 'It has been asked: "Since the purifying [wind] appears to be one, how can it be [called] one and a half?"'

'Because everything grows to maturity (*adhyārdhnot*) in it, it is [called] one and a half (*adhyardha*).'

'Which is the one God?'

'The breath of life, and that is Brahman, the beyond (*tya*). So have [we] been taught.'

10. [Śākalya said:] 'If a man were to know that "person" whose dwelling is the earth, whose sphere (*loka*) is fire, whose light is the mind, and who is the goal of every self, then would he be one who really knows, Yājñavalkya?'

[Yājñavalkya said:] 'I do know that "person", the goal of every self of whom you speak. It is the "person" in the body. But tell [me], Śākalya, what is his [tutelary] deity?'

'The Immortal', said he.

[Verses 11–18, which give a list of similar 'persons' and the corresponding 'deities', and verses 19–25, on the points of the compass, their 'deities' and 'bases', are omitted.]

26. [Śākalya said:] 'On what are you and [your] self based?'

[Yājñavalkya said:] 'On the in-breath.'

'On what is the in-breath based?'

'On the out-breath.'

'On what is the out-breath based?'

'On the "diffused" breath.'

'On what is the "diffused" breath based?'

27 Or, 'blowing'.

'On the "upper" breath.'

'On what is the "upper" breath based?'

'On the "concentrated" breath.

'This Self – [what can one say of it but] "No, no!" It is impalpable, for it cannot be grasped; indestructible, for it cannot be destroyed; free from attachment, for it is not attached [to anything], not bound. It does not quaver nor can it be hurt.

'These are the eight dwellings, the eight spheres (*loka*), the eight gods, the eight "persons".[28] Who splits apart and puts together these "persons" and then passes beyond them, he is the "Person" of the Upanishads about whom I question you. If you do not tell me who he is, your head will fall off.'

But Śākalya did not know him, and so his head did fall off. And robbers made away with his bones, thinking they were something else.

27. Then [Yājñavalkya] said: 'Venerable Brāhmans, let any one of you who so wishes question me; or do you all question me. Or I will question any of you who so wishes, or I will question all of you.'

But none of the Brāhmans dared to [question him].

28. Then he questioned them with these verses:

As a mighty tree, the forest's lord,
So, in very truth, is Man.
His hairs are [like] the leaves,
His skin the outer bark.

From his skin the blood flows forth
[As] sap from the bark [of the tree]:
When he is wounded, sap goes out
As from a stricken tree.

His flesh is [like] the mass of wood(?),
His sinews tough [like] the inner bark;
His bones are the wood within,
His marrow wrought like pith.

As a tree, when felled, grows up again
From the root, a new [creation],
So mortal [Man], when felled by death –
From what root will *he* grow up?

28 Enumerated in verses 10–17.

Say not 'from seed', for that springs forth
From one who is alive.
The tree, it seems, grows up from grain;
When dead, it straightaway comes to be.

Along with the tree tear out the roots –
It will not rise again:
So mortal [Man], when felled by death –
From what root will *he* grow up?

Once born, he is not born [again],
Who should again beget him?

Brahman is understanding (*vijñāna*), bliss,
[Self-]giving, giver's goal,
[The goal] of him who [patient] stands,
 Knowing It the while.

Book Four

IV, i

1. Janaka, [king] of Videha was sitting down when Yājñavalkya approached him. [The king] said to him: 'Yājñavalkya, what have you come for? Is it cows you want or subtle arguments?'

'Both, Your Majesty', said he.

2. 'Let us hear what people have been telling you', [continued Yājñavalkya.]

'Jitvan Śailini told me that Brahman is speech.'

'For Śailini to say that Brahman is speech is [about as significant] as for him to say that he has a mother or a father or a teacher; for what is the use of a man who cannot speak? But did he tell you its home and support?'

'No, he did not.'

'Your Majesty, [such a Brahman as this stands] on one leg only.'

'Well, Yājñavalkya, tell us yourself.'

'Its home is speech itself, and space is its support. It should be revered as cognition (*prajñā*).'

'What is the essence of cognition, Yājñavalkya?'

'Again speech, Your Majesty', said he. 'It is by speaking, sire, that a friend is recognized (*prajñā-*). By speech, Your Majesty, the *Ṛg-Veda*, *Yajur-Veda*, *Sāma-Veda*, the *Atharva-Veda*, [the hymns of] the Aṅgirases, the collections of stories, the ancient tales, wisdom (*vidyā*), the secret doctrines (*upaniṣad*), the verses, aphorisms, commentaries and commentaries on commentaries, what is offered up in sacrifice and as an oblation, food and drink, this world and the next and all contingent beings are cognized. Speech it is, sire, that is the highest Brahman. [And] speech does not forsake the man who, thus knowing, reveres it; all beings (*bhūta*) flow into him. He becomes a god and goes to the gods.'

'I will give you a thousand [cows] with a bull the size of an elephant', said Janaka, [king] of Videha.

'My father [always] thought', said Yājñavalkya, 'that one should not accept [gifts] without first imparting instruction.'

3. 'Let us hear what people have been telling you', [continued Yājñavalkya.]

'Udaṅka Śaulbāyana told me that Brahman is the breath of life.'

'For Śaulbāyana to say that Brahman is the breath of life is [about as significant] as for him to say that he has a mother or a father or a teacher; for what is the use of a lifeless man? But did he tell you its home and support?'

'No, he did not.'

'Your Majesty, [such a Brahman as this stands] on one leg only.'

'Well, Yājñavalkya, tell us yourself.'

'Its home is the breath of life itself, and space is its support. It should be revered as love (*priyam*).'

What is the essence of love, Yājñavalkya?'

'Again the breath of life, Your Majesty', said he. 'For love (*kāma*) of life, sire, a man will offer in sacrifice what should be sacrificed, and will accept [gifts] from one from whom he should not accept [them]. For love of life, Your Majesty, a man lives in fear of being killed wherever he may go. The breath of life it is, sire, that is the highest Brahman. [And] the breath of life does not forsake the man who, thus knowing, reveres it; all beings flow into him. He becomes a god and goes to the gods.'

'I will give you a thousand [cows] with a bull the size of an elephant', said Janaka, [king] of Videha.

'My father [always] thought', said Yājñavalkya, 'that one should not accept [gifts] without first imparting instruction.'

4. Let us hear what people have been telling you', [continued Yājñavalkya.]

'Barku Vārṣṇa told me that Brahman is sight.'

'For Vārṣṇa to say that Brahman is sight is [about as

significant] as for him to say that he has a mother or a father or a teacher; for what is the use of a sightless man? But did he tell you its home and support?'

'No, he did not.'

'Your Majesty, [such a Brahman as this stands] on one leg only.'

'Well, Yājñavalkya, tell us yourself.'

'Its home is the eye, and space is its support. It should be revered as truth.'

'What is the essence of truth, Yājñavalkya?'

'Again sight, Your Majesty', said he. 'If you say to a man who can see, "Can you see?" and he replies, "I can", that is the truth. Sight it is, sire, that is the highest Brahman. [And] sight does not forsake the man who, thus knowing, reveres it; all beings flow into him. He becomes a god and goes to the gods.'

'I will give you a thousand [cows] with a bull the size of an elephant', said Janaka, [king] of Videha.

'My father [always] thought', said Yājñavalkya, 'that one should not accept [gifts] without first imparting instruction.'

5. Let us hear what people have been telling you', [continued Yājñavalkya.]

'Gardabhīvipīta Bhāradvāja told me that Brahman is hearing.'

'For Bhāradvāja to say that Brahman is hearing is [about as significant] as for him to say that he has a mother or a father or a teacher; for what is the use of a deaf man? But did he tell you its home and support?'

'No, he did not.'

'Your Majesty, [such a Brahman as this stands] on one leg only.'

'Well, Yājñavalkya, tell us yourself.'

'Its home is the ear, and space is its support. It should be revered as the infinite.'

'What is the essence of the infinite, Yājñavalkya?'

'The points of the compass, Your Majesty', said he. 'That is why, sire, in whatever direction one goes, there is no end to it, for the points of the compass are infinite. Sire, the points of the compass are the same as hearing. Hearing it is, sire, that is the highest Brahman. [And] hearing does not forsake the man who, thus knowing, reveres it; all beings flow into him. He becomes a god and goes to the gods.'

'I will give you a thousand [cows] with a bull the size of an elephant', said Janaka, [king] of Videha.

'My father [always] thought', said Yājñavalkya, 'that one should not accept [gifts] without first imparting instruction.'

6. 'Let us hear what people have been telling you!', [continued Yājñavalkya.]

'Satyakāma Jābāla told me that Brahman is mind.'

'For Jābāla to say that Brahman is mind is [about as significant] as for him to say that he has a mother or a father or a teacher; for what is the use of a mindless man? But did he tell you its home and support? '

'No, he did not.'

'Your Majesty, [such a Brahman as this stands] on one leg only.'

'Well, Yājñavalkya, tell us yourself.'

'Its home is the mind itself, and space is its support. It should be revered as bliss.'

'What is the essence of bliss, Yājñavalkya?'

'Again mind, Your Majesty', said he. 'With the mind a man betroths himself to a woman, and a son is born by her in his own likeness; and [a son] is [very] bliss. The mind it is, sire, that is the highest Brahman. [And] the mind does not forsake the man who, thus knowing, reveres it; all beings flow into him. He becomes a god and goes to the gods.'

'I will give you a thousand [cows] with a bull the size of an elephant', said Janaka, [king] of Videha.

'My father [always] thought', said Yājñavalkya, 'that one should not accept [gifts] without first imparting instruction.'

7. 'Let us hear what people have been telling you', [continued Yājñavalkya.]

'Vidagdha Śākalya told me that Brahman is the heart.'

'For Śākalya to say that Brahman is the heart is [about as significant] as for him to say that he has a mother or a father or a teacher; for what is the use of a heartless man? But did he tell you its home and support?'

'No, he did not.'

'Your Majesty, [such a Brahman as this stands] on one leg only.'

'Well, Yājñavalkya, tell us yourself.'

'Its home is the heart itself, and space is its support. It should be revered as stability (*sthiti*).'

'What is the essence of stability, Yājñavalkya?'

'Again the heart, Your Majesty', said he. 'Of all contingent beings, sire, the support is the heart: all contingent beings are established on the heart. The heart it is, sire, that is the highest

Brahman. [And] the heart does not forsake the man who, thus knowing, reveres it; all beings flow into him. He becomes a god and goes to the gods.'

'I will give you a thousand [cows] with a bull the size of an elephant', said Janaka, [king] of Videha.

'My father [always] thought', said Yājñavalkya, 'that one should not accept [gifts] without first imparting instruction.'

IV, ii

1. Janaka, [king] of Videha, came down from his couch and said: 'All honour to you, Yājñavalkya. Will you instruct me?'

[And Yājñavalkya] said: 'As a man about to set out on a long journey might make ready (*samādhā-*) a chariot or a ship, so too has your [own] self been made ready (and concentrated upon itself, *samāhita*) by these secret teachings (*upaniṣad*). You are highly respected and wealthy, you have studied the Veda and been told the secret teachings. [Even so,] when you are set free (*vimuc-*) from this world, where will you go?'

'Good sir, I do not know where I shall go.'

'Then I will tell you where you will go.'

'Speak on, good sir.'

2. 'The "person" in the right eye is named Indha, the "kindler", but though he really *is* Indha, men call him Indra – obscurely. For the gods, it seems, love the obscure and hate the obvious.

3. 'Now that semblance of a "person" in the left eye is his wife, Virāj. The place where they meet in mutual praise is the space within the heart. Their food is the clot of blood within the heart. Their covering is something like a fine mesh within the heart. The path they move along is the channel that goes up from the heart. Like a hair a thousandfold divided are these channels, called *hitā*, which are established in the heart. Through these this liquid flows. That is why this [self composed of Indha and Virāj] seems to eat a more refined [form of] food than the bodily self.

4. 'The eastern quarter is his eastward breaths; the southern quarter is his southward breaths; the western quarter is his westward breaths; the northern quarter is his northward breaths; the zenith is his upward breaths; the nadir is his downward breaths. All the quarters are all his breaths.

'This Self – [what can one say of it but] "No, no!" It is impalpable, for it cannot be grasped; indestructible, for it cannot be destroyed; free from attachment, for it is not attached [to anything], not bound. It does not quaver, nor can it be hurt.

'Now indeed, Janaka, freedom from fear is yours!' Thus spake Yājñavalkya.

'May freedom from fear be yours, venerable Yājñavalkya,' said Janaka, [king] of Videha, 'for it is you, sir, who teach freedom from fear. All honour to you. Here are the Videhas and here am I [at your service].'

IV, iii

1. Yājñavalkya was going to visit Janaka, [king] of Videha and he thought [within himself]: 'I will not speak.'

But later Janaka, [king] of Videha and Yājñavalkya held converse together at the oblation of the fire, and Yājñavalkya granted him a boon. He chose to ask any question he wished, and [Yājñavalkya] granted him this [boon]. This was the first question the king asked him:

2. 'Yājñavalkya, what is the light of man (*puruṣa*)?'

'The sun is his light, Your Majesty', said he. 'Lighted by the sun alone a man sits down, moves away, does his work and comes back.'

'Very true, Yājñavalkya.'

3. 'When the sun has set, Yājñavalkya, what is the light of man then?'

'The moon becomes his light then. Lighted by the moon alone he sits down, moves away, does his work and comes back.'

'Very true, Yājñavalkya.'

4. 'When both sun and moon have set, Yājñavalkya, what is the light of man then?'

'Fire becomes his light then. Lighted by fire alone he sits down, moves away, does his work and comes back.'

'Very true, Yājñavalkya.'

5. 'When both sun and moon have set, Yājñavalkya, and the fire has gone out, what is the light of man then?'

'The voice becomes his light then. Lighted by the voice alone he sits down, moves away, does his work and comes back. That is why, sire, even when a man cannot distinguish his own hands, he will go towards [any place] where a voice is raised.'

'Very true, Yājñavalkya.'

6. 'When both sun and moon have set, Yājñavalkya, when the

fire has gone out and [all] voices are stilled, what is the light of man then?'

'The self becomes his light then. Lighted by the self alone he sits down, moves away, does his work and comes back.'

7. 'Which one is the self?'

'[Abiding] among the senses there is a "person" who consists of understanding (*vijñāna*), a light within the heart: this is he. Remaining ever the same (*samāna*), he skirts both worlds, seemingly thinking, seemingly moving. For, having fallen asleep, he transcends this world – the forms of death.

8. 'This "person", on being born and on being embodied, is conjoined with evil things. When he departs and dies he leaves evil things behind.

9. 'This "person" has two states [of consciousness] (*sthāna*), that of this world and that of the other world. There is a third twilight state [of consciousness], – that of sleep. Standing in this twilight state, he sees the [other] two, that of this world and that of the other world. Now, however, when he approaches the state [of consciousness] of the other world, he fares forth [towards it] and descries both evil and joyful (*ānanda*) things.

'When he falls asleep, he takes with him [all] the materials (*mātrā*) of this all-embracing world. Himself, he destroys them and himself builds them up [again]; and he dreams [in a world lighted] by his own brilliance, by his own light. Then is this "person" light by his own light.

10. 'There there are no chariots, no spans, no paths; but he brings forth [from himself] chariots, spans and paths. There there are no joys, no pleasures, no delights. There there are no tanks, no lotus-pools, no rivers; but he brings forth [from himself] tanks, lotus-pools and rivers: for he is a creator (*kartṛ*).

11. 'On this there are these verses:

By sleep he mashes down the things of body;
Unsleeping, the sleeping [senses] he surveys:
White light (*śukra*) assuming, back to his [former] state
He returns – the Golden Person, lonely swan.

12. Guarding his lower nest with the breath of life,
Forth from the nest, immortal, on he flies.
Where'er he will, immortal, on he goes –
The Golden Person, lonely swan!

13. In the realm of dream aloft, beneath, he roams,
A god – how manifold the forms he fashions!
With women he takes his pleasure, laughs – or else
Sees dreadful sights: so does it seem to him.

There are some who see his pleasure-grove:
Him no one sees at all.

14. 'There is a saying: "You should not awaken a man stretched out [in sleep]." Hard to cure indeed is the man to whom this ["person"] does not return.

'Now, some say that this is no different from (*eva*) the state of wakefulness, for he sees the same things whether awake or asleep. [But the difference is that] there (in sleep) this "person" is light by his own light.'

[Said Janaka:] 'Venerable sir, I will give you a thousand [cows]. Say on, [for your words show the way] to liberation [from our earthly state].'

15. 'In this deep serenity[29] he finds his joy, roams around, seeing good and evil. Then he hurries back in whatever manner suits him (*pratinyāya*), in accordance with his original nature (*pratiyoni*), to [the realm of] dream. Whatever he sees there, he is not followed by it; for this "person" is free from attachment.'

'Very true, Yājñavalkya. Venerable sir, I will give you a thousand [cows]. Say on, [for your words show the way] to liberation.'

16. 'In dream he finds his joy, roams around, seeing good and evil. Then he hurries back in whatever manner suits him, in accordance with his original nature, to the realm of wakefulness. Whatever he sees there, he is not followed by it; for this "person" is free from attachment.'

'Very true, Yājñavalkya. Venerable sir, I will give you a thousand [cows]. Say on, [for your words show the way] to liberation.'

17. 'In this realm of wakefulness he finds his joy, roams around, seeing good and evil. Then he hurries back in whatever manner suits him, in accordance with his original nature, to the realm of dream.

18. 'As a great fish might skirt both banks [of a river], both the nearer and the farther, so does this "person" skirt both realms – the realm of sleep and the realm of wakefulness.

29 i.e. 'dreamless sleep'.

19. 'As a falcon or some [other] bird, flying round in space, tires, folds its wings and is carried [down] to its nest, so too does this "person" hasten to this realm where, sleeping, he desires nothing whatever, and where he sees no dream.

20. 'Like a hair a thousand times divided are the channels [in] his [heart] called *hitā*, so minute are they, full of white, blue, yellow, green and red.

'Now, when it seems to him that he is being killed, or overpowered, or chased by an elephant, or that he is falling into a pit, he is [only] imagining in ignorance the horrors he sees when he is awake. But when, like a god or king, he thinks, "I surely am this [whole universe: I am] whole", that is his highest state of being (*loka*).

21. 'This is that form of his which is beyond desire, free from evil, free from fear.

'Just as a man, closely embraced by his loving wife, knows nothing without, nothing within, so does this "person", closely embraced by the Self that consists of wisdom (*prājña*), know nothing without, nothing within. That is his [true] form in which [all] his desires are fulfilled, in which Self [alone] is his desire, in which he has no desire, no sorrow.

22. 'There a father is no longer a father, a mother no longer a mother; states of being (*loka*) are no longer states of being, gods are no longer gods, the Vedas no longer Vedas. There a thief is no longer a thief, a slayer of an embryo no longer a slayer of an embryo, an outcaste no longer an outcaste,[30] a wandering friar no longer a wandering friar, an ascetic no longer an ascetic. He is not followed by good, not followed by evil; for then he will have passed beyond all sorrow of the heart.

23. 'Though he does not see, yet it is by seeing that he does not see; for there is no disjunction between seer and sight since [both] are indestructible. But there is no second thing other than himself and separate that he might see it.

24. 'Though he does not smell, yet it is by smelling that he does not smell; for there is no disjunction between smeller and smell since [both] are indestructible. But there is no second thing other than himself and separate that he might smell it.

25. 'Though he does not taste, yet it is by tasting that he does

30 Two types of outcaste are mentioned.

not taste; for there is no disjunction between taster and taste since [both] are indestructible. But there is no second thing other than himself and separate that he might taste it.

26. 'Though he does not speak, yet it is by speaking that he does not speak; for there is no disjunction between speaker and speech since [both] are indestructible. But there is no second thing other than himself and separate that he might speak to it.

27. 'Though he does not hear, yet it is by hearing that he does not hear; for there is no disjunction between hearer and hearing since [both] are indestructible. But there is no second thing other than himself and separate that he might hear it.

28. 'Though he does not think, yet it is by thinking that he does not think; for there is no disjunction between thinker and thought since [both] are indestructible. But there is no second thing other than himself and separate that he might think on it.

29. 'Though he does not touch, yet it is by touching that he does not touch; for there is no disjunction between toucher and touch since [both] are indestructible. But there is no second thing other than himself and separate that he might touch it.

30. 'Though he does not understand (*vijñā-*), yet it is by understanding that he does not understand; for there is no disjunction between understander and understanding since [both] are indestructible. But there is no second thing other than himself and separate that he might understand it.

31. 'When there seems to be another, then one can see another, one can smell another, one can taste another, one can speak to another, one can hear another, one can think on another, one can touch another, one can understand another.

32. 'An ocean, One, the seer becomes, without duality: this, sire, is the Brahman-world.'[31]

Thus did Yājñavalkya teach him.

'This is his highest path,[32] this his highest prize (*sampat*), this his highest world, this his highest bliss. This is that bliss of his on but a fraction of which other things (*bhūta*) live.

33. 'Take a man who is rich and prosperous, master over others, possessing everything possible that could minister to human enjoyment: that is the highest [measure of] bliss on the human scale.

31 Or, 'the man whose world is Brahman'.

32 Or, 'goal'.

'Now, a hundred [measures of] bliss on the human scale make one [measure of] bliss on the scale of the world-conquering ancestors.

'A hundred [measures of] bliss on the scale of the world-conquering ancestors make one [measure of] bliss of the world of the Gandharvas.

'A hundred [measures of] bliss of the world of the Gandharvas make one [measure of] bliss of the gods who have won divinity by their works (*karma*).

'A hundred [measures of] bliss of the gods who have won divinity by their works make one [measure of] bliss of the gods who are destined to be gods by birth and of the man well-versed in scripture who is not crooked nor smitten with desire.

'A hundred [measures of] bliss of the gods destined to be gods by birth make one [measure of] bliss of the world of Prajāpati and of the man well versed in scripture who is not crooked nor smitten with desire.

'A hundred [measures of] bliss of the world of Prajāpati make one [measure of] bliss of the Brahman-world and of the man well versed in scripture who is not crooked nor smitten with desire.

'This, sire, is indeed the highest bliss -- the Brahman-world, (that state of being which is Brahman).'

Thus spake Yājñavalkya.

'Venerable sir,' [said Janaka,] 'I will give you a thousand [cows]. Say on, [for your words show the way] to liberation.'

Then Yājñavalkya was afraid. 'The king is wise ['indeed', thought he], 'he has driven me out of every position (from which I could conceal the highest truth from him).'

[But he continued.] 'In this realm of dream,' [said he,] 'he finds his joy, roams around, seeing good and evil. Then he hurries back in whatever manner suits him, in accordance with his original nature, to the realm of wakefulness.

35. 'As a heavily-loaded cart moves along creaking, so does the bodily self, mounted by the self who consists of wisdom (*prājña*), move along groaning as he breathes his last.

36. 'When this "person" grows thin from old age, grows thin through fever, then does he detach (*pramuc-*) himself from his limbs as a mango or a fig or a berry detaches itself from its stalk. He hurries back in whatever manner suits him, in accordance with his original nature, to the breath of life (*prāṇa*).

37. 'As policemen, magistrates, charioteers and village headmen wait for the king when he comes [back from a journey] with food and drink and dwelling-places [all ready], saying, "Here he comes, here he comes", so do all contingent beings wait for the man who thus knows, saying, "Here comes Brahman, here he comes."

38. 'As policemen, magistrates, charioteers and village headmen gather round the king as he is about to go away, so at the time of death do all the bodily faculties (*prāṇa*) gather round this self when he is about to breathe his last.'

IV, iv

1. [And Yājñavalkya went on:] 'When this self grows weak and seems all confused, then do the bodily faculties (*prāṇa*) gather round him. He collects around him those elements of light (*tejas*)[33] and descends right down (*eva*) into the heart. When the "person" present in the eye turns away, back [towards the sun], he no longer recognizes forms.

2. '"He is becoming one, he does not see", they say. "He is becoming one, he does not smell", they say. "He is becoming one, he does not taste", they say. "He is becoming one, he does not speak", they say. "He is becoming one, he does not hear", they say. "He is becoming one, he does not think", they say. "He is becoming one, he does not feel", they say. "He is becoming one, he does not understand (*vijñā*)', they say.

'The apex of the heart lights up, and [lighted] by this light the self departs through the eye or the head or some other part of the body. As he departs, the breath of life follows after him; and as the breath of life departs, all the bodily faculties follow after it. He is then [re-]united with the understanding (*vijñāna*, ability to recognize things), and follows after the understanding.[34] His wisdom (*vidyā*) and his works (*karma*) and his knowledge of the past (*pūrvaprajñā*) lay hold of him.

3. 'As a caterpillar, drawing near to the tip of a blade of grass, prepares its next step and draws [it]self up towards it, so does this self, striking the body aside and dispelling ignorance (*avidyā*),

33 Or, 'heat' or 'energy'.

34 Reading *sa vijñānam*. If *savijñānam* is read, the translation must be, 'he follows after what has understanding'.

prepare its next step and draw [it]self up (for its plunge into the Brahman-world).

4. 'As a goldsmith, making use of the material of a [golden] object, forges another new and more beautiful form, so does this self, striking the body aside and dispelling ignorance, devise (*kṛ-*) another new and more beautiful form, – be it [the form] of one of the ancestors or of a Gandharva or of a god or of one in the Prajāpati[-world] or of one in the Brahman[-world] or of any other being (*bhūta*).

5. 'This Self is Brahman indeed: it consists of understanding (*vijñāna*), mind, breath, sight and hearing; of earth, water, wind and space, light (*tejas*) and darkness (*atejas*),[35] desire and desirelessness, anger and the lack of it, right (*dharma*) and wrong: it consists of all things. This is what is meant by the saying: "It consists of this: it consists of that."

'As a man acts (*karma*), as he behaves, so does he become. Whoso does good, becomes good: whoso does evil, becomes evil. By good (*puṇya*) works (*karma*) a man becomes holy (*puṇya*), by evil [works] he becomes evil.

'But some have said: "This 'person' consists of desire alone. As is his desire, so will his will (*kratu*) be; as is his will, so will he act (*karma kṛ-*); as he acts, so will he attain."

6. 'On this there is this verse:

To what his mind [and] character (*liṅga*) are attached,
To that attached a man goes with his works (*karma*).
Whatever deeds he does on earth,
Their rewards he reaps.
From the other world he comes back here –
To the world of deed and work (*karma*).

'So much for the man of desire.

'Now [we come to] the man without desire:

'He is devoid of desire, free from desire; [all] his desires have been fulfilled: the Self [alone] is his desire. His bodily functions (*prāṇa*)[36] do not depart [when he departs this world]. Being very Brahman to Brahman does he go.

7. On this there is this verse:

35 Or, 'heat and cold', or 'energy and the lack of it'.
36 Or, 'vital breaths'.

When all desires which shelter in the heart
Detach themselves (*pramuc-*), then does a mortal man
Become immortal: to Brahman he wins through.

'As the slough of a snake lies on an ant-hill, dead, cast off, so too does this body lie. Then is this incorporeal, immortal spirit (breath of life, *prāṇa*) Brahman indeed, light (*tejas*) indeed.'

'Venerable sir, I will give you a thousand [cows]', said Janaka, [king] of Videha.

8. [And Yājñavalkya continued:] 'On this there are these verses:

The ancient narrow far-flung path
Has touched me: I have found it!
Knowers of Brahman, wise, proceed along it
[From this world] freed and raised on high,
Along to Paradise.

9. On it, they say, are white and blue,
Yellow and green and red:
This is the path that Brahman[37] found:
Knowers of Brahman proceed along it,
Workers of good – irradiant (*taijasa*).

10. Blind darkness enter they
Who reverence unwisdom (*avidyā*):
Into darkness blinder yet
[Go they] who delight in wisdom.

11. Some worlds there are called "void of bliss",
Within blind darkness swathed:
To these at death such folk pass on
As know not wisdom – unawake.

12. Should a man [truly] understand the Self,
Knowing this that: "I am He",
What could he wish for – what desire
That he should to this body cleave?

13. Whoso has found the Self and wakened It
Deep buried in this abyss of ambiguity:
All-maker he – for everything he makes and does:
His is the world: the world itself is he!

37 Or, 'Brahmā'.

14. While yet on earth we may come to know It.
If thou hast here not known [It], great is the destruction!
Whoso knows This becomes immortal,
The rest must suffer misery indeed.

15. Should a man descry Him suddenly,
This Self, this God,
Lord of what was and what is yet to be,
How should he shrink from Him?

16. Before whose face the year
Revolves with [all] its days –
To Him the gods pay homage –
Life, light of lights, and immortality.

17. On whom the peoples five
And space [itself] are founded –
Myself immortal, wise (*vidvān*), I know Him
The Self – Immortal – Brahman!

18. Breath of breath, eye of eye,
Ear of ear, and mind of mind:
Who knows him thus, has understood
Primeval Brahman who from the beginning is.

19. Descry This with your mind:
Herein there's no diversity at all.
Death beyond death is all the lot
Of him who sees in This what seems to be diverse.

20. Descry It in its Oneness (*ekadhā*),
Immeasurable, firm (*dhruva*),
Transcending space, immaculate,
Unborn, abiding (*dhruva*), great –
[This is] the Self!

21. Let a wise Brāhman, knowing Him,
Bend his mind towards Him:
Let him not meditate on many words;
These can but tire the voice.

22. 'This is indeed the great unborn Self which consists of understanding (*vijñāna*) among the human faculties (*prāṇa*). In the space within the heart lies the Ruler of all, the Lord of all, the King of all. He neither increases by good works nor does he

diminish by evil ones. He is the Lord of all, He the King of beings, He their Protector. He is the causeway which holds these worlds apart lest they should split asunder.

'He it is whom Brāhmans strive to know by reciting the Veda, by sacrifice and the giving of alms, by fierce austerities and fasting. Once a man has come to know Him, he becomes a "silent sage" (*muni*). Desiring Him alone as a state of being (*loka*), wandering friars leave their homes.

'This is what the men of old knew well, [and knowing it,] they had no wish for offspring. "What should we do with offspring?" [so they said,] "for we possess this Self, – this [immortal] state of being (*loka*)." Rising above their desire for sons, their desire for riches, their desire for [exalted] states of being, they wander forth to lead a beggar's life. For there is no difference between a desire for sons and a desire for riches; and there is no difference between a desire for riches and a desire for [exalted] states of being: all of them are nothing more than desire.

'This Self – [what can one say of it but,] "No, no!" It is impalpable, for it cannot be grasped; indestructible, for it cannot be destroyed; free from attachment, for it is not attached [to anything], not bound. It does not quaver, nor can it be hurt.

'Whoso [thus knows] – these two thoughts do not occur to him, "So I have done evil," or, "So I have done what is [good and] fair." He shrugs them off (*tar-*). What he has done and what he has left undone does not torment him.

23. 'This is laid down in a Ṛg-Vedic verse;

> Such is a Brāhman's eternal majesty:
> By works (*karma*) he grows no greater, grows no less.
> Seek out the track of it! for knowing Him,
> By no evil work wilt thou be defiled.

'Hence the man who thus knows will be at peace, tamed, quietly contented, long-suffering, recollected (*samāhita*), for he will see the Self in [him]self: he will see all things as the Self. Evil does not touch (*tar-*) him: all evil he shrugs off (*tar-*). Evil does not torment (*tap-*) him: all evil he burns (*tap-*) out. Free from evil, free from doubt, immaculate, he becomes a Brāhman (in very truth, for Brahman now indwells him). This, sire, is the Brahman-world, (this the state of being which *is* Brahman). This it is that has been granted *you*.'

Thus spake Yājñavalkya.

'Venerable sir,' [said Janaka,] 'I will give you the whole of my kingdom[38] and myself to be your slave.'

24. [But Yājñavalkya continued:] 'This indeed is the great, unborn Self, eater of food, giver of good things; and good things will that man find who thus knows.

25. 'This indeed, the great, unborn Self, that knows neither age nor death nor fear, is Brahman – yes, Brahman, free from fear! Whoso knows this becomes Brahman, free from fear.'

IV, v

1 Now, Yājñavalkya had two wives, Maitreyī and Kātyāyanī. Of these Maitreyī liked to discuss Brahman while Kātyāyanī possessed only such knowledge as is proper to a woman. At that time Yājñavalkya was about to adopt another way of life (that is, he was about to give up the way of life of a householder and retire to the forest to pursue a life of meditation).

2. 'Maitreyī,' said Yājñavalkya, 'I will shortly be giving up my present way of life in order to pursue the life of a wandering friar. Well then, let me make a settlement between you and Kātyāyanī here.'

[Verses 3–12 are omitted as they are almost identical with II, iv. 2–11. Verses 13–15 round off what Yājñavalkya had left undisclosed in the earlier version.]

13. 'As a mass of salt [dissolved in water] has neither a "within" nor a "without", but is wholly a mass of taste, so too this Self has neither a "within" nor a "without", but is wholly a mass of wisdom (*prajñāna*). Out of the elements (*bhūta*) do [all contingent beings] arise and along with them are they destroyed. After death there is no consciousness (*saṁjñā*): this is what I say.' Thus spake Yājñavalkya.

14. But Maitreyī said: 'In this, good sir, you have thrown me into the utmost confusion. Indeed, I really do not understand this [Self].'

But he said: 'There is surely nothing confusing in what I say. The Self is wholly indestructible: of its very nature (*dharma*) it cannot be annihilated.

38 Text, 'the Vedehas'.

15. 'For where there is any semblance of duality, there does one see another, there does one smell another, there does one taste another, there does one speak to another, there does one hear another, there does one think of another, there does one touch another, there does one understand another. But when all has become one's very Self, then with what should one see whom? With what should one smell whom? With what should one taste whom? With what should one speak to whom? With what should one hear whom? With what should one think of whom? With what should one touch whom ? With what should one understand whom? With what should one understand Him by whom one understands this whole universe?

'This Self – [what can one say of it but,] "No, no!" It is impalpable, for it cannot be grasped; indestructible, for it cannot be destroyed; free from attachment, for it is not attached [to anything], not bound. It does not quaver, nor can it be hurt.

'With what indeed should one understand the Understander?

'Maitreyī, [now] you have been told the [full] teaching. Of such is immortality.'

So saying, Yājñavalkya took his leave.

[Chapter vi, which gives the chain of the teachers of this doctrine, is omitted.]

Book Five

V, i

Oṁ.

Fullness beyond, fullness here:
Fullness from fullness doth proceed.
From fullness fullness take away:
Fullness yet remains.

Oṁ. 'Brahman is space (*kha*), – primeval windy space.' So said the son of Kauravyāyaṇī. This is the knowledge which Brāhmans know: by this I know [all] that is to be known.

V, ii

1. The threefold offspring of Prajāpati, – gods, men and demons, – dwelt with their father, Prajāpati, as chaste students of

sacred knowledge. After they had stayed [with him for some time] as students, the gods said: 'Speak to us, sir.'

To them he uttered this [one] syllable: '*Da*. Did you understand?'

'We did understand,' they said. 'What you said to us was "*dāmyata*, restrain yourselves."'

'Yes (*oṁ*),' he said, 'you did understand.'

2. Then the men said to him: 'Speak to us, sir.'

To them he uttered this [one] syllable: '*Da*. Did you understand?'

'We did understand', they said. 'What you said to us was "*datta*, give".'

'Yes,' he said, 'you did understand.'

3. The demons said to him: 'Speak to us, sir.:

To them he uttered this [one] syllable: '*Da*. Did you understand?'

'We did understand,' they said. 'What you said to us was "*dayadhvam*, be compassionate".'

'Yes,' he said, 'you did understand.'

This is indeed what the divine voice, the thunder, echoes '*Da – da – da*: restrain yourselves, give, be compassionate.' This threefold lesson must be learnt: restraint, giving and compassion.

V, iii

The heart is the same as Prajāpati, it is Brahman, it is the All. The word *hṛdayam*, 'heart', has three syllables.

Hṛ is one syllable. Both his own people and strangers bring offerings (*abhi-hṛ-*) to the man who thus knows.

Da is one syllable. Both his own people and strangers give (*dā-*) to the man who thus knows.

Yam is one syllable. He who thus knows goes to Paradise.

V, iv

This indeed is that. It was that, the truth.[39] He who knows this great and strange being (*yakṣa*), the first-born, [who is] the truth and Brahman, overcomes these worlds.

39 Or, 'the real'.

'Could he be overcome who thus knows that this great and strange being, the first-born, is the truth and Brahman?'

'[No,] for Brahman is Truth.'

[Chapter v, a creation story full of magical correspondences, and chapter vi are omitted.]

V, vii

It is said that lightning (*vidyut*) is Brahman. [It is called] *vidyut* because it destroys (*vidāna*). For the man who knows that lightning is Brahman, it destroys [all] evil: for lightning *is* Brahman.

[Chapters viii and ix are omitted.]

V, x

When a man departs from this world, he goes to the wind. There [the wind] opens up before him like the hole in a chariot-wheel. Through it he rises aloft till he comes to the sun. [The sun] then opens up before him like the hole in a musical instrument. Through it he rises aloft till he comes to the moon. [The moon] then opens up before him like a hole in a drum. Through it he rises aloft till he comes to a world where there is neither heat[40] nor snow, and there he dwells for countless years.

[Chapter xi is omitted.]

V, xii

Some say that Brahman is food. But this is not so, for food goes bad without the breath of life.

Others say that Brahman is the breath of life. But this is not so, for without food the breath of life dries up.

Only when these two natural phenomena (*devatā*) become one single substance (*ekadhā*), do they reach the highest state.

In this connection Prātṛda said to his father: 'What good could I do to one who knows this? What evil could I do?'

[His father] replied [beckoning] with his hand: 'Do not [talk like that,] Prātṛda, for who could reach the highest state by becoming a single substance with these two?'

40 Or, 'sorrow'.

He also said to him: '[The syllable] *vi* is food, for all these contingent beings indwell (*viś-*) food; [the syllable] *ram* is the breath of life, for all these contingent beings take pleasure (*ram-*) in life. So all contingent beings indwell and take pleasure in the man who thus knows.'

[Chapters xiii, xiv and xv (which is identical with *Īśā*, 15–18, pp. 165–6) are omitted.]

Book Six

VI, i

[The characteristic excellence of six bodily functions, and the value of the knowledge thereof][41]

1. Oṁ. Verily, he who knows the chiefest and best, becomes the chiefest and best of his own [people].

Breath (*prāṇa*), verily, is chiefest and best. He who knows this becomes the chiefest and best of his own [people] and even of those of whom he wishes so to become.

2. Verily, he who knows the most excellent becomes the most excellent of his own [people].

Speech, verily, is the most excellent. He who knows this becomes the most excellent of his own [people] and even of those of whom he wishes so to become.

3. Verily, he who knows the firm basis (*prati-ṣṭhā*) has a firm basis (verb *prati-ṣṭhā*) on even ground, has a firm basis on rough ground.

The Eye, verily, is a firm basis, for with the eye both on even ground and on rough ground one has a firm basis. He has a firm basis on even ground, he has a firm basis on rough ground, who knows this.

4. Verily, he who knows attainment – for him, indeed, is attained what wish he wishes.

The Ear, verily, is attainment, for in the ear all these Vedas are attained. The wish that he wishes is attained for him who knows this.

5. Verily, he who knows the abode becomes the abode of his own [people], an abode of folk.

41 A parallel passage in simpler form is *Chāndogya Upanishad* V, i. 1–5.

The Mind, verily, is an abode. He becomes an abode of his own [people], an abode of folk, who knows this.

6. Verily, he who knows procreation (*prajāti*) procreates himself with progeny and cattle.

Semen, verily, is procreation. He procreates himself with progeny and cattle, who knows this.

7. These bodily organs (*prāṇa*) were disputing among themselves, each vaunting its own superiority. They went to Brahman and asked him which of them was the best. He replied: 'That one is the best on whose departure the body seems to be at its worst.'

8. The voice went off and stayed away for a year. On its return it said: 'How did you manage to live without me?'

They replied: '[We were] like the dumb, not speaking with the voice, [but] breathing with breath, seeing with the eye, hearing with the ear, knowing with the mind, begetting with semen. That is how we lived.' The voice entered [the body again].

9. The eye went off and stayed away for a year. On its return it said: 'How did you manage to live without me?'

They replied: '[We were] like the blind, not seeing with the eye, [but] breathing with breath, speaking with the voice, hearing with the ear, knowing with the mind, begetting with semen. That is how we lived.' The eye entered [the body again].

10. The ear went off and stayed away for a year. On its return it said: 'How did you manage to live without me?'

They replied: '[We were] like the deaf, not hearing with the ear, [but] breathing with breath, speaking with the voice, seeing with the eye, knowing with the mind, begetting with semen. That is how we lived.' The ear entered [the body again].

11. The mind went off and stayed away for a year. On its return it said: 'How did you manage to live without me?'

They replied: '[We were] like the feeble-minded, not knowing with the mind, [but] breathing with breath, speaking with the voice, seeing with the eye, hearing with the ear, begetting with semen. That is how we lived.' The mind entered [the body again].

12. The semen went off and stayed away for a year. On its return it said: 'How did you manage to live without me?'

They replied: '[We were] like eunuchs, not begetting with semen, [but] breathing with breath, speaking with the voice, seeing with the eye, hearing with the ear, knowing with the mind. That is how we lived.' The semen entered [the body again].

13. The breath of life was on the point of going off. As a great and goodly stallion from the Indus country might tear up the pegs to which it is tethered all together, so was the breath of life [on the point of] tearing up the [other] bodily organs. They said: 'Good sir, do not go away; for we will never manage to live without you.'

'Then make me an offering', [said the breath of life].

'So be it', [said they].

14. The voice said: 'In so far as I am most excellent, you [too] are most excellent.'

'In so far as I am a prop and support, you [too] are a prop and support', said the eye.

'In so far as I am success, you [too] are success', said the ear.

'In so far as I am a home, you [too] are a home', said the mind.

'In so far as I am procreation, you [too] are procreation', said the semen.

'Then what is my food, what is my dwelling?' [said the breath of life.]

'Everything that exists is your food, right down to dogs, worms and the insects that crawl and fly; and your dwelling is water.'

What is not food is not eaten or accepted by one who thus knows this food of the breath of life. Men who are conversant with scripture and who know this, take a sip [of water] before they eat and do the same when they have finished eating. In so doing they believe that they cover the nakedness of that breath of life.

VI, ii

1. Śvetaketu Āruṇeya once went to an assembly of the Pañcālas. He approached [a certain] Jaivali Pravāhaṇa, who was surrounded by servants. Looking up, [Jaivali] addressed him thus:

'Young man!'

'Sir', he replied.

'Have you been instructed by your father?'

'Yes indeed (*oṁ*)', said he.

2. 'Do you know how these creatures here go off in different directions when they depart?'

'No,' he said.

'Do you know how they come back again to this world?'

'No', he said.

'Do you know how [it is that] that world up there is not filled up with all those many [souls] which depart [from here] again and again?'

'No', he said.

'Do you know at which oblation offered up water comes to have a human voice, rises up and speaks?'

'No', he said.

'Do you know [how one obtains] access to the "path of the gods" or the "path of the ancestors", that is, what must one do to arrive at these two paths? For we have heard the word of the seer:

> Two paths there are for mortal man, I've heard –
> The path of the ancestors and the path of the gods:
> On these all things that move converge,
> [All things] that between the Father and the Mother[42] [dwell].'

'I do not know [the answer to] a single one of these [questions]', said he.

3. [Jaivali] then invited him to stay on, but the boy brushed [the invitation] aside and hurried away. He went up to his father and said to him: 'Formerly, sir, you used to speak of us as being instructed.'

'What is the matter now, you clever [boy?' the father said].

'Some fellow of the princely class asked me five questions, and I did not know [the answer to] one of them.'

'What were they?'

'These', and he repeated the [various] heads.

4. [The father] said: 'You should know me, child, and how I have [always] told you everything I know. But come, let us go there and stay, leading the chaste life of a student of sacred knowledge.'

'Sir, go there yourself!'

So Gautama [Āruṇi] went to where Jaivali Pravāhaṇa's house was. He offered him a seat, ordered water to be brought for him and gave him the customary offerings. Then he said: 'We will grant a boon to the venerable Gautama.'

5. [The other] said: 'You have promised me this boon. Well then, tell me the words you said in the young man's presence.'

6. 'Gautama,' he said, 'that is a boon appropriate to the gods; mention one appropriate to men.'

7. 'It is well known', said [Gautama], 'that I have my full share

42 i.e. 'heaven and earth'.

of gold, cattle, horses, maidservants, carpets and clothing. Please do not ungenerously measure out for me something that is great, infinite and boundless.'

'Then, Gautama, you should ask properly.'

'Sir, I come to you as a pupil.' This is the formula used by the men of old when they came as pupils [to a teacher]. Having [thus] acknowledged himself a pupil, he stayed on.

8. 'May neither you nor your forefathers do us harm!' said [Jaivali]. 'Although this wisdom has never dwelt with any Brāhman at all hitherto, I shall nevertheless tell it to you; for who could refuse you when you speak as you do?'

[Verses 9–12, which are almost identical with *Chāndogya* V, iv–vii (p. 126), and describe the next world, the rain-cloud, this world, and man as fires, are omitted.]

13. 'Woman is a fire, Gautama: the phallus is her fuel; the hairs are her smoke; the vulva is her flame; when a man penetrates her, that is her coal; the ecstasy is her sparks.

'In this very fire the gods offer semen; from this oblation man (*puruṣa*) comes to be. He lives out his allotted span. And when he dies he is carried off to the [funeral] pyre. His fire becomes [real] fire, his fuel [real] fuel, his smoke [real] smoke, his flame [real] flame, his coal [real] coal, his sparks [real] sparks. In this very fire the gods offer up man. From this oblation a [new] man arises, bright in colour.

14. 'Those who know this and those too who in the forest revere faith as truth, merge into the flame. From the flame [they pass on] into the day, from the day into the half-month of the full moon, from the half-month of the full moon into the six months during which the sun moves northwards, from [those] months to the world of the gods, from the world of the gods to the sun, from the sun to the realm of lightning. [Then] a Person who is [all] mind draws near to these realms of lightning and leads them on to the Brahman-worlds. In those Brahman-worlds they live for long ages. For them there is no return.

15. 'But those who win for themselves many a world by sacrifice, the giving of alms and self-mortification merge into the smoke. From the smoke [they pass on] into the night, from the night into the half-month in which the moon wanes, from the half-month in which the moon wanes into the six months in which the sun moves southwards, from [those] months to the world of the

ancestors, from the world of the ancestors to the moon. When they reach the moon, they turn into food, and the gods then eat them up even as [they eat] King Soma, (the moon,) with cries of "Wax! Wane!" When this [experience] passes away from them, they pass on into space, from space into the wind, from the wind into rain, from rain into the earth. When they reach the earth, they turn into food. Then they are again offered up in the fire of a man, and after that in the fire of a woman, [and then] they are born, only to face [these] worlds again: and so they are caught up in the cycle [again and again].

'But those who do not know these two paths become insects that crawl or fly, or else snakes.'

[Chapters iii (an incantation for obtaining a wish), iv (an incantation for fruitful sexual intercourse) and v, which gives the chain of teachers, are omitted.]

CHĀNDOGYA UPANISHAD

Book One

[Chapter i, extolling the syllable Oṁ, is omitted.]

I, ii

[Verses 1–6 discuss the battle between the gods and demons. The gods revere the syllable Oṁ as the breath in the nose, as speech, the eye, the ear and the mind. All these the demons succeed in corrupting.]

7. Then [the gods] revered this breath in the mouth as the syllable Oṁ (*udgīthā*). When the demons struck it, they were smashed to pieces, just as [a clod of earth] would be smashed to pieces on striking a solid stone.

8. Just as [a clod of earth] would be smashed to pieces on striking a solid stone, so too would anyone who bears ill-will towards one who knows this or who does him harm, be smashed to pieces, for he is a solid stone.

9. With this [breath in the mouth] he does not distinguish what is fragrant from what is foul-smelling, for it is devoid of [all] evil. With whatever he eats or drinks by means of it, he supports the other vital breaths. When at the last he can no longer find that [breath] he departs, leaving the mouth open.

[Verses 10–14 are omitted.]

I, iii

1. Now [we shall speak of the syllable Oṁ] in connection with natural phenomena (*adhidaivata*).

Let a man revere [the sun] up there which radiates heat as the syllable Oṁ; for on rising it sings aloud for the sake of [all] creatures; on rising it strikes down darkness and fear. So too shall he who knows this smite down darkness and fear.

2. This, [the breath in the mouth,] and that, [the sun in the sky,] are the same (*samāna*). This is hot, and that is hot: this is called *svara*,[1] sound, and that is called *svara, pratyāsvara*, 'sound and echo'. That is why a man should revere both this and that as the syllable Oṁ.

[The remainder of this chapter, as well as chapters iv to viii, which deal with technicalities of the sacred chant, are omitted.]

I, ix

1. 'What is the goal of this world?'[2] said [Śīlaka Śalavatya].

'Space', said [Pravāhaṇa]; 'for all these contingent beings originate from space, and to space do they return. For space is greater (and more ancient) than they: space is the final goal.

2. 'This is the supremely desirable (*parovarīyān*) [manifestation of] the syllable Oṁ: [and] it is infinite. Whoso thus knows and reveres this supremely desirable [manifestation of] the syllable Oṁ, wins what is supremely desirable and conquers supremely desirable states of being (*loka*).

3. Atidhanvan Śaunaka, after expounding this [manifestation of the syllable Oṁ] to Udaraśāṇḍilya, said: 'To the extent that this supremely desirable [manifestation of] the syllable Oṁ shall be known among your offspring, to that extent will they enjoy a supremely desirable life in this world [4] and an [exalted] state (*loka*) in the next. Whoso thus knows and reveres it, shall enjoy a supremely desirable life in this world and an [exalted] state in the next – an [exalted] state in the next.'

[Chapters x and xi, 1–3, are omitted. A beggar, Uṣasti Cākrāyaṇa, is called upon to perform the sacrifice.]

I, xi

4. Then the priest who sings the introductory words approached him and said: 'Sir, you said to me: "Your reverence, if you sing the introductory words without knowing to what natural

1 A pun on *svara*, 'sound', and *svar*, 'sun'.
2 Or, 'What does this world go back to?'

phenomenon (*devatā*) they refer, your head will fall off." Which [then] is that natural phenomenon?'

5. 'Breath,' said he; 'for all contingent beings here merge into breath, (the air,) [when they die] and rise up into breath [when they are born]. This is the natural phenomenon referred to by the introductory words. Had you sung them without knowing this, your head would have fallen off, just as I told you.'

6. Then the priest who chants the hymns approached him and said: 'Sir, you said to me: "Your reverence, if you chant the hymns without knowing to what natural phenomenon they refer, your head will fall off." Which [then] is that natural phenomenon?'

7. 'The sun,' said he; 'for all contingent beings here chant the praises of the sun when it is up. That is the natural phenomenon referred to by the hymns. Had you chanted them without knowing this, your head would have fallen off, just as I told you.'

8. Then the assistant of the priest who chants the hymns approached him and said: 'Sir, you said to me, "Your reverence, if you chant your part of the ritual without knowing to what natural phenomenon it refers, your head will fall off." Which [then] is that natural phenomenon?'

9. 'Food,' said he; 'for all contingent beings here live by absorbing food. That is the natural phenomenon referred to by your part of the ritual. Had you chanted it without knowing this, your head would have fallen off, just as I told you – just as I told you.'

I, xii

1. Next we come to the chant of the dogs.

Baka Dālbhya or, [as he was also called,] Glāva Maitreya, retired to study the Veda. [2] [One day] a white dog appeared on the scene, and other dogs gathered round him saying: 'Venerable sir, get us some food by singing; we are hungry.'

3. [The white dog] said to them: 'Gather round me here tomorrow morning.' So Baka Dālbhya, that is, Glāva Maitreya, kept watch.

4. [The next day] the dogs appeared making the same motions as [priests] make when, hand in hand, they start chanting the hymn of praise called *Bahiṣpavamāna*. Then they sat down together and said: 'Hiṁ! Oṁ, let us eat; Oṁ, let us drink! Oṁ, may the god Varuṇa, may Prajāpati and Savitṛ bring food here ! O Lord of food, bring food here – bring it here!'

[Chapter xiii, on magical correspondences between various sounds and natural phenomena, is omitted.]

Book Two

[Chapters i–xxii, which describe magical correspondences between various sounds and natural phenomena, are omitted.]

II, xxiii

1. There are three branches of religion (*dharma*). The first consists of sacrifice, study of the Veda and the giving of alms. The second is mortification. The third is to dwell as a student of sacred knowledge in the house of a teacher and to behave with the utmost humility in his house. All these gain the worlds allotted to the virtuous [as their reward]. He who stands firm in Brahman wins through to immortality.

2. Prajāpati brooded over the worlds. From these, thus brooded on, welled up the threefold wisdom, (the three Vedas). He brooded on this [too]; [and] from it, thus brooded on, welled up these syllables – *bhūr*, *bhuvas*, *suvar*.

3. He brooded upon these, [and] from these, thus brooded on, the syllable Oṁ welled up. Just as a whole pile of leaves might be pierced through and held together by a stake, so is all speech pierced through and held together by the syllable Oṁ. Surely Oṁ is this whole universe – Oṁ is this whole universe!

[Chapter xxiv, on the rewards of sacrifices, is omitted.]

Book Three

[Chapters i–x, dealing with the sun seen as honey extracted from the Vedas, are omitted.]

III, xi

1. Thenceforth [the sun], after rising up on high, will never again rise or set: all alone will it stand in the midst. On this there is this verse:

There indeed it never sets,
Nor does it ever rise at all:
By the truth of this, ye gods,
May I never be robbed of Brahman!

2. For the man who knows the secret doctrine (*upaniṣad*) of Brahman it neither rises nor sets: it is always day for him.

3. Brahmā told this to Prajāpati, Prajāpati to Manu, Manu to his offspring. This is the Brahman that his father taught to Uddālaka Āruṇi, his eldest son.

4. This is the Brahman that a father may teach to his eldest son or to a worthy pupil, but to no one else at all. Even if a man were to be given the [whole earth], girdled [as it is] by the waters and full of treasure, he should yet say: 'Assuredly, this is more than that – this is more than that.'

III, xii

1. The Gāyatrī verse [p. 3] is the whole universe, whatever has come to be; and the Gāyatrī is voice, for voice sings forth and protects this whole universe that has come to be.

2. What the Gāyatrī is, that is what this earth is, for it is on the [earth] that this whole universe has come to be, on it is it established; it does not extend beyond it.

3. What the earth is, that is what this body in man is here; for these vital breaths are established on it; they do not extend beyond it.

4. What this body in man is, that is the heart within the selfsame man; for on it these vital breaths are established; they do not extend beyond it.

5. This Gāyatrī has four quarters and is sixfold. A verse of the *Ṛg-Veda* has commented on this:

6. This is the measure of his greatness,
But greater yet is primal Man (*puruṣa*):
All beings form a quarter of him,
Three-quarters are the immortal in heaven. [p. 13]

7. What is called Brahman, that is what this space outside a man is; and what that space outside a man is, [8] that is what this space within a man is; and what that space within a man is, [9] that is what this space within the heart is. That is the 'full' –

inactive, undeveloping (*apravartin*). Whoso knows this wins good fortune (*śrī*), full inactive, undeveloping.

[Chapter xiii; verses 1–6, on the vital breaths, are omitted.]

III, xiii

7. Now, the light which shines beyond the heavens, on to the back of all things, on to the back of every single thing, in the highest and most exalted worlds, that is indeed the same as the light within man.

8. When a man feels the heat in the body [of another] by touching it, he sees that [light]. When he stops up his ears and hears something like a rumbling or the crackling of a blazing fire, he hears that [light]. So it should be revered as something seen and heard. Whoso knows this will be [well-seen] and [his name will be] noised abroad – whoso knows this.

III, xiv

1. This whole universe is Brahman. Let a man in all tranquillity revere it as *tajjalān* – (as that from which all things are born, into which they dissolve and in which they breathe and move).[3]

2. Now, man (*puruṣa*) is possessed of an active will (*kratu*). As is his will in this world, so does he, on departing hence, become. Let a man exercise his will.

3. He who consists of mind, whose body is the breath of life (*prāṇa*), whose form is light, whose idea (*saṅkalpa*) is the real, whose self is space, through whom are all works, all desires, all scents, all tastes, who encompasses all this universe, who does not speak and has no care – [4] he is my Self within the heart, smaller than a grain of rice or a barley-corn, or a mustard-seed, or a grain of millet, or the kernel of a grain of millet; this is my Self within my heart, greater than the earth, greater than the atmosphere, greater than the sky, greater than all these worlds.

5. All works, all desires, all scents, all tastes belong to it: it encompasses all this universe, does not speak and has no care. This my Self within the heart is that Brahman. When I depart from hence I shall merge into it. He who believes this will never doubt.

So did Śāṇḍilya say, – so did he say.

3 So, according to the commentary of Śaṅkara.

[Chapters xv (taking refuge in various 'deities') and xvi (life seen as the Soma sacrifice) are omitted.]

III, xvii

1. When a man hungers and thirsts, taking no pleasure, that is the initiatory rite (*dīkṣā*).

2. When he eats and drinks and takes his pleasure, he takes part in the *Upasada* ceremonies (in which it is permitted to eat).

3. When he laughs and eats and copulates, he takes part in the chants and recitations.

4. Mortification, the giving of alms, uprightness, refusal to do harm (*ahiṁsā*), truthfulness – these are one's gifts to the priests.

5. Hence it is said: 'He will procreate, he has procreated'[4] – that is his second birth. Death is the ablution he performs after the ceremony.

6. When Ghora Āṅgirasa told this to Kṛṣṇa, son of Devakī, he also said – for he had passed beyond thirst: 'When the end approaches, let a man lay hold of these three [thoughts]: "You are something that can never be destroyed; you are something that can never fall or fail; you are something quickened (*saṁśita*) by the breath of life."'

On this there are the following two verses from the *Ṛg-Veda*:

Of the primordial seed
[The early-morning light they see
That higher than heaven gleams].

[Emerging] from the darkness round about
We see the highest light,
The [all-]highest sun we see:
To the sun, God among [all the] gods
We have attained – to the highest light –
Yes, to the highest light.

III, xviii

1. Let a man revere Brahman as mind. So much with reference to the self.

Next with reference to natural phenomena (*adhidaivata*).

4 This also means: 'He will press out [the Soma-juice], he has pressed it out.'

[Let a man revere] Brahman as space. This is the twofold teaching with reference both to the self and to natural phenomena.

2. This Brahman has four quarters, – one quarter is voice, one breath, one the eye and one the ear. So much with reference to the self.

Next with reference to natural phenomena: one quarter is fire, one wind, one the sun, one the points of the compass. This is the twofold teaching with reference both to the self and to natural phenomena.

3. The voice is one quarter of Brahman. It shines and gives warmth with fire as its light. Whoever knows this shines and gives warmth by his renown and glory and the vital power (*varcas*) of Brahman.

4. Breath too is one quarter of Brahman. It shines and gives warmth with the wind as its light. Whoever knows this shines and gives warmth by his renown and glory and the vital power of Brahman.

5. The eye is one quarter of Brahman. It shines and gives warmth with the sun as its light. Whoever knows this shines and gives warmth by his renown and glory and the vital power of Brahman.

6. The ear is one quarter of Brahman. It shines and gives warmth with the points of the compass as its light. Whoever knows this shines and gives warmth by his renown and glory and the vital power of Brahman – whoever knows this.

III, xix

1. 'The sun is Brahman,' so runs the teaching. Now follows an amplification of this:

In the beginning this [universe] was Not-Being: [Yet] it was Being [too]. It developed. It turned into an egg. For the measure of a year it lay [there]. It was split [in two]. These two egg-shells became [the one] silver, [the other] gold.

2. The silver one is this earth, the golden one the sky up there. The outer membrane is the mountains, the inner membrane cloud and mist. The veins are the rivers. The fluid like goat's milk(?) is the ocean.

3. Now what was then born was the sun up there. When it was born, shouts and cries of joy rose up towards it, as did all contingent beings and all [their] aspirations (*kāma*). And so at its

rising and whenever it returns, shouts and cries of joy rise up towards it, as do all contingent beings and all [their] aspirations.

4. Whoever knows this in this way and reveres the sun as Brahman may expect heartening shouts to follow and encourage him – to follow and encourage him.

Book Four

IV, i

1. [Once upon a time] there lived one Jānaśruti, the great-grandson [of Janaśruta], a man of faith and generous, who gave away much in alms and supplied many a cooked meal [to his people]. He built rest-houses everywhere, hoping that people would [thus] everywhere be eating his food.

2. One night some flamingoes flew by, and one flamingo was saying to another: 'Hey, hey ! Short-sight, Short-sight! The light of Jānaśruti, the great-grandson [of Janaśruta], is as extensive as the sky. Do not touch it if you do not want to get burnt!'

3. The other one then answered [saying]: 'Now, what has this man got that you speak of him as if he was Raikva, the man with a cart?'

'Tell me about this Raikva, the man with a cart.'

4. 'Just as [in a game of dice] the lower throws go to the highest, to the winner, so do all the good deeds performed by [living] creatures go to him; and I say the same about whoever knows what he knows.'

5. Now Jānaśruti, the great-grandson [of Janaśruta], overheard this. Rising up, he said to an attendant: 'Well, my friend, do you speak of me as if I were Raikva, the man with a cart?'

'Tell me about Raikva, the man with a cart.'

6. 'Just as [in a game of dice] all the lower throws go to the highest, to the winner, so do all the good deeds performed by [living] creatures go to him; and I say the same about whoever knows what he knows.'

7. The attendant went to look for him, but came back saying he could not find him. So Jānaśruti] said to him: 'Well, then, go wherever you would [naturally] look for a Brāhman.'

8. [So the attendant] approached a man who was scratching his

scabs under a cart and said to him: 'Venerable sir, are you Raikva, the man with a cart?'

'That's who I am', he admitted, and the attendant went back and told [the king] that he had found him.

IV, ii

1. So Jānaśruti, the great-grandson [of Janaśruta], took six hundred cows, a golden necklace, and a chariot drawn by she-mules, went up to [Raikva] and said to him:

2. 'Raikva, here are six hundred cows, a golden necklace, and a chariot drawn by she-mules. Now, venerable sir, teach me about the divinity you revere.'

3. The other answered him and said: 'You can keep your necklace and cows, you low creature (*śūdra*)!'

Then again did Jānaśruti, the great-grandson [of Janaśruta], take a thousand cows, a golden necklace, a chariot drawn by she-mules, and his daughter [too], and went up [to him] and said to him:

4. 'Raikva, here are a thousand cows, a golden necklace, and this chariot drawn by she-mules, and here is a wife, and here is the village in which you live. Now, venerable sir, will you teach me?'

5. Lifting up her face, he said: 'You low creature, though you have brought [all] these [cows] along, it is only because of this face that you will make me talk.'

So [the villages] in the country of the Mahāvṛṣas where Raikva lived were, with the permission of Jānaśruti, called Raikvaparṇa.

Then he said to him:

IV, iii

1. 'It is the wind that consumes all (*saṁvarga*); for when a fire blows out, it simply goes to the wind; when the sun sets, it too goes to the wind; and when the moon sets, it also goes to the wind.

2. 'When water dries up, *it* goes to the wind; for it is the wind that consumes all these. So much for natural phenomena (*adhidaivata*).

3. 'Now with regard to the self:

'It is the breath of life that consumes all; for when a man is asleep, the voice simply enters [this] breath, as do eye, ear and mind; for it is the breath of life that consumes all these.

4. 'These are the two all-consumers, the wind among natural phenomena (*deva*), the breath of life among bodily functions (*prāṇa*).

5. 'Now, [once upon a time] when Śaunaka Kāpeya and Atiprātarin Kākṣaseni were [at table] surrounded [by attendants], a student of sacred knowledge came begging, but they gave him nothing.

6. 'Then he said:

> '"One God, protector of the world, has swallowed up
> Four great-souled beings: Kāpeya, who is He?
> Him mortal men do not discern, Atiprātarin,
> Though manifold his dwellings.

'"Indeed, no food was given to a man to whom it rightfully belongs."

7. 'Then Śaunaka Kāpeya, pondering [on this] retorted:

> '"The Self [it is], father of the gods and [every] creature,
> With tusks of gold devouring, truly wise:
> Great is his majesty, they say:
> Himself uneaten he devours
> Even what is not food.

'"Student of sacred knowledge, thus do we revere it (Brahman)." [And turning to the attendants,] he said: "Give him alms." [8] So they gave to him.

'These five[5] and the other five make ten, and that is the highest throw at dice. And so, in all regions, ten, the highest throw, is food. That [food] is primal matter (*virāj*), the eater of food, by which the whole universe was seen. Whoso knows this, comes to see the whole universe: he becomes an eater of food – whoso knows this.'

IV, iv

1. [Once upon a time] Satyakāma, son of Jabālā, addressed his mother, Jabālā: 'Madam, I wish to lead the life of a chaste student of sacred knowledge. What is my parentage?'

2. She said to him: 'My poor boy, I do not know what your

5 The natural phenomena and bodily functions mentioned in verses 1–3.

parentage is. In my youth I used to wander round a good deal serving as a maid, and it was then that I conceived you: so I do not know what your parentage is. But [at least] my name is Jabālā, and yours is Satyakāma; so you might as well call yourself Satyakāma Jābāla.'

3. So he went off to [a certain] Hāridrumata Gautama and said: 'I wish to live the life of a chaste student of sacred knowledge with you and I would like to be your pupil.'

4. [Gautama] said to him: 'What is your parentage, my dear boy?'

'I do not know, sir, what my parentage is,' he replied. 'I did ask my mother, and she answered and told me that in her youth she used to wander round a good deal serving as a maid, and it was then that she conceived me: so she did not know what my parentage was. Her name, [she said,] was Jabālā, and mine was Satyakāma. So, sir, I am Satyakāma Jābāla.'

5. 'No one but a Brāhman could put the matter so clearly', said [Gautama]. 'Bring fuel, my dear boy; I will accept you as a pupil. You have not deviated from the truth.'

After he had accepted him as a pupil, he selected four hundred lean and feeble cows and told him to keep an eye on them. As he drove them on, he said: 'I shall not come back with less than a thousand.' So he lived away for many years, and when the number [of cows] had reached a thousand –

IV, v

1. The bull [of the herd] spoke to him [saying], 'Satyakāma!'

'Sir?' he replied.

'My dear boy, there are now a thousand of us; take us to the teacher's house, [2] and I will tell you a quarter of Brahman.'

'Tell me, sir.'

He told him. 'One part [of it] is the East, one part the West, one part the South and one part the North. You see, my dear boy, this quarter of Brahman is in four parts; "luminous" is its name.

3. 'Whoever thus knows that this quarter of Brahman is in four parts and that it is called the "luminous", whoever reveres it as such, himself becomes luminous in this world. Yes, whoever thus knows that this quarter of Brahman is in four parts and that it is called the "luminous", whoever reveres it as such, wins [for himself] luminous states of being (*loka*).'

IV, vi

1. 'The fire will tell you [another] quarter.'

On the following day he drove the cows on. At the place where they bivouacked in the evening, he built up a fire, penned in the cows, put fuel [on the fire] and sat down behind it, facing east.

2. [And] the fire spoke to him [saying], 'Satyakāma!'

'Sir?' he replied.

3. 'My dear boy, I will tell you a quarter of Brahman.'

'Tell me, sir.'

It told him. 'One part [of it] is the earth, one part the atmosphere, one part the sky and one part the sea. You see, my dear boy, this quarter of Brahman is in four parts: "infinite" is its name.

4. 'Whoever thus knows that this quarter of Brahman is in four parts and that it is called "infinite", whoever reveres it as such, himself becomes infinite in this world. Yes, whoever knows that this quarter of Brahman is in four parts and that it is called "infinite", whoever reveres it as such, wins [for himself] infinite states of being.'

IV, vii

1. 'A flamingo will tell you [another] quarter.'

On the following day he drove the cows on. At the place where they bivouacked in the evening, he built up a fire, penned in the cows, put fuel [on the fire] and sat down behind it, facing east.

2. [Sure enough] a flamingo flew down towards him and spoke to him [saying], 'Satyakāma!'

'Sir?' he replied.

3. 'My dear boy, I will tell you a quarter of Brahman.'

'Tell me, sir.'

It told him. 'One part [of it] is fire, one part the sun, one part the moon and one part the lightning. You see, my dear boy, this quarter of Brahman is in four parts: "effulgent" is its name.

4. 'Whoever thus knows that this quarter of Brahman is in four parts and that it is called "effulgent", whoever reveres it as such, himself becomes effulgent in this world. Yes, whoever thus knows that this quarter of Brahman is in four parts and that it is called "effulgent", whoever reveres it as such, wins [for himself] effulgent states of being.'

IV, viii

1. 'A diver-bird will tell you [yet another] quarter.'

On the following day he drove the cows on. At the place where they bivouacked in the evening, he built up a fire, penned in the cows, put fuel [on the fire] and sat down behind it, facing east.

2. [Sure enough] a diver-bird flew down towards him and spoke to him [saying], 'Satyakāma!'

'Sir?' he replied.

3. 'My dear boy, I will tell you a quarter of Brahman.'

'Tell me, sir.'

It told him. 'One part [of it] is breath, one part sight, one part hearing, and one part the mind. You see, my dear boy, this quarter of Brahman is in four parts: "homely" (*āyatanavat*, "possessing a home") is its name.

4. 'Whoever thus knows that this quarter of Brahman is in four parts and that it is called "homely", whoever reveres it as such, himself becomes "homely" in this world. Yes, whoever knows that this quarter of Brahman is in four parts and that it is called "homely", whoever reveres it as such, wins [for himself] homely states of being.'

IV, ix

1. Then he reached the house of [his] teacher. The teacher spoke to him [saying], 'Satyakāma!'

'Sir', he replied.

2. 'My dear boy, you are radiant as is a man who knows Brahman. Now, who has been instructing you?'

'Not human beings,' he confessed, 'but it is you alone whom I should like to teach me; [3] for I have heard from men like you that wisdom learnt from a teacher produces the best results.'

Then [the teacher] repeated the very [words the others had spoken]. None of it was omitted – nothing was omitted.

IV, x

1. [Later] Upakosala Kāmalāyana lived with Satyakāma Jābāla as a student of sacred knowledge. For twelve years he tended his [sacred] fires. Then [Satyakāma] sent his other pupils home, but he did not send [Upakosala] home.

2. His wife said to him: 'This student of sacred knowledge has [duly] mortified himself and tended the fires splendidly. Do not let the fires reproach you,[6] but teach him.' But he went away on a journey without having taught him.

3. But [Upakosala] fell ill and lost his appetite; and the teacher's wife said to him, 'Eat, young man; why do you not eat?' But he [only] said: 'Many are the desires in man, distracting him in all directions. I am riddled with every kind of illness; I will not eat.'

4. Then the fires said among themselves: '[This] student of sacred knowledge has [duly] mortified himself and tended us splendidly. Come, let us teach him.' And they said to him:

'The breath of life is Brahman; pleasure (*ka*) is Brahman; space (*kha*) is Brahman.'

5. 'I understand how the breath of life is Brahman,' he said, 'but I do not understand how pleasure and space are so.'

'What pleasure is,' they said, 'that too is space. What space is, that too is pleasure.' And they explained to him about the breath of life and space (*ākāśa*).

IV, xi

1. Then did the householder's fire instruct him.

'Earth – fire – food – sun:' so did it say. 'The Person who is seen in the sun – He am I: He am I indeed.'

2. [All the fires speak:] 'Whoever thus knows and reveres this [fire] wards off evil deeds, wins [exalted] states of being (*lokībhū-*), lives a long and vigorous life, lives long and gloriously (*jyok*). His progeny is not cut short. In him – the man who knows and reveres this [fire] – we are well pleased and serve him (*upabhuñj-*) in this world and the next.'

IV, xii

1. Then did the southern sacrificial fire instruct him.

'Water – the points of the compass – stars – moon:' so did it say. 'The Person who is seen in the moon – He am I: He am I indeed.'

2. [All the fires speak:] 'Whoever thus knows and reveres this [fire] wards off evil deeds, wins [exalted] states of being, lives a

6 Or, 'Do not let the fires speak [to him] before you.'

long and vigorous life, lives long and gloriously. His progeny is not cut short. In him – the man who knows and reveres this [fire] – we are well pleased and serve him in this world and the next.'

IV, xiii

1. Then did the eastern sacrificial fire instruct him.

'Breath of life – space – sky – lightning:' so did it say. 'The Person who is seen in the lightning – He am I: He am I indeed.'

2. [All the fires speak:] 'Whoever thus knows and reveres this [fire] wards off evil deeds, wins [exalted] states of being, lives a long and vigorous life, lives long and gloriously. His progeny is not cut short. In him – the man who knows and reveres this [fire] – we are well pleased and serve him in this world and the next.'

IV, xiv

1. [The fires] said: 'Upakosala, my dear, now you know about us and about [your]self;[7] but it is for your teacher to tell you the way (*gati*).'

His teacher came back and spoke to him thus: 'Upakosala', he said.

2. 'Sir', he replied.

'My dear boy, your face is radiant as is [the face] of one who knows Brahman. Now, who has been instructing you?'

'Who do you think should have instructed me, sir?' Here he seemed to deny [what had happened to him]. 'They look like this now, though they can look quite different.' Here he alluded to the fires.

'Well, my dear boy, what did they tell you?'

'This —,' he confessed.

3. 'Indeed, my boy, they spoke to you of [exalted] states of being. But I will tell you something too: As water does not stick to a lotus leaf, so do evil deeds (*karma*) not stick to the man who knows this.'

'Please speak out, then', he said.

And then to him he said:

7 Or, 'the Self'.

IV, xv

1. 'This Person who is seen in the eye – he is the Self,' said he: 'He is immortality, freedom from fear: Brahman is He. Even if they were to pour ghee or water on to the [eye], it would flow away towards the edges.

2. '"Convergence of the Beautiful" (*saṁyadvāma*) they call him; for all beauteous things converge upon him [as] all beauteous things converge on the man who knows this.

3. '"Bringer of the Beautiful" (*vāmānīḥ*) is he too, for all beauteous things he brings [as] the man who knows this brings [with him] all beauteous things.

4. '"Bringer of Light" (*bhāmanīḥ*) is he too, for in all the worlds he shines [as] the man who knows this shines in all the worlds.

5. 'Now, whether or not the funeral rites are performed for such men as these, they merge into a flame, from the flame into the day, from the day into the half-month of the full moon, from the half-month of the full moon into the six months during which the sun moves northwards, from [those] months into the year, from the year into the sun, from the sun into the moon, from the moon into lightning. There there is a Person who is other than human. He leads them on to Brahman. This is the path of the gods, the path of Brahman. Those who follow this [path] never come back to human life – they never come back.'

[Chapters xvi and xvii, on aspects of the sacrifice, are omitted.]

Book Five

[Chapters i and ii are omitted, being almost identical with *Bṛhadāraṇyaka* Upanishad VI, chapters i and ii.]

V, iii[8]

1. Śvetaketu Āruṇeya once went to an assembly of the Pañcālas, and [a certain] Pravāhaṇa Jaibali addressed him thus:

'Young man, has your father instructed you?'

8 cf. *Bṛhadāraṇyaka* VI, ii.

'Yes indeed, sir', he said.

2. 'Do you know where [living] creatures go [when they depart] from here?'

'No, sir.'

'Do you know how they come back again?'

'No, sir.'

'Do you know the partings of the two paths, the way of the gods and the way of the ancestors?'

'No, sir.'

3. 'Do you know how [it is that] that world up there is not filled up?'

'No, sir.'

'Do you know how [it is that] at the fifth oblation water comes to have a human voice?'

'No indeed, sir.'

4. 'Then, how could you say that you had been instructed? How, indeed, could anyone who does not know these things say that he has been instructed?'

Much depressed, he returned to his father's house and said to him:

'You have not instructed me at all and yet, sir, you said that you had done so. [5] Some fellow of the princely class asked me five questions, and I could not unravel one of them.'

'As you have repeated them to me', [the father] said, 'I do not know [the answer to] one of them. Had I known of them, how should I not have told you?'

6. Then Gautama [i.e. Śvetaketu's father] went off to the king's house, and on his arrival [the king] paid him due honour. Next morning he went up to him as he was entering the assembly-hall and said to him:

'Venerable Gautama, choose a boon from among such things as men possess.'

'Keep such things for yourself, Your Majesty', said he. 'Rather, tell me the words you said in this young man's presence.'

7. [But the king] was troubled. Then he bade him stay [with him] awhile and said: 'As to what you have said, this wisdom has never yet reached the Brāhmans before you, and that is why in all the worlds sovereignty (*praśāsana*)[9] has belonged to the princely class alone.' Then he said to him:

9 Or, 'teaching'.

V, iv

1. 'Gautama, the world up there is a fire: the sun is its fuel; the sun's rays its smoke; the day its flame; the moon its coal; the stars its sparks.

2. 'In this very fire the gods offer faith; from this oblation King Soma comes to be.'

V, v

1. 'Gautama, the rain-cloud is a fire: the wind is its fuel; cloud its smoke; lightning its flame; the thunderbolt its coal; hailstones its sparks.

2. 'In this very fire the gods offer King Soma; from this oblation rain comes to be.'

V, vi

1. 'Gautama, the earth is a fire: the year is its fuel; space its smoke; night its flame; the points of the compass its coal; the intermediate points of the compass its sparks.

2. 'In this very fire the gods offer rain; from this oblation food comes to be.'

V, vii

1. 'Gautama, man is a fire: the voice is his fuel; breath his smoke; the tongue his flame; the eyes his coal; the ears his sparks.

2. 'In this very fire the gods offer food; from this oblation semen comes to be.'

V, viii

1. 'Gautama, woman is a fire: the phallus is her fuel; when a man solicits her, this is her smoke; the vulva is her flame; when he penetrates her, this is her coal; the ecstasy is her sparks.

2. 'In this very fire the gods offer semen; from this oblation the embryo comes to be.'

V, ix

1. 'So [it is that] at the fifth oblation water comes to have a human voice.

'Enveloped in the membrane the embryo lies within [the womb] for nine, ten, or however many months it may be, and is then born.

2. 'Once born he lives out his allotted span. When dead he is carried off from here to the [funeral] pyre [to go from there to that] allotted [place] from which he came, from which he arose.'

V, x

1. 'Those who know thus as well as those who worship in the forest knowing that self-mortification is the same as faith, merge into the flame [of the funeral pyre]; from the flame [they pass on] into the day, from the day into the half-month of the full moon, from the half-month of the full moon into the six months during which the sun moves northwards, [2] from [those] months into the year, from the year into the sun, from the sun into the moon, from the moon into the lightning. There, there is a Person who is other than human. He leads them on to Brahman. This path is the "way of the gods".

3. 'But those who in their villages lay great store by sacrifice, good works and the giving of alms, merge into smoke, from smoke [they pass on] into the night, from the night into the latter half of the month, from the latter half of the month into the six months in which the sun moves southwards. These do not reach the year. [4] From [those] months they [merge] into the world of the ancestors, from the world of the ancestors into space, from space into the moon which is King Soma, the food of the gods. This the gods eat up.

5. 'There they remain until the residue [of their good works] is exhausted, and then they once again return on the same path. [They merge] into space, and from space into the wind. After becoming wind, they become smoke; after becoming smoke, they become mist; [6] after becoming mist, they become cloud; after becoming cloud, they pour forth as rain. [Then] they are born here as rice or barley, herbs or trees, sesame or beans. To emerge from these is very difficult. For only if someone or other eats [him as] food and pours [him out as] semen, can he be born again.

7. 'Those whose conduct on earth has given pleasure, can hope to enter a pleasant womb, that is, the womb of a Brāhman, or a woman of the princely class, or a woman of the peasant class; but those whose conduct on earth has been foul can expect to enter a foul and stinking womb, that is, the womb of a bitch or a pig or an outcaste. [8] But those small and continually returning creatures (like flies and worms) are not to be found on either of these two paths: [theirs is] a third condition, [for of them it is said:] "Be born and die."

'That is why the world up there is not filled up, and that is why a man should take good care of himself. On this there is the following verse:

9. Stealer of gold, drinker of wine,
Defiler of his teacher's bed,
Slayer of Brāhmans, these are the four
Who fall [in the scale of being]; the fifth
Is he who associates with these.

10. 'But whoever thus knows these five fires is not defiled by evil even though he associate with such people. Pure and clean, he reaches the world of the good and pure (*puṇya*) – whoever thus knows, whoever thus knows.'

V, xi

1. Prācīnaśāla Aupamanyava, Satyayajña Pauluṣi, Indradyumna Bhāllaveya, Jana Śārkarākṣya and Budila Āśvatarāśvi, all of them owners of stately mansions and greatly learned in the scriptures, once came together to consider [the problem of] what the Self is and what Brahman is.

2. [Knowing that] Uddālaka Āruṇi was just then making a study of the universal (*vaiśvānara*) Self, they agreed to approach him, and did so.

3. He, however, thought to himself: 'These owners of stately mansions, who are so greatly learned in the scriptures, are going to ask me questions all of which I may not be able to answer. Well, I shall direct them to another teacher.'

4. So he said to them: 'Gentlemen, Aśvapati Paikeya is just now making a study of the universal Self; let us approach him.' And so they did.

5. When they arrived he saw to it that they were received with all due honour. On getting up the following morning he said:

'Within my realm there is no thief,
  No miser, no drinker of wine,
No man without a sacred fire,
  No dunce, no lecher, no whore!

6. 'Gentlemen, I am about to arrange for the performance of a sacrifice, and I will give you gentlemen as much wealth as I give to each of the priests. Please stay [with me], sirs.'

7. But they said: 'A man should speak only about the subject with which he is conversant. At the moment you are making a study of the universal Self; please tell us about that.'

8. 'I shall give you your answer tomorrow morning', said he. The following morning they came back with fuel in their hands, but he, without accepting them officially as pupils, spoke to them as follows:

V, xii

1. 'Aupamanyava, what is the Self that you revere?'

'The sky, Your Majesty', he said.

'The brilliant [sky] which you revere as the Self is certainly the universal Self. That is why the Soma-juice is seen to be pressed out again and again in your family.

2. 'You eat food and see what is agreeable [to you]; and whoever thus reveres this universal Self eats food and sees what is agreeable [to him]. [Moreover,] the vital power (*varcas*) of Brahman abides in his family. But this is only the head of the Self,' said he. 'Your head would have fallen off if you had not come to me.'

V, xiii

1. Then he said to Satyayajña Pauluṣi: 'Prācīnayogya, what is the Self that you revere?'

'The sun, Your Majesty', he said.

'[The sun] which possesses every form and which you revere as the Self is certainly the universal Self. That is why things of every shape and form are seen in your family, [2] such as a chariot drawn by a she-mule all ready to set out, a maidservant and a golden necklace.

'You eat food and see what is agreeable [to you]; and whoever thus reveres this universal Self eats food and sees what is agreeable [to him]. [Moreover,] the vital power of Brahman abides in his family. But this is only the eye of the Self,' he said. 'You would have gone blind if you had not come to me.'

V, xiv

1. Then he said to Indradyumna Bhāllaveya: 'Vaiyāghrapadya, what is the Self that you revere?'

'The wind, Your Majesty', he said.

'[The wind] which follows various paths and which you revere as the Self is certainly the universal Self. That is why the offerings to you are so various, and various are the rows of chariots that follow you.

2. 'You eat food and see what is agreeable [to you]; and whoever thus reveres this universal Self eats food and sees what is agreeable [to him]. [Moreover,] the vital power of Brahman abides in his family. But this is only the life-breath of the Self,' said he. 'Your life-breath would have departed if you had not come to me.'

V, xv

1. Then he said to Jana: 'Śārkarākṣya, what is the Self that you revere?'

'Space, Your Majesty', he said.

'Broad [space] which you revere as the Self is certainly the universal Self. That is why you have a broad [quiver of] offspring and wealth.

2. 'You eat food and see what is agreeable [to you]; and whoever thus reveres this universal Self eats food and sees what is agreeable [to him]. [Moreover,] the vital power of Brahman abides in his family. But this is only the body of the Self,' said he. 'Your body would have wasted away if you had not come to me.'

V, xvi

1. Then he said to Budila Āśvatarāśvi: 'Vaiyāghrapadya, what is the Self that you revere?'

'Water, Your Majesty', he said.

'That treasure which you revere as the Self is certainly the universal Self. That is why you are rich in treasure and prosperous.

2. 'You eat food and see what is agreeable [to you]; and whoever thus reveres this universal Self eats food and sees what is agreeable [to him]. [Moreover,] the vital power of Brahman abides in his family. But this is only the bladder of the Self,' said he. 'Your bladder would have burst if you had not come to me.'

V, xvii

1. Then he said to Uddālaka Āruṇi: 'Gautama, what is the Self that you revere?'

'The earth, Your Majesty', he said.

'This firm basis which you revere as the Self is certainly the universal Self. That is why you are firmly based as far as offspring and cattle are concerned.

2. 'You eat food and see what is agreeable [to you]; and whoever thus reveres this universal Self eats food and sees what is agreeable [to him]. [Moreover,] the vital power of Brahman abides in his family. But this is only the feet of the Self,' said he. 'Your feet would have withered away if you had not come to me.'

V, xviii

1. Then he said to them [all]: 'You know, you eat food, although you [only] know this universal Self as if it were something separate. But whoever reveres this universal Self, as having the measure of a span and [yet] as having limitless dimensions(?), eats food in all worlds, all creatures, all selves.

2. 'The head of this universal Self is indeed the brilliant [sky], its eye is [the sun] which possesses every form, its breath is [the wind] whose nature is to follow various paths, its body is broad [space], its bladder is the wealth [of water], its feet are the earth, its breast is the sacrificial altar, its hair is the sacrificial strew, its heart is the householder's fire, its mind is the southern sacrificial fire and its mouth is the eastern sacrificial fire.'

[Chapters xix to xxiv, concerning various oblations, are omitted.]

Book Six

VI, i

1. [Once upon a time] there lived [a man called] Śvetaketu Āruṇeya. To him his father said: 'Śvetaketu, you should [now] live the life of a chaste student of sacred knowledge. No one in our family, my dear boy, is uneducated, a [mere] hanger on, as you might say, of the Brāhman class.'

2. So at the age of twelve he went to [a master], and when, at the age of twenty-four, he had studied all the Vedas, he returned, conceited, priding himself on his learning, and obdurate.

3. Then his father said to him: 'Śvetaketu, my boy, since you are now conceited and obdurate, and pride yourself on your learning, did you also ask about that teaching by which what had [hitherto] not been heard, is heard; what had [hitherto] not been thought of, is thought of; and what had [hitherto] not been known, is known?'

'Now, sir, what manner of teaching is that?'

4. 'My dear boy, just as all that is made up of clay can be known by one lump of clay – its modifications are verbalizations, [mere] names – the reality is just "clay-ness".

5. 'And, dear boy, just as all that is made of copper can be known by one copper ornament – its modifications are verbalizations, [mere] names – the reality is just copper.

6. 'And, dear boy, just as all that is made of iron can be known by one pair of nail-scissors – its modifications are verbalizations, [mere] names – the reality is just iron – so, dear boy, is that teaching.'

7. 'Now, I am sure those venerable gentlemen did not know this; for if they had known it, why should they not have told me? Do you, sir, then tell me.'

'My dear boy, I will', said he.

VI, ii

1. 'In the beginning, my dear, this [universe] was Being only – one only – without a second. True, some say that in the beginning this [universe] was Not-Being only – one only – without a second, and that from that Not-Being Being was born.

2. 'But, my dear, whence could this be?' said he. 'How could Being be born from Not-Being? No, it was Being alone that was this [universe] in the beginning – one only, without a second.

3. 'It had this thought: "Would that I were many; fain would I procreate!" It emitted light-and-heat (*tejas*). This light-and-heat [too] had the thought: "Would that I were many; fain would I procreate!" And it emitted water. So whenever a man is very hot[10] or sweats from the heat (*tejas*), water is produced.

4. 'This water [too] had the thought: "Would that I were many; fain would I procreate!" It emitted food. So whenever it rains, there is food in abundance; for it is from water that edible food is produced.

VI, iii

1. 'There are only three origins[11] of all these beings, [whether they be] born of an egg, a living being, or a sprout.

2. 'That same [primal] substance (*devatā*) had this thought: "Come, let me enter into these three [secondary] substances with this [my] living Self and [thereby] differentiate name and form (individuality).

3. 'Let me make each of them threefold.' [So] that same [primal] substance entered into these three [secondary] substances with his own [*eva*) living Self and [thereby] differentiated name and form. [4] Each one of them he made threefold.

'Now, my dear boy, learn from me how each one of these three substances becomes threefold.

VI, iv

1. 'In fire whatever is red in colour (*rūpa*) is the form (*rūpa*) of light-and-heat; whatever is white is [the form] of water; whatever is black is [the form] of food. The essence of fire[12] has [now] left the fire; the modification is a verbalization, a [mere] name. The reality is just the three forms (*rūpa*).

2. 'In the sun whatever is red in colour is the form of light-and-heat; whatever is white is [the form] of water; whatever is black is

10 Or, 'grieves'.
11 Lit. 'seed'.
12 *Agnitva*, 'fire-ness'.

[the form] of food. The essence of the sun has [now] left the sun; the modification is a verbalization, a [mere] name. The reality is just the three forms.

3. 'In the moon whatever is red in colour is the form of light-and-heat; whatever is white is [the form] of water; whatever is black is [the form] of food. The essence of the moon has [now] left the moon; the modification is a verbalization, a [mere] name. The reality is just the three forms.

4. 'In the lightning whatever is red in colour is the form of light-and-heat; whatever is white is [the form] of water; whatever is black is [the form] of food. The essence of lightning has left the lightning; the modification is a verbalization, a [mere] name. The reality is just the three forms.

5. 'It is precisely this that those owners of stately mansions who were greatly learned in the scriptures[13] knew in olden times when they said: "No one today can bring up any [idea] which has never been heard of, thought of, or known before." [Starting] from these [three forms] they knew [everything].

6. 'They knew that whatever appeared red was the form of light-and-heat; they knew that whatever appeared white was the form of water; they knew that whatever appeared black was the form of food.

7. 'What seemed to be unknown, they knew, was a compound of these same substances (*devatā*).

'Now, my dear boy, learn from me how each of these three substances [itself] becomes threefold when it enters into the sphere of man.

VI, v

1. 'Food, when eaten, is disposed of in three ways. Its coarsest element becomes faeces, the intermediate one flesh and the finest one the mind.

2. 'Water, when drunk, is disposed of in three ways. Its coarsest element becomes urine, the intermediate one blood and the finest one breath.

3. 'Light-and-heat, when absorbed, is disposed of in three ways. Its coarsest element becomes bone, the intermediate one marrow and the finest one voice.

13 See v, xi. 1.

4. 'For the mind, dear boy, is composed of food, breath is composed of water, while the voice is composed of light-and-heat.'

'Good sir, will you kindly instruct me further?'

'I will, my dear child,' said he.

VI, vi

1. 'My dear boy, when curds are churned, the finest part rises upwards and turns into butter. [2] So too, dear boy, when food is eaten, the finest part rises upwards and becomes mind. [3] When water is drunk, dear boy, the finest part rises upwards and becomes breath. [4] When light-and-heat is absorbed, dear boy, the finest part rises upwards and becomes the voice.

5. 'For, my dear child, the mind is composed of food, breath is composed of water, while the voice is composed of light-and-heat.'

'Good sir, will you kindly instruct me further?'

'I will, my dear child,' said he.

VI, vii

1. 'A human being, dear boy, consists of sixteen parts.

'Do not eat for fifteen days, but drink as much water as you like, for the breath of life is composed of water and will not be cut off so long as you drink.'

2. So for fifteen days he ate nothing. He then approached [his father] and said: 'Sir, what shall I recite?'

'Recite verses from the *Ṛg-Veda*, the *Sāma-Veda* and the *Yajur-Veda*', said he.

'I am afraid they do not come to my mind,' he replied.

3. 'My dear boy,' he said to him, 'if a single piece of coal the size of a firefly was all that was left of a large [fire] which had already been lighted, then [the fire] would not burn much by means of it. So too, my dear, only one of your sixteen parts may be left, and that is not enough for you to remember the Vedas by. Eat, and then you will [be able to] learn from me.'

4. [The boy] ate, and approached [his father]; and he [was able to] answer anything he asked him.

5. [The father] said to him: 'My dear boy, if a single piece of coal the size of a firefly was all that was left of a large [fire] which had already been lighted, and if it was then made to blaze up by putting straw on it, then by these means there would be quite a

big fire. [6] So too, my dear, although only one of your sixteen parts was left, that [part,] once it had been strengthened by food, blazed up, and that was enough for you to remember the Vedas by – for the mind is composed of food, dear boy, breath is composed of water, while the voice is composed of light-and-heat.'

This, then, did he learn from him – this did he learn.

VI, viii

1. Uddālaka Āruṇi said to his son, Śvetaketu: 'My child, learn from me the true nature of sleep.

'When a man is properly (*nāma*) asleep (*svapiti*), then, dear boy, is he suffused in Being – he will have returned to his own (*svam apīta*). That is why it is said of him "*svapiti*, he is asleep"; for he will have returned to his own (*svam apīto bhavati*).

2. 'Just as a bird, tied to a string, will fly around in all directions and finding no resting-place anywhere else, will resort to the very [string] that keeps it captive, so too, my dear, the mind will fly around in all directions and, finding no resting-place anywhere else, will come to rest in the breath of life; for, my child, the mind is the captive of the breath of life.

3. '[Now,] dear boy, learn from me about hunger and thirst. When a man is really hungry, it is the water that carries off what he has eaten. For just as we speak of a carrier off of cattle or a carrier off of horses or a carrier off of men, so do we speak of water as a carrier off of food.

'In this context, my dear boy, you must know that this [body] is a sprout which has sprung up; and there is no [sprout] without a root.

4. 'What could its root be but food? So too, my child, [if you think of] food as a sprout, then you must look for water as its root; and, dear boy, [if you think of] water as the sprout, then you must look for light-and-heat as its root; and, dear boy, [if you think of] light-and-heat as the sprout, you must look for Being as its root.

'My dearest child, all these creatures [here] have Being as their root, Being as their resting-place (*āyatana*), Being as their foundation.

5. 'Now, when a man is really thirsty, it is the light-and-heat that carries off what he has drunk. For just as we speak of a carrier off of cattle or a carrier off of horses or a carrier off of men, so too do we speak of light-and-heat as a carrier off of water.

'In this context, my dear boy, you must know that this [body] is a sprout which has sprung up; and there is no [sprout] without a root.

6. 'What could its root be but water? And, my child, [if you think of] water as the sprout, you must look for light-and-heat as its root; and, dear boy, [if you think of] light-and-heat as the sprout, you must look for Being as its root.

'My dearest child, all these creatures [here] have Being as their root, Being as their resting-place, Being as their foundation.

'My dear boy, I have already told you how each of these substances (*devatā*) [itself] becomes threefold when it enters into the sphere of man.

'My dear boy, when a man dies, his voice is absorbed (*saṁpad-*) into the mind, his mind into breath, breath into light-and-heat and light-and-heat into the highest substance.

7. 'This finest essence, – the whole universe has it as its Self: That is the Real: That is the Self: That *you* are, Svetaketu!'

'Good sir, will you kindly instruct me further?'

'I will my dear child', said he.

VI, ix

1. 'As bees, dear boy, make honey by collecting the juices of many trees and reduce the juice to a unity, [2] yet [those juices] cannot perceive any distinction there [so that any of them might know:] "I am the juice of this tree", or "I am the juice of that tree", [so too], my dearest boy, all these creatures [here], once they have merged (*saṁpad-*) into Being do not know that they have merged into Being.

3. 'Whatever they are in this world, whether tiger or lion, wolf or boar, worm or moth, gnat or fly, that they become again (*ā-bhū*).

4. 'This finest essence – the whole universe has it as its Self: That is the Real: That is the Self: That *you* are, Śvetaketu!'

'Good sir, will you kindly instruct me further?'

'I will, my dear child', said he.

VI, x

1. '[Look at] these rivers, my dear: from east to west, from west to east they flow – from ocean to ocean they go. They become the

ocean itself so that, once there, they no longer know: "This one am I, that one am I."

2. 'Even so, my dear, all these [living] creatures, arising out of Being, do not know that they have arisen out of Being.

'Whatever they are in this world, whether tiger or lion, wolf or boar, worm or moth, gnat or fly, that they become again.

3. 'This finest essence – the whole universe has it as its Self: That is the Real: That is the Self: That *you* are, Śvetaketu!'

'Good sir, will you kindly instruct me further?'

'I will, my dear child,' said he.

VI, xi

1. '[Look at] this great tree, my dear. If you were to strike at its root, it would bleed but live on; if you were to strike it in the middle, it would bleed but live on; if you were to strike it at the top, it would bleed but live on. Strengthened[14] by the living Self, it still stands, drinking in the moisture and exulting.

2. 'If life leaves one of its branches, it dries up; if it leaves a second, that too dries up; if it leaves a third, that too dries up. If it leaves the whole [tree], the whole [tree] dries up. This, my dear boy, is how you ought to understand it,' said he.

3. 'When the life has gone out of it, this [body] dies; [but] the life does not die.

'This finest essence – the whole universe has it as its Self: That is the Real: That is the Self: That *you* are, Śvetaketu!'

'Good sir, will you kindly instruct me further?'

'I will, my dear child,' said he.

VI, xii

1. 'Bring me a fig from over there.'

'Here you are, sir.'

'Cut it open.'

'[There it is,] cut open, sir.'

'What do you see there?'

'These rather small seeds, sir.'

'Would you, please, cut one of them up?'

'[Here is one,] cut up, sir.'

14 Or, 'pervaded' (*anuprabhūta*).

'What do you see there?'

'Nothing at all, sir.'

2. Then he said to him: 'My dear boy, it is true that you cannot perceive this finest essence, but it is equally true that this huge fig tree grows up from this same finest essence.

3. 'My dear child, have faith.

'This finest essence – the whole universe has it as its Self: That is the Real: That is the Self: That *you* are, Śvetaketu!'

'Good sir, will you kindly instruct me further?'

'I will, my dear child', said he.

VI, xiii

1. 'Put this piece of salt in the water and come to me tomorrow morning.'

[Śvetaketu] did as he was told. [Then his father] said to him:

'[Do you remember] that piece of salt you put in the water yesterday evening? Would you be good enough to bring it here?'

He groped for it but could not find it. It had completely dissolved.

2. 'Would you please sip it at this end? What is it like?' he said.

'Salt.'

'Sip it in the middle. What is it like?'

'Salt.'

'Sip it at the far end. What is it like?'

'Salt.'

'Throw it away, and then come to me.'

He did as he was told; but [that did not stop the salt from] remaining ever the same.

[His father] said to him: 'My dear child, it is true that you cannot perceive Being here, but it is equally true that it *is* here.

3. 'This finest essence – the whole universe has it as its Self: That is the Real: That is the Self: That *you* are, Śvetaketu!'

'Good sir, will you kindly instruct me further?'

'I will, my dear child', said he.

VI, xiv

1. 'And now a parable.

'A certain man was led blindfold from [the land of] the Gandhāras and left in an uninhabited place. He was tossed around, whether east or north or south or west [he did not know], for he had been brought there blindfold and been abandoned blindfold.

2. '[Then a certain man came up to him and] removed the bandage [from his eyes], saying, "[The land of] the Gandhāras is in that direction; that is the direction you should take."

'[And so,] being a sensible man, he [went] from village to village asking [his way], and once he had been shown the way he arrived home in [the land of] the Gandhāras.

'So too does the man who has a teacher [to show him the way] know that he will remain [in this phenomenal world] only so long as he is not released (*vimuc-*): then he will arrive home.

3. 'This finest essence – the whole universe has it as its Self: That is the Real: That is the Self: That *you* are, Śvetaketu!'

'Good sir, will you kindly instruct me further?'

'I will, my dear child', said he.

VI, xv

1. 'Again, my dear boy, when a man is gravely ill, his relatives gather round him and ask him again and again if he recognizes them. So long as his voice does not merge into his mind, his mind into breath, breath into light-and-heat, and light-and-heat into the highest substance (*devatā*), he will recognize (*jñā-*) [them].

2. 'Then, when his voice does merge into his mind, his mind into breath, breath into light-and-heat, light-and-heat into the highest substance, then he will not recognize [them].

3. 'This finest essence – the whole universe has it as its Self: That is the Real: That is the Self: That *you* are, Śvetaketu!'

'Good sir, will you kindly instruct me further?'

'I will, my dear child', said he.

VI, xvi

1. 'Again, my dear boy, people bring a man handcuffed [to face the ordeal], crying out, "He has committed a robbery, he has stolen, heat the axe for him!" If he is guilty, he makes himself out to be what he is not (*anṛtam ātmānaṁ kurute*), speaks untruly (*anṛta*), clothes [him]self (*ātmānam*) in untruth. He takes hold of the red-hot axe and is burnt. Then he is killed.

2. 'If, however, he is innocent, he shows himself to be what he

is (*satya*), speaks the truth (*satya*), clothes [him]self in truth. He takes hold of the red-hot axe and is not burnt. Then he is released (*muc-*).

3. 'So, just as such a man is not burnt [because he embodies Truth], so does this whole universe have this [Truth] as its Self. That is the Real (*satya*, Truth): That is the Self: that *you* are, Śvetaketu!'

This did he understand from him – this did he understand.

Book Seven

VII, i

1. Nārada approached Sanatkumāra and said to him: 'Teach [me], sir.'

[Sanatkumāra] said: 'Tell me what you know, and I will then develop it further for you.'

2. [Nārada] said: 'I know the *Ṛg-Veda*, sir, the *Yajur-Veda* and the *Sāma-Veda*; fourthly [I know] the *Atharva-Veda* and fifthly the ancient collections of stories (*itihāsa-purāṇa*). [I also know] the "Veda of Vedas" (grammar), the funeral rites for the dead, arithmetic, divination, chronometry, logic, politics, the etymological interpretation (*devavidyā*) and semantic interpretation (*brahmavidyā*) of the scriptures, the way to approach disembodied spirits, archery,[15] astronomy, the art of dealing with snakes, and the fine arts. [All] this, sir, do I know.

3. 'And so, sir, I am conversant with the sacred writings (*mantra*), but I do not know the Self. But I have heard from men like you that any man who knows the Self transcends unhappiness; and I *am* unhappy, sir. Do you then, sir, enable me to transcend unhappiness.'

[Sanatkumāra] replied: 'Everything that you have been studying is no more than a name.

4. 'The *Ṛg-Veda*, the *Yajur-Veda* and the *Sāma-Veda* are no more than a name. Your fourth and fifth, that is, the *Atharva-Veda* and the ancient collections of stories [are no more than a name. And no more than a name are] the "Veda of Vedas" (grammar), the funeral rites of the dead, arithmetic, divination,

15 Or, 'the art of rulership'.

chronometry, logic, politics, the etymological and semantic interpretations of the scriptures, the way to approach disembodied spirits, archery, astronomy, the art of dealing with snakes, and the fine arts. All this is merely a name. Revere the name.

5. 'Whoso reveres the name as Brahman, gains freedom of movement (*kāmacāra*) in the whole sphere of name – whoso reveres the name as Brahman.'

'Is there anything greater than the name, sir?'

'There is indeed something greater than the name.'

'Then, sir, will you please tell me what it is?'

VII, ii

1. 'Speech is greater than the name; for speech makes the *Ṛg-Veda*, the *Yajur-Veda* and the *Sāma-Veda* known; so too your fourth and fifth, that is, the *Atharva-Veda* and the ancient collections of stories, grammar, the funeral rites of the dead, arithmetic, divination, chronometry, logic, politics, the etymological and semantic interpretations of the scriptures, the way to approach disembodied spirits, archery, astronomy, the art of dealing with snakes, and the fine arts. [Speech too makes known] heaven and earth, wind and space, water and fire (*tejas*), gods and men, beasts and birds, grasses and trees, animals right down to worms, moths and ants, right (*dharma*) and wrong, truth and falsehood, good and evil, pleasant and unpleasant. Were it indeed not for speech, there would be no knowledge of right and wrong, truth and falsehood, good and evil, pleasant and unpleasant: for it is speech that makes all this known. Revere speech.

2. 'Whoso reveres speech as Brahman gains freedom of movement in the whole sphere of speech – whoso reveres speech as Brahman.'

'Is there anything greater than speech, sir?'

'There is indeed something greater than speech.'

'Then, sir, will you please tell me what it is?'

VII, iii

1. 'Mind is greater than speech. For just as a man's fist can contain two acorns or two berries or two nuts, so does mind contain both speech and name. If a man by his mind has a mind

to study the sacred texts (*mantra*), he then studies them; [if he has a mind] to perform any [sacred] action, he then performs it; [if he has a mind] to wish for sons and cattle, he then wishes for them; [if he has a mind] to wish for this world and the next, he then wishes for them. Mind is the Self; for mind is the [whole] world: mind is Brahman. Revere mind.

2. 'Whoso reveres mind as Brahman gains freedom of movement in the whole sphere of mind – whoso reveres mind as Brahman.'

'Is there anything greater than mind, sir?'

'There is indeed something greater than mind.'

'Then, sir, will you please tell me what it is?'

VII, iv

1. 'Will[16] is greater than mind. For when a man wills something, then he has it in mind, then he utters speech and formulates it in a name. In the name the sacred formulas become one as do [sacred] actions in the sacred formulas.

2. '[All] these meet in one place only – in the will. Will is their very self, and will is their foundation. Heaven and earth were willed into existence; wind and space were willed into existence; water and fire were willed into existence. Because these were willed into existence,[17] rain was willed into existence; because rain was willed into existence, food was willed into existence; because food was willed into existence, living creatures (*prāṇa*) were willed into existence; because living creatures were willed into existence, the sacred formulas were willed into existence; because the sacred formulas were willed into existence, [sacred] actions were willed into existence; because [sacred] actions were willed into existence, the world was willed into existence; because the world was willed into existence, all is willed into existence. Such is will. Revere will.

3. 'Whoso reveres will as Brahman [attains to] states of being (*loka*) ordered and willed (*klpta*); being himself abiding, firmly based and unperturbed, he attains to states of being that are [likewise] abiding, firmly based and unperturbed. He gains freedom of movement in the whole sphere of will – whoso reveres will as Brahman.'

16 Or, 'conception'. Śaṅkara comments: 'Ability to distinguish between what ought to be and what ought not.'

17 Or, 'by the will of these'. So, too, in the following clauses.

'Is there anything greater than will, sir?'
'There is indeed something greater than will.'
'Then, sir, will you please tell me what it is.'

VII, v

1. 'Thought is greater than will. For when a man thinks, then he wills, then he has it in mind, then he utters speech and formulates it in a name. In name the sacred formulas become one as do [sacred] actions in the sacred formulas.

2. '[All] these meet in one place only – in thought. Thought is their very self, and thought is their foundation. And so even if a man knows a great deal but is unthinking, people say of him: "He is nothing, whatever he may know. For if he were [really] wise, he would not be so very unthinking." On the other hand, even if a man knows only a little but knows how to think, people are anxious to listen to him. For thought is the one point at which [all] these [other faculties] meet: thought is [their] self, thought [their] foundation. Revere thought.

3. 'Whoso reveres thought as Brahman [attains to] states of being (*loka*) that have been properly thought out; being himself abiding, firmly based and unperturbed, he attains to abiding, firmly based and unperturbed states of being. He gains freedom of movement in the whole sphere of thought – whoso reveres thought as Brahman.'
'Is there anything greater than thought, sir?'
'There is indeed something greater than thought.'
'Then, sir, will you please tell me what it is.'

VII, vi

1. 'Meditation (*dhyāna*) is greater than thought. The earth seems to meditate; atmosphere and sky seem to meditate; the waters and the mountains seem to meditate, as do gods and men. That is why whenever men achieve greatness on earth, they may be said to have received their [due] portion of the fruits of meditation. So, while small men are quarrelsome, slanderous gossips, the great may be said to have received their [due] portion of the fruits of meditation. Revere meditation.

2. 'Whoso reveres meditation as Brahman gains freedom of

movement in the whole sphere of meditation – whoso reveres meditation as Brahman.'

'Is there anything greater than meditation, sir?'

'There is indeed something greater than meditation.'

'Then, sir, will you please tell me what it is?'

VII, vii

1. 'Understanding (*vijñāna*) is greater than meditation. For it is with the understanding that one understands the *Ṛg-Veda*, the *Yajur-Veda* and the *Sāma-Veda*, the *Atharva-Veda* and the ancient collections of stories as fourth and fifth, grammar, the funeral rites of the dead, arithmetic, divination, chronometry, logic, politics, the etymological and semantic interpretations of the scriptures, the way to approach disembodied spirits, archery,[18] astronomy, the art of dealing with snakes, and the fine arts. It is with the understanding too that one understands heaven and earth, wind and space, water and fire, gods and men, beasts and birds, grasses and trees, animals right down to worms, moths and ants, right and wrong, truth and falsehood, good and evil, pleasant and unpleasant, food and taste,[19] this world and the next. Revere the understanding.

2. 'Whoso reveres the understanding as Brahman attains to states of being characterized by understanding and wisdom (*jñāna*). He gains freedom of movement in the whole sphere of understanding – whoso reveres understanding as Brahman.'

'Is there anything greater than understanding, sir?'

'There is indeed something greater than understanding.'

'Then, sir, will you please tell me what it is.'

VII, viii

1. 'Strength is greater than understanding. For one strong man can make a hundred men of understanding tremble. If a man is strong, he will engage in manly effort (*utthātā*); and, so engaged, he will serve [the wise]. Serving [the wise], he will become familiar [with them, and] once familiar [with them], he will become one who [truly] sees, hears, thinks (*mantṛ*), is aware (*boddhṛ*), acts

18 Or, 'the art of rulership'.
19 Or, 'drink'.

and understands. It is by strength alone that the earth and atmosphere and sky subsist, that the mountains subsist, that gods and men subsist, that beasts and birds subsist, that grasses and trees subsist, that animals right down to worms, moths and ants subsist, that the world [itself] subsists. Revere strength.

2. 'Whoso reveres strength as Brahman gains freedom of movement in the whole sphere of strength – whoso reveres strength as Brahman.'

'Is there anything greater than strength, sir?'

'There is indeed something greater than strength.'

'Then, sir, will you please tell me what it is.'

VII, ix

1. 'Food is greater than strength. For if a man should abstain from food for ten days, although he might still live, he would not be able to see, hear, think, be aware [of anything], act or understand. Once he starts to eat again, however, he will be able to see, hear, think, be aware [of things], act and understand. Revere food.

2. 'Whoso reveres food as Brahman attains to states of being (*loka*) rich in food and drink. He gains freedom of movement in the whole sphere of food – whoso reveres food as Brahman.'

'Is there anything greater than food, sir?'

'There is indeed something greater than food.'

'Then, sir, will you please tell me what it is?'

VII, x

1. 'Water is greater than food. This being so, if the rains are deficient, living creatures become ill, thinking that there will be a dearth of food; but if the rains are abundant, living creatures will be overjoyed, thinking that there will be plenty of food. Truly, earth and atmosphere and sky are nothing but water transmuted into different forms; the mountains, gods and men, beasts and birds, grasses and trees, animals right down to worms, moths and ants are nothing but water transmuted into different forms. Revere water.

2. 'Whoso reveres water as Brahman, obtains all his desires and will be well satisfied. He gains freedom of movement in the whole sphere of water – whoso reveres water as Brahman.'

'Is there anything greater than water, sir?'

'There is indeed something greater than water.'

'Then, sir, will you please tell me what it is?'

VII, xi

1. 'Heat (*tejas*) is greater than water. For heat seizes hold of the wind and warms up space. Then people say: "It is hot: it is burning hot: it is going to rain." It is heat that gives the first indication [of the coming rains] and that pours down water. Then, with the lightning flashing upwards and sideways, the thunder roars. And so people say: "There is thunder and lightning: it is going to rain." It is heat that gives the first indication [of the coming rains] and that pours down the water. Revere heat.

2. 'Whoso reveres heat as Brahman, himself becomes brilliant (*tejasvin*) and attains to brilliant, shining states of being from which all darkness has been expelled. He gains freedom of movement in the whole sphere of heat – whoso reveres heat as Brahman.'

'Is there anything greater than heat, sir?'

'There is indeed something greater than heat.'

'Then, sir, will you please tell me what it is?'

VII, xii

1. 'Space is greater than heat. For in space are both the sun and moon, lightning, stars and fire. Through space a man calls, through space he hears and through space he answers. In space does a man take his pleasure and in space is he distressed: in space is he born and for space is he born. Revere space.

2. 'Whoso reveres space as Brahman attains to states of being that are spacious, luminous, unconfined, broadly extended. He gains freedom of movement in the whole sphere of space – whoso reveres space as Brahman.'

'Is there anything greater than space, sir?'

'There is indeed something greater than space.'

'Then, sir, will you please tell me what it is?'

VII, xiii

1. 'Memory is greater than space. This being so, if there was a crowd of people who had no memory, they would hear nothing,

have a mind to nothing, recognize (*vijñā-*) nothing. But if their memory was intact, then they would hear, have a mind [to do something] and recognize [people and things]; for it is by memory that one recognizes one's sons and cattle. Revere memory.

2. 'Whoso reveres memory as Brahman, gains freedom of movement in the whole sphere of memory – whoso reveres memory as Brahman.'

'Is there anything greater than memory, sir?'

There is indeed something greater than memory.'

'Then, sir, will you please tell me what it is?'

VII, xiv

1. 'Hope is greater than memory. For it is only when kindled by hope that memory learns the sacred formulas, performs [sacred] actions, wishes for sons and cattle, wishes for this world and the next. Revere hope.

2. 'Whoso reveres hope as Brahman – all his desires are fulfilled by hope, all his prayers come true; he gains freedom of movement in the whole sphere of hope – whoso reveres hope as Brahman.'

'Is there anything greater than hope, sir?'

'There is indeed something greater than hope.'

'Then, sir, will you please tell me what it is?'

VII, xv

1. 'The breath of life is greater than hope. For just as the spokes [of a wheel] are fixed in the hub, so is everything fixed in this breath of life. By life (*prāṇa*) does life [itself] go on: life gives life – gives [it back] to life.[20] Life is father, life mother, life brother and sister, life the teacher and life the Brāhman.

2. '[And so,] if a man, showing even a little harshness, answers back his father or mother, brother or sister, teacher or a Brāhman, people will say to him: "A curse on you, you have killed your father", or "You have killed your mother" – or your brother or sister or teacher or a Brāhman.

3. 'But if, when the breath of life has left such as he, someone were [to strike them] with a stake, cast them aside(?) and burn them up completely, no one would say to him: "You have killed

20 Or, 'a living creature'.

your father," or "You have killed your mother" – or your brother or sister or teacher or a Brāhman.

4. 'For truly the breath of life is all these things; and the man who sees that this is so, has it thus in mind and understands that it is so, becomes a master of dialectic (*ativādin*). Should people say to him, "You are a master of dialectic," he should reply, "That is perfectly true." He should not deny it.

VII, xvi

'Now the man who shows himself a master of dialectic shows it by [speaking] the truth.'

'I too, sir, would show myself to be a master of dialectic by [speaking] the truth.'

'Then [you] should really want to understand the truth.'

'Sir, I do want to understand the truth.'

VII, xvii

'When one understands, then one speaks the truth. No one speaks the truth without understanding. Only by understanding does one speak the truth. So [you] should really want to understand understanding (*vijñāna*).'

'Sir, I do want to understand understanding.'

VII, xviii

'When one thinks, then one understands. No one understands without thinking. Only by thinking first can one understand. So [you] should really want to understand thought.'

'Sir, I do want to understand thought.'

VII, xix

'When one has faith, then one thinks. No one thinks until he has faith. Only by having faith does one think. So [you] should really want to understand faith.'

'Sir, I really do want to understand faith.'

VII, xx

'When one has an ideal (*?nististhati*),[21] then one has faith. No one has faith without having an ideal. Only by having an ideal does one have faith. So [you] should really want to understand what it is to have an ideal.'

'Sir, I really do want to understand such an ideal.'

VII, xxi

'When one acts, then one has an ideal. No one has an ideal without acting first. Only by acting first has one an ideal. So [you] should really want to understand action (*kṛti*).'

'Sir, I really do want to understand action.'

VII, xxii

'When one is blessed with happiness (*sukha*), then does one act. No one acts without being blessed with happiness first. Only by being blessed with happiness first, does one act. So [you] should really want to understand happiness.'

'Sir, I really do want to understand happiness.'

VII, xxiii

'Happiness is nothing less than the Infinite (*bhūman*): there is no happiness in what is small (finite). Only the Infinite is happiness. So [you] should really want to understand the Infinite.'

'Sir, I do want to understand the Infinite.'

VII, xxiv

'Where one sees nothing else, hears nothing else, knows (*vijñā-*) nothing else, that is the Infinite. But where one sees something else, hears something else, knows something else, that is something small [because finite]. The Infinite is the same as the immortal; the small [and finite] is the same as what is mortal.'

'Sir, on what is this [Infinite] based?'

'On its own greatness, or else – not on any greatness at all.

21 Or, 'grows forth'.

Cows and horses men here on earth call "greatness" – so too elephants, gold, slaves, wives, fields and dwelling-places. This is not the way I talk: this is not the way I talk,' said he, 'for [in these cases] one is based on another.'

VII, xxv

1. 'This [Infinite] is below, it is above, it is to the west, to the east, to the south, to the north. Truly it is this whole universe.

'Next the teaching concerning the ego.

'I am below, I am above, I am to the west, to the east, to the south, to the north. Truly I am this whole universe.

2. 'Next the teaching concerning the Self. The Self is below, the Self is above, the Self is to the west, to the east, to the south, to the north. Truly the Self is this whole universe.

'The man who sees and thinks and understands (*vijñā-*) in this way has pleasure in the Self, plays with the Self, lies with the Self and has his joy with the Self: he becomes an independent sovereign. In all the worlds (and in every state of being) freedom of movement is his. But [all] those who understand [reality] in any way that is different from this, are subjects of another sovereign:[22] their states of being (*loka*) are perishable, and in all the worlds (and states of being) they have no freedom of movement.'

VII, xxvi

1. 'For the man who sees and thinks and understands in this way, life (*prāṇa*) [wells up] from the Self; hope and memory [well up] from the Self; space, heat and water [well up] from the Self; appearance and disappearance, food and strength [well up] from the Self; understanding, meditation, thought, will,[23] mind, speech and name [well up] from the Self; sacred formulas and [sacred] actions, nay, this whole universe [wells up] from the Self. [2] On this there are the following verses:

> The seer does not see death,
> Nor sickness nor yet sorrow:
> Seeing the All, the seer
> Attains the All in every way.

22 Or, 'sovereign over others'.
23 Or, 'conception'.

Onefold, threefold it becomes,
Fivefold, sevenfold, nine –
Again they say elevenfold,
One hundred-and-elevenfold,
And twenty-thousandfold.

'If your food is pure, your whole nature will be pure: if your whole nature is pure, your memory will be unfailing: if you have mastered your memory, all the knots [of doubt within your heart] will be loosened. To such a one from whom all stains have been wiped away the blessed Sanatkumāra shows the [further] shore beyond darkness. He is called "Skanda", "he who leaps [from shore to shore]" – Skanda is he called.'

Book Eight

VIII, i

1. [The teacher speaks:]

'Now, in this city of Brahman there is a dwelling-place, a tiny lotus-flower; within that there is a tiny space. What is within that is what [you] should seek: that is what [you] should really want to understand.'

2. If [his pupils] should say to him: '[Granted that] there is a dwelling-place, a tiny lotus-flower, within this city of Brahman, and that within that there is a tiny space, what, then, is to be found there that [we] should seek out and really want to understand?'

3. Then he should say: 'As wide as this space [around us], so wide is this space within the heart. In it both sky and earth are concentrated, both fire and wind, both sun and moon, lightning and the stars, what a man possesses here on earth and what he does not possess: everything is concentrated in this [tiny space within the heart].'

4. If they should say to him: 'If all this is concentrated within this city of Brahman – all beings and all desires – what is left of it all when old age overtakes it and it falls apart?'

5. Then should he say: 'It does not grow old with [the body's] ageing nor is it slain when [the body] is slain. This is the true city of Brahman; in it are concentrated [all] desires. This is the Self, exempt from evil, untouched by age or death or sorrow, untouched

by hunger or thirst: [this is the Self] whose desire is the real, whose idea[24] is the real.

'As here on earth people act as they are bidden, living out their lives [conditioned] by the ends on which they have set their hearts, be it a kingdom or [only] a plot of land –

6. 'As here on earth the worldly station (*loka*) that is won by work (*karma*) must perish, so too must the [heavenly] state (*loka*) won by merit perish in the next world.

'[All] those who go hence without having found the Self and these real [objects of] desire, will have no freedom of movement in any state of being (*loka*). But those who go hence, having found the Self and these real [objects of] desire, will have freedom of movement in every state of being.'

VIII, ii

1. If a man should desire the world of fathers, by a mere act of will[25] fathers will rise up together before him. By possessing the world of fathers he will be magnified.[26]

2. And if he should desire the world of mothers, by a mere act of will mothers will rise up together before him. By possessing the world of mothers he will be magnified.

3. And if he should desire the world of brothers, by a mere act of will brothers will rise up together before him. By possessing the world of brothers he will be magnified.

4. And if he should desire the world of sisters, by a mere act of will sisters will rise up together before him. By possessing the world of sisters he will be magnified.

5. And if he should desire the world of comrades, by a mere act of will comrades will rise up together before him. By possessing the world of comrades he will be magnified.

6. And if he should desire the world of perfumes and garlands, by a mere act of will perfumes and garlands will rise up together before him. By possessing the world of perfumes and garlands he will be magnified.

7. And if he should desire the world of food and drink, by a mere act of will food and drink will rise up together before him. By possessing the world of food and drink he will be magnified.

24 Or, 'will' (*saṅkalpa*).
25 Or, 'conception' (*saṅkalpa*), and so in the following verses.
26 Or, 'happy', and so in the following verses.

8. And if he should desire the world of song and music, by a mere act of will song and music will rise up together before him. By possessing the world of song and music he will be magnified.

9. And if he should desire the world of women, by a mere act of will women will rise up together before him. By possessing the world of women he will be magnified.

10. On whatever end a man sets his heart, whatever [object of] desire he desires, by a mere act of will that same [end and object] rises up before him and, possessed of it, he is [duly] magnified.

VIII, iii

1. 'These desires,[27] [though directed to what is] real,[28] are [none the less] covered over with unreality. Though they are real themselves, their covering is unreal.

'Never on earth can a man bring back one close to him once he has departed this life so that he can see him. [2] Yet whatever. he may long for among the living and the dead, or whatever else he may long for and cannot obtain, all that will he find if he will but go to that [city of Brahman within the heart]; for there it is that his real desires are, [though now they are] covered over with unreality.

'For, just as [a group of people] who do not know the country (*akṣetrajña*) might wander about and pass over a hidden hoard of gold time and again without finding it, so too do all these creatures go on day after day without finding the Brahman-world within them (*eta*), for they are led astray by unreality.

3. 'Truly, this Self is in the heart. And the etymology of *hṛdayam*, "heart", is this: *hṛdy ayam* "He is in the heart". Hence it is [called] *hṛdayam*, "heart". Whoever understands it in this way, day in and day out, goes to the heavenly world.

4. 'Then this deep serenity which, rising up from this body, attains the highest light, reveals itself in its own [true] form: this is the Self.' So said he. 'This is the immortal, [this] freedom from fear: this is Brahman. And the name of Brahman is this, – Reality: [and Reality is Truth].

5. 'In this word *satīyam*, "Reality and Truth", there are three syllables: *sat*, which means "immortal", *ti*, which means "mortal",

27 Enumerated in VIII, ii.

28 *Satya* and *anṛta*. these words also mean 'true' and 'false'.

and *yam*, which means "by this the two are held together". Because the two are held together by this [element, it is called] *yam* [$\sqrt{}$*yam*, meaning to "control" or "hold together"]. Whoever understands it in this way day in and day out, goes to the heavenly world.'

VIII, iv

1. Now, the Self is a causeway[29] which holds these worlds apart lest they should split asunder. On this causeway there passes neither day nor night, neither old age nor death nor sorrow, neither deeds well done nor deeds ill done. All evils recoil from it, for in this Brahman-world evil has ever been laid low.

2. And so, let the blind pass along this causeway and he will regain his sight; let the wounded [pass along it] and he will be healed; let the fevered [pass along it] and his fever will be calmed. And so it is that once a man has passed along this causeway, night will reveal itself as day indeed, for this Brahman-world is once and for all (*sakṛt*) light [by its own light].

3. To them alone belongs this Brahman-world who discover it by living the Brahman-life.[30] In all the worlds they have [full] freedom of movement.

VIII, v

1. What is commonly called sacrifice is really the chaste life of a student of sacred knowledge, for only by leading such a life can a wise man (*jñātṛ*) find the [Brahman-world].

What is commonly called the sacrificial offering is really the chaste life of a student of sacred knowledge, for only by leading such a life and after having searched for it[31] can a man find the Self.

2. What is commonly called the protracted sacrifice is really the chaste life of a student of sacred knowledge, for only by leading such a life can a man win the protection of the real (*sat*) Self.

What is commonly called a vow of silence (*mauni*) is really the chaste life of a student of sacred knowledge, for only by leading

29 Or, 'bridge'.
30 i.e. the chaste life of a student of sacred knowledge.
31 Or, 'sacrificed'.

such a life can a man discover the Self and [thereby learn how to] think.

3. What is commonly called a vow of perpetual fasting is really the chaste life of a student of sacred knowledge, for the Self that a man finds by leading such a life is never destroyed.

What is commonly called the vow of the forest-dweller is really the chaste life of a student of sacred knowledge.

In the Brahman-world, in the third heaven from here, there are two seas called Ara and Nya. There too is the lake *Airam Madīyam* ('Refreshment and Ecstasy'). There too is the fig-tree *Somasavana* ('Soma-dripping'), the city of Brahman called *Aparājita* ('Unconquered') and the golden [palace] built by the Lord (*prabhuvimita*).

4. But only those who, by leading the chaste life of a student of sacred knowledge, find these two seas, Ara and Nya, in the Brahman-world, enjoy this Brahman-world and [full] freedom of movement in all states of being (*loka*).

VIII, vi

1. Now, these channels within the heart arise from a minute substance which is reddish-brown – white, blue, yellow and red. So too the sun up there – it too is reddish-brown, white, blue, yellow and red.

2. Just as a broad highway leads to two villages – this one here and that one over there – so do these rays of the sun lead to the two worlds – this one down here and that one up there. [And] these [rays] stretch out from the sun up there and filter into these channels down here, [and, reversing the process,] they stretch out from these channels and filter [back] to the sun.

3. Now, when a man is sound asleep, integrated within himself (*samasta*) and quite serene, and when he is not conscious of dreaming, then he slips into these channels and no evil can touch him, for he is then swathed in the light (*tejas*) [of the sun].

4. Again, when a man is reduced to a state of [great] weakness, people will gather round him, sitting [at his bedside], and will ask him again and again whether he recognizes (*jñā-*) them. So long as he has not left the body, he [still] recognizes [them].

5. But when he leaves the body behind, then, surrounded by these same rays of light, he strides on upwards. Uttering [the sacred

syllable] Oṁ, he ascends aloft.[32] In as short a time as it takes to think of it (*kṣipyen manas*) he reaches the sun: for this, truly, is the gate of the world by which the wise may enter, by which the unwise are held back. On this there is the following verse:

> One hundred and one are the channels of the heart.
> Of these but one extends right up to the head:
> Ascend thereby to immortality!
> The rest, at thy departing,
> Everywhere get lost.

VIII, vii

1. 'The Self is exempt from evil, untouched by age or death or sorrow, untouched by hunger or thirst: its desire is the real, its idea[33] is the real. This is what [you] must seek out, this is what [you] must want to understand. Whoso has found this Self and understands it, wins all states of being (*loka*) and all [objects of] desire.' Thus spake Prajāpati.

2. Both the gods and the demons were apprised [of what he had said]. They said: 'Come, let us seek out that Self; for once a man has sought him out he will win all states of being and all [objects of] desire.'

Then Indra from among the gods and Virocana from among the demons sallied forth, and these two, without knowing what the other did, came with fuel in hand into the presence of Prajāpati.

3. For thirty-two years they lived the chaste life of a student of sacred knowledge. And Prajāpati said to them: 'What is it you seek by living [here so long]?'

Then the two of them replied: 'The Self is exempt from evil, untouched by either age or death or sorrow, untouched by hunger or thirst: its desire is the real, its idea is the real. This is what [you] must seek out, this is what [you] must want to understand. Whoso has found this Self and understands it, wins all states of being and all [objects of] desire. Good sir, such were your words, or so do men report them. This is what we sought when we came to live [here].'

4. And Prajāpati said to them: 'This Person who can be seen in

32 Text corrupt.
33 Or, 'will'.

the eye is that very Self.' So said he. 'This is the immortal, [this] the free from fear: this is Brahman!'

'But, good sir, what of that [Person] who can be observed in water or in a mirror, which is he?'

'The very same is observed in all these cases.'

VIII, viii

1. 'Look at [your]selves in a dish of water, and report to me anything you do not understand about [your]selves.'[34]

So the two of them looked into a dish of water; and Prajāpati said to them: 'What do you see?'

And they said: 'We see all of it, good sir – a self corresponding exactly [to our own bodies] right up to the hairs on our bodies and the finger-nails.'

2. And Prajāpati said to them: 'Attire yourselves gorgeously, put on fine raiment, adorn yourselves and then look [again] into the dish of water.' And so did they do.

And Prajāpati said to them: 'What did you see?'

3. And they said: 'Just as we ourselves here, good sir, are gorgeously attired, clad in fine raiment and [richly] adorned, so are they gorgeously attired, clad in fine raiment and [richly] adorned.'

'This is the Self,' said he; 'this the immortal, [this] the free from fear: this is Brahman!'

And the two of them, their hearts at peace, went their way.

4. And Prajāpati, gazing after them, said: 'There they go, understanding nothing and without having discovered the Self. All who hold *such* a doctrine (*upaniṣad*), be they gods or demons, can but go down to defeat.'

And Virocana, his heart at peace, returned to the demons and preached to them this doctrine: 'Let [one]self[35] be magnified![36] Let [one]self be carefully tended! Whoso magnifies [him]self and carefully tends [him]self here and now, wins the two worlds, both this one and the next.'

5. That is why even now men say on earth [when they run across] a man who gives no alms, has no faith, and offers no

34 Or, 'the Self'.
35 i.e. the body.
36 Or, 'be happy'.

sacrifice: 'Oh! what a demon!' for such is the doctrine of the demons. They deck out the body of the dead with what they have begged, [adorning it] with clothes and ornaments – for that is what they call them – thinking that they will win the next world thereby.

VIII, ix

1. But Indra, even before he had rejoined the gods, saw this danger. ['True,' he thought,] 'when this body is gorgeously attired, clad in fine raiment and [richly] adorned, so too will that [self] be gorgeously attired, clad in fine raiment and [richly] adorned; but should this [body] be blind or lame or maimed, then that [self] too will be blind or lame or maimed; and when once this body is destroyed, it too must follow it in its destruction. I see nothing enjoyable in this.'

2. [So,] with fuel in hand, back he went.

And Prajāpati said to him: 'Bountiful [Indra], with heart at peace you went your way together with Virocana, yet now you have returned. What is it you want?'

But [Indra] said: 'Good sir, when this body is gorgeously attired, clad in fine raiment and [richly] adorned, so too will that [self] be gorgeously attired, clad in fine raiment and [richly] adorned; but should this [body] be blind or lame or maimed, then that [self] too will be blind or lame or maimed; and when once this body is destroyed, it must follow it in its destruction. I see nothing enjoyable in this.'

3. 'Such indeed must be his fate, Bountiful [Indra],' said [Prajāpati], 'but I shall explain this [Self] to you further. Stay [with me] for another thirty-two years.' So he stayed [with him] for another thirty-two years. And [then Prajāpati] spoke to him:

VIII, x

1. 'He who roams abroad in dream, glorying in himself – this is the Self,' said [Prajāpati], 'this the immortal, [this] the free from fear: this is Brahman.'

And with heart at peace he went his way. But even before he had rejoined the gods, he saw this danger.

['True,' he thought,] 'even if this body is blind or lame, that [other self] will be neither blind nor lame; it is not in any way harmed by the body's ailments; [2] it is not killed when the [body] is killed, nor lame when the [body] is lame; and yet it does have the impression of being killed, of being stripped, of undergoing unpleasant experiences and even of weeping. I see nothing enjoyable in this.'

3. [So,] with fuel in hand, back he went.

And Prajāpati said to him: 'Bountiful [Indra], with heart at peace you went your way, yet now you have returned. What is it you want?'

But [Indra] said: 'Good sir, now even if this body is blind and lame, that [other self] will be neither blind nor lame; it is not in any way harmed by the body's ailments; [4] it is not killed when the [body] is killed, nor lame when the [body] is lame; and yet it does have the impression of being killed, of being stripped, of undergoing unpleasant experiences and even of weeping. I see nothing enjoyable in this.'

'Such indeed must be his fate, Bountiful [Indra],' said [Prajāpati,] 'but I shall explain this [Self] to you further. Stay [with me] for another thirty-two years.' So he stayed [with him] for another thirty-two years. And [then Prajāpati] spoke to him:

VIII, xi

1. 'Now, when a man is sound asleep, integrated within himself (*samasta*) and quite serene, and when he is not conscious of dreaming – this is the Self,' said [Prajāpati], 'this the immortal, [this] the free from fear: this is Brahman!'

And with heart at peace he went his way. But even before he had rejoined the gods he saw this danger.

[He thought:] 'Such a man, it seems to me, has no present knowledge of [him]self so that he could say, "This I am", nor, for that matter, [has he any knowledge] of these creatures [here]. Surely he might as well be a man annihilated. I see nothing enjoyable in this.'

2. [So,] with fuel in hand, back he went.

And Prajāpati said to him: 'Bountiful [Indra], with heart at peace you went your way, yet now you have returned. What is it you want?'

But [Indra] said: 'Good sir, such a man, it seems to me, has no present knowledge of [him]self so that he could say, "This I am", nor, for that matter, [has he any knowledge] of these creatures

[here]. Surely he might as well be a man annihilated. I see nothing enjoyable in this.'

3. 'Such indeed must be his fate, Bountiful [Indra],' said Prajāpati, 'but I shall explain this [Self] to you further, for it is not otherwise than this. Stay [with me] for another five years.' So he stayed [with him] for another five years, which makes a hundred and one years altogether. Hence we have the saying: 'For a hundred and one years the Bountiful [Indra] lived the life of a chaste student of sacred knowledge with Prajāpati.'

And [then Prajāpati] spoke to him:

VIII, xii

1. 'Bountiful one! For sure this body is mortal, held in the grip of death. Yet it is the dwelling-place of the immortal, incorporeal Self. [And this Self,] while still in the body, is held in the grip of pleasure and pain; and so long as it remains in the body there is no means of ridding it of pleasure and pain. But once it is freed from the body, pleasure and pain cannot [so much as] touch it.

2. 'The wind has no body. Clouds, thunder and lightning – these too have no body. So, just as these arise from [the broad expanse of] space up there and plunge into the highest light, revealing themselves each in its own form, [3] so too does this deep serenity arise out of this body and plunge into the highest light, revealing itself in its own form. Such a one is a superman (*uttara puruṣa*); and there he roves around, laughing, playing, taking his pleasure with women, chariots, or friends and remembering no more that excrescence [which was] his body.[37]

'As a draught-animal is yoked to a wagon, so is this breath of life yoked to the body.

4. 'Now, when the eye gazes upon space, it is the Person in the eye [who actually sees]: the eye itself [is merely the instrument] of sight.

'Again, when a man is conscious of smelling something, it is the Self [that smells], the nose [is only the instrument] of smell.

'And when a man is conscious of wanting to say something, it is the Self [that is so conscious], the voice [is only the instrument] of speech.

37 Or, 'the body into which he was born'.

'And when a man is conscious of hearing something, it is the Self [that hears], the ear [is only the instrument] of hearing.

5. 'And when a man is conscious of thinking of something, it is the Self [that thinks], the mind is its divine eye. With this divine eye, the mind, this Self sees these [objects of] desire and rejoices.

6. 'Assuredly, the gods in the Brahman-world revere this Self. And so all states of being (*loka*) and all [objects of] desire are in their hands. Let a man but discover this Self and understand it, then will he make his own all states of being and all [objects of] desire.' Thus spake Prajāpati: thus spake Prajāpati.

VIII, xiii

From the dark I go to the dappled: from the dappled I go to the dark.

Shaking off evil as a horse [shakes off] its hairs, shaking off the body as the moon delivers herself from the eclipse, with self perfected (*kṛtātman*), I merge into the unmade Brahman-world – I merge [into the Brahman-world].

VIII, xiv

Space it is indeed which brings out name and form. That within which they are, is Brahman, the immortal, the Self.

I go to the palace and assembly-hall of Prajāpati.

I am the glory (*yaśas*) of the Brāhmans, the glory of princes, the glory of the people.

Glory have I won! Glory of glories am I! May I never go near the white and toothless – the toothless, white and slimy.[38] To that drivelling thing may I never go!

VIII, xv

This did Brahmā tell to Prajāpati, Prajāpati to Manu, and Manu to his descendants.

The man who has studied the Veda in his teacher's family in accordance with the prescribed ordinances and in the time left over after he has performed his duties for his teacher; and who, after returning home, has continued his Vedic studies in his house

38 i.e. old age.

and in a clean place; who has produced virtuous [sons]; and who has concentrated all his faculties (*indriya*) on the Self, taking care to hurt no living thing (*ahiṁsan*) except in sacrifice – such a man, if he perseveres in this throughout life, will reach the Brahman-world and will not return again – he will not return again.

ĪŚĀ UPANISHAD

1. This whole universe must be pervaded by a Lord –
Whatever moves in this moving [world].
Abandon it, and then enjoy:
Covet not the goods of anyone at all.

2. Performing [ritual] works on earth a man
May wish to live a hundred years:
This, not otherwise, is true for thee;
A man is not defiled by works.

3. Some worlds there are called 'devilish'
In blind darkness swathed:
To these at death such folk pass on
As [seek to] slay the self.

4. Unmoving – One – swifter than thought (*manas*) –
The gods could not seize hold of It as it sped before [them]:
Standing, It overtakes [all] others as they run;
In It the wind incites activity.

5. It moves. It moves not.
It is far, yet It is near:
It is within this whole universe,
And yet It is without it.

6. Those who see all beings in the Self,
And the Self in all beings
Will never shrink from It.[1]

7. When once one understands that in oneself[2]
The Self's become all beings,
When once one's seen the unity,
What room is there for sorrow? What room for perplexity?

1 Var. 'will never doubt It'.
2 Or, 'at what time'.

8. He, the wise Sage, all-conquering, self-existent,
Encompassed that which is resplendent,
Incorporeal, invulnerable,
Devoid of sinews, pure, unpierced by evil:
[All] things He ordered each according to its nature
For years unending.

9. Blind darkness enter they
Who revere the uncompounded (*asambhūti*):[3]
Into a darkness blinder yet
[Go they] who delight in the compounded.[4]

10. Other, they say, than what becomes (*sambhava*),
Other, they say, than what does not become:
So from wise men have we heard
Who instructed us therein.

11. Coming to be (*sambhūti*) and perishing –
Who knows these both together,
By 'perishing' surpasses death,
By 'coming to be'[5] wins deathlessness.

12. Blind darkness enter they
Who reverence unwisdom (*avidyā*):
Into a darkness blinder yet
[Go they] who delight in wisdom.

13. Other, they say, than wisdom,
Other than unwisdom [too], they say:
So from wise men have we heard
Who instructed us therein.

14. Wisdom and unwisdom –
Who knows these both together,
By 'unwisdom' surpasses death,
By 'wisdom' reaches deathlessness.

15. Wind and immortal breath,
And then this body whose end is in ashes:

3 Or, 'not coming to be'.
4 Cf. p. 95.
5 Var. 'not coming to be'.

Oṁ, O mind (*kratu*) remember; what's done remember;
O mind, remember; what's done remember.[6]

16. Lead us, O god of fire, along fair paths to riches,
Thou who knowest every way;
Repel from us the fault that leads astray.
May we compile for thee a most fulsome hymn of homage!

17. The face of truth is hidden
By the golden vessel [of the sun]:
That Person yonder in the sun,
I in truth am He.

18. O Pūṣan, single seer, O god of death,
O sun, born of Prajāpati,
Display thy rays, diffuse thy light;
That form of thine which is most fair I see:
That Person yonder, I am He.

6 Var. 'O mind remember; the world(?) (*klibe*) remember; what's done remember.'

KAṬHA UPANISHAD

I

1. [A certain] Uśan, son of Vajaśravas, gave away all his property. He had a son called Naciketas;

2. And as [the kine to be distributed as] the fee for the sacrifice performed were being brought near, faith entered into him, boy though he was, and he thought:

3. 'They drink water, eat grass, give milk, insensitive:
Joyless the worlds to which the giver of these must go!'

4. He said to his father, 'Daddy, to whom will you give *me*?' [And he said it] a second and third time. [His father] said to him, 'I'll give you to death.'

[Naciketas speaks:]
5. Of many the first to go,
Of many the middlemost,
What is Yama (Death) to do with me,
For today I'm his concern?

6. Look back, [how fared] the first,
Look forward, [how fare] the last:
Like corn a man grows up,
Like corn he's born again.

7. Like fire a Brāhman guest
Enters a house:
To appease [his fiery anger],
Bring water, [Yama,] Vivasvat's son.

8. Hope and expectation, conviviality and good cheer,
Sacrifice, its merit, sons, cattle – all of this
The Brāhman wrests away from the man of little wit
In whose house he, nothing eating, dwells.

[Yama, the god of death, returning after three days' absence and finding that Naciketas has not received the hospitality due to Brāhmans, says:]

9. Since for three nights, O Brāhman, thou hast dwelt
In [this] my house, an honoured guest, [yet] nothing eating,
I now salute thee, Brāhman, may it go well with me.
Three boons [I grant] thee, choose [what thou wilt].

[Naciketas speaks:]
10. Let my father's ill-will (*saṁkalpa*) be stilled, let him be well disposed,
Let his anger with me melt away, O Death:
Let him greet me kindly, dismissed by thee;
Of the three boons this the first I choose.

[Yama speaks:]
11. Thy father, Auddālaka Āruṇi, as before
Will be well pleased [with thee] dismissed by me;[1]
His anger spent, how sweet his sleep at night will be,
When he [again] beholds thee from the jaws of Death set free!

[Naciketas speaks:]
12. In paradise there's no [such thing as] fear;
Thou art not there, nor shrinks one from old age.
Hunger and thirst, these two transcending,
Sorrow surpassing, a man makes merry in paradise.

13. O death, thou understandest the fire that leads to paradise;
Declare it [then] to me, for I have faith:
The heavenly worlds partake of (*bhaj-*) immortality;
This do I choose as my second boon.

[Yama speaks:]
14. This [too] will I declare to thee – take note of it;
The fire that leads to paradise, I know it well.
Know that [this fire] can win [thee] worlds unending,
It is the ground (*pratiṣṭhā*) [of all], hidden in secret places.

15. [And so] he told him of [this] fire, the world's beginning,
[He told him] of the firebricks, how many and how to be disposed.

1 Reading *prasṛṣṭe*.

And [Naciketas] repeated [all] just as he had said it:
Well satisfied with him Death spake again.

16. [So] great-souled [Death], well pleased, spake to him [again]:
'To thee again today I grant another boon:
This fire shall bear thy name, no other;
Accept this garland[2] variously contrived.

17. Who thrice performs the Nāciketa rite,
With the three [Vedas] concludes a pact,
And performs the three works [prescribed],
He transcends both birth and death:
Knowing that God adorable who knows
What is from Brahman born,
And realizing Him,
He attains to peace and what is absolute.[3]

18. Who thrice performs the Nāciketa rite,
And understands all three,
Who, knowing them, builds up the Nāciketa fire,
He thrusts afar Death's fetters, sorrow surpassing,
And makes full merry in the heavenly world.

19. This is the Nāciketa fire, thy very own,
Leading to paradise;
This didst thou choose as thy second boon:
This fire will men proclaim as thine indeed.
Naciketas, [now] thy third boon choose!'

[Naciketas speaks:]
20. When a man is dead, this doubt remains:
Some say, 'He is', others again, 'He is not'.
This would I know, by thee instructed –
This is the third of the boons [I crave].

[Yama speaks:]
21. Of old the gods themselves this doubt assailed –
How hard is it to know! How subtle a matter (*dharma*)!
Choose thou another boon, O Naciketas;
Insist not overmuch, hold me excused in this.

2 Translation uncertain.
3 Or, 'absolutely'.

[Naciketas speaks:]
22. 'Of old indeed the gods themselves this doubt assailed –
How hard is it to know!' So, Death, hast thou declared.
Thou alone canst tell it forth; none other is there like thee:
No other boon is there equal to this in any wise.

[Yama speaks:]
23. Choose sons and grandsons to live a hundred years,
[Choose] wealth in cattle, horses, elephants and gold,
Choose wide property in land, and thou myself
Live out thy years as many as thou wilt.

24. Or shouldst thou think this a boon [at all] equivalent,
Choose riches and long life;
Be thou of the great ones in the land:
I grant thee enjoyment of all thou canst desire!

25. Whatever a man could possibly desire
In [this] the world of men,
However hard to win,
Ask anything thou wilt at thy good pleasure –
Fair women, chariots, instruments of music.
The like of these cannot be won by [other] men –
All these I give thee, bend them to thy service.
O Naciketas, ask me no further concerning death.

[Naciketas speaks:]
26. The morrows of a man, O Death, wear down
The power of all the senses.
A life though [lived] entire is short indeed;
Keep [then] thy chariots, keep thy songs and dances!

27. With riches can man never be satisfied:
When once we've seen thee, [how] shall we riches win?
So long we'll live as thou [for us] ordainest;
This, then, is the only boon that I would claim.

28. What mortal man, grown old and wretched here below,
Could meet immortals, strangers to old age,
Know them, and [still] meditate on colours, pleasures, joys,
Finding [some] comfort in this life however long.

29. Wherein men, puzzled, doubt, O Death, [that tell us];
What [happens] at the great departing tell us!

That is the boon that's hidden in secret places:
Therefore no other [boon] doth Nacitekas choose.

II

[Yama speaks:]
1. The better part is one thing, the agreeable another;
Though different their goals both restrict a man:
For him who takes the better of the two all's well,
But he who chooses the agreeable fails to attain his goal.

2. 'Better' and 'agreeable' present themselves to man:
Considering them carefully the wise man discriminates,
Preferring the better to what only pleasure brings:
Dull men prefer the 'agreeable' –
For the getting and keeping[4] [of what they crave].

3. Thou, Naciketas, has well considered [all objects of] desire,
[All] that's agreeable in form – thou has rejected them;
Thou wouldst not accept this garland of wealth compacted
In which how many a man has been [dragged down,] submerged!

4. Different, opposed, wide separated these –
Unwisdom (*avidyā*) and what men as wisdom know:
Wisdom [it is that] Naciketas seeks, I see;
Not thou to be distracted by manifold desire!

5. Self-wise, puffed up with learning, some
Turn round and round [imprisoned] in unwisdom['s realm];
Hither and thither rushing, round they go, the fools,
Like blind men guided by the blind!

6. No glimmering have such of man's last destiny –
Unheeding, childish fools, by wealth deluded:
'This world alone exists, there is no other', so think they;
Again and ever again they fall into my hands.

7. Many there are who never come to hear of Him,[5]
Many, though hearing of Him, know Him not:

4 Reading *yogakṣemād*.
5 i.e. the Self.

Blessed (*āścarya*) the man who, skilled therein, proclaims Him,
grasps Him;
Blessed the man who learns from one so skilled and knows Him !

8. How difficult for man, though meditating much,
To know Him from the lips of vulgar men:
[Yet] unless another tells of Him, the way (*gati*) to Him is barred,
For than all subtleties of reason He's more subtile –
Logic He defies.

9. No reasoning, [no logic,] can attain to this Idea;
Let another preach it, then is it easily cognized.
[And yet] hast thou achieved it, for steadfast in truth art thou:
May there never be another like thee, Naciketas, dear,
To question [me about it].

10. I know that what's called treasure is impermanent,
For by things unstable the Stable cannot be obtained.
Have I, then, builded up the Nāciketa fire –
By things impermanent have I the Permanent attained?

11. The winning of desires is the foundation of the world,
The unending fruit of sacrifice is the bourn of fearlessness:
[All this] hast thou rejected, wise and steadfast,
For thou hast seen that this foundation broadly based
Is [Brahman,] worthy of great praise.

12. Let a wise man think upon that God,
Let him engage in spiritual exercise (*yoga*) related to the Self
(*adhyātma*):
[Let him think upon that God,] so hard to see,
Deep hidden in the depths, dwelling in a secret place,
Firm-fixed (*-stha*) in the abyss, primordial;
Then will he put behind him both sorrow and [unstable] joy.

13. Let a man hear this and understand,
Let him take hold upon this subtile [God],
Let him uproot all things of law,[6] – rejoice,
For he has won That in which [alone] he should find joy:
A house wide open is Naciketas [now], I see.

6 Reading *dharmyam*. Var. *dharmam*: 'Having attained to this subtile matter, let him uproot [all else]'.

[Naciketas speaks:]
14. Other than righteousness (*dharma*), other than unrighteousness,
Other than what's done or left undone,
Other than what has been and what is yet to be –
This that thou seest, tell it forth!

[Yama speaks:]
15. The single word[7] announced by all the Vedas,
Proclaimed by all ascetic practices,
[The word] in search of which men practise chastity,
This word I tell [thee now] in brief.
Oṁ – this is it.

16. The Imperishable Brahman this,
This the Imperishable Beyond (*para*):
Whoso this Imperishable comes to know –
What he desires is his.

17. Depend on This, the best;
Depend on This, the ultimate (*para*):
Who knows that on This [alone all things] depend,
In the Brahman-world is magnified.

18. This wise one is not born nor dies;
From nowhere has He [sprung] nor has He anyone become;
Unborn is He, eternal, everlasting and primeval –
He is not slain when the body is slain.

19. Should the killer think 'I kill',
Or the killed 'I have been killed',
Both these have no [right] knowledge:
He kills not, is not killed.

20. More subtile than the subtile, greater than the great,
The Self is hidden in the heart[8] of creatures [here]:
The man without desire (*kratu*), [all] sorrow spent, beholds It,
The majesty of the Self, by the grace of the Ordainer.[9]

21. Seated he strides afar,
Lying down he ranges everywhere:

7 Or, 'state' or 'goal'.
8 Elsewhere translated as 'secret place'.
9 Or, 'Creator', cf. *Śvetāsvatara*, III, 20. Var. 'with his elements serene'.

This God is joy and joylessness[10]
Who but I can understand Him?

22. In bodies bodiless,
In things unstable still, abiding,
The Self, the great Lord all pervading –
Thinking on Him the wise man knows no grief.

23. This Self cannot be won by preaching [Him],
Not by sacrifice[11] or much lore heard;
By him alone can He be won whom He elects:
To him this Self reveals his own [true] form (*tanū*).

24. Not he who has not ceased from doing wrong,
Nor he who knows no peace, no concentration (*asamāhita*),
Nor he whose mind is filled with restlessness,
Can grasp Him, wise and clever though he be.

25. [Though some there be] for whom the dignity
Of both Brāhman and prince are as a dish of rice
With death its sauce [and condiment] –
[Yet] where He is – [this] who really knows?

III

1. [Like] light and shade [there are] two [selves]:
[One] here on earth imbibes the law (*ṛta*) of his own deeds:[12]
[The other,] though hidden in the secret places [of the heart],
[Dwells] in the uttermost beyond.
So say [the seers] who Brahman know,
The owner of five fires and of three Nāciketa fires.

2. May we master the Nāciketa fire,
[Sure] bridge for men who sacrifice,
Seeking to reach the [further] shore
Beyond the reach of fear –
[The bridge that leads to] Brahman,
Imperishable, supreme.

10 Or, 'perpetually joyful'.
11 Or, 'intellect'.
12 Var. 'of his deeds well done'.

3. Know this:
The self is the owner of the chariot,
The chariot is the body,
Soul (*buddhi*) is the [body's] charioteer,
Mind the reins [that curb it].

4. Senses, they say, are the [chariot's] steeds,
Their objects the tract before them:
What, then, is the subject of experience?
'Self, sense and mind conjoined', wise men reply.

5. Who knows not how to discriminate (*avijñānavat*)
With mind undisciplined (*a-yukta*) the while –
Like vicious steeds untamed, his senses
He cannot master – he their charioteer.

6. But he who does know how to discriminate
With mind [controlled and] disciplined –
Like well-trained steeds, his senses
He masters [fully] – he their charioteer.

7. But he who knows not how to discriminate,
Mindless, never pure,
He reaches not that [highest] state (*pada*), returns
To this round of never-ending birth and death (*saṁsāra*).

8. But he who does know how to discriminate,
Mindful, always pure,
He gains [indeed] that [highest] state
From which he's never born again.

9. The man whose charioteer is wisdom (*vijñāna*),
Whose reins a mind [controlled],
Reaches the journey's end [indeed],
Vishnu's final state (*pada*).[13]

10. Higher than the senses are the [senses'] objects,
Higher than these the mind,
Higher than mind is soul (*buddhi*),
Higher than soul the self, the 'great'.

11. Higher than the 'great' the Unmanifest,
Higher than that the 'Person':

13 Or, 'step, pace' referring to Viṣṇu's pacing out of the universe (p. 4).

Than 'Person' there's nothing higher;
He is the goal, He the All-highest Way.[14]

12. This is the Self, deep-hidden in all beings,
[The Self that] shines not forth –
Yet it *can* be seen by men who see things subtile,
By the subtle soul (*buddhi*), [man's] noblest [part].

13. Let the wise man hold tongue and mind in check,
Submit them to the intellectual (*jñāna*) self;
Let him submit this intellect to the self [called] 'great',
And this to [that] Self which is [forever] still (*śānta*).

14. Arise! Awake! Your boons you've won!
[Awake and] understand [them]!
A sharpened razor's edge is hard to cross –
The dangers of the path – wise seers proclaim them!

15. Beyond the 'great', abiding, endless, beginningless,
Soundless, intangible, It knows not form or taste or smell,
Eternal, changeless – [such It is,] discern It!
[For only so] can ye escape the jaws of death.

16. Wise men who hear and utter forth this deathless tale
Concerning Naciketas, told by Death –
These shall win greatness in the Brahman-world.

17. Whoso, well versed therein, shall spread abroad
This highest mystery
Among assembled Brāhmans or at the commemoration of the dead,
He is conformed to infinity;
To infinity he's conformed!

IV

1. The self-existent [Lord] bored holes facing the outside world;
Therefore a man looks outward, not into [him]self.
A certain sage, in search of immortality,
Turned his eyes inward and saw the self within.

14 Or, 'refuge'.

2. Fools pursue desires outside themselves,
Fall into the snares of widespread death:
But wise men, discerning immortality,
Seek not the Stable here among unstable things.

3. By what [one knows] of form and taste and smell,
Sound, touch and sexual union,
By that [same thing] one knows:
'What of all this abides?'
This in truth is That.

4. By what one sees these both –
The state of sleep, the state of wakefulness,
'That is the self, the "great", the lord',
So think the wise, unsorrowing.

5. Who knows this honey-eating self,
The living [self] so close at hand,
Lord of what was and what is yet to be,
He shrinks not from him.
This in truth is That.

6. Who descried him[15] from among contingent beings
As first-born of fervid penance (*tapas*),[16]
As entering into the secret place [and there] abiding,
He is the first-born of the waters.
This in truth is That.

7. Who comes to be by the breath of life (*prāṇa*),
Who entered into the secret place [and there] abides,
Aditi, pregnant with divinity,
Was born from among contingent beings.[17]
This in truth is That.

8. The all-knowing [fire] concealed between the fire-sticks,
Like an embryo well nurtured by a woman with child,
Should every day be reverenced by wakeful men,
Bearing their offerings to him, the fire.
This in truth is That.

15 Sc. the 'Golden Embyro' (p. 5–16).
16 Or, 'as being born before heat'.
17 The grammar of this section is peculiar and the translation uncertain.

9. From whence the sun arises,
To whither it goes down,
Thereon are all the gods suspended;
None passes beyond this.

This in truth is That.

10. What [we see] here is also there beyond;
What there, that too is here:
Death beyond death does he incur
Who sees in this what seems to be (*iva*) diverse!

11. Grasp this with your mind:
Herein there's no diversity at all.
Death beyond death is all the lot
Of him who sees in this what seems to be diverse.

12. Of the measure of a thumb, the 'Person'
Abides within the self,
Lord of what was and what is yet to be:
No need to shrink from Him.

This in truth is That.

13. Of the measure of a thumb, [this] 'Person',
Resembling a smokeless flame,
Lord of what was and of what is yet to be:
He is today, tomorrow He.

This in truth is That.

14. As rain that falls in craggy places
Loses itself, dispersed throughout the mountains,
So does the man who sees things (*dharma*) as diverse,
[Himself] become dispersed in their pursuit.

15. As water pure into pure [water] poured
Becomes even as (*tādṛg*) [that pure water] is,
So too becomes the self of him –
The silent sage who knows.

V

1. Whoso draws nigh to the city of eleven gates[18]
Of him who is not born, whose thought is not perverse,

18 i.e. the body.

He grieves not, for he has won deliverance:
Deliverance is his!

This in truth is That.

2. As swan he dwells in the pure [sky],
As god (*vasu*) he dwells in the atmosphere,
As priest he dwells by the altar,
As guest he dwells in the house:
Among men he dwells, in vows,
In Law (*ṛta*) and in the firmament;
Of water born, of kine, of Law (*ṛta*),
Of rock – [He], the great cosmic Law (*ṛta*)!

3. He leads the out-breath upward
And casts the in-breath downward:
To this Dwarf seated at the centre
All gods pay reverence.

4. When the embodied soul whose dwelling is the body
Dissolves and from the body is released,
What then of this remains?

This in truth is That.

5. Neither by breathing in nor yet by breathing out
Lives any mortal man:
By something else they live
On which the two [breaths] depend.

6. Lo! I will declare to thee this mystery
Of Brahman never-failing,
And of what the self becomes
When it comes to [the hour of] death.

7. Some to the womb return –
Embodied souls, to receive another body;
Others pass into a lifeless stone (*sthāṇu*)
In accordance with their works (*karma*),
In accordance with [the tradition] they had heard (*śruta*).

8. When all things sleep, [that] Person is awake,
Assessing all desires:
That is the Pure, that Brahman,
That the Immortal, so they say:
In It all the worlds are stablished;

Beyond it none can pass.
This in truth is That.

9. As the one fire ensconced within the house
Takes on the forms of all that's in it,
So the One Inmost Self of every being
Takes on their several forms, [remaining] without [the while].

10. As the one wind, once entered into a house,
Takes on the forms of all that's in it,
So the One Inmost Self of every being
Takes on their several forms, [remaining] without [the while].

11. Just as the sun, the eye of all the world,
Is not defiled by the eye's outward blemishes,
So the One Inmost Self of every being
Is not defiled by the suffering of the world –
[But remains] outside [it].

12. One and all-mastering is the Inmost Self of every being;
He makes the one form manifold:
Wise men who see Him as subsistent in [their] selves,
Taste everlasting joy (*sukha*) – no others.

13. Permanent among impermanents, conscious among the conscious.
The One among the many, Disposer of desires:
Wise men who see Him as subsistent in [their] selves,[19]
Taste of everlasting peace – no others.

14. 'That is this,' so think [the wise]
Concerning that all-highest bliss which none can indicate.
How, then, should I discern It?
Does It shine of itself or but reflect the brilliance?[20]

15. There the sun shines not, nor moon nor stars;
These lightnings shine not [there] – let alone this fire.
All things shine with the shining of this light,
This whole world reflects its radiance.

19 Or, 'self-subsistent'.
20 Var. 'Does It shine or does It not?'

VI

1. With roots above and boughs beneath
This immortal fig tree [stands];
That is the Pure, that Brahman,
That the Immortal, so men say:
In it all the worlds are stablished;
Beyond it none can pass.
This in truth is That.

2. This whole moving world, whatever is,
Stirs in the breath of life (*prāṇa*), deriving from it:
The great fear [this], the upraised thunderbolt;
Whoso shall know it [thus], becomes immortal.

3. For fear of It the fire burns bright,
For fear [of It] the sun gives forth its heat,
For fear [of It] the gods of storm and wind,
And Death, the fifth, [hither and thither] fly.

4. Could one but know It here [and now]
Before the body's breaking up . . . !
[Falling] from such [a state] a man is doomed
To bodily existence in the 'created' (*sarga*) worlds.

5. In the self one sees as in a mirror,
In the world of the ancestors as in a dream,
In the world of the heavenly minstrels as across the waters,
In the world of Brahman as into light and shade.

6. Separately the senses come to be,
[Separately] they rise and fall,
Separately are they produced – so thinking
The wise man grieves no more.

7. Higher than the senses is the mind,
Higher than mind the soul (*sattva*),
Higher than soul, the self, the 'great',
Higher than [this] 'great' the Unmanifest.

8. Higher than [this] Unmanifest the 'Person',
Pervading all, untraceable (*aliṅga*):[21]

21 Or, 'sexless'.

When once a creature knows Him, he is freed (*muc-*),
And goes on to immortality.

9. His form is not something that can be seen;
No one beholds Him with the eye;
By heart and mind and soul (*manīṣ*) is He conceived of:
Whoso knows this becomes immortal.

10. When the five senses (*jñāna*) stand, [their action stilled,]
Likewise the mind; and when the soul (*buddhi*)
No longer moves or acts –
Such, have men said, is the all-highest Way.[22]

11. 'Yoga', this is how they think of it –
[It means] to check the senses firmly, still them:
Then is a man freed from heedlessness,
For Yoga is origin and end.

12. [This Self] cannot be apprehended
By voice or mind or eye:
How, then, can He be understood,
Unless we say – HE IS?

13. HE IS – so must we understand Him,
And as the true essence (*tattva*) of the two:[23]
HE IS – when once we understand Him thus,
The nature of his essence is limpidly shown forth.

14. When all desires that shelter in the heart
Of [mortal] man are cast aside (*pramuc-*),
Then mortal puts on immortality –
Thence to Brahman he attains.

15. When here [and now] the knots [of doubt]
Are all cut out from the heart,
Mortal puts on immortality:
Thus far the teaching goes.

16. A hundred veins (*nāḍi*) and one pervade the heart;
Of these [but] one extends up to the head:
By ascending this [a self] fares on to immortality;
The rest, at death (*utkramaṇa*) are dissipated everywhere.

22 Or, 'goal', or 'state', or 'refuge'.
23 Sc. the absolute and the relative.

17. Of the measure of a thumb is [this] Person,
The Inmost Self, in the heart of creatures abiding ever.
Stand firm! and from thy body wrench Him out
Like pith extracted from a reed.
Pure and immortal He: so know Him!
So know Him: pure and immortal He!

18. So did Naciketas learn this [holy] science
By Death declared, and all the arts of Yoga:[24]
Immaculate, immortal, to Brahman he won through;
And so shall all who know what appertains to Self.

May he bring aid to both of us, may He bring profit to both of us. May we together make a manly effort; may this lesson bring us glory; may we never hate each other. Oṁ. Peace – peace – peace.

24 Or, 'all the ways of putting it into practice'.

MĀṆḌŪKYA UPANISHAD

1. Hari[1] Oṁ. This syllable 'Oṁ' is this whole universe. And the interpretation thereof is this:

What was and is and is yet to be –
  All of it is Oṁ;
And whatever else the three times transcends, –
  That too is Oṁ.

2. For all this [world] is Brahman. This Self is Brahman. This Self has four quarters.

3. The waking state, conscious (*prājña*) of what is without, seven-limbed, with nineteen mouths, experiencing what is gross, common to all men (*vaiśvānara*), is the first quarter.

4. The state of dream, conscious of what is within, seven-limbed, with nineteen mouths, experiencing what is subtle, composed of light (*taijasa*), is the second quarter.

5. When a man is asleep and desires nothing whatever, dreams no dream, that is deep sleep (*suṣupta*).

The state of deep sleep, unified, a very mass of wisdom (*prajñāna*), composed of bliss, experiencing bliss, with thought as its mouth, wise (*prājña*), is the third quarter.

6. This is the Lord of all, This the omniscient. This is the Inner Controller: This is the source of all, for it is both the origin and the end of contingent beings.

7. Conscious (*prājña*) of neither within nor without, nor of both together, not a mass of wisdom (*prajñā*), neither wise nor unwise, unseen, one with whom there is no commerce, impalpable,[2] devoid of distinguishing mark, unthinkable, indescribable, its essence the firm conviction of the oneness of itself, bringing all development (*prapañca*) to an end, tranquil and mild, devoid of

1 A name of Viṣṇu.
2 Or, 'incomprehensible'.

duality, such do they deem this fourth to be. That is the Self: that is what should be known.

8. [Now,] this is the Self in its relationship to syllables: it is Oṁ. As to the letters, the quarters [enumerated above] are the letters; and the letters are the quarters – *A, U. M.*[3]

9. The waking state, common to all men, is *A*, the first letter, signifying *āpti*, 'obtaining', or *ādimattva*, 'what is in the beginning'. For he who knows this obtains all his desires and becomes the beginning.

10. The state of dream, composed of light, is *U*. the second letter, signifying *utkarṣa*, 'exaltation', or *ubhayatva*, 'partaking of both'. He who knows this exalts the continuum of knowledge and becomes like [Brahman]. In his family there is none who does not know Brahman.

11. The state of deep sleep, the wise, is *M*, the third letter, signifying *miti*, 'building up' [or 'measuring'], or *apīti*, 'absorption'. He who knows this builds up [or measures] the whole universe in very deed and is absorbed [into it].

12. The fourth is beyond [all] letters: there can be no commerce with it; it brings [all] development to an end; it is mild and devoid of duality. Such is Oṁ, the very Self indeed. He who knows this merges of his own accord (*ātmanā*) into the Self – yes, he who knows this.

3 *Oṁ* analysed as *A* + *U* + *M*.

ŚVETĀŚVATARA UPANISHAD

I

Students of Brahman say:

1. What is the cause? [What] Brahman? Whence did we come to be?
By whom or what do we live? On what are we established?
By whom directed do we pursue our several ways
In pleasure and in pain? Knowers of Brahman, [tell us!]

2. How is the first origin to be conceived? As time,
Inherent Nature, fate, chance, the elements, a person (*puruṣa*)?
Or a conjunction of these? [I think] not, given the nature of the self;
For the self [itself] is powerless over whatever causes pleasure and pain.[1]

3. [Sages] well-practised (*yoga*)[2] in meditation have beheld
God's native (*ātma-*) power deep-hidden by his attributes (*guṇa*).
He, the One, surveys, directs all causes –
All those [we spoke of] from time to self.

4. [We understand] Him [as a wheel]
With one felly, with a triple tyre,[3]
With sixteen ends and fifty spokes
And twenty counter-spokes,
With six sets of eights:[4]
Its one[5] rope has every form:

1 Or, 'because of the existence of pleasure and pain'.
2 Or, 'practised in meditation and Yoga'.
3 i.e. the three constituents of Nature.
4 The numbers refer to different categories in the Sāṅkhya system.
5 i.e. desire.

Three separate paths[6] it follows;
Its one illusion (*moha*) is doubly caused.[7]

5. We understand Him as a river of five streams[8]
From five sources?[9] – crooked, cruel –
Its waves the five vital breaths,
Its primal fount fivefold perception (*buddhi*);
Its five whirlpools swirl wildly
With fivefold misery:
Fifty tributaries it has, five branches.

6. This is the great wheel of Brahman
Giving life and livelihood to all,
Subsists in all:
In it the swan [of the soul] is hither and thither tossed.
'One is the self, another
He who impels to action',
So thinking, a man[10] rejoices:
Hence and hereby he passes on to immortality.

7. [Of old] was this highest Brahman proclaimed in song:
In It there is a trinity, firm-based, imperishable.
Knowers of Brahman, discerning what lies within It,
Merged in Brahman, intent on It,
Were freed from [the bondage of] the womb.

8. What is here conjoined together –
Perishable and imperishable,
Manifest and unmanifest –
All this doth the Lord sustain;
But for lack of mastery the self is bound,
Its [very] nature to enjoy experience:
[But] once it knows [its] God,
From all fetters is it freed!

9. Two unborn [males] there are: one knows, the other knows not;
One Master, Lord, the other lacking mastery.

6 Of righteousness, unrighteousness and wisdom.
7 i.e. by good and evil actions.
8 i.e. the senses.
9 i.e. the five elements.
10 Or, 'favoured by Him'.

One unborn female there is too, close linked
To what enjoys experience and to the experience enjoyed.
And there is the self unbounded
Of universal form: it neither works nor acts.
Find out [this] trinity. That is Brahman.

10. Perishable is Nature (*pradhāna*);
Immortal and imperishable [the self]:
Both the perishable and the self
Doth the One God Hara[11] rule.
By meditating on Him, by constant striving,[12]
By becoming what one really is (*tattvabhāva*),[13]
The whole world of appearance (*māyā*) will once again
Be lost to sight (*nivṛtti*) at last.

11. Once God is known, all fetters fall away,
[All] cares dissolve,
Birth and death are left behind;
And thirdly, by meditating on Him
At [the time of] the body's breaking up
There is mastery supreme (*viśvaiśvarya*): his desires fulfilled
[A man is then] absolute, alone (*kevala*).

12. This must be known – the Eternal Self-subsistent:[14]
For than That there's nothing higher to be known.
The enjoyer of experience – the thing experienced –
The one who provides the impulse –
Know these! and all is said.
This is the triple Brahman.

13. Just as the form of fire when it returns to its source
Cannot be seen though its subtle form (*liṅga*) is not destroyed,
For it can again be grasped at its very source, the fire-drill;
So too can both [be grasped] by [uttering]
Within one's body [the single syllable,] Oṁ.

14. Make thy body the lower fire-stick,
[The syllable] Oṁ the upper;

11 A name of Śiva. Perhaps the whole phrase should be translated thus: 'The immortal and imperishable is Hara: [He,] the One God rules both the perishable and the self.'

12 Or, 'by uniting [with Him]'.

13 Or, 'by becoming [His] essence'.

14 Or, 'subsisting in selves'.

Make use of meditation like the friction [of the sticks],
Then wilt thou see God, like hidden [fire].

15. As oil in sesame, as butter in cream,
As water in river beds, as fire between the fire-sticks,
So is that Self to be grasped within the self
[Of him] who by austerity beholds Him in [very] truth –

16. The Self who all pervades
As butter inheres in cream,
Root of[15] self-knowledge, [root of] ascetic practice –
That is Brahman, [that] the highest teaching (*upaniṣad*).[16]

II

1. First harnessing his mind and thoughts
To what is real (*tattva*),
Savitṛ[17] discerned the light of fire
And brought it to[18] the earth.

2. With mind [well] harnessed we
Attend on(?) Savitṛ, the god,
With power directed heavenward.

3. By mind has [Savitṛ] harnessed the gods
That to bright heaven they may go in thought
To make a mighty light:
May Savitṛ urge them on!

4. The wise sages of the mighty Sage
Harness their minds, harness their thoughts:
The One who knows the ordinances has decreed the [due] oblations.
How mighty is the praise of [this] god, Savitṛ!

5. For you I harness the ancient prayer (*brahman*) with adoration:
May my verses go forth on the path of the sun!
Let all the sons of the Immortal hearken [to them]; –
[The sons of the Immortal] who dwell in celestial abodes!

15 Or, 'rooted in'.
16 Or, 'that is the highest teaching concerning Brahman'.
17 A sun-god.
18 Or, 'from'.

6. Where the fire is kindled,
Where the wind is made to serve it (?),
Where the Soma overflows,
There does the mind arise.

7. With Savitṛ to urge us on,
Let us take our pleasure in the ancient prayer (*brahman*):
There must thou seek (*kṛ-*) thine origin,
For thy good works have not disdained thee.

8. Holding the body straight with head, neck and chest in line,
With senses and the mind withdrawn into the heart,
Let a wise man on Brahman's raft cross over
All the rivers [of this life] so fraught with peril.

9. Restraining here his breath, his movements well controlled,
Let a wise man breathe in through the nostrils, his breath reduced;
Free from distraction, let him hold his mind in check
Like a chariot harnessed to vicious steeds.

10. Let him meditate in a clean and level [spot]
From pebbles, fire and gravel free,
Pleasing to the mind by reason of [soft] sounds,
Water and dwelling-places, not offensive to the eye –
A secret spot protected from the wind.

11. Fog, smoke, sun, fire and wind,
Fire-flies, lightning, crystal, and the moon –
In Yoga these are the visions (*rūpa*) that anticipate
The [fuller] revelations [seen] in Brahman.

12. When the fivefold attributes (*guṇa*) of Yoga come to be and grow,
[The attributes] of earth, water, fire, wind and space –
Then is there no sickness, age or death
For him who has won himself a body of Yogic fire.

13. Lightness, good health, freedom from harassment,
A clean complexion and a pleasant voice,
A fragrant odour and but slight excretions
Announce the first steps on Yoga['s path].

14. Even as a mirror with dirt begrimed
Shines brightly once it is well cleaned,
So too the embodied soul, once it has seen
Self as it really is (*tattva*),
Becomes one, its goal achieved, from sorrow free.

15. When by means of self as it really is as with a lamp
An integrated (*yukta*) man sees Brahman as It really is (*tattva*),
[Then will he know] the unborn,[19] undying[19] God, the Pure,[19]
Beyond all essences as they really are,[19]
[And] knowing Him, from all fetters he'll be freed.

16. This is the God who pervades all regions:
He is the first-born, He is in the womb.
He is born indeed and will be born again:
Over against [his] creatures does He stand,
His face turned every way.

17. This is the God in fire and in the waters;
The whole world has He entered;
In healing plants is He, He it is in the trees:
To this God all hail, all hail!

III

1. He is the One who, spreading wide his net,
Rules with his sovereign powers:
By his sovereign powers all worlds He rules.
He is One [and One abides]
As [others] come to be and grow together.
Whoso knows this becomes immortal.

2. For One is Rudra – they stand not for a second –
Who all the worlds doth rule by his sovereign powers:
Over against [his] creatures stands He, protector;
All worlds He emanated,
[All worlds] will He roll up at the end of time.

3. His eyes on every side, on every side his face,
On every side his arms, his feet on every side:

19 These epithets could be taken as agreeing with 'Brahman'.

With arms and wings He together forges
Heaven and earth, begetting them, [He,] God, the One![20]

4. He, of gods the source and origin,
All-sovereign Rudra, mighty Seer,
Of old begat the Golden Embryo:[21]
May He conjoin us with a lucid mind (*buddhi*)!

5. Dweller in the mountains, Thyself reveal to us
In thy fairest form (*tanu*), [great] Rudra,
In a form auspicious (*śiva*), [a form] not cruel,
[A form] that displays no evil!

6. Dweller in the mountains, make thine arrow kind (*śiva*),
[The arrow] Thou carriest in thy hand to shoot it:
Protector of the mountains, do no hurt
To man or beast.

7. Higher than this,[22] than Brahman higher,[23] the mighty [God],
Hidden in all beings, in each according to his kind,
The One, all things encompassing, the Lord –
By knowing Him a man becomes immortal.

8. I know that mighty Person,
Sun-coloured beyond the darkness:
By knowing Him indeed a man surpasses death;
No other path is there on which to go.

9. Beyond Him is nothing whatsoever, no other thing;
No one is more minute than He, no one more vast:
Like a sturdy tree firm-fixed in heaven He stands,
The One, the Person, this whole universe full filling!

10. Than this[24] yet more exalted
Is That which has no form, no imperfection:
Whoso knows this becomes immortal,
The rest must suffer misery.

11. The face, the head, the neck of all is He,
In the heart of every being He makes his home,

20 *Ṛg-Veda*, x, lxxxi, 3, p. 11.
21 See p. 15–16.
22 Sc. the 'Golden Embryo'.
23 Or (with a slight variation), 'is the highest Brahman'.
24 Sc. the universe. It can scarcely refer to Rudra. Or, 'for this reason'.

All things pervading, Blessed Lord (*bhagavat*);
Hence is [He called] 'Benign', *Śiva*, penetrating everywhere.

12. A mighty Lord indeed is He, the Person;
He speeds existence on its course:
Over this prize[25] immaculate
He rules, a light unchanging.

13. This Person of the measure of a thumb, the Inmost Self,
Forever dwells within the hearts of men,
By heart and thought and mind to be conceived of:[26]
Whoso knows this becomes immortal.

14. A thousand heads [this] Person has,
A thousand eyes, a thousand feet:
Encompassing the earth on every side
He outdistances it by ten fingers' breadth.[27]

15. All this universe [this] Person is,
What was and what is yet to be,
The Lord of immortality
[And of all] that thrives on food.

16. With hands and feet on every side,
On every side eyes, heads and mouths,
With ears on every side He stands,
All things encompassing that the world contains.

17. All attributes of sense doth he light up,[28]
[Himself] devoid of all [attributes of] sense,
[He,] sovereign Lord of all,
Of all the mighty shelter.

18. In the city of nine doors[29] the embodied soul
[Like] a great bird flutters outward,
Though the whole world's in its power,
What moves and what stands still.

19. Handless and footless He yet speeds and grasps,
Eyeless he sees and earless hears:

25 Sc. *mukti*, 'spiritual liberation'.
26 Or, 'fashioned'.
27 See p. 13.
28 Or, 'seems to possess' or 'reflects'.
29 i.e. the body.

[All that is] knowable He knows,
Though of Him there is no knower:
Him men have called the primeval mighty Person.

20. More subtile than the subtile, greater than the great,
The Self is hidden in the heart of creatures here;
By the Ordainer's[30] grace does a man whose sorrow's spent
Descry the Lord who active will transcend in majesty.

21. I know this undecaying primal Self of all,
Everywhere roving, for [all things] he pervades:
[Re]birth by Him is ended,[31] so have [the wise] proclaimed;
For students of Brahman say He is eternal.

IV

1. The One, [himself] uncoloured,
Widely disposes colours manifold
By the practice (*yoga*) of his power
(Now hidden is his purpose!):
Into Him all things dissolve at the end [of time],
[As] in the beginning [all things from Him emerged]:
He is God! May He conjoin us with a lucid mind (*buddhi*)!

2. That assuredly is fire, That the sun,
That the wind, and That the moon;
That is the Pure, That Brahman,
That is the waters, That the Lord of Creatures!

3. Thou art woman, Thou art man,
Thou art the lad and the maiden too,
Thou art the old man tottering on his staff:
Once born thou comest to be, thy face turned every way![32]

4. A dark-blue moth art Thou, green [parrot] with red eyes,
Pregnant with lightning – seasons, seas:
Thyself beginningless, all things dost Thou pervade;
From Thee all worlds were born.

30 Or, 'Creator's'.
31 Or, 'He is exempt from birth'.
32 *Atharva-Veda*, x. viii. 27, pp. 32–3.

5. With the one unborn female, red, white and black,
Who gives birth to many a creature like unto herself,
Lies the one male unborn, taking his delight.
Another Male unborn forsakes her, for she has had her pleasure.

6. Two birds, close-linked companions,
Cling to the selfsame tree;
Of these the one eats of the sweet fruit,
The other, nothing eating, looks on intent.

7. On the selfsame tree a person is plunged in [grief],
Mourning his lack of mastery, perplexed;
When he sees the other, the Lord, rejoicing
In his majesty, his sorrow melts away.

8. That syllable[33] of the Vedic hymn (*ṛc*) whereon
In highest heaven all the gods are seated –
What shall the Vedic hymns avail the man
Who knows not Him [who indwells that syllable]?
The men who know it, lo, they are here assembled!

9. Hymns, sacrifices, rites and ordinances,
What was and what is yet to be,
[All] that the Vedas proclaim –
All this does He who is possessed of creative power (*māyā*) emit
From that [same syllable]; and by the same creative power (*māyā*)
The other is therein constrained.

10. Creative power (*māyā*) is Nature (*prakṛti*), this must be known,
And He who possesses it (*māyin*) is the Mighty Lord:
By things that are but parts of Him
This whole world is pervaded.

11. It is He alone who approaches every womb,[34]
In Him [alone] does this universe grow together and dissolve;
He is the Lord who grants [us] favours,
God, the adorable:
Discerning Him a man wins peace for ever.

12. He, of gods the source and origin,
All-sovereign Rudra, mighty Seer,

33 i.e. Oṁ: or, 'imperishable being'.
34 Or, 'rules over every source'.

Of old beheld the Golden Embryo[35] when he was born:
May He conjoin us with a lucid mind!

13. King of the gods is He,
All worlds in Him are fixed!
His is the kingdom over fourfooted and twofooted beasts:
To what God shall we offer our oblations?

14. More subtile than the subtile, in the midst of chaos
All things He emanates – how manifold his forms! –
All things encompasses [though He is but] One:
Whoso should know Him, *Śiva*, the Benign, wins peace forever.

15. For sure protector of the world in time is He,
Sovereign of all, hidden in all creatures;
In Him are seers of Brahman and the gods united:
By knowing Him death's fetters are cut loose.

16. By knowing *Śiva*, the Benign, in all creatures hidden,
Surpassing subtile, even as cream surpasses butter,
By knowing God, the One Encompasser of all,
A man is from all fetters freed.

17. He is God, All-maker, of exalted Self (*mahātman*),
Forever dwelling in the hearts of men,
By heart and thought and mind to be conceived of:[36]
Whoso knows this becomes immortal.

18. When there is no darkness, no day nor night,
No Being, no Not-Being – Śiva alone (*kevala*) [is this];
This the imperishable, this the choice [light] of Savitṛ:
From this primeval wisdom (*prajñā*) issued forth!

19. Above, athwart, or in the middle –
Nowhere hath anyone caught hold of him:
Of Him there is no likeness,
Great Glory is his name.

20. His form cannot be glimpsed,
None may see Him with the eye:
Whoso should know Him with heart and mind
As dwelling in the heart, becomes immortal!

35 See pp. 15, 28.
36 Or, 'fashioned'.

21. 'Unborn is He', so saying,
Let a man in fear approach Him:
O Rudra [show] thy right [auspicious] cheek,
Protect me with it ever!

22. Do us no hurt in child or offspring,
In life or kine or horses;
Slay not our men in anger, Rudra!
Bearing oblations we invoke Thee ever.

V

1. In the imperishable infinite city[37] of Brahman
Two things there are –
Wisdom (*vidyā*) and unwisdom, hidden, established there:
Perishable is unwisdom, but wisdom is immortal:
Who over wisdom and unwisdom rules, He is Another.

2. It is He alone who approaches every womb,[38]
[Who rules] all forms and every cause,
Who bears in his thoughts the tawny seer[39]
As in the beginning he was engendered,
And gazes on him as he is born.

3. One after another this God spreads wide his many nets
In this [earthly] field only to draw them in [again]:
So too the Lord of Self so great (*mahātman*) sends out
Rulers, though He [alone] wields the all-sovereign power.

4. As the sun shines forth, illumining
All regions, above, below, athwart,
So does this One God, the Blessed Lord (*bhagavat*), adorable,
Hold sway over whatever creature (*svabhāva*) issues from the womb.

5. Source of all things, He ripens every creature (*svabhāva*),
When ripe transmutes them all:
Over this whole universe He alone holds sway,
Assigning their proper attributes to all.

37 Reading *pure* for *pare*.
38 Or, 'rules over every source'.
39 Sc. the 'Golden Embryo' mentioned above.

6. That which is hidden in the secret Upanishads of the Veda
Brahmā knows to be the source of Brahman:[40]
The ancient gods and seers who knew It
Shared in its nature and became immortal.

7. Ruler of the vital breaths,[41] [the individual self]
Has attributes, does works and reaps their fruits,
Enjoys what he has done, assuming all manner of forms:
He's made of Nature's three constituents,[42]
Three paths are open to him:[43]
So does he roam [the world, conditioned] by his works.

8. Of the measure of a thumb, the sun's equal in appearance –
When conjoined with will (*saṅkalpa*) and ego, such is he;
But with soul (*buddhi*) and self as his [only] attributes (*guṇa*)
He seems another – no larger than the fine point of an awl.

9. Think of this living (*jīva*) self as but a part
Of a hundredth part of the tip of a hair
Divided a hundred times!
And [yet] to infinity is it conformed.

10. It is not male, not female,
Nor yet hermaphrodite;
Whatever body it receives,
By that is it protected.

11. By delusions bred by touch, sight and imagination
(*saṅkalpana*),[44]
By watering it with food and drink,
The self is made to grow, is born:
The embodied [self] in [different] states takes on
Forms in accordance with its [former] works,
Each in its order due.

12. Many the forms both gross and subtile
That the embodied [self] clothes with[45] its own attributes –
With attributes [derived] from works

40 Or, 'to have Brahman as its source'.
41 Or 'lord of life'.
42 See pp. 279 ff.
43 i.e. righteousness, unrighteousness and wisdom.
44 Or, 'touch, sight, imagination and delusion'.
45 Or, 'chooses as'.

And attributes [derived] from self:
But He is seen to be another – the cause of this conjunction.

13. Endless and beginningless is God:
In the midst of chaos He
All things doth emanate – how manifold his forms! –
The One Encompasser of all:
By knowing Him a man is from every fetter freed.

14. *Śiva*, the Benign, is God:
Maker of what becomes (*bhāva*) and what does not become:
Affection (*bhāva*) can lay hold of Him,[46] 'Homeless'[47] is his name:
Maker of [all] creation (*sarga*), [maker of its] parts:
Whoso should know Him, the body casts aside!

VI

1. 'Inherent Nature', some sages say,
'Time', others – both deluded!
No, it is the majesty of God in the world [made manifest]
That turns and sets in motion Brahman's [awful] wheel!

2. For from all eternity this whole universe
Doth He encompass:
He knows, He the architect of time,
Possessed of attributes, omniscient:

By Him are works (*karma*) commanded,
[By Him do works] evolve –
[Works] we think of [as diffused among the elements,]
Among earth and water, fire, wind and space.

3. His work accomplished He takes his rest,
Then once again conjoins (*yoga*) Himself
With principle after principle (*tattva*)[48] –
With one, with two, with three, or eight,[49]
With time, and the subtile attributes (*guṇa*) of self.

46 Or, 'He can be grasped in [the process of] becoming': or, 'He can be grasped by the mind.'

47 Lit. 'without nest'.

48 Or, 'with the essence of essence'.

49 The figures refer to the categories of the Sāṁkhya system.

4. [All] works does He initiate,
[And works] are never free from quality (*guṇa*):
All modes of being (*bhāva*) He directs.
When once these cease to be, the work once done must perish.
When works have perished, He goes on:
Other than essence is He,
[Other than any 'thing' even as it really is.]

5. He is the Beginning, the efficient cause of the conjoining,[50]
Seen as beyond the three times – partless too:
Of old did we worship Him, this God adorable,
Become becoming, in his thought subsisting, omniform!

6. Higher and other is He than [world-]tree, time and forms:
From Him the world evolves, fully diversified:
Righteousness He brings, evil repels, Master of good fortune,
Immortal, self-subsistent,[51] of all the home and ground (*dhāma*);
So must He be known.

7. Of lords supreme Great Lord,
Of gods the highest God,
Of kings the highest King – utterly beyond!
So should we know Him – God,
Lord of the worlds, adorable!

8. There is naught He needs to do, he works not with any tool:
Like unto Him is none, none greater [than He] is known:
Manifold is his exalted power, [as manifold] revealed:
His works of power and wisdom inhere in his very nature (*svābhāvika*).

9. No one in the [whole] world is his master,
No one his ruler; no outward sign (*liṅga*) has He:
He is the Cause, Lord of the senses' lord.[52]
No one begat Him, no one is his lord.

10. Like a spider the One God
Involves Himself in threads
Of primal Nature (*pradhāna*) born

50 i.e. of *puruṣa* ('person', spirit) and *prakṛti* (Nature).
51 Or, 'subsisting in selves'.
52 i.e. the individual self: or, 'of the masters of tools (*karaṇa*)'.

From out his very essence (*svabhāva*):
May He grant us entry into Brahman!

11. The One God, in all contingent beings hidden,
Pervading all, of all beings the Inmost Self,
Of [all] works (*karma*) the overseer, in Him all beings dwell,
Witness, observer, absolute, alone (*kevala*),
Devoid of attributes!

12. This One holds sway among the inactive many,
Makes the one seed manifold;
Wise men who see Him in their selves subsistent,[53]
Taste everlasting joy (*sukha*) – no others.

13. Eternal among eternals, conscious (*cetana*) among the conscious,
The One among the many, he disposes over desires:
He is the Cause, He can be comprehended
In theory (*sāṁkhya*) as in spiritual exercise (*yoga*);
Knowing this God a man is from every fetter freed.

14. There the sun shines not, nor moon, nor stars;
These lightnings shine not there, let alone this fire:
All things shine with the shining of this light,
This whole universe reflects his radiance![54]

15. The One [great] swan in the middle of this world
Is the same as the fire in ocean['s depths] deep hidden:
By knowing Him indeed a man surpasses death;
No other path is there on which to go.

16. Maker of all is He, all-knowing, source of selves,[55]
He knows, He the architect of time,
Possessed of [all] attributes, omniscient:
Lord of primeval Nature, [Lord of all] knowers of the field,[56]
Lord of the constituents of Nature (*guṇa*),
Cause of the round of birth and death (*sàmsāra*),
[Cause of] deliverance,
[Cause of our] sojourn here and of [our] imprisonment.

53 Or, 'as self-subsistent'.
54 Cf. p. 180.
55 Or, 'of Himself': or, 'having Self as source'.
56 See pp. 266–70.

17. Being all this,[57] He is immortal, subsistent as the Lord,
Wise, present everywhere, protector of this world:
For all eternity He rules this moving world,
There is no other cause [like Him] in sovereignty!

18. Of old did he raise up (*vidhā-*) Brahmā,
[Of old] entrust him with the Vedas:
On liberation bent I fly to his sheltering care –
[The care] of the God who illumines self and soul (*ātmabuddhi*).[58]

19. No parts has He, no part in action,
Tranquil, unblemished and unflecked,
The highest bridge to immortality,
Like a fire whose fuel is spent.

20. When men shall roll up space
As though it were a piece of leather,
Then will there be an end of suffering
For him who knew not God![59]

21. By much austerity and by the grace of God
Did the wise Śvetāśvatara make Brahman rightly known
To those who had gone furthest on the ascetic path –
Vessel of purity supreme, to the company of seers well pleasing.

22. This highest mystery of the Veda's end
Was propounded in an earlier age;
Let it not be told to an unquiet man,
Or to one who is neither son nor pupil.

23. To the great-souled man who loyally
And greatly loves (*bhakti*) [his] God,
Who loves his spiritual master even as his God,
The matter of this discourse will shine with clearest light –
With clearest light will shine.

57 Or, 'consisting of That (i.e. Brahman)'.

58 Or, 'who illumines his own intellect'. Var. 'who has the grace of making himself known'. Many other translations are possible.

59 Or, 'apart from knowing God'.

THE BHAGAVAD-GĪTĀ

THE BHAGAVAD-GĪTĀ

I

Dhṛtarāṣṭra said:
1. On the field of justice, the Kuru-field,
My men and the sons of Pāṇḍu too
Stand massed together, intent on war.
What, Sañjaya, did they do?

Sañjaya said:
2. Then did Duryodhana, the king,
Surveying the host of Pāṇḍu's sons
Drawn up in ranks, approach
His teacher (Droṇa) saying:

3. 'Teacher, behold this mighty host
Of Pāṇḍu's sons
Drawn up by the son of Drupada,
Thine own disciple, wise and skilled.

4. Here are men, brave and mighty archers,
Equals of Bhīma and Arjuna in [the art of] war –
Yuyudhāna, Virāṭa,
And Drupada, the mighty charioteer,

5. Dhṛṣṭaketu, Cekitāna,
And Kāśī's valiant king,
Purujit, Kuntibhoja,
And the Śibi's king, foremost of fighting men,

6. High-mettled Yudhāmanyu
And valiant Uttamaujas,
Subhadrā's son and the sons of Draupadī –
All of them mighty charioteers.

7. Listen too, thou best of Brāhmans,
To [the list of] those outstanding on our side,

Leaders of my army.
Of these I speak to thee that thou mayst know.

8. Thyself Bhīṣma, and Karṇa too,
And Kṛpa, victor in the fight,
Ashvatthāman and Vikarṇa,
And Somadatta's son as well.

9. Many another hero too
Will risk his life for me.
Various are their arms and weapons,
And all of them are skilled at war.

10. Imperfect are those our forces
Which Bhīṣma guards,
But perfect these their forces
Under [great] Bhīma's care.

11. So stand firm in all your ranks
Each in his appointed place;
Guard Bhīṣma above all others,
Every one of you!'

12. [And] (Bhīṣma,) the aged grandsire of the Kuru clan,
To give him cheer,
Cried out with a loud cry like lion's roar
And undaunted blew his conch.

13. Then conches, cymbals, drums,
Tabors and kettledrums,
Burst into sudden sound;
Tumultuous was the din.

14. Then too did (Kṛṣṇa), Madhu's son and Pāṇḍu's [third-] born (Arjuna,)
Standing erect on their great chariot
Yoked to [snow-]white steeds,
Their godly conches loudly blow.

15. [The conch called] Pañcajanya did Kṛṣṇa blow,
[The conch called] Devadatta Arjuna;
The mighty conch [called] Pauṇḍra
Blew Bhīma of dreadful deeds.

16. [The conch called] Anantavijaya
Blew Kuntī's son, Yudhiṣṭhira, the king:
Sughosha and Manipuṣpaka
[Blew] Nakula and Sahadeva.

17. And Kāśī's king, archer supreme,
And Śikhaṇḍin, the great charioteer,
Dhṛṣṭadyumna, Virāta too,
And unconquered Sātyaki,

18. Drupada and the sons of Draupadī,
And Subhadrā's strong-armed son,
Blew each his conch
[Resounding] from every side.

19. At the din [they made] the hearts
Of Dhṛtarāṣṭra's sons were rent:
And heaven and earth it made
Tumultuously resound.

20. Then (Arjuna,) whose banner is an ape,
Gazed upon the serried ranks
Of Dhṛtarāṣṭra's sons. The clash of arms
Began. He lifted up his bow.

21. To Kṛṣṇa then
These words he spake:
'Halt thou my chariot [here]
Between the armies twain,

22. That I may see these men drawn up,
Spoiling for the fight,
[That I may see] with whom I must do battle
In this enterprise of war.

23. I see them [now], intent on strife,
Assembled here;
All eager they to please by waging war
[Old] Dhṛtarāṣṭra's baleful son.'

24. Thus Arjuna: and Kṛṣṇa,
Hearkening to his words,
Brought that splendid chariot to a halt
Between the armies twain.

25. And there in front of them Bhīṣma and Droṇa stood
And all the [assembled] kings;
And Kṛṣṇa said: 'Arjuna, behold
These Kurus gathered [here].'

26. And Arjuna beheld
Fathers, grandsires,
Venerable teachers, uncles, brothers, sons,
Grandsons and comrades,

27. Fathers-in-law and friends
Standing there in either host.
And the son of Kuntī, seeing them,
All his kinsmen thus arrayed,

28. Was filled with deep compassion
And, desponding, spake these words:
'Kṛṣṇa, when these mine own folk I see
Standing [before me], spoiling for the fight,

29. My limbs give way [beneath me],
My mouth dries up, and trembling
Takes hold upon my frame:
My body's hairs stand up [in dread].

30. [My bow,] Gāṇḍīva, slips from my hand,
My very skin is all ablaze;
I cannot stand, my mind
Seems to wander [all distraught].

31. And portents too I see
Boding naught but ill.
Should I strike down in battle mine own folk,
No good therein see I.

32. Kṛṣṇa, I hanker not for victory,
Nor for the kingdom, nor yet for things of pleasure.
What use to us a kingdom, friend,
What use enjoyment or life [itself] ?

33. Those for whose sake we covet
Kingdom, delights and things of pleasure,
Here stand they, arrayed for battle,
Surrendering both wealth and life.

34. They are our venerable teachers, fathers, sons,
They too our grandsires, uncles,
Fathers-in-law, grandsons,
Brothers-in-law, kinsmen all;

35. These would I nowise slay
Though they slay [me], my friend,
Not for dominion over the three [wide] worlds,
How much less for [this paltry] earth.

36. And should we slaughter Dhṛtarāṣṭra's sons,
Kṛṣṇa, what sweetness then is ours?
Evil, and only evil, would come to dwell with us,
Should we slay them, hate us as they may.

37. Therefore have we no right to kill
The sons of Dhṛtarāṣṭra, our own kinsmen [as they are].
Should we lay low our own folk, Kṛṣṇa,
How could we find any joy?

38. And even if, bereft of sense by greed,
They cannot see
That to ruin a family is wickedness (*doṣa*)
And to break one's word[1] a crime,

39. How should we not be wise enough
To turn aside from this evil thing?
For the annihilation of a family
We know full well is wickedness.

40. Annihilate a family, and with it
Collapse the eternal laws that rule the family.
Once law's destroyed, then lawlessness
Overwhelms all [we know as] family.

41. With lawlessness triumphant, Kṛṣṇa,
The family's [chaste] women are debauched;
From debauchery of the women [too]
Confusion of caste is born.

42. Yes, [caste-]confusion leads to hell –
[The hell prepared] for those who wreck
The family and for the family [so wrecked].

1 Or, 'injury to a friend'.

So too their ancestors fall down [to hell],
Cheated of their offerings of food and drink.

43. These evil ways of men who wreck the family,
[These evil ways] that bring on caste-confusion,
[These are the ways] that bring caste-law to naught
And the eternal family laws.

44. A sure abode in hell there is
For men who bring to naught
The laws that rule the family:
So, Kṛṣṇa, have we heard.

45. Ah, ah: so are we [really] bent
On committing a monstrous evil deed?
Coveting the sweet joys of sovereignty,
[Look at us,] all poised to slaughter our own folk!

46. O let the sons of Dhṛtarāṣṭra, arms in hand,
Slay me in battle, though I,
Unarmed myself, will offer no defence;
Therein were greater happiness for me!'

47. So saying Arjuna sat down
Upon the chariot-seat [though] battle [had begun],
Let slip his bow and arrows,
His mind distraught with grief.

II

Sañjaya said:
1. To him thus in compassion plunged,
His eyes distraught and filled with tears,
[To him] desponding Kṛṣṇa spake
These words.

The Blessed Lord said:
2. Whence comes this faintness on thee?
[Now] at this crisis-hour?
This ill beseems a noble, wins none a heavenly state,
But brings dishonour, Arjuna.

3. Play not the eunuch, son of Pṛthā
For this ill beseems thee:

Give up this vile faintheartedness,
Arise, O scorcher of the foe.

Arjuna said:
4. Kṛṣṇa, how can I in battle
With Bhīṣma and Droṇa fight,
Raining on them my arrows?
For they are worthy of respect.

5. For better were it here on earth to eat a beggar's food
Than to slay preceptors of great dignity.
Were I to slay here my preceptors, ambitious though they may be,
Then should I be partaking of blood-sullied food.

6. Besides we do not know which is the better part,
Whether that we should win the victory or that they should conquer us.
There facing us stand Dhṛtarāṣṭra's sons:
Should we kill them, ourselves would scarce desire to live.

7. My very being (*svabhāva*) is assailed by compassion's harmful taint.
With mind perplexed concerning right and wrong (*dharma*) [I turn] to thee and ask:
Which is the better course? Tell me, and [let thy words be] definite and clear;
For I am thy disciple: teach me, for all my trust's in thee.

8. I cannot see what could dispel
My grief, [this] parching of the senses –
Not though on earth I were to win an empire –
Unrivalled, prosperous, – or lordship over the gods themselves.

Sañjaya said:
9. So speaking Arjuna, scorcher of the foe,
To Kṛṣṇa said:
'I will not fight':
And having spoken held his peace.

10. And Kṛṣṇa faintly smiled
Between the armies twain,
And spake these words to Arjuna
In his [deep] despondency.

The Blessed Lord said:
11. Thou sorrowest for men who do not need thy sorrow,
And speakest words that [in part] are wise.[2]
Wise men know no sorrow
For the living or the dead.

12. Never was there a time when I was not,
Nor thou, nor yet these lords of men;
Nor will there be a time when we shall cease to be –
All of us hereafter.

13. Just as in this body the embodied soul
Must pass through childhood, youth and age,
So too [at death] will he take another body up:
In this a thoughtful man is not perplexed.

14. But contacts with the world outside
Give rise to heat and cold, pleasure and pain:
They come and go, impermanent;
Arjuna, put up with them!

15. For wise men there are,
The same in pleasure as in pain
Whom these [contacts] leave undaunted:
Such are conformed to immortality.

16. Of what is not there is no becoming;
Of what *is* there is no ceasing to be:
For the boundary-line between the two
Is seen by men who see things as they really are.

17. Indestructible [alone] is That – know this –
By Which this whole [universe] was spun.[3]
No one at all can bring destruction
On This which passes not away.

18. Finite, they say, are these [our] bodies
[Indwelt] by an[4] eternal embodied soul –
[A soul] indestructible, incommensurable.[5]
Fight then, O scion of Bharata!

2 Var. 'Thou dost not speak as a wise man would'.
3 Or, 'pervaded'.
4 Or, 'the'.
5 Or, 'unfathomable'.

19. Who thinks that he[6] can be a slayer,
Who thinks that he is slain,
Both these have no [right] knowledge:
He slays not, is not slain.

20. Never is he born nor dies;
Never did he come to be, nor will he ever come to be again:
Unborn, eternal, everlasting he – primeval:
He is not slain when the body is slain.[7]

21. If a man knows him as indestructible,
Eternal, unborn, never to pass away,
How and whom can he cause to be slain
Or slay?

22. As a man casts off his worn-out clothes
And takes on other new ones [in their place],
So does the embodied soul cast off his worn-out bodies
And enters others new.

23. He cannot be cut by sword,
Nor burnt by fire;
The waters cannot wet him,
Nor the wind dry him up.

24. Uncuttable, unburnable,
Unwettable, undryable
Is he – eternal, roving everywhere,
Firm-set, unmoving, everlasting.

25. Unmanifest, unthinkable,
Unchanging is he called:
So realize that he is thus
And put away thy useless grief.

26. And even if thou thinkst that he
Is constantly [re-]born and constantly [re-]dies,
Even so, [my] strong-armed [friend],
Thou lamentest him in vain.

27. For sure is the death of all that comes to birth,
Sure the birth of all that dies.

6 i.e. the embodied soul.
7 Cf. p. 173.

So in a matter that no one can prevent
Thou hast no cause to grieve.

28. Unmanifest are the beginnings of contingent beings,
Manifest their middle course,
Unmanifest again their ends:
What cause for mourning here?

29. By a rare privilege[8] may someone behold him,
And by a rare privilege indeed may another tell of him,
And by a rare privilege may such another hear[9] him,
Yet even having heard there's none that knows him.

30. Never can this embodied soul be slain
In the body of anyone [at all].
And so for no contingent being
Hast thou any cause for sorrow.

31. Likewise consider thine own (caste-)duty (*dharma*),
Then too hast thou no cause to quail;
For better than a fight prescribed by duty
Is nothing for a man of the princely class.

32. Happy the warriors indeed
Who become involved in war –
[A war] like this presented by pure chance
And opening the gates of paradise!

33. But if thou wilt not wage this war –
Prescribed by thy (caste-)duty,
Then, by casting off both honour and (caste-)duty,
Thou wilt bring evil[10] on thyself.

34. Yes, this thy dishonour will become a byword
In the mouths of men in ages yet to come;
And dishonour in a man well-trained to honour
[Is an ill] surpassing death.

35. 'From fear he fled the battlefield' –
So will they think, the mighty charioteers.

8 Or, 'As a marvel'.
9 Or, 'hear of'.
10 Or, 'incur guilt'.

Greatly esteemed by them before,
Thou wilt bring upon thyself contempt.

36. Many a word that is better left unsaid
Will such men say as wish thee ill,
Disputing thy competence.
What could cause thee greater pain than this?

37. If thou art slain, thou winnest paradise;
And if thou gain the victory, thine the earth to enjoy.
Arise, then, son of Kuntī,
Resolved to fight the fight.

38. [First learn to] treat pleasure and pain as things equivalent,
Then profit and loss, victory and defeat;
Then gird thyself for battle.
Thus wilt thou bring no evil on thyself.[11]

39. This wisdom (*buddhi*) has been revealed to thee in theory (*sāṁkhya*);
Listen now to how it should be practised (*yoga*):
If by this wisdom thou art exercised (*yukta*),
Thou wilt put off the bondage inherent in [all] works (*karma*).

40. Herein no effort goes to seed,
Nor is there any slipping back:
Even a little of this discipline (*dharma*)
Saves from the monstrous terror [of rebirth].

41. The essence of the soul (*buddhi*) is will (*vyavasāya*),
If it is single here [on earth]:
But many-branched and infinite
Are the souls of men devoid of will.

42–4. The essence of the soul is will –
[The soul] of men who cling to pleasure and to power,
Their minds seduced by [flowery words],
Are not equipped for enstasy (*samādhi*).

Such men give vent to flowery words,
The fools,
Delighting in the Veda's lore,
Saying there is naught else.

11 Or, 'incur [no] guilt'.

Desire their essence, paradise their goal –
[Their words] tell of [re-]birth as fruit of works,
Expatiate about the niceties of ritual
By which pleasure and power can be achieved.

45. [All nature is made up of] three 'constituents' (*guṇa*):
These are the Veda's goal. Have done with them:
Have done with [all] dualities (*dvandva*), stand ever firm on
Goodness;[12]
Think not of gain or keeping the thing gained, but be thyself.

46. As much use as there is in a water-tank
Flooded with water on every side,
So much is there in all the Vedas
For the Brāhman who discerns.

47. Work alone is thy proper business,
Never the fruits [it may produce];
Let not your motive be the fruit of work,
Nor your attachment to [mere] worklessness (*akarma*).

48. Stand fast in Yoga, surrendering attachment;
In success and failure be the same,
And then get busy with thy works.
Yoga means 'sameness' and 'indifference' (*samatva*).

49. For lower far is the [path of] active work [for its own sake]
Than the Yoga of the soul (*buddhi*).
Seek refuge in the soul!
[How] pitiful are they whose motive is the fruit [of works]!

50. Whoso is integrated by [the Yoga of] the soul
Discards both good and evil works;
Brace thyself (*yuj-*) then for [this] Yoga!
Yoga is skill in [performing] works.

51. For those wise men who are integrated by [the Yoga of]
the soul,
Who have renounced the fruit that's born of works,
These will be freed from the bondage of [re-]birth
And fare on to that region that knows no ill.

12 Or, 'courage' or, 'truth'.

52. When thy soul shall pass beyond
Delusion's turbid quicksands,
Then wilt thou learn disgust
For what has been heard [ere now][13]
And for what may yet be heard.

53. When once thy soul, by Scripture (*śruti*) once bewildered,
Stands motionless and still,
Immovable in enstasy,
Then shalt thou win [the prize which is] Yoga, [integration].

Arjuna said:
54. [Tell me,] Kṛṣṇa, what is the mark of the man of steady (*sthita*) wisdom,
The man immersed in enstasy?
How does he speak – this man of steadied thought?
How sit? How walk?

The Blessed Lord said:
55. When a man puts from him all desires
That prey upon the mind,
Himself (*ātmanā*) contented in the self alone,
Then is he called a man of steady wisdom.

56. Whose mind is undismayed [though beset] by [many a] sorrow,
Who for pleasure has no further longing,
From whom [all] passion (*rāga*), fear, and wrath have fled,
Such a man is called a sage of steadied thought.

57. Who has no love (*abhisneha*) for any thing,
Who rejoices not at whatever good befalls him,
Nor hates the bad that comes his way,
Firm-stablished is the wisdom of such a man.

58. And when he draws in on every side
His senses from their proper objects,
As a tortoise might its limbs,
Firm-stablished is the wisdom of such a man.

59. For the embodied soul who eats no more
Objects of sense must disappear –

13 Meaning the Veda.

Save only the [recollected] flavour – and that too
Must vanish at the vision of the Highest.

60. And yet however much
A wise man strive,
The senses' tearing violence
May seduce his mind by force.

61. [Then] let him sit, curbing them all –
Integrated (*yukta*) – intent on Me:
For firm-stablished is that man's wisdom
Whose senses are subdued.

62. Let a man [but] think of the things of sense –
Attachment to them is born:
From attachment springs desire,
From desire is anger born.

63. From anger comes bewilderment
From the wandering of the mind (*smṛti*),
From this the destruction of the soul:[14]
With soul destroyed the man is lost.

64. But he who roves among the things of sense,
His senses subdued to self, from hate and passion free,
And is self-possessed [himself],
Is not far off from calm serenity (*prasāda*).

65. And from him thus becalmed
All sorrows flee away:
For once his thoughts are calmed, then soon
Will his soul (*buddhi*) stand firmly [in its ground].

66. No soul (*buddhi*) has he who knows not integration (*ayukta*);
In him there's no development (*bhāvanā*):
For the undeveloped there is no peace.
Whence should there be joy (*sukha*) to a peaceless man?

67. Hither and thither the senses rove,
And when the mind is attuned to them,
It sweeps away [whatever of] wisdom a man may possess,
As the wind a ship at sea.

14 *Buddhi*: or 'intellect'.

68. And so, whose senses are withheld
From the objects proper to them,
Wherever they may be,
Firm-stablished is the wisdom of such a man.

69. In what for all [other] folk is night,
Therein the man of self-restraint is [wide-]awake.
What time all [other] folk are awake,
That time is night for the sage who sees.

70. As the waters flow in to the sea,
Full filled, unmoving in its depths,
So too do all desires flow into the [heart of] man:
And such a man wins peace – not the desirer of desires.

71. The man who puts off all desires
And roams around from longing freed,
Who does not even think, 'This I am', or 'This is mine',
Draws near to peace.

72. This is the fixed, still state (*sthiti*) of Brahman;
He who wins through to this is nevermore perplexed.
Standing therein at the time of death
To the Nirvāṇa that is Brahman too[15] he goes!

III

Arjuna said:
1. If, Kṛṣṇa, thou think'st that wisdom (*buddhi*)
Is a loftier [course] than [the mere doing of] deeds,
Then why dost thou command me
To do a hideous deed?

2. Thou dost confuse my intellect, or so it seems,
With strangely muddled words:
So tell me with authority the one [simple way]
Whereby I may attain the better part.

The Blessed Lord said:
3. Of old did I proclaim the twofold law (*niṣṭhā*)
[That] in this world [holds sway] –

15 Or, 'the Nirvāṇa of Brahman'.

For the men of theory (*sāṃkhya*) wisdom's Yoga,
For men of action (*yogin*) the Yoga of works (*karma*).

4. Not by leaving works undone
Does a man win freedom from the [bond of] work,
Nor by renunciation alone
Can he win perfection['s prize].

5. Not for a moment can a man
Stand still and do no work;
For every man is powerless and forced to work
By the 'constituents' born of Nature.

6. Whoso controls his limbs through which he acts
But sits remembering in his mind
Sense-objects, deludes himself:
He's called a hypocrite.

7. How much more excellent he all unattached,
Who with his mind controls [those] limbs,
And through those limbs [themselves] by which he acts
Embarks on the Yogic exercise (*yoga*) of works!

8. Do thou the work that is prescribed for thee,
For to work is better than to do no work at all;
For he who does not work will not succeed
Even in keeping his body in good repair.

9. This world is bound by bonds of work
Save where that work is done for sacrifice.
Work to this end, then, Arjuna,
From [all] attachment freed.

10. Of old the Lord of Creatures (Prajāpati) said,
Emitting creation (*prajā*) and with it sacrifice:
'By this shall ye prolong your lineage,
Let this be to you the cow that yields
The milk of all that ye desire.

11. With this shall ye sustain the gods,
So that the gods may sustain you [in return]:
Sustaining one another [thus]
Ye shall achieve the highest good.

12. For, so sustained by sacrifice, the gods
Will give you the food of your desire.
Whoso enjoys their gift, yet gives nothing [in return],
Is a thief, no more nor less.'

13. Good men who eat of the leavings of the sacrifice
Are freed from every taint;
But evil are they, and evil do they eat
Who cook [their food] for their own [selfish] sakes.

14. From food [all] contingent beings are born,
And food from rain;
And rain derives from sacrifice,
And sacrifice from works (*karma*).

15. From Brahman[16] work arises, know you this,
And Brahman from the Imperishable[17] is born;
Therefore is Brahman, penetrating everywhere,
Forever based on the sacrifice.

16. So was the wheel in motion set;
And whoso fails to match his turning [with the turning of the wheel],
Living an evil life, the senses his pleasure-ground,
Lives out his life in vain.

17. Nay, let a man take pleasure in self alone,
In self his satisfaction find,
In self alone content:
[Let him do this, for then]
There is naught he needs to do.

18. In works done and works undone
On earth what interest has he?
What interest in all contingent beings?
On none of them does he depend.

19. And so, detached, perform unceasingly
The works that must be done
For the man detached who labours on (*karma*),
To the Highest must win through.

16 Meaning 'manifest Nature'.
17 Or, 'the syllable Oṁ'.

20. For only by working on (*karma*) did Janaka
And his like attain perfection.
Or if again for the welfare[18] of the world thou carest,
Then shouldst thou work [and act].

21. [For] whatever the noblest does,
That too will others do:
The standard that he sets
All the world will follow.

22. In the three worlds there's nothing
That I must do at all,
Nor anything unattained which I have not attained;
Yet work [is the element] in which I move.

23. For were I not tirelessly
To busy myself with works,
Then would men everywhere
Follow in my footsteps.

24. If I were not to do my work,
These worlds would fall to ruin,
And I should be a worker of confusion,
Destroying these [my] creatures.

25. As witless [fools] perform their works
Attached to the work [they do],
So, unattached, should the wise man do,
Longing to bring about the welfare of the world.

26. Let not the wise man split the mind (*buddhi*)
Of witless men attached to work:
Let him encourage[19] all [manner of] works,
[Himself,] though busy, controlled and integrated (*yukta*).

27. It is Nature's [three] 'constituents'
That do all works wherever [works are done];
[But] he whose self is by the ego fooled,
Thinks, 'It is I who do.'

28. But he who knows how 'constituents' and works
Are parcelled into categories, seeing things as they are,

18 Or, 'control'.
19 Or, 'cause them to enjoy'.

Thinks thus: 'Constituents on constituents act',
[And so thinking] remains detached.

29. By the constituents of Nature fooled
Are men attached to the constituents' works:
Such men, dull-witted, only know in part.
Let not the knower of the whole
Upset [the knower of the part].

30. Cast all thy works on Me,
Thy mind in self withdrawn (*adhyātmacetas*);
Have neither hope, nor thought that 'This is mine':
Cast off this fever! Fight!

31. Whoso shall practise constantly
This my doctrine, firm in faith,
Not envying, [not cavilling,]
He too shall find release from [the bondage that is] work.

32. But whoso refuses to perform my doctrine,
Envious [yet, and cavilling],
Of every [form of] wisdom fooled,
Is lost, the witless [dunce]! Be sure of that.

33. As is a man's own nature,
So must he act, however wise he be.
All beings follow Nature:
What can repression do?

34. In all the senses passion and hate
Are seated, [turned] to their proper objects:
Let none fall victim to their power,
For these are brigands on his road.

35. Better one's own duty (*dharma*) [to perform], though void of merit,
Than to do another's well:
Better to die within [the sphere of] one's own duty:
Perilous is the duty of other men.

Arjuna said:
36. By what impelled does [mortal] man
Do evil,
Unwilling though he be?
He's driven to it by force, or so it seems to me.

The Blessed Lord said:
37. Desire it is: Anger it is:
Arising from the 'constituent' of Passion –
All-devouring, fount of wickedness:
Know this to be thine enemy on earth.

38. As fire is swathed in smoke,
As mirror [fouled] by dust,
As embryo all covered up by the membrane-envelope,
So is this [world] obscured by this.

39. This the wise man's eternal foe;
By this is wisdom overcast:
Whatever form it will it takes[20]
A fire insatiate!

40. Senses, mind and soul (*buddhi*), they say,
Are the places where it lurks;
Through these it fences wisdom in,
Leading astray the embodied soul.

41. Therefore restrain
The senses first:
Strike down this evil thing! –
Destroyer [alike] of what we learn from holy books
And what we learn from life.

42. Exalted are the senses, or so they say;
Higher than they the mind;
Yet higher than the mind is soul (*buddhi*):
What is beyond the soul is he.[21]

43. Know him who is yet higher than the soul;
And of thyself (*ātmanā*)[22] make firm [this] self.
Vanquish the enemy, Arjuna!
[Swift is he] to change his form,[23]
And hard is he to conquer!

20 Or, 'in the form of desire'.
21 i.e. the 'self'. Some have referred it to desire.
22 Or, 'by means of the self'.
23 Or, 'in the form of desire'.

IV

The Blessed Lord said:
1. This changeless way of life (*yoga*) did I
To Vivasvat [once] proclaim;
To Manu Vivasvat told it,
And Manu to Ikṣvāku passed it on.

2. Thus was the tradition from one to another handed on,
The Royal Seers came to know it;
[But] in the long course of time
The way of life (*yoga*) on earth was lost.

3. This is the same primeval way of life (*yoga*)
That I preach to thee today;
For thou art loyal, devoted (*bhakta*), and my comrade,
And this is the highest mystery.

Arjuna said:
4. Later thy birth,
Earlier Vivasvat's:
How should I understand thy words,
That in the beginning thou didst proclaim it?

The Blessed Lord said:
5. Many a birth have I passed through,
And [many a birth] hast thou:
I know them all,
Thou knowest not.

6. Unborn am I, changeless is my Self;
Of [all] contingent beings I am the Lord!
Yet by my creative energy (*māyā*) I consort
With Nature – which is mine – and come to be [in time].

7. For whenever the law of righteousness (*dharma*)
Withers away, and lawlessness (*adharma*)
Raises its head
Then do I generate Myself [on earth].

8. For the protection of the good,
For the destruction of evildoers,
For the setting up of righteousness,
I come into being, age after age.

9. Who knows my godly birth and mode of operation (*karma*)
Thus as they really are,
He, his body left behind, is never born again:
He comes to Me.

10. Many are they who, passion, fear and anger spent,
Inhere in Me, making Me their sanctuary:
Made pure by wisdom and hard penances,[24]
They come [to share in] the manner of my being.

11. In whatsoever way [devoted] men approach Me,
In that same way do I return their love (*bhaj-*).
Whatever their occupation and wherever they may be,
Men follow the path I trace.

12. Desiring success in their (ritual) acts (*karma*),
Men worship here the gods;
For swiftly in the world of men
Comes success, engendered by the act [itself].

13. The four-caste system did I generate
With categories of 'constituents' and works;
Of this I am the doer, know thou this –
And yet I am the Changeless One
Who does not do [or act].

14. Works can never affect Me.
I have no yearning for their fruits.
Whoso should know that this is how I am
Escapes the bondage [forged] by works.

15. This knowing, the ancients too did work,
Though seeking [all the while] release [from temporal life]:
So do thou work [and act]
As the ancients did in the days of old.

16. What is work? What worklessness?
Herein even sages are perplexed.
So shall I preach to thee concerning work;
And once thou hast understood my words,
From ill thou'lt win release.

24 Or, 'by the hard penances of wisdom'.

17. For a man must understand
[The nature] of work, of work ill-done,
And worklessness, [all three]:
Profound, [hard to unravel,] are the ways of work!

18. The man who sees worklessness in work [itself],
And work in worklessness,
Is wise among his fellows,
Integrated (*yukta*), performing every work.

19. When all a man's emprises
Have neither motive nor desire [for fruit] –
His works burnt up in wisdom's fire –
Then wise men call him learned.

20. When he's cast off [all] attachment to the fruit of works,
Ever content, on none dependent,
Though he embark on work [himself],
In fact he does no work at all.

21. Nothing hoping, his thought and mind (*ātman*) restrained,
Giving up all possessions,
He only does such work
As is needed for the body's maintenance,
And so avoids defilement.

22. Content to take whatever chance may bring his way,
Surmounting all dualities (*dvandva*), knowing no envy,
The same in failure and success,
Though working [still], he is not bound.

23. Attachments gone, deliverance won,
His thoughts are fixed on wisdom:
He works for sacrifice [alone],
And all the work [he ever did]
Entirely melts away.

24. The offering is Brahman, Brahman the sacrificial ghee
Offered by Brahman in Brahman's fire:
Who fixes all his thought (*samādhi*) on this sacrificial rite (*karma*)
[Indwelt by] Brahman, to Brahman must he go.

25. Some Yogins offer sacrifice
To the gods as their sole object,
In the fire of Brahman others

Offer sacrifice as sacrifice
[Which has merit in itself].

26. Yet others offer the senses – hearing and the rest –
In the fires of self-restraint;
Others the senses' proper objects – sounds and the like –
In the fires of the senses.

27. And others offer up all works of sense,
All works of vital breath,
In the fire of the practice (*yoga*) of self-control
By wisdom kindled.

28. Some offer up their wealth, some their hard penances,
Some spiritual exercise (*yoga*), and some again
Make study and knowledge [of Scripture] their sacrifice –
Religious men whose vows are strict.

29. Some offer the inward breath in the outward,
Likewise the outward in the inward,
Checking the flow of both,
On breath control intent.

30. Others restrict their food
And offer up breaths in breaths.
All these know the [meaning of] sacrifice,
For by sacrifice all their defilements are made away.

31. Eating the leavings of the sacrifice,
The food of immortality,
They come to eternal Brahman.
This world is not for him who performs no sacrifice –
Much less another [world].

32. So, many and various are the sacrifices
Spread out athwart the mouth of Brahman.
They spring from work, all of them; be sure of this,
[For] once thou knowest this, thy deliverance is sure.

33. Better than the sacrifice of wealth
Is the sacrifice of wisdom.
All works without exception
In wisdom find their consummation.

34. Learn to know this by humble reverence [of the wise],
By questioning, by service,
[For] the wise who see things as they really are
Will teach thee wisdom.

35. Once thou hast known this, wilt thou never again
Be perplexed [as now thou art]:
By [knowing] this thou wilt behold [all] beings
In [thy]self – yes, everyone of them – and then in Me.

36. Nay, though thou wert the very worst
Among all evil-doers,
[Yet, once thou hast mounted] wisdom's bark,
Thou wilt surmount all this tortuous [stream of life].

37. As a kindled fire
Reduces its fuel to ashes,
So does the fire of wisdom
Reduce all works to ashes.

38. Nothing on earth resembles wisdom
In its power to cleanse [and purify];
And thus in time a man may find himself
Within [him]self – a man perfected in spiritual exercise (*yoga*).

39. A man of faith, intent on wisdom,
His senses [all] restrained, will wisdom win;
And, wisdom won, he'll come right soon
To perfect[25] peace.

40. The man, unwise, devoid of faith,
Doubting at heart (*ātman*), must perish:
No part in this world has the man of doubt,
Nor in the next, nor yet in happiness.

41. Let a man in spiritual exercise (*yoga*) all works renounce,
Let him by wisdom his doubts dispel,
Let him be himself (*ātmavat*) and then
[Whatever] his works [may be], they will never bind him [more].

42. And so, [take up] the sword of wisdom, cut
This doubt of thine, unwisdom's child,

25 Lit. 'highest'.

Still lurking in thy heart:
Prepare for action[26] [now], stand up!

V

Arjuna said:
1. 'Renounce [all] works': [such is the course] thou recommendest:
And then again [thou sayest]: 'Perform them (*yoga*).'
Which is the better of these two?
Tell me this in clear, decisive [words].

The Blessed Lord said:
2. Renouncing works – performing them (*yoga*) –
Both lead to the highest good;
But of the two to engage in (*yoga*) works
Is more excellent than to renounce them.

3. This is the mark of the man
Whose renunciation is abiding:
He hates not, nor desires,
For, surmounting all dualities (*nirdvandva*), how easily
He wins release from bondage!

4. 'There must be a difference between theory (*sāṁkhya*) and practice (*yoga*)',
So say the simple-minded, not the wise.
Apply thyself to only one, whole-heartedly,
And win the fruit of both.

5. [True,] the men of theory attain a [high] estate,
But that [same state] achieves the man of practice too;
For theory and practice are all one:
Who sees [that this is true], he sees [indeed].

6. Hard to attain is [true] renunciation
Without practising [some] Yogic exercise (*yoga*):
The sage well-versed in Yogic exercise and integrated (*yoga-yukta*)
Right soon to Brahman goes.

26 Or, 'resort to Yoga'.

7. Well-versed in Yogic exercise, his self made clean,
With mind (*ātman*) and sense subdued,
His self become the [very] self of every being,
Though working yet, he suffers no defilement.

8. 'Lo, nothing do I do':
So thinks the integrated (*yukta*) man
Who knows things as they really are –
Seeing the while and hearing, touching, smelling,
Eating, walking, sleeping, breathing,

9. Talking, emitting, grasping,
Opening and shutting the eyes:
'The senses are busied with their proper objects:
[What has that to do with me?'
This is the way] he thinks.

10. And on he works, though he's [long] renounced attachment,
Ascribing his works to Brahman;[27]
Yet evil cannot touch him,
As water [cannot touch] the petal of a lotus.

11. With body, mind and soul (*buddhi*), and senses too –
[With these] alone and isolated [from the self] –
Do Yogins practise work
Renouncing [all] attachment for the cleansing of the self.

12. The integrated man, renouncing the fruit of works,
Gains an abiding peace:
The man not integrated, whose works are prompted by desire,
Holds fast to fruits and thus remains enslaved.

13. [And so,] all works renouncing with his mind,
Quietly he sits in full control
Within [this] body,[28] city of nine gates:
He neither works nor makes another work.

14. Nor agency nor worldly works
Does [the body's] lord engender,[29]
Nor yet the bond that work to fruit conjoins;
It is Nature (*svabhāva*) that initiates the action.

27 Or, 'casting his works on God (*brahman*)'.
28 Reading *dehe*.
29 Or, 'The Lord of the world does not engender agency or work'.

15. The good and evil works of anyone at all
He takes not on – that all-pervading lord.[30]
By ignorance is wisdom overspread;
Thereby are creatures fooled.

16. But some there are whose ignorance of self
By wisdom is destroyed:
Their wisdom, like the sun,
Sheds [a ray of] light on That All-highest.

17. Souls (*buddhi*) bent on That, selves bent on That,
With That their aim and That their aspiration,
They stride [along the path] from which there's no return,
[All] taints by wisdom washed away.

18. [These] wise ones see the selfsame thing (*sama*)
In a Brāhman, wise and courteous,
As in a cow or elephant
Nay, as in a dog or outcaste.

19. While yet in this world, [the world of] emanation [and decay]
They've conquered, for their minds are stilled in That which ever is the same (*sāmya*):
For devoid of imperfection and ever the same (*sama*) is Brahman;
Therefore in Brahman [stilled] they stand.

20. Winning some pleasant thing [the sage] will not rejoice,
Nor shrink disquietened when the unpleasant comes his way;
Steadfast and stilled his soul (*buddhi*), [all] unconfused,
He will know Brahman, in Brahman [stilled] he'll stand.

21. His self detached from contacts with the outside world,
In self he finds his joy (*sukha*);
His self in Brahman integrated by spiritual exercise (*brahma-yogayuktātmā*)
He finds imperishable joy.

22. For the pleasures men derive from contacts
Assuredly give rise to pain,
Having a beginning and an end.
In these the wise take no delight.

30 Or, 'Lord'.

23. Let a man, remaining in this world,
And before he is released from the body['s bondage]
Stand fast against the onset of anger and desire;
Only so in joy will he be integrated.

24. His joy within, his bliss within,
His light within, that Yogin
Becomes Brahman and draws nigh
To Nirvāṇa that is Brahman too.[31]

25. Nirvāṇa that is Brahman is the lot
Of seers in whom [all] taint of imperfection is destroyed;
Their doubts dispelled, [all] self-controlled,
They take their pleasure in the weal
Of all contingent beings.

26. Around these holy men whose thoughts are fast controlled,
Estranged from anger and desire,
Knowing [at last] the self,
Nirvāṇa that is Brahman fares.

27. [All] contacts with things outside he puts aside,
Fixing his gaze between the eyebrows;
Inward and outward breaths he makes the same
As they pass up and down the nostrils;

28. With sense and mind and soul (*buddhi*) restrained,
The sage on deliverance intent,
Who has forever banished fear, anger and desire
Is truly liberated.

29. [Then] does he learn to know Me, who alone enjoy
The sacrifice and fierce austerities, great Lord
Of all the worlds, friend of all contingent beings,
[And knowing Me] he reaches peace.

VI

The Blessed Lord said:
1. The man who does the work that is his to do,
Yet covets not its fruits,

31 Or, 'the Nirvāṇa of Brahman'.

He [it is who] at once renounces and yet works on (*yogin*),
Not he who builds no sacrificial fire and does no work.

2. What men call renunciation
Is practice (*yoga*) too; this must thou know.
For without renouncing [all] set purpose (*saṅkalpa*)
None can engage in spiritual exercise (*yogin*).

3. For the sage who would climb [the heights of] spiritual exercise (*yoga*),
Works are said to be the means;
But for that same sage who has reached that peak
They say quiescence is the means.

4. For when a man knows no attachment
To objects of sense or to the deeds [he does],
When all set purpose he's renounced,
Then has he climbed [the heights of] spiritual exercise (*yoga*),
Or so they say.

5. Raise self by self,
Let not the self droop down;
For self's friend is self indeed,
So too is self self's enemy.

6. Self is friend to the self of him
Whose self is by the self subdued;
But for the man bereft of self
Self will act as an enemy indeed.

7. The higher self of the self-subdued
Who quietness knows, is rapt in enstasy[32] –
In cold as in heat, in pleasure as in pain,'
Likewise in honour or disgrace.

8. With self content in wisdom learnt
From holy books and wisdom learnt from life,
With sense subdued, unmoving in the heights,
The Yogin [stands]: 'Integrated', so he's called;
Alike to him are clods of earth, stones, gold.

9. Outstanding he whose soul (*buddhi*)
Views in the self-same way

32 Or, 'The self . . . is supremely rapt in enstasy'.

Friends, comrades, enemies, those indifferent,
Neutrals, the men he hates and those who are his kin –
The good and the evil too.

10. Let the Yogin ever integrate [him]self
Standing in a place apart,
Alone, his thoughts and self restrained,
Devoid of [earthly] hope, nothing possessing.

11. Let him for himself set up
A steady seat in a clean place,
Neither too high nor yet too low,
With cloth or hides or grass bestrewn.

12. There let him sit and make his mind a single point;
Let him restrain the motions of his thought and senses,
And engage in spiritual exercise (*yoga*)
To purify the self.

13. Remaining still, let him keep body, head and neck
In a straight line, unmoving;
Let him fix his gaze on the tip of his own nose,
Not looking round about him.

14. [There] let him sit, his self all stilled,
His fear all gone, firm in his vow of chastity,
His mind controlled, his thoughts on Me,
Integrated, [yet] intent on Me.

15. Thus let the Yogin ever integrate [him]self,
His mind restrained;
Then will he approach that peace
Which has Nirvāṇa as its end
And which subsists in Me.

16. Yoga is not for him who eats too much.
Nor yet for him who does not eat at all,
Nor for him who is all too prone to sleep,
Nor yet for him who [always] stays awake.

17. [Rather] is Yoga [made] for him
Who knows the mean (*yukta*) in food and recreation,
Who knows the mean in all his deeds and gestures,
Who knows the mean in sleeping as in waking:
[This is the Yoga] that slaughters pain.

18. When thought, held well in check,
Sinks into the self alone,
Then is a man from longing freed, though all desires assail him:
They call him 'integrated'.

19. As a lamp might stand in a windless place,
Unflickering – this likeness have we heard
Of such Yogins who control their thought
And practise the integration of the self.

20. When thought by Yogic exercise is checked
And comes to rest,
And when by self one sees the self in self
And finds content therein,

21. That is the utmost joy which transcends [all things of] sense,
And which soul (*buddhi*) [alone] can grasp.
When he knows this and [knowing it] stands still,
Departing not an inch from the Reality [he sees],

22. He wins a prize beyond all others –
Or so he thinks.
Therein he [firmly] stands,
Unmoved by any suffering, however grievous it may be.

23. This he should know is what is meant by 'Yoga' –
The unlinking of the link with suffering and pain.
This is the Yoga which must be brought about (*yuj-*)
With firm resolve and mind all undismayed.

24. Let him all desires renounce whose origin
Lies in the will (*saṁkalpa*), all of them without remainder;
Let him restrain in every way
By mind alone the senses' busy throng:

25. His soul (*buddhi*) held fast in steadfastness,
Little by little he'll come to rest;
Stilling the mind in self,
He must think of nothing at all.

26. Whenever the fickle mind
Unsteady roves around,
From thence he'll bring it back
And subject it to the self.

27. For upon this man of Yoga whose mind is stilled
The highest joy descends:
[All] passion laid to rest, free from [all] stain,
Brahman he becomes.

28. [And] thus [all] flaws transcending,
The man of Yoga, constant in integrating self,
With ease attains the highest joy,
Brahman's [saving] touch.

29. With self by Yoga integrated, [now] he sees
The self in all beings standing,
All beings in the self:
The same in everything he sees.

30. Who sees Me everywhere,
Who sees the All in Me,
For him I am not lost,
Nor is he lost for Me.

31. Who loves and worships (*bhaj-*) Me, embracing unity,
As abiding in all beings,
In whatever state he be,
That man of Yoga abides in Me.

32. By analogy with self who sees
The same [essence] everywhere
In pleasure as in pain,
He among Yogins is supreme, or so men think.

Arjuna said:
33. So fickle [is my mind] that I cannot descry
The still, firm-stablished state
Of this Yoga thou hast preached
As 'being the same [in everything]'.

34. For fickle is the mind,
Impetuous, exceeding strong:
How difficult to curb it!
As easy to curb the wind, I'd say.

The Blessed Lord said:
35. Herein there is no doubt,
Hard is the mind to curb and fickle;

But by untiring effort and by transcending passion
  It can be held in check.

36. Hard to come by is this self-control (*yoga*)
By one whose self is not restrained; this [too] I think;
But the man who strives, [all] self-controlled,
Can win it if he but use [the appropriate] means.

Arjuna said:
37. [Suppose] a man of faith should strive in vain,
His restless mind from Yoga weaned –
He fails to win the perfect prize [proffered] by Yoga –
  What path does he tread then?[33]

38. Does he, both objects unachieved, come crashing down
And perish like a riven cloud,
  His firm foundation gone,
  Bemused on Brahman's path?

39. Kṛṣṇa, this doubt thou canst dispel for me
  So that none of it remains,
  For there seems to be no other
Who can dispel this doubt [of mine].

The Blessed Lord said:
40. Not in this world nor in the next
Is such a man destroyed or lost:
No doer of fair works will tread
An evil path, my friend, no, none whatever.

41. The worlds of doers of good works he'll win,
  And dwell there endless years;
And then will he be born again, this man who failed in Yoga,
In the house of pious men by fortune blest.

42. Or else he will be born in a family
Of real Yogins possessed of insight;
But such a birth as this on earth
  Is yet harder to win.

43. There is he united with the soul (*buddhi*)
As it had matured in his former body;

33 Or, 'What goal does he reach?'

And once again he [girds his loins,]
Struggling for [Yoga's] highest prize.

44. By [the force of] that same struggle he'd waged in former times
He's swept away though helpless [of himself];
For even he who does no more
Than wish to know what Yoga is,
Transcends that 'Brahman' which is [no more than] wordy rites.

45. But cleansed of taint, that man of Yoga
Strives on with utmost zeal,
Through many, many births [at last] perfected;
And then the highest path he treads.[34]

46. Higher than the [mere] ascetic is the Yogin held to be,
Yes, higher than the man of wisdom,
Higher than the man of works:
Be, then, a Yogin, Arjuna!

47. But of all the men of Yoga
The man of faith who loves and honours (*bhaj-*) Me,
His inmost self absorbed in Me,
He is the most fully integrated: this do I believe.

VII

The Blessed Lord said:
1. Attach thy mind to Me:
Engaged in Yogic exercise, put thy trust in Me:
[This doing] listen how thou mayest come to know Me
In my entirety, all doubt dispelled.

2. This wisdom derived from sacred writ
And the wisdom of experience
I shall proclaim to thee, leaving nothing unsaid.
This knowing, never again will any other thing
That needs to be known remain.

3. Among thousands of men but one, maybe,
Will strive for self-perfection;

34 Or, 'reaches the highest goal'.

And even among these [athletes] who have won perfection['s
crown]
But one, maybe, will come to know Me as I really am.

4. Eightfold divided is my Nature – thus:
Earth, water, fire and air,
Space, mind, and also soul (*buddhi*),
The ego [last].

5. This is the lower: but other than this
I have a higher Nature; this too must thou know.
[And this is] Nature seen as life
By which this universe (*jagat*) is kept in being.

6. From these[35] [two Natures] all beings take their origin
Be very sure of this.
Of the whole [wide] universe
The origin and the dissolution too am I.

7. Higher than I
There's nothing whatsoever:
On Me the universe (*sarvam*) is strung
Like clustered pearls upon a thread.

8. In water I am the flavour,
In sun and moon the light,
In all the Vedas Oṁ [the sacred syllable],
In space I'm sound: in man [his] manliness am I.

9. Pure fragrance in the earth am I,
Flame's onset in the fire;
[And] life [am I] in all contingent beings,
In ascetics [their] fierce austerity.

10. Know that I am the eternal seed
Of all contingent beings:
Reason in the rational,
Glory in the glorious am I.

11. Power in the powerful I –
[Such power] as knows nor passion nor desire:
Desire am I in contingent beings,
[But such desire as is] not at war with right (*dharma*).

35 Or, 'this'.

12. Know too that all states of being, whether they be
Of [Nature's constituent] Goodness, Passion or Darkness,
Proceed from Me;
But I am not in them, they are in Me.

13. By these three states of being
Inhering in the 'constituents'
This whole universe is led astray,
And does not understand
That I am far beyond them:
I neither change nor pass away.

14. For [all] this is my creative power (*māyā*),
Divine, hard to transcend.
Whoso shall put his trust in Me alone,
Shall pass beyond this [my] uncanny power (*māyā*).

15. Doers of evil, deluded, base,
Put not their trust in Me;
Their minds seduced by this uncanny power,
They cleave to a devilish form of life (*bhāva*).

16. Fourfold are the doers of good
Who love and worship (*bhaj-*) Me –
The afflicted, the man who seeks for wisdom,
The man who strives for gain, and the man who wisdom knows.

17. Of these the man of wisdom, ever integrated,
Who loves and worships (*bhakti*) One alone, excels:
To such a man I am exceeding dear,
And he is dear to Me.

18. All these are noble and exalted,
But the man of wisdom is my very self, so must I hold.
His self [already] integrated, he puts his trust in Me,
The [one] All-Highest way.[36]

19. At the end of many a birth
The man of wisdom resigns himself to Me,
[Knowing that Kṛṣṇa,] Vasudeva's son, is All:
A man so great of soul (*mahātman*) is exceeding hard to find.

36 Or, 'goal', or 'refuge'.

20. [All] wisdom swept away by manifold desires,
Men put their trust in other gods,
Relying on diverse rules and precepts:
For their own nature forces them thereto.

21. Whatever form, [whatever god,] a devotee
With faith desires to honour,
That very faith do I confirm in him,
Making it unswerving and secure.

22. Firm stablished (*yukta*) in that faith,
He seeks to reverence that [god],
And thence he gains all he desires,
Though it is I who am the true dispenser.

23. But finite is the reward (*phala*)
Of such men of little wit:
Whoso worships the gods, to the gods will [surely] go,
[But] whoso loves and worships (*bhakta*) Me,
To Me will come indeed.

24. Fools think I am the Unmanifest
In manifest form displayed:
They know nothing of my higher state,
The Unchangeable, All-Highest.

25. Because my creative power (*yoga-māyā*) conceals Me,
I am not revealed to all:
This world, deluded, knows Me not –
[Me,] the Unborn and Changeless.

26. All beings past and present,
And yet to come
I know:
But none there is that knoweth Me.

27. By dualities (*dvandva*) are men confused, and these arise
From desire and hate;
Thereby are all contingent beings
Bewildered the moment they are born.

28. But some there are for whom [all] ill is ended –
Doers of what is good and pure:
Released [at last] from the confusion of duality,
Steadfast in their vows, they love and worship (*bhaj-*) Me.

29. Whoso shall strive to win release from age and death,
Putting his trust in Me,
Will come to know That Brahman in Its wholeness,
What appertains to self[37] and the whole [mystery] of works.

30. Whoso shall know Me and all that appertains
To contingent being, to the divine and to the sacrifice,
Will come to know Me at the time of passing on,
For integrated their thought will be.

VIII

Arjuna said:
1. What is That Brahman? What that which appertains to self?
[And] what, O best of men, are works (*karma*)?
What is that called which appertains to contingent beings?
What that which appertains to the divine?

2. Who and in what manner is he
Who appertains to the sacrifice here in this body?
And how, at the time of passing on,
Mayst thou be known by men of self-restraint?

The Blessed Lord said:
3. The Imperishable[38] is Brahman, the All-Highest,
Nature (*svabhāva*), they say, is what appertains to self:
Creative force (*visarga*) is known as 'works' (*karma*),
For it gives rise to the [separate] natures of contingent beings.

4. To contingent beings a perishable nature appertains,
To the divine [pure] spirit (*puruṣa*);
But it is I myself who appertain to the sacrifice
Here in this body, O best of men who bodies bear.

5. Whoso at the hour of death,
Abandoning his mortal frame,
Bears Me in mind and passes on,
Accedes to my Divinity (*mad-bhāva*): have no doubt of that.

6. Whatever state (*bhāva*) a man may bear in mind
When the time comes at last to cast the mortal frame aside,

37 Most translators have 'overself' and the like, contrary to Upanishadic usage.
38 Or, 'the sacred syllable Oṁ'.

Even to that state does he accede,
For ever does that state of being make him grow into itself (*tadbhāva-bhāvita*).

7. Then muse upon Me always,
And go to war;
For if thou finest mind and soul (*buddhi*) on Me,
To Me shalt thou most surely come.

8. Let a man's thoughts be integrated with the discipline (*yoga*)
Of constant striving: let them not stray to anything else [at all];
So by meditating on the divine All-Highest Person,
[That man to that All-Highest] goes.

9. For [He it is who is called] the Ancient Seer,
Governor [of all things, yet] smaller than the small,
Ordainer[39] of all, in form unthinkable,
Sun-coloured beyond the darkness. Let a man meditate on Him [as such].

10. With mind unmoving when his turn comes to die,
Steadied (*yukta*) by loyal love (*bhakti*) and Yogic power,
Forcing the breath between the eyebrows duly,
[So will such a man] draw nigh to the divine All-Highest Person.

11. The imperishable state[40] of which the Vedic scholars speak,
Which sages enter, [all their] passion spent,
For love of which men lead a life of chastity,
[That state] will I proclaim to thee in brief.

12. Let a man close up all [the body's] gates,
Stem his mind within his heart,
Fix his breath within his head,
Engrossed in Yogic concentration.

13. Let him utter [the word] Oṁ, Brahman in one syllable,
Keeping Me in mind;
Then when his time is come to leave aside the body,
He'll tread the highest Way.[41]

39 Or, 'creator', or 'supporter'.
40 Or, 'word'.
41 Or, 'Go to the highest goal or refuge'.

14. How easily am I won by him
Who bears Me in mind unceasingly,
Thinking of nothing else at all –
A Yogin integrated ever.

15. Coming right nigh to Me, these great of soul,
Are never born again.
For rebirth is full of suffering, knows nothing that abides:
[Free from it now] they attain the all-highest prize (*saṁsiddhi*).

16. The worlds right up to Brahmā's realm
[Dissolve and] evolve again;
But he who comes right nigh to Me
Shall never be born again.

17. For a thousand ages lasts
One day of Brahmā,
And for a thousand ages one such night:
This knowing, men will know [what is meant by] day and night.

18. At the day's dawning all things manifest
Spring forth from the Unmanifest;
And then at nightfall they dissolve again
In [that same mystery] surnamed 'Unmanifest'.

19. Yea, this whole host of beings
Comes ever anew to be; at fall of night
It dissolves away all helpless;
At dawn of day it rises up [again].

20. But beyond that there is [yet] another mode of being –
Beyond the Unmanifest another Unmanifest, eternal:
This is He who passes not away
When all contingent beings pass away.

21. Unmanifest surnamed 'Imperishable' –
This, men say, is the All-Highest Way,[42]
And this once won, there is no more returning:
This is my all-highest home.[43]

22. That is [indeed] the highest Person (Spirit);
By love and worship (*bhakti*) is He won, and nowise else.[44]

42 Or, 'goal' or 'refuge'.
43 *dhāma*: or, 'law' or 'light'.
44 Or, 'not confounding any other with Him'.

In Him do all contingent beings subsist;
By Him this universe was spun.[45]

23. Some to return, some never to return,
Yogins set forth when they pass on;
The times [and seasons of them all]
I shall [now] declare.

24. Fire, light, day, the moon's light fortnight,
The six months of the sun's northern course –
Dying in these to Brahman do they go,
The men who Brahman know.

25. Smoke, night, the moon's dark fortnight,
The six months of the sun's southern course –
[Dying] in these, a Yogin wins the light of the moon,
And back he comes again.

26. These courses – light and dark – are deemed
To be unchanging [laws] on earth.
One leads to [the place of] no return,
By the other one returns again.

27. Knowing these courses twain
No Yogin is bemused.
So, Arjuna, ever be
In Yoga integrated.

28. For knowledge of the Veda, for sacrifice, for grim austerities,
For gifts of alms a meed of merit is laid down;
All this the Yogin leaves behind who knows this [secret teaching;]
[And knowing it] he draws right nigh to the highest primal state (*sthāna*).

IX

The Blessed Lord said:
1. But most secret and mysterious
Is the teaching I will [now] reveal –
[A teaching] based on Holy Writ, consonant with experience:

45 Or, 'pervaded'.

To thee [will I proclaim it,] for in thee there is no envy;
And knowing it, thou shalt be free from ill.

2. Science of kings, mystery of kings
Is this, – distilling the purest essence,
To the understanding evident, with righteousness enhanced,
How easy to carry out! [Yet] it abides forever.

3. Men who put no faith
In this law of righteousness (*dharma*),
Fail to reach Me and must return
To the road of recurring death.

4. By Me, Unmanifest in form,
This whole universe was spun:[46]
In Me subsist all beings,
I do not subsist in them.

5. And [yet] contingent beings do not subsist in Me –
Behold my sovereign power (*yoga*)!
My Self sustains [all] beings, it does not subsist in them;
It causes them to be.

6. As in [wide] space subsists the mighty wind,
Blowing [at will] ever and everywhere,
So too do all contingent beings
Subsist in Me: so must thou understand.

7. All contingent beings pass
Into material Nature which is Mine
When an aeon comes to an end; and then again
When another aeon starts, I emanate them forth.

8. Firm-fixed in my material Nature
Ever again I emanate
This whole mighty host of beings,
Powerless themselves – from Nature comes the power.

9. These works of mine
Bind Me not nor limit Me:
As one indifferent I sit
Among these works, detached.[47]

46 Or, 'pervaded'.
47 Or, 'detached from these works'.

10. [A world of] moving and unmoving things
Material Nature brings to birth, while I look on and supervise:
This is the cause and this the means
By which the world revolves.

11. For that a human form I have assumed
Fools scorn Me,
Knowing nothing of my higher nature (*bhāva*) –
Great Lord of [all] contingent beings.

12. Vain their hopes and vain their deeds,
Vain their 'gnosis', void their wit;
A monstrous, devilish nature they embrace
Which leads them [far] astray.

13. But great-souled men take up their stand
In a nature [all] divine;
And so, with minds intent on naught but Me,
They love and worship (*bhaj-*) Me,
Knowing Me to be the Beginning of all that is,
As Him who cannot pass away.

14. Me do they ever glorify,
[For Me] they strive, full firm their vows;
To Me they bow down, devoted in their love (*bhakti*),
And integrated ever [in themselves], they pay me worship (*upās-*).

15. Others again with wisdom's sacrifice
Make sacrifice to Me and worship Me
As One and yet as Manifold,
With face turned every way, in many a guise.

16. I am the rite, the sacrifice,
The offering for the dead, the healing herb;
I am the sacred formula, the sacred butter am I,
I am the fire, and I the oblation [offered in the fire].

17. I am the father of this world,
Mother, ordainer,[48] grandsire, [all] that need be known;
Vessel of purity [am I, the sacred syllable] Oṁ;
And the three Vedas am I too.

48 Or, 'creator' or 'sustainer'.

18. [I am] the Way,[49] sustainer, Lord and witness,
[True] home and refuge, friend –
Origin and dissolution and the stable state between –
A treasure-house, the seed that passes not away.

19. It is I who pour out heat, hold back
The rain and send it forth;
Death am I and deathlessness,
What is not and that which IS.

20. Trusting in the three Vedas, the Soma-drinkers, purged of ritual fault (*pāpa*),
Worship Me with sacrifice, seeking to go to paradise:
These win through to the pure world of the lord of the gods
And taste in heaven the gods' celestial joys.

21. [But] once they have [to the full] enjoyed the broad expanse of paradise,
Their merit exhausted, they come back to the world of men.
And so it is that those who stick fast to the three Vedas [only]
Receive [a reward] that comes and goes; for it is desire that they desire.

22. For those men who meditate upon Me, no other [thought in mind],
Who do me honour, ever persevere,
I bring attainment
And possession of what has been attained.

23. [Yet] even those who worship other gods with love (*bhakta*)
And sacrifice to them, full filled with faith,
Do really worship Me,
Though the rite differ from the norm.

24. For it is I who of all acts of sacrifice
Am Recipient and Lord,
But they do not know Me as I really am,
And so they fall [back into the world of men].

25. To the gods go the gods' devotees,
To the ancestors their votaries,

49 Or, 'goal'.

To disembodied spirits the worshippers of these,
But those who sacrifice to Me shall come to Me.

26. Be it a leaf, or flower, or fruit, or water
That a zealous soul may offer with love's devotion (*bhakti*),
That do I [willingly] accept,
For it was love (*bhakti*) that made the offering.

27. Whatever thou dost, whatever thou eatest,
Whatever thou dost offer up in sacrifice or give away in alms,
Whatever penance thou mayst perform,
Offer it up to me.

28. So from [those] bonds which works [of their very nature forge],
Whose fruits are fair or foul, thou shalt be freed:
Thy self [now] integrated by renunciation and spiritual exercise (*yoga*),
Free, thou shalt draw nigh to Me.

29. In all contingent beings the same[50] am I;
None do I hate and none do I fondly love (*priya*);
But those who commune (*bhaj-*) with me in love's devotion (*bhakti*)
[Abide] in Me, and I in them.

30. However evil a man's livelihood may be,
Let him but worship Me with love (*bhaj-*) and serve (*bhaj-*) no other,
Then shall he be reckoned among the good indeed,
For his resolve is right.

31. Right soon will his self be filled with righteousness (*dharmātmā*)
And win eternal rest (*śānti*).
Arjuna, of this be sure:
None who pays me worship of loyalty and love (*bhakta*) is ever lost.

32. For whosoever makes Me his haven,
Base-born though he may be,

50 Or, 'indifferent'.

Yes, women too, and artisans, even serfs –
Theirs it is to tread the highest Way.[51]

33. How much more, then, Brāhmans, pure and good,
And royal seers who know devoted love (*bhakta*).
Since thy lot has fallen in this world, impermanent and joyless,
Commune with Me in love (*bhaj-*)!

34. On Me thy mind, for Me thy loving service (*bhakta*),
For Me thy sacrifice, and to Me be thy prostrations:
Let [thine own] self be integrated, and then
Shalt thou come to Me, thy striving bent on Me.

X

The Blessed Lord said:
1. [Now] once again, my strong-armed [friend],
Give ear to my all-highest word
Which I shall speak to thee [alone],
For therein is thy delight[52] and thy welfare is my wish.

2. None knows from whence I came[53] –
Nor gods' celestial hosts nor mighty seers:
For I am the Beginning of the gods [themselves]
As of the mighty seers and all in every way.

3. Whoso shall know Me as Unborn, Beginningless,
Great Lord of [all] the worlds,
Shall never know delusion among men,
From every evil freed.

4. Intellect (*buddhi*), wisdom, freedom from delusion,
Long-suffering, truth, restraint, tranquillity,
Pleasure and pain, coming-to-be and passing away,[54]
Fear and fearlessness as well,

5. Refusal to do harm, equanimity (*samatā*), content,
Austerity, open-handedness, fame and infamy –
Such are the dispositions (*bhāvā*) of contingent beings,
And from Me in all their diversity they arise.

51 Or, 'goal'.
52 Or, 'For thou art [beloved of Me]'.
53 Lit. 'my origin'. Var. 'lordly power'.
54 Or, 'exaltation and depression'.

6. The seven mighty seers of old,
Likewise the Manus four,[55]
Sharing in my mode of being,[56] were born [the children] of [my] mind;
From them [arose] these creatures in the world.

7. Whoso should know my far-flung power and how I use it (*yoga*):[57]
[Whoso should know these] as they really are,
Is [truly] integrated (*yujyate*); and this his integration (*yoga*)
Can never be undone. Herein there is no doubt.

8. The source of all am I;
From Me all things proceed:
This knowing, wise men commune with (*bhaj-*) Me,
Full filled with warm affection.[58]

9. On Me their thoughts, their life they'd sacrifice for Me;
[And so] enlightening one another
And telling my story constantly,
They take their pleasure and delight.

10. And since these men are ever integrated
And commune with (*bhaj-*) Me in love (*prīti*),
I give them an integrated soul[59]
By which they may draw nigh to Me.

11. Out of compassion for these same men
[All] darkness born of ignorance I dispel
With wisdom's shining lamp;
[Yet all the while] I still abide in the [true] nature of my Self.[60]

Arjuna said:
12–13. All-Highest Brahman, highest home (*dhāma*),
All-highest vessel of Purity art Thou.
All seers agree that Thou
Art the Person, eternal and divine,

55 Or, 'The seventy mighty seers, the four ancients, and the Manus too'.
56 Or, 'originating from Me'.
57 Or, 'creative power'.
58 *Bhāva*: or, 'with [the right] disposition' or 'perseverance'.
59 *Buddhiyoga*, cf. 11. 49. Or 'discipline of mind'.
60 Or, 'abiding in their selves', but this forces the Sanskrit.

Primeval God, unborn and all-pervading Lord.
So too Nārada, the godly seer,
Asita, Devala and Vyāsa [have declared];
And Thou Thyself dost tell me so.

14. All this Thou tellest me is true;
So, Kṛṣṇa, I believe,
For, Blessed Lord, nor gods nor demons
Acknowledge [this] manifest [world] as thine.[61]

15. By Thy Self Thou thyself dost know
Thy Self, O Thou, the All-Highest Person,
[Thou that] bestowest being on contingent beings,
[Thou] the Lord of [all] contingent beings,
[Thou] God of gods and Lord of [all] the world.

16. Tell me, I pray Thee, leaving naught unsaid,
Of the fair and far-flung powers [that centre] on thy Self,[62]
By which Thou dost pervade these worlds,
Standing [unchanged the while].

17. How am I to know Thee, Thou master of Yogic power,
Though I think upon Thee always?
And in what several modes of being
Should I think about Thee, Blessed Lord?

18. Tell me again in detail full
Of thy far-flung power and how thou usest it (*yoga*);[63]
For as I listen to thy undying words,
I cannot have enough.

The Blessed Lord said:
19. Lo, I shall tell thee
Of the fair and far-flung powers [that centre] on my Self,[64]
Those of them, at least, that are fundamental,
For of the details[65] there is no end.

20. I am the Self established
In the heart of all contingent beings;

61 Or, 'know thy manifestation'.
62 Reading *vibhūtīr ātmanaḥ subhāḥ*.
63 Or, 'creative power'.
64 Reading *vibhūtīr ātmanaḥ subhāḥ*.
65 Or 'extent'.

I am the beginning, the middle, and the end
Of all contingent beings too.

21. Among the Ādityas Viṣṇu am I,
Among lights the radiant sun,
Among the Maruts Marīci am I,
Among stars I am the moon.

22. Of the Vedas the *Sāma-Veda* am I,
Indra among the gods;
Among the senses I am mind,
Amongst contingent beings thought.

23. Among the Rudras Śiva am I,
Among sprites and monsters the Lord of Wealth (Kuvera),
Of the Vasus I am Fire,
Among the mountains I am Meru.

24. Of household priests know that I
Am the chief, Bṛhaspati,
Among warlords I am Skanda, [god of war,]
Among lakes I am the Ocean.

25. Bhṛgu I am among the mighty seers,
Among utterances the single syllable [Oṁ],
Among sacrifices I am the sacrifice of muttered prayer,
Among things immovable the Himalayas,

26. Among all trees the holy fig tree,
Nārada among the celestial seers,
Citraratha among the heavenly minstrels,
Among perfected beings Kapila, the silent sage.

27. Among horses know that I
Am Uccaiḥśravas, (Indra's steed,) from nectar born,
Among princely elephants [Indra's called] Airāvata:
Among men I am the King.

28. Of weapons I am the thunderbolt,
Of cows the milch-cow of desires.
I am Kandarpa, [god of love,] generating seed:
Among serpents I am Vāsuki, [the serpent king].

29. Of Nāga-serpents Ananta am I,
Of water-dwellers Varuṇa;

Of the ancestors I am Aryaman,
Among those who subdue I am Yama, [the god of death].

30. Among demons Prahlāda am I,
Among those who reckon Time;
Among beasts I am [the lion], the king of beasts,
And among birds Garuḍa, [Viṣṇu's bird].

31. Among those who purify I am the Wind,
Rāma I am among men-at-arms;
Among water-monsters I am the crocodile,[66]
Among rivers [the Ganges, surnamed] Jāhnavī.

32. Among emanations the beginning and the end
And the middle too am I;
Among sciences I am the science concerned with Self,
Of those who speak I am [their very] speech.

33. Among the letters of the alphabet I am 'A',
Among grammatical compounds the *dvandva*.
In very truth I am imperishable Time,
I the ordainer[67] with face turned every way.

34. I am Death that snatches all away,
And the origin of creatures yet to be.
Among feminine nouns[68] I am fame, fortune, speech,
Memory, intelligence, steadfastness, long-suffering.[69]

35. Among chants the Great Chant am I,
Among metres the Gāyatrī,
Among months I am [the first,] Mārgaśīrṣa,
Among seasons flower-bearing [spring].

36. I am the dicing of tricksters,
Glory of the glorious;
Victory and firm resolve am I.
And the courage of the brave.[70]

37. Among Vṛṣṇi clansmen I am [Kṛṣṇa,] Vasudeva's son,
Among Pāṇḍu's sons I am Arjuna;

66 Or, 'shark' or 'dolphin'.
67 Or, 'creator'.
68 Lit. 'women'.
69 All these nouns are feminine in Sanskrit.
70 Or, 'goodness of the good'.

Among sages I am Vyāsa,
Among psalmists the psalmist, Uśanas.

38. Of those who subdue the rod of chastisement am I,
And the statecraft of those who seek the upper hand;
The very silence of hidden, secret things am I,
And the wisdom of the wise.

39. What is the seed of all
Contingent beings, that too am I:
No being there is, whether moving or unmoving,
That could exist apart from Me.

40. Of [these] my far-flung powers divine
There is no end;
As much as I have said concerning them
Must serve as an example.

41. Whatever being shows wide power,
Prosperity or strength,
Be sure that this derives
From [but] a fragment of my glory.

42. But where's the use for thee
To know so much?
This whole universe I hold apart [supporting it]
With [but] a fragment [of Myself], yet I abide [unchanging].

XI

Arjuna said:
1. Out of thy gracious favour to me Thou
Hast uttered the all-highest mystery
Called 'what appertains to Self',[71]
And by that word [of thine] banished is my perplexity.

2. For I have heard of the coming-to-be
And passing away of contingent beings;
[This hast Thou told me] in detail full,
As well as the majesty of [thine own] Self which passes not away.

3. Even as Thou hast described [thy] Self to be,
So must it be, O Lord Most High;

71 See note on VII. 29, p. 243.

[But] fain would I *see* the [bodily] form
Of Thee as Lord, All-Highest Person.

4. If, Lord, Thou thinkest that I can
Thus see Thee, then show Thou forth,
Lord of creative power (*yoga*),
[This] Self that passes not away.

The Blessed Lord said:
5. Son of Pṛthā, behold my forms
In their hundreds and their thousands;
How various are they, how divine,
How many-hued and multiform!

6. Ādityas, Rudras, Vasus, the Aśvins twain,
The Maruts too – behold them!
Marvels never seen before – how many!
Arjuna, behold them!

7. Do thou today this whole universe behold
Centred here in One, with all that it contains
Of moving and unmoving things;
[Behold] it in my body,
And whatsoever else thou fain wouldst see.

8. But never canst thou see Me
With this thy [natural] eye.
A celestial eye I'll give thee:
Behold my creative power (*yoga*)[72] as Lord!

Sañjaya said:
9. So saying Hari,[73]
The great Lord of Yogic power,
Revealed to the son of Pṛthā
His all-highest sovereign form –

10. [A form] with many a mouth and eye
And countless marvellous aspects;
Many [indeed] were its divine adornments,
Many the celestial weapons raised on high.

72 Var. 'form'.
73 A name of Viṣṇu-Kṛṣṇa.

11. Garlands and robes celestial He wore,
Fragrance divine was his anointing:
[Behold] this God whose every [mark] spells wonder,
The infinite, facing every way!

12. If in [bright] heaven together should arise
The shining brilliance of a thousand suns,
Then would that [perhaps] resemble
The brilliance of that God so great of Self.

13. Then did the son of Pāṇḍu see
The whole [wide] universe in One converged,
There in the body of the God of gods,
Yet divided out in multiplicity.

14. Then filled with amazement Arjuna,
His hair on end, hands joined in reverent greeting,
Bowing his head before the God,
[These words] spake out:

Arjuna said:
15. O God, the gods in thy body I behold,
And all the hosts of every kind of being;
Brahmā, the Lord, [I see], throned on the lotus-seat,
Celestial serpents and all the [ancient] seers.

16. Arms, bellies, mouths and eyes all manifold –
So do I see Thee wherever I may look – infinite thy form.
End, middle or beginning in Thee I cannot see,
O Monarch Universal, [manifest] in every form.

17. Thine the crown, the mace, the discus –
A mass of glory shining on all sides,
So do I see Thee – yet how hard art Thou to see – for on every side,
There's brilliant light of blazing fire and sun. O, who should comprehend it?[74]

18. Thou art the Imperishable, [thou] wisdom's highest goal,
Thou, of this universe the last prop and resting-place,
Thou the changeless, [thou] the guardian of eternal law (*dharma*),
Thou art the eternal Person; [at last] I understand!

74 Lit, 'immeasurable', or 'incomprehensible'.

19. Beginning, middle, end Thou knowest not – how infinite thy strength!
How numberless thine arms – thine eyes the sun and moon!
So do I see Thee – thy mouth a flaming fire
Burning up this whole [universe] with its blazing glory.

20. For by Thee alone is this space between heaven and earth
Pervaded – all points of the compass [by Thee pervaded too];
Gazing on this, thy marvellous, frightening form,
The three worlds shudder, All-Highest Self (*mahātman*)!

21. Lo, the hosts of gods are entering into Thee:
Some, terror-struck, extol Thee, hands together pressed;
Great seers and men perfected in serried ranks
Cry out, 'All hail', and praise Thee with copious hyms of praise.

22. Rudras, Ādityas, Vasus, Sādhyas,
All-gods, Aśvins, Maruts and [the ancestors] who quaff the stream,
Minstrels divine, sprites, demons and the host of perfected saints,
Gaze upon Thee, all utterly amazed.

23. Gazing upon thy mighty form
With its myriad mouths, eyes, arms, thighs, feet,
Bellies, and sharp, gruesome tusks,
The worlds [all] shudder [in affright] – how much more I!

24. Ablaze with many coloured [flames] Thou touch'st the sky,
Thy mouths wide open, gaping, thine eyes distended, blazing;
I see Thee, and my inmost self is shaken:
I cannot bear it, I find no peace, O Viṣṇu!

25. I see thy mouths with jagged, ghastly tusks
Reminding [me] of Time's [devouring] fire:
I cannot find my bearings, I see no refuge;
Have mercy, God of gods, Home of the universe!

26. Lo, all these sons of Dhṛtarāṣṭra
Accompanied by a host of kings,
Bhīṣma, Droṇa and [Karṇa,] son of the charioteer,
And those foremost in battle of our party too,

27. Rush [blindly] into thy [gaping] mouths
That with their horrid tusks strike [them] with terror.

Some stick in the gaps between thy teeth,
See them! – their heads to powder ground!

28. As many swelling, seething streams
Rush headlong into the [one great] sea,
So do these heroes of this world of men
Enter thy blazing mouths.

29. As moths, in bursting, hurtling haste
Rush into a lighted blaze to their destruction,
So do the worlds, well-trained in hasty violence,[75]
Pour into thy mouths to their own undoing.

30. On every side thou lickest, lickest up – devouring –
Worlds, universes, everything – with burning mouths;
Viṣṇu! thy dreadful rays of light fill the whole universe
With flames of glory, scorching [everywhere].

31. Tell me, who art Thou, thy form so cruel?
Homage to Thee, Thou best of gods, have mercy!
Fain would I know Thee as Thou art in the beginning,
For what Thou workest (*pravṛtti*) I do not understand.

The Blessed Lord said:
32. Time am I, wreaker of the world's destruction,
Matured – [grimly] resolved (*pravṛtta*) here to swallow up the worlds.
Do what thou wilt, all these warriors shall cease to be,
Drawn up [there] in their opposing ranks.

33. And so arise, win glory,
Conquer thine enemies and enjoy a prosperous kingdom!
Long since have these men in truth been slain by Me,
Thine it is to be the mere occasion.

34. Bhīṣma, Droṇa, Jayadratha,
Karṇa and all the other men of war
Are [as good as] slain by Me. Slay them then – why falter?
Fight! [for] thou shalt conquer thine enemies in battle.

Sañjaya said:
35. Hearing these words of Kṛṣṇa, [Arjuna,]

75 This is the same phrase in Sanskrit as that translated as 'in bursting, hurtling haste' two lines above.

Wearer of the crown, hands joined in veneration, trembling,
Bowed down again to Kṛṣṇa and spake again
With stammering voice, as terrified he did obeisance.

Arjuna said:
36. Full just it is that in praise of Thee
The world should find its pleasure and its joy,
That monsters by terror [tamed] should scatter in all directions,
And that all who've won perfection should do Thee homage.

37. For why should they not revere Thee, great as is thy Self,
More to be prized art Thou than Brahmā,[76] [Thou] the first Creator,
Gods' Lord, the world's [abiding] home, unending.
Thou art the Imperishable, Being, Not-Being and what surpasses both.[77]

38. Thou art the Primal God, Primeval Person,
Thou of this universe the last prop and resting-place,
Thou the knower and what is to be known, [Thou our] final home (*dhāma*),
O Thou whose forms are infinite, by whom the whole [universe] was spun.[78]

39. Thou art [the wind-god] Vāyu, Yama [the god of death],
The god of fire (Agni) and water (Varuṇa) and the moon:
Prajāpati art Thou, and the primordial Ancestor:
All hail, all hail to Thee, [all hail] a thousandfold,
And yet again, All hail, all hail!

40. All hail [to Thee] when I stand before Thee,
[All Hail] when I stand behind Thee,
All hail to Thee wherever I may be,
[All hail to Thee], Thou All!
How infinite thy strength, how limitless thy prowess!
All dost Thou bring to consummation,[79] hence art Thou All.

41. How rashly have I called Thee comrade, for so I thought of Thee,

76 Or, 'Brahman'. The whole phrase could mean 'Most reverend creator of Brahmā (or Brahman)'.
77 Or, 'that All-Highest' with some MSS.
78 Or, 'pervaded'.
79 Or, 'comprisest'.

[How rashly said,] 'Hey Kṛṣṇa, Hey Yādava, Hey comrade!'
Little did I know of this thy majesty,
Distraught was I, . . . or was it that I loved Thee?

42. Sometimes in jest I showed Thee disrespect
As we played or rested or sat or ate at table,
Sometimes together, sometimes in sight of others:
I crave thy pardon, O Lord, unfathomable, unfallen.

43. Thou art the father of the moving and unmoving world,
Thou its venerable teacher, most highly prized;
None is there like Thee – how could there be a greater? –
In these three worlds, O matchless is thy power.

44. And so I bow to Thee, prostrate my body,
Crave grace of Thee, [my] Lord adorable;
Bear with me, I pray Thee, as father [bears] with son,
Or friend with friend, or lover with the one he loves.

45. Things never seen before I've seen, and ecstatic is my joy;
Yet fear and trembling possess my mind.
Show me, then, God, that [same human] form [I knew],
Have mercy, Lord of gods, Home of the universe!

46. Fain would I see Thee with [thy familiar] crown and mace,
Discus in hand, just as Thou used to be;
Take up again thy four-armed form,
O Thousand-armed, to whom every form belongs.

The Blessed Lord said:
47. Because I desired to show thee favour, Arjuna,
By my Self's mysterious power (*ātmayoga*) I showed thee this my All-Highest form –
Glorious, all-embracing, infinite, primeval –
Which none has seen before save thee.

48. Not by the Vedas, not by sacrifice,
Not by [much] study or the giving of alms,
Not by rituals or grim ascetic practice,
Can I be seen in such a form in the world of men:
To Thee alone have I revealed it.

49. Thou needst not tremble nor need thy spirit be perplexed,
Though thou hast seen this form of mine, awful, grim.

Banish all fear, be glad at heart: behold again
That same [familiar human] form [thou knewest].

Sañjaya said:
50. Thus speaking did the son of Vasudeva
Show his [human] form to Arjuna again,
Comforting him in his fear.
For once again the high-souled (*mahātman*) [Kṛṣṇa]
Assumed the body of a friend.

Arjuna said:
51. Now that I see [again] thy human form,
Friendly and kind,
I have returned to my senses
And regained my normal state.

The Blessed Lord said:
52. Right hard to see is this my form
Which thou hast seen:
This is the form the gods themselves
Forever crave to see.

53. Not by the Vedas or grim ascetic practice,
Not by the giving of alms or sacrifice
Can I be seen in such a form
As thou didst see Me.

54. But by worship of love (*bhakti*) addressed to Me alone
Can I be known and seen
In such a form and as I really am:
[So can my lovers] enter into Me.

55. Do works for Me, make Me thy highest goal,
Be loyal in love (*bhakta*) to Me,
Cast off [all other] attachments,
Have no hatred for any being at all:
For all who do thus shall come to Me.

XII

Arjuna said:
1. Of those who are thus ever integrated
And serve Thee with loyal devotion (*bhakta*),

And those who [revere] the Imperishable Unmanifest,
Which are the most skilled in spiritual exercise (*yoga*)?

The Blessed Lord said:
2. Those I deem to be the most integrated
Who fix their thoughts on Me
And serve Me, ever integrated [in themselves],
Filled with the highest faith.

3. But those who serve the indeterminate,
Imperishable Unmanifest,
Unthinkable, though coursing everywhere,
Sublime, aloof, unmoving, firm,

4. Who hold in check the complex of their senses,
In all things equal-minded,
In others' weal rejoicing,
Those too attain to Me.

5. [But] greater is the toil of those
Whose thinking clings to the Unmanifest;
For difficult [indeed] it is for embodied men
To reach and tread the unmanifested Way.[80]

6. But those who cast off all their works on Me,
Solely intent on Me,
And meditate on Me in spiritual exercise (*yoga*),
Leaving no room for others, [and so really] do Me service,

7. These will I lift up on high
Out of the ocean of recurring death,
And that right soon,
For their thoughts are fixed on Me.

8. On Me alone let thy mind dwell,
Stir up thy soul (*buddhi*) to enter Me;
Thenceforth in very truth (*eva*)
In Me thou'lt find thy home.

9. But if thou art unable in all steadfastness
To concentrate thy thoughts on Me,
Then seek to win Me
By effort unremitting.

80 Or, 'goal'.

10. And if for such effort thou lack'st the strength,
Then work and act for Me, make this thy goal;
For even if thou workest only for my sake,
Thou shalt receive the prize.

11. And then again if even this exceeds thy powers,
Gird up thy loins,[81] renounce
The fruit of all thy works
With self restrained.

12. For better is wisdom than [mere] effort,
Better than wisdom meditation;
And better than meditation to renounce the fruits of works:
Renunciation leads straightway to peace.

13. Let a man feel hatred for no contingent being,
Let him be friendly, compassionate,
Let him be done with thoughts of 'I' and 'mine',
The same in pleasure as in pain, long-suffering,

14. Content and ever integrated,
His self restrained, his purpose firm,
Let his mind and soul (*buddhi*) be steeped in Me,
Let him worship Me with love (*bhakta*):
Then will I love him [in return].

15. That man I love from whom the people do not shrink,
And who does not shrink from them,
Who's free from exaltation, fear,
Impatience and excitement.

16. I love the man who has no expectation,
Is pure and skilled, indifferent,
Who has no worries, and gives up
All [selfish] enterprise, wrapt up in (*bhakta*) Me.

17. I love the man who hates not, nor exults,
Who mourns not nor desires,
Who puts away both pleasant and unpleasant things,
Who's loyal, devoted and devout (*bhaktimat*).

18–19. I love the man who is the same
To friend and foe, [the same]

81 Reading *udyogam* with some MSS for *mad-yogam*.

Whether he be respected or despised,
The same in heat and cold, in pleasure as in pain,

Who's put away attachment and remains
Unmoved by praise or blame, who's taciturn,
Contented with whatever comes his way, of steady mind,
Homeless, [but] loyal, devoted and devout.

20. But as for those who reverence these deathless [words]
Of righteousness (*dharmya*) which I have just now spoken,
Putting their faith [in them], making Me their goal,
My loving devotees (*bhakta*) – these do I love exceedingly.

XIII

Arjuna said:
0.[82] What is Nature? What the 'person'?
What the 'field', and what its knower?
This, Kṛṣṇa, would I know.
What too is knowledge? What that which should be known?

The Blessed Lord said:
1. This body
Is called the 'field',
And he who knows it is the 'knower of the field',
Or so it has been said by men who know it.

2. Know that I am the 'knower of the field'
In every field;
Knowledge of [this] field and [this] knower of the field
I deem to be [true] knowledge.

3. What the field is and what it is like,
What are its changes and which derives from which,
And who He is [the knower of the field,] and what his powers[83]
Hear now from Me in brief.

4. In many ways has it been sung by seers,
In varied hymns, each in its separate way,
In aphoristic verses concerning Brahman,
Well reasoned and conclusive.

82 Most MSS omit this verse.
83 Var. 'nature'.

5. Gross elements, the ego,
Intellect (*buddhi*), the Unmanifest,
The eleven senses
And the five sense-objects on which the senses thrive,

6. Desire, hate, pleasure, pain,
Sensus communis,[84] thought and constancy –
These, in briefest span, are called the 'field'
Together with its changes.

7. To shun conceit and tricky ways,
To wish none harm, to be long-suffering and upright,
To reverence one's preceptor, purity,
Steadfastness, self-restraint,

8. Detachment from the things of sense,
And selflessness most certainly,
Insight into birth, death, old age, disease and pain –
And what constitutes their worthlessness,

9. To be detached and not to cling
To sons, wives, houses and the like,
A constant equal-mindedness
Whatever happens, pleasing or unpleasing,

10. Unswerving loyalty and love (*bhakti*) for Me
With spiritual exercise (*yoga*) on no other bent,
To dwell apart in desert place,
To take no pleasure in the company of men,

11. Constant devotion to the wisdom appertaining to self,
To see where knowledge of reality must lead,
[All] this is 'knowledge' – or so it has been said.
Ignorance is what is otherwise than this.

12. [And now] shall I tell thee that which should be known:
Once a man knows it, he attains to immortality.
All-Highest[85] Brahman is It called – beginningless –
Call it not 'Being', [call it] not 'Not-Being'.

13. Hands and feet It has on every side,
On every side eyes, heads, mouths and ears;

84 Uncertain.
85 Var. 'dependent on Me', 'suffused in Me'.

In the world all things encompassing
[Changeless] It abides.

14. Devoid of all the senses,
It yet sheds light on[86] all their qualities,
[From all] detached, and yet supporting all;
Free from Nature's constituents,[87] It yet experiences them.

15. Within all beings, yet without them;
Unmoved, It moves in very truth;
So subtle It is you cannot comprehend It;
Far off It stands, and yet how near It is!

16. Undivided, in beings It abides
Seeming divided:
This is That which should be known –
[The One] who upholds, devours and generates [all] beings.

17. Light of lights,
'Beyond the darkness' It is called;
[True] knowledge, what should be known, accessible to knowledge,
Abiding in the heart of all.

18. And so in brief I have explained
The 'field' and 'knowledge' and 'that which should be known';
The man who loves and worships (*bhakta*) Me, on knowing this,
Becomes fit [to share in] my own mode of being.

19. 'Person' and 'Nature': [what are these?]
Both are beginningless, this know.
And know that change and quality[88]
Arise from Nature.

20. Nature, they say, is [itself] the cause
Of cause,[89] effect and agency,
While 'person' is said to be the cause
In the experience of pleasure and of pain.

21. For [this] 'person' is lodged in Nature,
Experiencing its 'constituents';

86 Or, 'has the semblance of'.
87 Or, 'qualities'.
88 Or, 'the constituents of Nature'.
89 Reading *kāraṇa*.

Because he attaches himself to these,
He comes to birth in good and evil wombs.

22. [And yet another One there is who,] surveying and approving,
Supports and [Himself] experiences [the constituents of Nature],
The Mighty Lord: 'All-Highest Self' some call Him,
'All-highest Person' in this body.

23. Who 'person' knows and Nature
And Nature's constituents to be such,
Whatever his station be in life,
He is not born again.

24. By meditation some themselves
See self in self,
Others by putting sound reason into practice (*sāṁkhyayoga*),
Yet others by the exercise (*yoga*) of works (*karma*).

25. But some, not knowing thus,
Hear it from others and revere it;
And even these, taking their stand on Scripture,[90]
Pass beyond death indeed.

26. Whatever being comes to be,
Be it motionless or moving,
[Derives its being] from the union
Of 'field' and 'Knower of the field': this know.

27. The same in all contingent beings,
Abiding [without change], the All-Highest Lord,
When all things fall to ruin, [Himself] knows no destruction:
Who sees Him, sees [indeed].

28. For seeing Him the same, the Lord,
Established everywhere,
He cannot of himself to [him]self[91] do hurt;
Hence he treads on the highest Way.[92]

29. Nature it is which in every way
Does works [and acts];

90 Or, 'what they hear'.
91 Or, 'the Self'.
92 Or, 'goal'.

No agent is the self: who sees it thus,
He sees indeed.

30. When once a man can see that [all] the diversity
Of contingent beings abides in One [alone],
And from That alone they radiate,
Then to Brahman he attains.

31. Because this All-Highest Self knows no beginning,
No quality,[93] it passes not away;
Though abiding in [many a] body,
He does not act nor is He defiled.

32. Just as the ether, roving everywhere,
Knows no defilement, so subtle [is its essence],
So does this Self, though everywhere abiding
And embodied, know no defilement.

33. As the one sun lights up
This whole universe,
So does the 'Knower of the field'
Illumine [this] whole 'field'.

34. Whoso with wisdom's eye discerns the difference
Between 'field' and 'Knower of the field',
And knows deliverance from beings in their material (*prakṛti*) form,
Treads on the highest Way.[94]

XIV

The Blessed Lord said:
1. [And now] again I shall proclaim
The highest wisdom, best of doctrines (*jñāna*);
On knowing this all sages, when they passed on hence,
Attained the highest prize.

2. With this wisdom as their bulwark
They reached a rank [in the order of existence] equivalent to (*sādharmya*) my own;

93 Or, 'constituent of Nature'.
94 Or, 'goes to the highest goal'. This alternative will no longer be noted.

And even when [the universe is once again] engendered, they are not born [again],
And when [again] it is dissolved, they know no trepidation.

3. Great Brahman is to Me a womb,
In it I plant the seed:
From this derives the origin
Of all contingent beings.

4. In whatever womb whatever form
Arises and grows together,
Of [all] those [forms] great Brahman is the womb,
I the father, giver of the seed.

5. Goodness – Passion – Darkness:
These are the 'constituents' from Nature sprung.
They bind the embodied soul
In the body, though [the soul itself is] changeless.

6. Among these Goodness, being immaculate,
Knowing no sickness, dispenses light,
[And yet] it binds by [causing the soul] to cling
To wisdom and to joy (*sukha*).

7. Passion is instinct with desire: this know.
From craving and attachment it wells up:
It binds the embodied soul
By [causing it] to cling to works.

8. From ignorance is Darkness born: mark this well.
All embodied souls it leads astray.
With fecklessness and sloth and sleepiness
It binds.

9. Goodness causes a man to cling to joy,
Passion to works;
But Darkness, stifling wisdom,
Attaches to fecklessness.

10. Once Passion and Darkness it dominates,
Goodness comes to grow;[95]
So Passion and Darkness
When they dominate the other two.

95 Reading *vardhate*.

11. When at all this body's gates
Wisdom's light arises,
Then must thou know
That Goodness has increased.

12. When Passion's waxing strong,
These [states] arise:
Greed, [purposeful] activity, committing oneself to works,
Ambition and disquiet.

13. When Darkness is surging up,
These [states] arise:
Unlighted darkness, unwillingness to act,
Delusion, fecklessness.

14. But when an embodied soul comes face to face with the body's dissolution,
And Goodness [then] prevails,
Then will he reach the spotless worlds
Of those who know the highest.

15. [Another] goes to his demise when Passion [predominates];
He will be born among such men as cling to works:
And as to him who dies when Darkness [has the upper hand],
He will be born in wombs of deluded fools.

16. Of works well done, they say,
The fruits belong to Goodness, being without spot:
Pain is the fruit of Passion,
Ignorance of Darkness.

17. From Goodness wisdom springs,
From Passion greed,
From Darkness delusion, fecklessness,
And ignorance – how not?

18. Upward is the path of those who abide in Goodness,
In the middle stand the men of Passion.
Stuck in the modes of the vilest constituent,
The men of Darkness go below.

19. When the watching [self] sees that there is no agent
Other than [these] constituents,
And knows what is beyond them,

Then will he come [to share]
In that mode of being which is Mine.

20. Transcending these three constituents
Which give the body its existence,[96]
From birth and death, old age and pain delivered,
The embodied soul wins immortality.

Arjuna said:
21. What signs, Lord, mark him out –
[This man] who has transcended the three constituents?
How does he behave? And how does he step out beyond
These three constituents?

The Blessed Lord said:
22. Radiance – activity – yes, delusion too –
When they arise, he hates them not;
And when [in turn] they cease,
He pines not after them.

23. Indifferent he sits,
By the 'constituents' unruffled:
'So the constituents are busy', thus he thinks:
Firm-based is he, unquivering,

24. The same in pleasure as in pain, and self-assured,
The same when faced with clods of earth or stones or gold;
For him, the wise, are friend and foe of equal weight,
Equal the praise or blame [with which men cover him];

25. Equal [his mind] in honour and disgrace,
Equal to ally and to enemy,
He renounces every [busy] enterprise:
'He has transcended the "constituents"': so must men say.

26. And as to those who do Me honour with spiritual exercise (*yoga*)
In loyalty and love (*bhakti*) undeviating,
Passed [clean] beyond these 'constituents',
To becoming Brahman they're conformed.

27. For I am the base supporting Brahman –
Immortal [Brahman] Which knows no change –

96 Or, 'arising from the body'.

[Supporting too] the eternal law of righteousness (*dharma*)
And absolute beatitude (*sukha*).

XV

The Blessed Lord said:
1. With roots above and boughs beneath,
They say, the undying fig tree [stands]:
Its leaves are the [Vedic] hymns:
Who knows it, knows the Veda.

2. Below, above, its branches straggle out,
Well nourished by the constituents; sense-objects are its twigs.
Below, its roots proliferate
Inseparably linked with works in the world of men.

3. No form of it can here be comprehended,
No end and no beginning, no sure abiding-place:
This fig tree with its roots so fatly nourished –
[Take] the stout axe of detachment and cut it down!

4. And then search out that [high] estate[97]
To which, when once men go, they come not back again.
I fly for succour to that Primeval Person
'From whom flowed forth primordial creativity (*pravṛtti*)'.

5. Not proud, not fooled, [all] taint of attachment crushed,
Ever abiding in what concerns the self, desire suppressed,
Released from [all] dualities made known in pleasure as in pain,
The undeluded march ahead to that state[98] which knows no change.

6. That [state] is not illumined
By sun or moon or fire:
Once men go thither, they come not back again,
For that is my all-highest home (*dhāma*).

7. In the world of living things a [minute] part of Me,
Eternal [still], becomes a living [self],
Drawing to itself the five senses and the mind
Which have their roots in Nature.

97 Or, 'place, region'. Var. *para*, 'the highest'.
98 Or, 'place, region'.

8. When [this] sovereign [self] takes on a body
And when he rises up therefrom,
He takes them [with him], moving on,
As the wind [wafts] scents away from their proper home.

9. Ear, eye, touch, taste and smell
He turns to due account;
So too the mind;
[With these] he moves among the things of sense.

10. Whether he rise up [from the body] or remain therein,
Or whether, through contact with the constituents, he tastes experience,
Fools do not perceive him;
But whoso possesses wisdom's eye sees him [indeed].

11. And Yogins, fighting the [spirit's] fight,
See him established in the self;
Not so those men whose self is unperfected –
However much they strive, witless, they see him not.

12. The splendour centred in the sun
Which bathes the whole world in light,
[The splendour] in the moon and fire –
Know that it [all] derives from Me.

13. [Thus] too I penetrate the earth and so sustain
[All] beings with my strength;
Becoming [the moon-plant] Soma, the very sap [of life],
I cause all healing herbs to grow.

14. Becoming the digestive fire, I dwell
In the body of all that breathes;
Conjoined with the inward and outward breaths,
I digest the fourfold food.

15. I make my dwelling in the hearts of all:
From Me stem memory, wisdom refuting [doubt].[99]
Through all the Vedas it is I that should be known,
For the Maker of the Veda's end[100] am I, and I the Vedas know.

99 Uncertain.
100 *Vedānta*, i.e. the Upanishads.

16. In this world there are these two 'persons' –
Perishable the one, Imperishable the other:
The perishable is all contingent beings,
The Imperishable they call 'the sublime, aloof' (*kūṭastha*).

17. But there is [yet] another Person, the [All-]Sublime (*uttama*),
Surnamed 'All-Highest Self':
The three worlds he enters and pervades,
Sustaining them – the Lord who passes not away.

18. Since I transcend the perishable,
And am more exalted than the Imperishable itself,
So am I extolled in common as in Vedic speech
As 'the Person [All-]Sublime'.

19. Whoever knows Me, unconfused,
As 'the Person [All-]Sublime',
Knows all and [knowing all] communes with (*bhaj-*) Me
With all his being (*bhāva*), all his love (*bhāva*).

20. And so have I [at last] revealed
This most mysterious doctrine:
Let a man but understand it, for then he'll be
A man who [truly] understands, his [life's] work done.

XVI

The Blessed Lord said:
1. Fearless and pure in heart,
Steadfast in the exercise (*yoga*) of wisdom,
Restrained and open-handed, performing sacrifice,
Intent on studying Holy Writ, ascetic and upright,

2. None hurting, truthful, from anger free,
Renouncing [all], at peace, averse to calumny,
Compassionate to [all] existent beings, free from nagging greed,
Gentle, modest, never fickle,

3. Ardent, patient, enduring, pure,
Not treacherous nor arrogant –
Such is the man who's born [to inherit]
A godly destiny.

4. A hypocrite, proud of himself and arrogant,
Angry, harsh and ignorant
Is the man who's born [to inherit]
A devilish destiny.

5. A godly destiny means deliverance,
A devilish one enslavement; this is the usual view.
But fret not, Ariuna, for thou art born
To a godly destiny.

6. Two orders of contingent beings in this world there are:
The godly and the devilish.
Of the godly I have discoursed enough,
Now listen to my words about the devilish.

7. Of creative action (*pravṛtti*) and its cessation (*nivṛtti*)
The devilish folk know nothing;
In them thou'lt find no purity nor yet
Seemly behaviour or truthfulness.

8. 'The world's devoid of truth,' they say,
'It has no ground, no ruling Lord;
It has not come to be by mutual causal law;
Desire alone has caused it,[101] nothing else.'

9. Fast holding to these views,
Lost souls (*ātman*) with feeble minds,
They embark on cruel and violent deeds – malignant
[In their lust] for the destruction of the world.

10. Insatiate desire's their starting-point –
Maddened are they by hypocrisy and pride,[102]
Clutching at false conceptions, deluded as they are,
Plying their several trades: impure are their resolves.

11. Unmeasured care is theirs
Right up to the time of death,
[For] they aim at nothing but to satisfy their lusts,
Convinced that this is all.

12. Bound by a hundred fetters [forged] by hope,
Obsessed by anger and desire,

101 Var. 'random, without any cause'.
102 Or, 'possessed by hypocrisy, pride and frenzy'.

They seek to build up wealth unjustly
To satisfy their lusts.

13. 'This have I gained today,
This whim I'll satisfy;
This wealth is mine, and much more too
Will be mine as time goes on.

14. He was an enemy of mine; I've killed him,
And many another too I'll kill.
I'm master [here], I take my pleasure [as I will];
I'm strong and happy and successful!

15. I'm rich and of a good family.
Who else can match himself with me?
I'll sacrifice and I'll give alms:
[Why not?] I'll have a marvellous time!'
So speaks [the fool] deluded in his ignorance!

16. [Their minds] unhinged by many a [foolish] fancy,
Caught up in delusion's snare,
Obsessed [by one thought only]; 'I must satisfy my lusts' –
Into foul hell they fall.

17. Puffed up with self-conceit, unbending,
Maddened by their pride in wealth,[103]
They offer sacrifices that are but sacrifice in name
And not in the way prescribed – the hypocrites!

18. Selfishness, force and pride,
Desire and anger – these do they rely on,
Envying and hating Me
Who dwell in their bodies as I dwell in all.

19. Birth after birth in this revolving round
These vilest among men, strangers to [all] good,
Obsessed with hate and cruel, I hurl
Into devilish wombs.

20. Caught up in devilish wombs,
Birth after birth deluded,
They never attain to Me:
And so they tread the lowest path.

103 Or, 'filled with the madness and pride of wealth'.

21. Desire – Anger – Greed:
This is the triple gate of hell,
Destruction of the self:
Therefore avoid these three.

22. When once a man is freed
From these three gates of darkness,
Then can he work for self's salvation (*śreyas*),
Thence tread the highest Way.

23. Whoso forsakes the ordinance of Scripture
And lives at the whim of his own desires,
Wins not perfection, [finds] no comfort (*sukha*),
[Treads not] the highest Way.

24. Therefore let Scripture be thy norm,
Determining what is right and wrong.
Once thou dost know what the ordinance of Scripture bids thee do,
Then shouldst thou here perform the works [therein prescribed].

XVII

Arjuna said:
1. [And yet there are some] who forsake the ordinance of Scripture,
And offer sacrifice, full filled with faith.
Kṛṣṇa, where do they stand?
On Goodness, Passion or on Darkness?

The Blessed Lord said:
2. Threefold is the faith of embodied souls;
[Each of the three] springs from [a man's own] nature.
[The first is] of Goodness, [the second] of Passion,
[The third] of Darkness. Listen to this.

3. Faith is connatural to the soul (*sattva*)
Of every man:
Man is instinct with faith:
As is his faith, so too must he be.

4. To the gods do men of Goodness offer sacrifice,
To sprites and monsters men of Passion;

To ghosts and the assembled spirits of the dead
The others – men of Darkness – offer sacrifice.

5–6. And this know too. Some men there are
Who, without regard to Scripture's words, savagely mortify [their flesh],
Buoyed up by hypocrisy and self-regard,
Yielding to the violence of passion and desire,

And so torment the mass of living things
Whose home their body is, the witless fools –
And [with] them Me Myself within [that same] body hidden:
How devilish their intentions!

7. Threefold again is food –
[Food] that agrees with each [different type of] man:
So too sacrifice, ascetic practice and the gift of alms.
Listen to the difference between them.

8. Food that promotes a fuller life, strength, health,
Vitality (*sattva*),[104] pleasure and good-feeling –
[Foods that are] savoury, rich in oil, and firm,
Heart-gladdening: these are agreeable to the man of Goodness.

9. Foods that are pungent, sour, salty, stinging hot,
Sharp, rough and burning – these are what
The man of Passion loves. And they it is that cause
Pain, misery and sickness.

10. Whatever's stale and tasteless
Rotten and decayed –
Leavings, what's unfit for sacrifice,
Is food agreeable to the man of Darkness.

11. The sacrifice approved by sacred ordinance
And offered up by men who would not taste its fruits,
Who concentrate their minds on this [alone]:
'In this sacrifice lies duty': [such sacrifice] belongs to Goodness.

12. But the sacrifice that is offered up by men
Who bear its fruits in mind,

104 Or, 'soul', 'mind' or 'courage'.

Or simply for vain display,
Know that [such sacrifice] belongs to Passion.

13. The sacrifice in which no proper rite is followed, no food distributed,
No sacred words recited, no Brāhman's fees paid up,
No faith enshrined – [such sacrifice]
Men say belongs to Darkness.

14. [Due] reverence of gods and Brāhmans,
Preceptors and wise men,
Purity, uprightness, chastity, refusal to do harm –
This is [true] penance of the body.

15. Words that do not cause disquiet,
[Words] truthful, kind and pleasing,
The constant practice too of sacred recitation –
This is the penance of the tongue.

16. Serenity of mind and friendliness,
Silence and self-restraint,
And the cleansing of one's affections (*bhāva*) –
This is the penance of the mind.

17. When men possessed of highest faith,
Integrated and indifferent to the fruits [of what they do],
Do penance in this threefold wise,
Men speak of penance in Goodness' way.

18. Some mortify themselves to win respect,
Honour and reverence, or from sheer hypocrisy:
Here [on earth] this must be called
Penance in Passion's ways – fickle and unsure.

19. Some mortify themselves following perverted theories,
Torturing themselves,
Or to destroy another:
This is called penance in Darkness' way.

20. Alms given because to give alms is a sacred duty
To one from whom no favour is expected in return
At the [right] place and time and to a [fit] recipient –
This is called alms given in Goodness' way.

21. But [alms] given in expectation of favours in return,
Or for the sake of fruits [to be reaped] hereafter,
[Alms] given too against the grain –
This is called alms given in Passion's way.

22. Alms given at the wrong place and time
To recipients unworthy
Without respect, contemptuously –
This is called [alms given] in Darkness' way.

23. Oṁ, THAT, IT IS: This has been handed down –
A threefold pointer to Brahman:
By It were allotted their proper place of old
Brāhmans, Vedas and sacrifice.

24. And so [all] acts of sacrifice, the giving of alms and penance
Enjoined by [Vedic] ordinances
And ever again enacted by Brahman's devotees
Begin with the utterance of [the one word] Oṁ.

25. THAT: [so saying,] do men who hanker for deliverance
Perform the various acts of sacrifice,
Penance and the gift of alms,
Having no thought for the fruits [they bring].

26. IT IS (*sat*): in this the meanings are conjoined
Of 'Being' and of 'good':
So too the [same] word *sat* is appropriately used
For works that call forth praise.

27. In sacrifice, in penance, in the gift of alms
[The same word] *sat* is used, meaning 'steadfastness':
And works performed with these purposes in mind,
[These] too are surnamed *sat*.

28. Whatever offering is made in unbelief,
Whatever given, whatever act of penance undertaken,
Whatever done – of that is said *asat*, 'it is not':
For naught it is in this world and the next.

XVIII

Arjuna said:
1. Kṛṣṇa, fain would I hear the truth

Concerning renunciation,
And apart from this
[The truth] of self-surrender.

The Blessed Lord said:
2. To give up works dictated by desire,
Wise men allow this to be renunciation;
Surrender of all the fruits [that accrue] to works
Discerning men call self-surrender.

3. '[All] works must be surrendered, [for works themselves are] tainted with defect':
So say some of the wise;
But others say that works of sacrifice, the gift of alms
And works of penance are not to be surrendered.

4. Hear then mine own decision
In [this matter of] surrender:
Threefold is [the act of] self-surrender;
So has it been declared.

5. Works of sacrifice, the gift of alms and works of penance
Are not to be surrendered; these must most certainly be done;
It is sacrifice, alms-giving and ascetic practice
That purify the wise.

6. But even those works should be done [in a spirit of self-surrender]
For [all] attachment to what you do and [all] the fruits [of what you do]
Must be surrendered.
This is my last decisive word.[105]

7. For to renounce a work enjoined [by Scripture]
Is inappropriate;
Deludedly to give this up
Is [the way] of Darkness. This [too] has been declared.

8. The man who gives up a deed simply because it causes pain
Or because he shrinks from bodily distress,
Commits an act of self-surrender that accords with Passion's way;
Assuredly he will not reap surrender's fruit.

105 Lit. 'thought'.

9. But if a work is done simply because it should be done
And is work enjoined [by Scripture],
And if [all] attachment, [all thought of] fruit is given up,
Then [that work is done] in Goodness' way, I deem.

10. The self-surrendered man, suffused with Goodness, wise,
Whose [every] doubt is cut away,
Hates not his uncongenial work
Nor cleaves to the congenial.

11. For one still in the body it is not possible
To surrender up all works without exception;
Rather it is he who surrenders up the *fruits* of works
Who deserves the name 'a self-surrendered man'.

12. Unwanted – wanted – mixed:
Threefold is the fruit of work –
[This they experience] at death who have not surrendered [self],
But not at all such men who have renounced.

13. In the system of the Sāṁkhyas
Five factors are laid down;
By these all works attain fruition.
Learn them from Me.

14. Material basis, agent,
Instruments of various kinds,
The vast variety of motions,
And fate, the fifth and last:

15. These are the five factors
Of whatever work a man may undertake,
Of body, speech or mind,
No matter whether right or wrong.

16. Since this is so, the man who sees in self alone
The agent, does not see [at all].
Untrained is his intelligence,
And evil are his thoughts.

17. A man who's reached a state where there is no sense of 'I',
Whose soul (*buddhi*) is undefiled –
Were he to slaughter [all] these worlds,
Slays nothing. He is not bound.

18. Knowledge – its object – knower: –
[These form] the threefold instrumental cause of action (*karma*).
Instrument – action – agent:
[Such is] action's threefold nexus.

19. Knowledge – action – agent: –
[These too are] three in kind, distinguished by 'constituent'.
The theory of 'constituents' contains it [all]:
Listen to the manner of these [three].

20. That [kind of] knowledge by which one sees
One mode of being, changeless, undivided
In all contingent beings, divided [as they are],
Is Goodness' [knowledge]. Be sure of this.

21. But that [kind of] knowledge which in all contingent beings
Discerns in separation all manner of modes of being,
Different and distinct –
This thou must know is knowledge [born] of Passion.

22. But that [kind of knowledge] which sticks to one effect
As if it were all – irrational,
Not bothering about the Real as the [true] object [of all knowledge],
This trifling [knowledge] is Darkness' own. So is it laid down.

23. The work (*karma*) of obligation, from [all] attachment free,
Performed without passion, without hate,
By one who hankers not for fruits,
Is called [the work] of Goodness.

24. The work in which much effort is expended
By one who seeks his own pleasure and desire
And ever thinks, 'It is I myself who do it',
Such [work]'s assigned to Passion.

25. The work embarked on by a man deluded
Who has no thought of consequence, nor cares at all
For the loss and hurt [he causes others] or for the human part
He plays himself, is called [a work] of Darkness.

26. The agent who, from attachment freed,
Steadfast and resolute,

Remains unchanged in failure or success,
And never speaks of 'I', is called [an agent] in Goodness' way.

27. The agent who pursues the fruits of works,
Passionate, greedy, intent on doing harm, impure,
A prey to exultation as to grief,
Is widely known [to act] in Passion's way.

28. The agent, inept (*ayukta*) and vulgar, stiff and proud,
A cheat, low-spoken,[106] slothful,
Who's subject to depression, who procrastinates,
Is called [an agent] in Darkness' way.

29. Divided threefold too are intellect (*buddhi*) and constancy
According to the constituents. Listen [to Me,
For I shall] tell it forth in all its many forms,
Omitting nothing.

30. The intellect that distinguishes between activity
And its cessation, between what should be done and what should not,
Between danger and security, bondage and release,
Is [an intellect] in Goodness' way.

31. The intellect by which lawful right (*dharma*) and lawless wrong,
What should be done and what should not
Are untruly understood,
Is [an intellect] in Passion's way.

32. The intellect which, by Darkness overcast,
Thinks right is wrong, law lawlessness,
All things their opposite,[107]
Is [an intellect] in Darkness' way.

33. The constancy by which a man holds fast
In check the works of mind and breath and sense,
Unswerving in self-discipline (*yoga*),
Is constancy in Goodness' way.

34. The constancy by which a man holds fast
[In balance] pleasure, self-interest and righteousness,

106 Or, 'dishonest'.
107 Or, 'all things contrary [to truth]'.

Yet clings to them, desirous of their fruits,
Is constancy in Passion's way.

35. [The constancy] by which a fool
Will not let go sleep, fear or grief,
Depression or exaltation,
Is constancy in Darkness' way.

36. Threefold too is pleasure:
Arjuna, hear this now from Me.
[That pleasure] which a man enjoys after much effort spent,
Making an end thereby of suffering,

37. Which at first seems more like poison
But in time transmutes itself into what seems to be
Ambrosia – is called pleasure in Goodness' way,
For it springs from that serenity which comes from apperception of the self.[108]

38. [That pleasure] which at first seems like ambrosia,
Arising when the senses meet the things of sense,
But in time transmutes itself into what seems to be
Poison, that pleasure, so it's said, is in Passion's way.

39. [That pleasure] which at first
And in the sequel leads the self astray,
Which derives from sleep and sloth and fecklessness,
Has been condemned[109] as pleasure in Darkness' way.

40. There is no existent thing in heaven or on earth
Nor yet among the gods,
Which is or ever could be free
From these three constituents from Nature sprung.

41. To Brāhmans, princes, artisans and serfs
Works have been variously assigned
By [these] constituents,
And they arise from the nature of things as they are (*svabhāva*).

42. Calm, self-restraint, ascetic practice, purity,
Long-suffering and uprightness,

108 *ātma-buddhi-prasāda*: Or, 'of one's own intellect (soul)' or 'of intellect and self'.

109 Lit. 'declared'.

Wisdom in theory as in practice, religious faith –
[These] are the works of Brāhmans, inhering in their nature.

43. High courage, ardour, endurance, skill,
In battle unwillingness to flee,
An open hand, a lordly mien –
[These] are the works of princes, inhering in their nature [too].

44. To till the fields, protect the kine and to engage in trade –
[These] are the works of artisans, inhering in their nature;
But works whose very soul is service
Inhere in the very nature of the serf.

45. By [doing] the work that is proper to him [and] rejoicing
[in the doing],
A man succeeds, perfects himself.
[Now] hear just how a man perfects himself
By [doing and] rejoicing in his proper work.

46. By dedicating the work that is proper [to his caste]
To Him who is the source of all beings' activity (*pravṛtti*),
By whom this whole universe was spun,[110]
A man attains perfection and success.

47. Better to do one's own [caste] duty, though devoid of merit,
Than to do another's, however well performed.
By doing the works prescribed by his own nature
A man meets with no defilement.

48. Never should a man give up the works to which he's born,
Defective though they be;
For every enterprise is choked
By defects, as fire by smoke.

49. With soul (*buddhi*) detached from everything,
With self subdued, all longing gone,
Renounce: and so thou'lt find complete success,
Perfection, works transcended (*naiṣkarmya*).

50. Perfection found, now learn from Me
How Brahman thou mayst reach.
This briefly [will I tell thee],
It is wisdom's highest bourn.

110 Or, 'pervaded'.

51. Let a man be integrated by his soul (*buddhi*), now cleansed,
Let him restrain [him]self with constancy,
Abandon things of sense – sound and all the rest –
Passion and hate let him cast out;

52. Let him live apart, eat lightly,
Restrain speech, body, mind,
Let him practise meditation constantly,
Let him cultivate dispassion;

53. Let him give up all thought of 'I', force, pride,
Desire and hatred and possessiveness,
Let him not think of anything as 'mine', at peace –
[If he does this,] to becoming Brahman he's conformed.

54. Brahman become, with self serene,
He grieves not nor desires;
The same to all contingent beings,
He gains the highest love and loyalty (*bhakti*) to Me.

55. By love and loyalty he comes to know Me as I really am,
How great I am and who;
And once he knows Me as I am,
He enters [Me] forthwith.

56. Let him then do all manner of works,
Putting his trust in Me;
For by my grace he will attain
To an eternal, changeless state (*pada*).

57. Give up in thought to Me all that thou dost;
Make Me thy goal:
Relying on the Yoga of the soul (*buddhi*),
Think on Me constantly.

58. Thinking on Me thou shalt surmount
All dangers by my grace,
But if through selfishness thou wilt not listen,
Then wilt thou [surely] perish.

59. [But] if thou shouldst think, relying on thine ego,
'I will not fight',
Vain is thy resolution,
[For] Nature will constrain thee.

60. Bound art thou by thine own works
Which spring from thine own nature;
[For] what, deluded, thou wouldst not do,
That wilt thou do perforce.

61. In the region of the heart of all
Contingent beings dwells the Lord,
Twirling them hither and thither by his uncanny power (*māyā*)
[Like puppets] fixed in a machine.

62. In Him alone seek refuge
With all thy being, all thy love (*bhāva*);
And by his grace shalt thou attain
An eternal state, the all-highest peace.

63. Of all mysteries most mysterious
This wisdom have I told thee;
Ponder on it in all its amplitude,
Then do whatever thou wilt.

64. And now again give ear to this my all-highest Word,
Of all the most mysterious:
'I love thee well.'
Therefore will I tell thee thy salvation (*hita*).

65. Bear Me in mind, love Me and worship Me (*bhakta*),
Sacrifice, prostrate thyself to Me:
So shalt thou come to Me, I promise thee
Truly, for thou art dear to Me.

66. Give up all things of law (*dharma*),
Turn to Me, thine only refuge,
[For] I will deliver thee
From all evils; have no care.

67. Never must thou tell this [Word] to one
Whose life is not austere, to one devoid of love and loyalty (*bhakta*),
To one who refuses to obey,
Or one who envies Me.

68. [But] whoever shall proclaim this all-highest mystery
To my loving devotees (*bhakta*),
Showing the while the highest love and loyalty (*bhakti*) to Me,
Shall come to Me in very truth.

69. No one among men can render Me
More pleasing service than a man like this;
Nor shall any other man on earth
Be more beloved of Me than he.

70. And whoso shall read this dialogue
Which I and thou have held concerning what is right (*dharmya*),
It will be as if he had offered Me a sacrifice
Of wisdom: so do I believe.

71. And the man of faith, not cavilling,
Who listens [to this my Word] –
He too shall win deliverance, and attain
To the goodly worlds of those whose works are pure.

72. Hast thou listened, Arjuna, [to these my words]
With mind on them alone intent?
And has the confusion [of thy mind]
That stemmed from ignorance, been dispelled?

Arjuna said:
73. Destroyed is the confusion; and through thy grace
I have regained a proper way of thinking (*smṛti*):
With doubts dispelled I stand
Ready to do thy bidding.

Sañjaya said:
74. So did I hear this wondrous dialogue
Of [Kṛṣṇa,] Vasudeva's son
And the high-souled Arjuna,
[And as I listened,] I shuddered with delight.

75. By Vyāsa's favour have I heard
This highest mystery,
This Yoga from [great] Kṛṣṇa, Yoga's Lord himself,
As he in person told it.

76. O king, as oft as I recall
This marvellous, holy dialogue
Of Arjuna and Kṛṣṇa
I thrill with joy, and thrill with joy again!

77. And as often as I recall that form of Viṣṇu –
Utterly marvellous –

How great is my amazement!
I thrill with joy, and thrill with joy again!

78. Wherever Kṛṣṇa, the Lord of Yoga, is,
Wherever Arjuna, Pṛthā's son,
There is good fortune, victory, success,
Sound policy assured. This do I believe.

From the

YĀJÑAVALKYA-SMṚTI

THE LAW BOOK OF YĀJÑAVALKYA

CHAPTER 1 (CONDUCT)

1. The sages venerated the lord of yogins, Yājñavalkya, and said, 'Teach us all the moral duties (*dharmān*) of the [four] estates, the [four] walks of life[1] and of those outside these (*varṇāśrametarāṇām*).'

The lord of yogins, who was [then] at Mithilā, reflected a while and spoke to the sages:

2. Know that these are the moral duties of the land where the blackbuck [naturally lives].[2]

3. The Vedas, together with the Purāṇas,[3] the [system of logic and natural philosophy called] Nyāya, the [exegetical school of] Mīmāṃsā, treatises on moral duty (*dharmaśāstra*), and the [six classes of work that are] necessary auxiliaries (*aṅga*) [to the Veda, namely pronunciation, prosody, grammar, word-derivation, astronomy and ritual (*kalpa*)] are the fourteen bases of knowledge and moral duty (*vidyānāṃ dharmasya ca*).

4–5. Manu, Atri, Viṣṇu, Hārīta, Yājñavalkya, Uśanas, Aṅgiras, Yama, Āpastamba, Saṃvarta, Kātyāyana, Bṛhaspati, Parāśara, Vyāsa, Śaṅkha, Likhita, Dakṣa, Gautama, Śātātapa and Vasiṣṭha are the promulgators of treatises on moral duty.

6. When something is given with faith, in [the correct] place, time and manner to a [worthy] recipient – all [these are the necessary conditions that] define [acts of] moral duty (*dharmalakṣaṇam*).

1 Those of student (*brahmacārin*), married man (*gṛhastha*), forest-dweller (*vānaprastha*), and renunciant who has internalized the Vedic fires (*sannyāsin*).

2 *Antilope cervicapra* (Linnaeus). These antelope live in open plains where there is scrub or cultivation. They avoid dense forest, mountains and marshland. Ideally the twice-born (for which see 1:39) were not to live outside the natural habitat of the blackbuck, which was coterminous with a large area of North Central India.

3 Viśvarūpa seeks to include the epics under this head. It is striking that they are not mentioned here.

7. Vedic revelation (*śrutiḥ*) and lower revelation (*smṛtiḥ*),[4] the conduct of good men, one's own preference, and desire born of good resolutions (*samyaksaṃkalpajaḥ*) are held to be the sources of [knowledge of] moral duties (*dharmamūlam*).
8. Among sacrifice, good conduct, self-control (*dama*), not harming living beings (*ahiṃsā*), giving and performing one's personal daily recitation (*svādhyāya*) – among all these works the highest moral duty (*paramo dharmaḥ*) is the perception of the soul through yoga.
9. An assembly [for settling matters of doubt] is [formed by] four men who know the Vedas and [the treatises on] moral duty, or by a group of men who know three Vedas.[5] What that [assembly] teaches is law (*dharmaḥ*). [In their absence what is taught by] one [man] who thoroughly knows about the soul [is law].

[*The Student*]

10. The [four] estates are those of the Brahmin, the Kṣatriya, the Vaiśya, and the Śūdra. The first three are twice-born.[6] Their rituals – beginning with [that at] insemination and ending with [that at] the cremation ground – are accompanied by [Vedic] mantras.
11. The rite at conception (*garbhādhānam*) takes place in [the wife's fertile] season;[7] that of the producing of a male child (*puṃsaḥ savanam*) takes place before the foetus moves; that of parting the mother's hair (*sīmantaḥ*) takes place in the sixth or eighth month; and the birth-rite, once [the child has] come forth.
12. On the eleventh day [is performed] the naming ceremony; in the fourth month, the ceremony of going out [from the house to be shown the sun and moon] (*niṣkramaḥ*); in the sixth month,

4 The word for Vedic revelation, *śruti*, means 'hearing' and that for lower revelation, *smṛti*, means 'remembering' (for which see Introduction pp. xx–xxi). The category of lower revelation is elastic; what Yājñavalkya understands thereby is probably what he has enumerated in verses 3–5, but Vijñāneśvara would include only treatises on *dharma*. Each member of the list in this verse is overruled by the previous member.

5 What is probably intended is that the fuller assembly contain at least four men: three who know a Veda each (excluding the *Atharva-Veda* as in 1:101) and one who knows treatises on moral duty. The smaller assembly is one of at least three men who know a Veda each. (This would be consistent with *Manusmṛti* 12:111–12.)

6 This appellation is explained in 1:39.

7 This is defined in 1:79.

that of the eating of [solid] food (*annaprāśanam*). [That of] the tonsure (*cūḍā*) should be performed according to family [practice].

13. Thereby the evil (*enaḥ*) that arises from semen and the womb is laid to rest. These rites [starting from the birth rite] are performed silently for female offspring; but the marriage ceremony [*is* performed] with mantras.

14. In the eighth year from conception or in the eighth [from birth] the Brahmin is to receive initiation[8] (*upanāyanam*), Kṣatriyas in the eleventh, Vaiśyas in the twelfth [or], some [say], according to family practice.

15. After initiating his pupil the preceptor should, after [teaching him] the great utterances,[9] teach him to recite the Veda and should instruct him in the rules of conduct relating to purity.

16. By day and at the junctions [of dawn and dusk] he should urinate and excrete with his sacred thread [looped] over his [right] ear, facing north, [but] facing south if at night.

17. Holding his penis he should stand up and assiduously cleanse [himself] with [handfuls of] earth and water that he lifts up[10] so that he removes all dirt and smell.

18. [After placing his hands] between his knees, seated in a pure place facing north or east the twice-born man should always sip water with the [part of the right hand called the] ford of brahman.

19. The bases of the little finger, the index and the thumb, and the forepart of the palm are respectively [called] the fords of Prajāpati, of the Ancestors, of brahman, and of the gods.

20. After thrice swallowing water and twice wiping his mouth he should touch the orifices [of his head] with water – but with water that is in its natural state, free of foam and bubbles.

21. The [three groups of] twice-born men are purified respectively

8 This is commonly associated with the investiture with the sacred triple thread that the twice-born are entitled to wear (usually hung over the left shoulder so that it hangs down the right side); but this investiture does not always seem to have been part of the ceremony. Among other rites the preceptor shows the initiand the sun, has him put a piece of firewood on the fire, ties a girdle about the boy's waist, and gives him a staff. This initiation entitles and binds the boy to Vedic study under the preceptor.

9 These are the names of the seven worlds of the orthodox brahmanical cosmos. In ascending order these are: *bhūḥ, bhuvaḥ, svaḥ, mahaḥ, janaḥ, tapaḥ, satya.*

10 Vijñāneśvara explains that this expresses that he may not cleanse himself *in* water.

by [water] reaching the heart, the throat and the palate, and a woman and a Śūdra by [water] touching at the tip [of the lips[11]].
22. Every day [in the morning] he should bathe, rub his body with mantras dedicated to water,[12] practise control over the vital breaths (*prāṇāyāmaḥ*), venerate the sun and recite the Gāyatrī.[13]
23. [While controlling his breath] he should thrice recite the Gāyatrī with the head[14] preceded by the utterances each in turn [prefaced] with the syllable *oṃ*. This is the control of the vital breaths.
24. [In the evening] after practising control over the vital breaths, sprinkling [the body with water] to the accompaniment of the [aforementioned] three verses of the *Ṛg-Veda* dedicated to water, he should sit reciting the Gāyatrī facing west until the stars rise.
25. At the morning junction he should remain facing east in the same way until the sun rises. At both junctions he should then perform what must be done for the fire.[15]
26. Then he should greet his elders saying, 'I, so and so, am here.' And he should attend on his preceptor concentratedly for the sake of his personal daily recitation (*svādhyāyārtham*).
27. And he should study when called on and he should give what he receives [on his alms round] to him. And he should always do what is to his [teacher's] benefit in deeds of thought, word and body.
28. The grateful, the gentle, the intelligent, the pure, the healthy, those who do not point out others' faults are to be instructed according to the law (*dharmataḥ*) – the good, the capable, the fit, those generous with their knowledge and wealth.
29. He should carry a staff, [wear] an animal skin, a sacred thread and a girdle.[16] To sustain himself he should go to Brahmins of impeccable character for alms.

11 Thus Aparārka; of the tongue according to Viśvarūpa.

12 Vijñāneśvara mentions the three verses of the *Ṛg-Veda* starting *āpo hi ṣṭhā* (X, ix.1–3): 'Waters, you are the ones who bring us the life force. Help us to find nourishment so that we may look upon great joy. Let us share in the most delicious sap that you have, as if you were loving mothers. Let us go straight to the house of the one for whom you waters give us life and give us birth.' (Doniger O'Flaherty's translation.)

13 The first item in this anthology.

14 The expression 'head' designates a mantra that starts 'Water, light, juice, nectar . . . ' (*Taittirīya-Āraṇyaka* 10.15.1).

15 He must feed the fire with firewood and oblations.

16 Manu (in 2:41–7) specifies the different materials that should be used for these accoutrements according to which estate the student belongs to.

30. Brahmins, Kṣatriyas, Vaiśyas should mark [their requests for alms when they go on] their alms round with the word 'Madam!' (*bhavacchabda-*) [placed] respectively at the beginning, middle and end [of their request].
31. After he has performed what must be done to [feed and kindle] the fire, he should, with the permission of his preceptor, eat in silence after peforming the rite [consisting of saying the prayer 'You are a bed for nectar' and of rinsing his mouth] that ensures nourishment (*āpośānakriyāpūrvaṃ*),[17] revering the food and not speaking ill of it.
32. One [observing the celibacy and austerity that are prescribed] in studentship (*brahmacarye*) should not eat [repeatedly just] one [person's] food [taken as alms] except in case of emergency (*anāpadi*). [But] a Brahmin [student] may of course eat at a rite for Ancestors (*śrāddhe*)[18] as long as he does not neglect the observances [of studentship].
33. [Those are that] he should avoid honey, meat, collyrium [for the eyes and ointment for the body],[19] food left over by another (*ucchiṣṭa*), bitter [speech], women, injuring living beings, looking at the sun, vulgar [speech], gossip and so on.
34. One who performs [a man's] rites[20] and hands on to him the Veda is [called] 'preceptor' (*guruḥ*). One who [merely] initiates him and gives him the Veda is called 'teacher' (*ācāryaḥ*).
35. [One who teaches] only part [of the Veda is called] 'instructor' (*upādhyāyaḥ*). He who performs sacrifices [on his behalf] is called the Ṛtvik (priest). These are to be revered in due order [the earliest mentioned first]. The mother is more venerable than [all of] these.
36. For each Veda [he should adhere to the observances enjoined for] studentship for twelve years or for five, or, according to some, until it has been learnt. In the sixteenth year [should be performed the ceremony of] the cutting of the hair (*keśāntaḥ*).
37. Up until [respectively] the sixteenth, the twenty-second and the twenty-fourth year is the last time for initiation of Brahmins, Kṣatriyas and Vaiśyas.
38. After that they fall, excluded from all rights to perform their moral duties (*sarvadharmabahiṣkṛtāḥ*). They lose [the right to

17 For the purpose of this rite see 1:106.
18 Such a rite is performed by one person; hence the appropriateness to the context here.
19 This double translation of *añjana* follows Vijñāneśvara.
20 All the rites from that at conception to initiation according to Vijñāneśvara.

receive] the Gāyatrī. They become outcastes (*vrātyāḥ*) until they perform the [sacrifice that restores the rights forfeited by not performing due purificatory life-cycle rites called the] *vrātyastoma*.

39. Because they are born first from a mother and a second time from being [initiated, when they are] tied with a girdle of muñja grass,[21] Brahmins, Kṣatriyas, and Vaiśyas are taught to be twice-born.

40. Greater than sacrifices and austerities and auspicious rites (*śubhānāṃ caiva karmaṇām*), the Veda alone brings about the supreme good for twice-born men.

41. The twice-born man who daily studies verses of the *Ṛg-Veda* pleases the gods with honey and with milk and the Ancestors with honey and with clarified butter (*ghṛta*).

42. One who daily studies verses of the *Yajur-Veda*, as much as he is able, pleases the gods with clarified butter (*ghṛta*) and with nectar and the Ancestors with clarified butter (*ājya*)[22] and with honey.

43. He who daily recites verses of the *Sāma-Veda* pleases the gods with soma and with clarified butter (*ghṛta*) and delights the Ancestors with honey and clarified butter (*sarpiḥ*).

44. The twice-born who daily recites verses of the *Atharva-Veda*, as much as he is able, pleases the gods with marrow and the Ancestors with honey and clarified butter (*sarpiḥ*).

45–46. Whoever studies, as much as he is able, the portion of the Vedic corpus that is in the form of question and answer (*vākovākyam*), the Purāṇas, the Nārāśaṃsī,[23] Gāthikā hymns,[24] the epics and the sciences (*vidyāḥ*), he pleases the gods with meat, milk, boiled rice and honey, and the Ancestors with honey and clarified butter (*sarpiḥ*).

21 *Saccharum arundinaceum* Retz. In fact only the Brahmins have their girdles of muñja grass; according to Manu (2:41), the Kṣatriyas have theirs made of a bowstring and the Vaiśyas have theirs of hemp.

22 *ghṛta*, *ājya*, and *sarpiḥ* have all been translated 'clarified butter'. The first is thick, the last is thin, but confusingly *ājya* appears to be used as a generic term.

23 The Nārāśaṃsī are hymns in praise of men. Aparārka cites the first line of *Atharva-Veda* XX, cxxvii as an example. *Atharva-Veda* XX, cxxvii–cxxxvi contain this sort of material. Vijñāneśvara takes the word to refer to mantras dedicated to Rudra.

24 Certain Vedic hymns are so called when they are sung rather than recited. Thus Charles Malamoud, *Le Svādhyāya – Récitation du Veda: Taittirīya-Āraṇyaka Livre II* (Paris: Institut de Civilisation Indienne, 1977), p. 175.

47. When these are pleased they please him with the bright fruits of all his desires. Whatever sacrifice he studies he receives its fruit.
48. The twice-born man who always keeps up his [daily] recitation enjoys three times the fruit of giving away treasure hoarded in the earth and [the fruit] of the greatest self-mortification (*tapasaḥ*) in this world (*iha*).
49. The perpetual student should live next to his teacher (*ācārya-sannidhau*), or, if he should be gone, by his [teacher's] daughter, his wife or by his fire.
50. If he wearies (*sādayan*) his body following these prescriptions, [and remains] in control of his organs of sense and action, he attains the world of Brahmā and is not born again in this world.

[*Marriage*]

51. After completing his Veda, or the practices undertaken [as part of studentship], or both, [and] after [thereupon] giving the preceptor a gift, or [if he cannot afford that, then] after getting his permission, he may bathe.[25]
52–3. A man who has not failed in [the observances of] his studentship should marry a woman with [auspicious] marks, one who has not been married to another before, one who pleases him (*kāntām*), not related to him by the offering of the balls of rice (*asapiṇḍām*),[26] younger, free of disease, one who has brothers,

25 The ritual bath (*snānam*) marks the end of the period of studentship. Those who have taken it are known as *snātakas*.

26 This stipulation is intended to define the degrees of consanguinity within which one may not marry. Balls (*piṇḍa*) of rice are regularly offered for the benefit of deceased Ancestors (see 1:217–69). Vijñāneśvara claims the phrase does not refer to the offering of rice-balls, pointing out that one may offer such rice-balls for the sake of those who are not relatives and whom one might therefore marry (as a pupil may for his teacher), and that one need not offer them to maternal relatives, whom one may not marry. Vijñāneśvara therefore ingeniously interprets *sapiṇḍa* to mean 'sharing part of the same flesh' (rather than 'sharing the offering of rice'), and he understands the second half of verse 53 as defining the limits of this kind of *sapiṇḍa* kinship to the seventh generation in the male line and the fifth in the female line. This means, following Vijñāneśvara, that if either the prospective groom or the prospective bride shares a common male ancestor in his or her father's line of descent within seven generations or in his or her mother's line within five generations, then they cannot marry. There may be female antecedents in the father's line of descent, but, by the 'frog's leap principle', the line does not thereby count as maternal or as an interrupted paternal line for

not born of a clan of the same sage (*asamānārṣagotrajām*).[27] [Marriage is permitted between those whose common male ancestor is] beyond the fifth [generation] from the mother and the seventh from the father.

54. [She should be] from a great family of men learned in the Vedas, renowned for ten [great] individuals in it, but not from one with the flaw of an hereditary disease, even if it should be rich.

55. The groom should be a man of the same estate, learned in the Vedas, with the same qualities, diligently inspected as to his masculinity,[28] young, wise, well-liked.

56. It has been taught [by others] that twice-born men may take a wife from a Śūdra; but this is not my opinion, because a [man's] soul is itself reborn [as his son] in that [wife].

57. Respectively Brahmins, Kṣatriyas and Vaiśyas may take three, two and one wife, in accordance with their estate.[29] A Śūdra [may take only one wife] of his own [estate].

---

those descended from males further down in the same line of descent. An example may clarify this:

> Two lines descend from one man (the numbers mark the generations and the letters the gender of the offspring):

1m → 2m→3f→4f→5f→6m→7m
1m → 2m→3f→4m→5f→6f→7f

Here 6m and 6f might have married, because in both lines the common ancestor is more than five generations away in the maternal line; but 7f and 7m might not, because, even though the common male ancestor is more than five generations away in 7f's maternal line, he is the seventh in 7m's paternal line.

27 Vijñāneśvara interprets this to mean 'not of the same family name (*gotra*), nor of the same lineage of sages (*ārṣa*)'. A *gotra* was an exogamous clan called by a patronymic derived from the name of a Vedic seer. The word *ārṣa*, used here as an adjective meaning 'of a sage' is assumed by Vijñāneśvara to be a synonym of the noun *pravara*, which denotes a list of one, two, three or five illustrious ancestors whose name a man invokes in certain ritual contexts. A particular list is fixed for each *gotra*. Probably because the term *gotra* had widely come to be used to denote smaller units of families and sub-families, Vijñāneśvara felt the need to read into the verse here an additional prohibition of marrying someone with the same *pravara*. Thus John Brough, *The Early Brahmanical System of Gotra and Pravara* (Cambridge University Press, 1953), pp. 6–7.

28 Vijñāneśvara quotes a verse to the effect that semen that floats and foamy urine are signs from which one can infer that a man will not be impotent.

29 Each of the twice-born except the Vaiśya may marry a woman of his own estate and one from each twice-born estate below him. A Vaiśya has no twice-born estate below him.

58. A marriage is called [a union] of Brahmā when, after inviting [the groom], the bride is adorned in accordance with [the family's] means and given away. A son born of that [sort of marriage] purifies twenty-one men[30] on both sides [of the union].
59. [It is a union] of the gods (*daivaḥ*) when the bride is given to a priest (*ṛtvije*) employed for a sacrifice [as his sacrificial fee] and [a union] of the sages (*ārṣaḥ*) [when the groom receives] a pair of cows. A son of the first [union] purifies fourteen and a son of the second [purifies] six.
60. When the bride is given with the words 'Perform your moral duty (*dharmam*) together' to one who asks for her, it is called [a union] of Prajāpati (*kāyaḥ*). The son of that [union purifies] six [antecedents and] six [descendants] of the same family together with himself.
61. A union of demons (*āsuraḥ*) results, when money is taken [in exchange for the bride]; that of celestial musicians (*gāndharvaḥ*) when it results from mutual agreement;[31] that of ogres (*rākṣasaḥ*) when it follows the capture [of the bride] in a fight; and that of ghouls (*paiśācaḥ*) when it follows the abduction [by deception] of a virgin.
62. Where the bride is of the same estate, her hand should be grasped, but when marrying a man of higher birth, a Kṣatriya woman should grasp an arrow and a Vaiśya woman should grasp a goad.
63. The father, grandfather, a brother, a male of the same family and the mother can give away the bride. If the first should be dead, the next should do it, if he is sane and healthy (*prakṛtisthaḥ*), [and if he too should be dead,] then the next.
64. One who fails to give her away attains [the fruit of] killing a foetus with each [fertile] period [of hers]. If there is no one, then a virgin should herself choose a suitable groom.
65. A bride is given once; he who takes her [after she has already been given (but is not yet actually married), in order to give her to another] gets the penalty that a thief receives; but even if she has been given away, he should take her [in order to give her away again], if a better groom than the previous should approach.

30 He frees from sin ten ancestors, himself, and ten descendants, according to Manu (3:38).

31 According to Mitramiśra this includes the *svayaṃvara*, a form of marriage often described in narrative literature in which the bride's father summons an assembly of eligible suitors, one of whom the bride may choose.

66. One who gives away [a bride] without proclaiming a fault [that she has] should pay the highest penalty,[32] as should one who abandons a bride who is without fault. One who falsely attributes faults to her [should pay as a fine] one hundred [*paṇas*].
67. A virgin and a woman who is no longer a virgin,[33] if they remarry, are called 'reborn' (*punarbhūḥ*). A woman who abandons her husband and out of lust goes to another man of the same estate is a wanton (*svairiṇī*).
68. When a son is required, a brother-in-law, or a man related [to the husband] by rice-ball offerings, or a man of the same lineage (*sagotraḥ*), may, with the permission of the elders, after smearing himself with clarified butter, go to a wife who has no son in [her fertile] season.
69. He should go to her until she conceives. [If he were to go to her] in any other circumstances he should fall [from his rights to perform the duties of the twice-born]. The son born to a man according to this rule is one 'born of the field' (*kṣetrajaḥ*).
70. An adulterous woman he should cause to live with her rights taken from her, dirty, living off mere mouthfuls of food, [constantly] reproached, sleeping on the ground.[34]
71. The moon gave them brightness, a celestial musician (*gandharvaḥ*) [gave] a sweet voice, and fire [gave] purity above all else, and that is why women are pure.
72. After adultery a woman becomes pure at her menses.[35] If she should conceive [in her adultery], then it is prescribed that she should be abandoned, as in cases where she commits a serious offence that causes her to fall [from the rights to the duties of the twice-born] such as abortion or killing her husband.
73. [If a man's wife] drinks alcohol, is sickly, cantankerous, barren, wastes money, is quarrelsome, gives birth [only] to female children, [or] is hostile to men, then he may take another wife.

32 This is later (1:366) defined as a fine of 1080 *paṇas*.

33 Vijñāneśvara interprets 'A virgin [who was married] and a woman who has had sex [before marriage] . . . '

34 Vijñāneśvara and Mitramiśra emphasize that this has no purificatory function. Mitramiśra quotes a verse to the effect that if the man she commits adultery with is of a lower estate, then she is to be killed.

35 Mitramiśra interprets the previous verse as a justification for the woman's becoming pure at her menses without needing to perform any penance. Aparārka however understands 'a woman becomes pure [by the performance of a penance] at her menses'.

74. But the superseded wife should [still] be maintained, otherwise great wrong is incurred. When a couple is well-suited, the three [life-aims of moral duty, wealth and pleasure] prosper.
75. Whether her husband is alive or dead, a wife who never goes to another man attains fame in this world and delights [in the next] with Umā.
76. If a man abandons a wife who obeys his commands, is skilful, gives birth to heroes, and speaks sweetly, he should be made to give [her] a third part [of his wealth or] the woman's maintenance, if he is poor.
77. Women should do what their husbands say; this is the highest moral duty (*dharmaḥ*) of a woman. If a man is sullied by having committed a serious offence that causes him to fall [from his rights to perform the duties of the twice-born], then she should wait for him until he is purified.[36]
78. [Respectively] through a son, a grandson and a great grandson a man attains worlds, eternity [for his succession] and heaven.[37] Therefore women are to be honoured and kept well-protected.
79. [Starting from her menses] there are sixteen nights in a woman's season. [Among those] he should have sex with her on the even nights [of the lunar month]. [Observing the sexual abstinence of] a student,[38] he should avoid the lunar junctions[39] and the first four days [after the beginning of her menstrual period].
80. Thus a man should go to his wife, when she is weakened [from fasting] (*kṣāmām*),[40] [should have sex with her not more

36 Vijñāneśvara takes this to mean that she is not subordinate to him until he is purified.

37 Reading *lokānantyadivaprāptiḥ* with Viśvarūpa (cf. Manu in 9:137).

38 Vijñāneśvara interprets this to mean that a man effectively observes the chastity of studentship, if he has sex with her only on the prescribed nights.

39 The days of the new moon, the full moon and the eighth and fourteenth days of the lunar fortnight. Sexual abstinence is required before the performance of important sacrifices such as those on the days of the new and of the full moon.

40 Vijñāneśvara interprets the verse in this way and explains that this is because when the woman has more [or stronger] semen (both sexes are reckoned to have semen) than the man, then the child will be female (cf. Manu in 3:49). Viśvarūpa however understands the verse to say that he should abstain from sex when she is weakened, just as he should when the moon is in Maghā and Mūla. (Maghā and Mūla are constellations on the ecliptic of the moon.) The ecliptic of the moon is divided into twenty-seven mansions (*nakṣatra*), which are named after the constellations in them.

than] once [in the same night] when the moon is favourable, [and] should beget a son that has [auspicious] marks. He should avoid [the nights when the moon is in the constellations] of Maghā and Mūla.

81. Alternatively [regardless of whether it is her season] he may also match his desire [with hers] (*yathākāmī*), remembering the boon granted to women,[41] having pleasure only in his own wife, for it is taught that women are to be cherished (*rakṣyāḥ*).

82. Women should be honoured with ornaments, clothes and food by their husbands, brothers, fathers, kinsmen on the male side, parents-in-law, brothers-in-law, and by [all] relatives.

83. A wife should keep the household equipment in order, she should be skilled, contented, economical, and she should revere the feet of her parents-in-law, devoted to her husband.

84. When her husband is abroad she should eschew games, ornamenting her body, watching gatherings and festivals, laughter, and visiting other people's houses.

85. The father should protect [her when she is] a virgin; the husband [when she is] a married woman; her sons, when she reaches old age; and, when there is none of these, their relatives. A woman should never be independent.

86. A woman without a husband should never be separated from father, mother, sons, brothers, parents-in-law [or] maternal uncles, otherwise she will draw blame upon herself (*garhaṇīyā*).

87. The woman who is intent on what her husband likes and on his well-being, whose conduct is fitting, whose organs of sense and action are controlled, attains fame in this world and, when she dies, the state than which there is no higher.

88. He should not make another wife [of lower estate] perform religious rites (*dharmakāryam*), if he has a wife of the same estate as himself. If he has a number of wives of the same estate as himself, then another [younger] one [should not be employed] in carrying out religious prescriptions without the eldest.

41 A certain Viśvarūpa, the domestic priest (*purohita*) of the gods, promised the gods their share of the sacrifice, but also, in secret, promised it to the demons (*asura*). Indra killed him and then begged the earth, trees, and women each to take a third part of his guilt in exchange for granting each a wish. The women asked to bear offspring from intercourse in season and to enjoy sex with their husbands until giving birth. This Indra granted and the guilt of the murder of Viśvarūpa appears every month as their menstrual flow. (Related in *Taittirīya-Saṃhitā* ii.5.1.)

89. When a husband has burnt a dutiful (*vṛttavatīm*) wife with [the sacred Vedic fires used for] the daily Vedic fire sacrifice (*agnihotreṇa*), he should without delay take [another] wife in the prescribed way and [other] fires.[42]

[*Estates and Castes*]

90. Sons that make the lineage thrive are born of the same caste [as their parents] in women of the same estate to men of the same estate in faultless marriages.[43]
91. From a Brahmin man is born a Mūrdhāvasikta to a Kṣatriya woman, an Ambaṣṭha to a Vaiśya woman, and a Niṣāda or a Pāraśava to a Śūdra woman.
92. It is taught that from a Kṣatriya man are born [respectively] a Māhiṣya and an Ugra to a Vaiśya woman and to a Śūdra woman. From a Vaiśya man [is born] a Karaṇa to a Śūdra woman. This is the rule that is taught [about what kinds of son are born] of [properly] married women.[44]
93. To a Brahmin woman from a Kṣatriya man is born a Sūta (charioteer) and from a Vaiśya man a Vaidehaka, but from a Śūdra man a Caṇḍāla (untouchable) who is beyond all moral codes of duty (*sarvadharmabahiṣkṛtaḥ*).

42 At the last rites he gives the fires to his dead wife (cf. Manu 5:167–9). Vijñāneśvara adds that he should use the household (*smārta*) fire, if he does not keep the Vedic fires. For information about the fires see 1.97 and note ad loc. That he should not delay is emphasized, because, as Mitramiśra explains, he should never be outside one of the four walks of life (enumerated ad 1:1). The second of these is that of the married man (*gṛhastha*), whose rituals require the participation of his wife.

43 I have throughout translated *varṇa* with 'estate' and *jāti* with 'caste'. In this passage an attempt is made to account for the plethora of castes known at the time of the redaction of the work as a result of miscegenation between the four estates. Estates make their appearance in the *Ṛg-Veda* (see, for example, X, xc.12 in this anthology); castes do not. That the account is a fictional rationalization of developments that happened long before the time of the redaction of the *Yājñavalkya-Smṛti* is suggested by the use of the past tense in 1:94. The names of the castes mentioned here point to other origins: Ambaṣṭha, Vaideha and Māgadha are derived from place names; Rathakāra means a carter and Māhiṣya a tender of buffaloes; Niṣāda is used elsewhere of tribal hunters and fishermen. Others of the names are commonly associated with particular occupations: a Karaṇa is typically a scribe, a Sūta is a charioteer and bard, and a Kṣattṛ is a doorkeeper.

44 i.e. in marriages in which the man is superior as to estate.

94. A Kṣatriya woman gave birth to a Māgadha son from a Vaiśya man, to a Kṣattṛ from a Śūdra man, a Vaiśya woman to an Āyogava from a Śūdra man.
95. To a Karaṇa woman from a Māhiṣya man is born a Rathakāra (carter). The bad and the good offspring are to be understood to result [respectively] from unions that are against the grain and from those that are with the grain.[45]
96. Supremacy of birth (*jātyutkarṣaḥ*) must be understood [to return] in the seventh or even in the fifth generation. If wrong actions[46] are performed [by the offspring of mixed marriages], then [their status remains] the same. As above, [offspring can be relatively] high and low [according to the kind of union from which they are born].[47]

[*The duties of a married householder*]

97. A married man should daily perform ritual action prescribed in texts of secondary authority (*karma smārtam*) in the fire [set at the time] of the marriage or inherited at the time of the distribution [of the family's wealth]. The ritual action prescribed in Vedic scripture (*śrautam*) [he should perform only] in the sacred Vedic fires.[48]
98. When he has dealt with bodily considerations and done what is prescribed for his cleanliness, a twice-born man should attend

45 Marriages that are with the grain are those in which the man is of a higher estate or caste.

46 i.e. adopting the means of livelihood of a low estate, according to Vijñāneśvara.

47 This verse is open to widely different interpretations and is probably deliberately so. Viśvarūpa explains by way of illustration that if a Mūrdhāvasikta woman marries a Brahmin and her female offspring marry Brahmin males in each generation, then the fifth generation will have the status of Brahmins. If she marries another Mūrdhāvasikta and her female offspring in each generation do the same, then the fifth generation will have the status of Kṣatriyas. Possible permutations are many and the commentators do not attempt to list them all.

48 The three Vedic fires are called the Gārhapatya, the Āhavanīya, and the Dakṣiṇa. The Vedic (*śrauta*) rites prescribed in Vedic texts (*śruti*) are performed with these. Sacrifices prescribed in texts of secondary revelation (*smṛti*) are performed into the household fire, which is also used for ordinary activities such as cooking. The household fire (called variously *avasatthya*, *aupāsana*, *gṛhya*, *smārta*) is the one that is either carried to the groom's house from the marriage ceremony or inherited at the time of the distribution of the family's wealth. (For a reminder of the distinction between *śruti* and *smṛti* see Introduction pp. xx–xxi).

to the rite prescribed at the morning junction[49] after cleaning his teeth.

99. After making oblations into the fires[50] he should, with focused mind, recite mantras dedicated to the sun. And [then] he should study the meaning of the Vedas and diverse treatises.

100. And he should approach the lord [of the land] in order to accomplish the aims of acquiring what he wants and of securing what he has (*yogakṣemārthasiddhaye*). And after bathing he should satisfy and revere the gods and the Ancestors.

101. In order to accomplish the sacrifice of recitation he should recite the Vedas, the *Atharvan*, the Purāṇas and the epics as much as he is able, and the spiritual science [of the Upanishads] (*vidyām cādhyātmikīm*).

102. The rite of offering portions of food (*balikarma*), [oblations offered with the exclamation] '*svadhā*', oblations into the fires, a man's daily recitation, and the honouring of guests are the [five] great sacrifices [respectively] to disembodied departed spirits (*bhūta*), Ancestors, gods, brahman and men.

103. He should take the portions of cooked food for the disembodied spirits from what remains from what has been oblated for the gods. For dogs, outcastes (*cāṇḍāla*) and crows he should scatter food on the ground.

104. Food is to be given daily to Ancestors and to men, and water. He should always do his daily recitation. He should not cook food [just] for himself.

105. After feeding children, married women living in their father's household, the elderly, pregnant women, the sick, girls, guests, and servants, the husband and wife should eat what remains.

106. By the prayers that nourish (*āpośānena*) before and after he eats, the twice-born man should ensure that the food is not naked and that it is nectar (*anagnam amṛtaṃ caiva*).[51]

107. He should give [food] to those who arrive as guests from the four estates in due order as he is able. A guest should not be turned away even in the evening; [he should be received] with conversation, a place on the ground, grass [spread upon it], and water.

108. After honouring them he should give alms to a beggar and

49 For the rite at the morning junction see 1:22–4.

50 i.e. the Vedic (*śrauta*) fires or, if he does not keep these, the household fire.

51 Before eating he says the prayer 'You are a bed for nectar' and sips water. After eating he says the prayer 'You are a covering for nectar' and sips water. Thus the food is 'covered' by water and a prayer at both ends.

to one who has undertaken special religious observances (*savratāya*). He should feed friends, in-laws, and blood-relatives who arrive at [meal-]time.

109. He should put a large bull or a large goat before one learned in the Vedas.[52] [He should offer] respect, a seat beside [himself], sweet food, and conversation that is pleasant and true.

110. Every year a Brahmin who has [completed his studentship and] bathed, a teacher (*ācāryaḥ*), a ruler, a friend, and a son-in-law are to be respectfully received, but officiating priests (*ṛtvijaḥ*) [are to be received] at every sacrifice.

111. He should treat as a guest a man travelling who is versed in the Vedas and one who has crossed to the further bank of the Veda.[53] These two are to be revered by a married man who wishes to reach the world of Brahmā.

112. He should have no desire for another man's cooked food unless he is invited by a man of impeccable character. He should avoid laxness of speech, hands and feet, and overeating.

113. A guest learned in the Vedas whom he has satisfied he should accompany out as far as the boundary.[54] The remainder of the day he should sit together with learned men, friends, and kinsmen.

114. After he has worshipped [the sun at] the evening junction, made oblations into the fires and worshipped them, he should eat surrounded by his servants without overfilling himself and then he should go to sleep.

115. He should get up at the moment of Brahmā[55] and think of his well-being. As far as he is able he should not neglect his [three life aims of] moral duty (*dharma*), wealth and pleasure, each in its proper time.

116. Men are revered for their knowlege, their rituals (*karma*), their age, their relatives, and their wealth in that order. When he has these in abundance, even a Śūdra earns respect in old age.

117. One should make way for an old man, someone carrying a

52 Vijñāneśvara explains that the animal is not given or slaughtered, but proferred as a gesture of respect.

53 Thus Vijñāneśvara; Aparārka interprets, 'He should know that a traveller is a guest and one who is versed in the Veda is one who has crossed to the further bank of the Veda.'

54 Aparārka explains that he should accompany guests to the boundary of his house, his village, or fields, depending on the degree of respect that should be accorded to them.

55 The last half of the last watch of the night.

burden, a king, one who has bathed [after completing his Vedic study], a woman, the infirm, a bridegroom, and someone in a vehicle. A king is to be venerated by these and one who has bathed [after completing his Vedic study] is to be venerated by a king.

118. Sacrificing, studying, and giving are [tasks] for a Kṣatriya and for a Vaiśya. In addition to these a Brahmin has to receive [gifts], to sacrifice and to teach.

119. The principal activity of a Kṣatriya is to protect men, for a Vaiśya it is taught to be lending upon interest, agriculture, trade and tending livestock.

120. For a Śūdra it is obedience to the twice-born and, if he cannot live by that, then he may be a tradesman. Otherwise he may live by various crafts, acting for the well-being of the twice-born.

121. A man should love his wife, be pure, support his servants, devote himself to the performance of ceremonies in honour of the Ancestors (*śrāddhakriyāratah*). He should not neglect the five sacrifices[56] [which are to be performed] with the mantra *namaḥ* ('homage!').

122. Not injuring living beings, truth, not stealing, purity, control of the organs of sense and action, giving, restraint, compassion, forbearance are the means of accomplishing the moral duty (*dharmasādhanam*) of all men.

123. He should behave in a manner that is seemly for his age, intellect, wealth, speech, dress, knowlege of the Veda, family and occupation, not crooked and not dishonest.

124. [Only] the twice-born man who has provisions of food for more than three years should drink soma. One who has a year's supply should perform the rites that precede [the drinking of] soma.[57]

125. The soma [sacrifice should be performed] every year, [the sacrifice of] an animal at each solstice. And the sacrifice to secure the harvest (*āgrayaṇeṣṭiḥ*) should be performed [once a year] and the four-monthly sacrifices [every four months].

126. If these are not possible then the twice-born man should

56 For the five sacrifices see 1:102.

57 These are the twice daily fire oblations (*agnihotra*); the new and full moon sacrifices (*darśapūrṇamāsa*) and the sacrifices described in the next verse (excluding the soma sacrifice itself).

perform the sacrifice called 'For All Men' (*vaiśvānarī*).[58] [An optional rite aimed at attaining a particular worldly goal] he should never perform in a manner that is deficient, [since] it [only] bears fruit if [all the necessary] ingredients are there.[59]
127. He will be born as an outcaste (*cāṇḍālaḥ*), if he begs the instruments for a sacrifice from a Śūdra. If he does not offer up what he has received in order to perform the sacrifice, then he becomes a vulture or a crow.
128. He may possess a granary full, or a pot full,[60] he may be one who has [enough food for his household] for three days, or even a man who has not enough for tomorrow, or he may live from gleaning. Each of these is superior to the last.

[*The duties of one who has completed his Vedic studies and taken the ritual bath which concludes them.*]

129. He should not seek wealth in a way that will interrupt his daily recitation, nor [just] from any source, nor by an occupation that is forbidden, and he should always [in any case] be content.
130. From a king, from a student who lives beside him, from a man for whom he performs sacrifices he may ask for money if he is oppressed with hunger. He should avoid hypocrites, sceptics, heretics and those who behave like herons.[61]
131. He should wear white garments, have short hair, beard and nails, be clean; he should not eat in the sight of his wife,[62] nor when he is wearing [only] one robe, nor when he is standing.
132. He should do nothing dangerous, should say nothing unpleasant without reason, nothing unhelpful, nor anything untrue. He should not be a thief or a usurer.
133. He should bear golden ornaments, the sacred thread, a staff

58 The *vaiśvānarī* is an annual sacrifice that makes up for all the shortcomings of the year that has passed.

59 The commentators are unanimous in assuming that it is optional rites (*kāmya*) that are referred to. In tantric Śaivism a similar notion is upheld: that rites performed for salvation can be effective even when there are deficiencies in the manner of performance, but that optional rites for the attainment of supernatural powers and pleasures are only effective if correctly performed to the letter.

60 The first, according to the Vijñāneśvara, is enough to feed a household for twelve days, the second for six.

61 Herons appear to look down out of modesty and to wade cautiously about as though afraid of hurting the aquatic animals they devour.

62 Vijñāneśvara explains that eating in front of his wife exposes him to the risk of begetting weak offspring.

of bamboo, a water jar. [An image of] a god, earth [taken from a sacred place],[63] a cow, a Brahmin and a tree he should keep on his right when he passes them.

134. He should not urinate in a river, in the shade, on a road, in a cow-pen, into water, on ash, nor towards fire, the sun, a cow, the moon, towards the dusk or the dawn, towards waters, towards a woman, nor towards a twice-born.

135. He should not look at the sun, at a naked woman, nor [at his wife] after sexual congress, nor[64] at urine or excrement, nor, when he is impure, at Rāhu[65] and the stars.

136. When it rains he should recite the entire mantra '[May] this thunderbolt [ward off evil] to me'[66] [and] he should not go about uncovered. And he should not sleep with his head to the west.

137. He should not cast saliva, blood, excrement, urine and semen into water. He should not warm his feet at the fire, nor should he step over it.

138. He should not drink water with cupped hands, he should not wake someone who is sleeping, he should not play with dice, nor with things [or people] that destroy his morals (*dharma-ghnaiḥ*), nor should he sleep [in the same place] with those who are ill.

139. He should avoid actions that are forbidden [in his particular country, village or family],[67] the smoke of a corpse, crossing a river [by swimming with his arms], and standing on hair, ash, chaff, charcoal and skulls.

140. He should not point out a drinking cow, he should not enter anywhere except by the door, he should not accept [anything] from an avaricious king who does what is prohibited by the treatises [on law].

141. In the matter of accepting things a butcher, an oil-presser,[68] a seller of liquor, a prostitute, and a king [of the sort mentioned in

63 Thus Vijñāneśvara; Aparārka and Mitramiśra both gloss with 'earth that has been raised up', but they offer no explanation.

64 Vijñāneśvara takes the *ca* ('and') to include a prohibition of looking at his own image reflected in water.

65 A demon who causes eclipses of the sun and moon by swallowing them.

66 *Pāraskaragṛhyasūtra* II.7.7. The brackets here enclose the part of the mantra not given in the verse.

67 Thus Vijñāneśvara; Aparārka understands 'actions that are injurious [to health and long life]'.

68 Thus Vijñāneśvara; according to Viśvarūpa 'a hunter'.

the preceding verse] are in order each ten times worse than the one before.

142. On the full moon day of Śrāvaṇa, or on a day [when the moon is] in the asterism Śravaṇa, or, if plants are starting to grow, [when the moon is] in the asterism Hasta on the fifth day of the month of Śrāvaṇa,[69] the ritual of the commencement (*upākarma*) of [Vedic] study should be performed.

143. In the month of Pauṣa under Rohiṇī or on the eighth day,[70] he should perform according to prescription the rite of giving up (*utsargam*)[71] the Vedas outside [the village] beside water.

144. When his student, priest, preceptor or relative dies, there should be no recitation for three days, so too after the rites of the commencement and giving up of study and after the death of one versed in the same branch of transmission of the Veda.[72]

145. When there is thunder at the junctions [of dawn and dusk], when there is a whirlwind, an earth-tremor, the fall of a meteorite, when he has completed a Veda, then [there should be no recitation] for a day and a night, as also when he has completed a forest book (*āraṇyakam*).

146. On the fifteenth, the fourteenth, the eighth [days of the lunar fortnight], at the birth of Rāhu,[73] at the junctions of the [six] seasons of the year, after eating at and receiving an invitation to a ceremony for the Ancestors [there should be no recitation].

147. When a sacrificial animal, a frog, a mongoose, a dog, a snake, a cat or a rat pass between [a teacher and his pupil], for a day and a night [there should be no recitation], as also when the standard of Indra is raised[74] and taken down.

69 Thus Vijñāneśvara and Aparārka; Viśvarūpa reads: 'or . . . in the asterism Hasta, *or* on the fifth day of Śrāvaṇa'. Śrāvaṇa is the lunar month that corresponds to July/August. Its name and that of the asterism Śravaṇa are derived from the verb *śru*, 'to listen', as is *śruti*, the expression for Vedic revelation used in 1:7. Śravaṇa and Hasta are asterisms on the ecliptic of the moon. (See note ad 1:80).

70 Pauṣa is the lunar month that corresponds to December/January. Rohiṇī is another asterism on the ecliptic of the moon.

71 The rite of *utsarga* marks the end of the term of Vedic study. Manu (4:94) states that the term should last four and a half months.

72 reading *svaśākhā-* in 144d.

73 i.e. when there is an eclipse of the sun or of the moon. (For Rāhu see note ad 1:135.)

74 This marks a royal festival said to commemorate Indra's giving a bamboo pole to a certain King Upacarivasu. Kings desiring prosperity should set up a

148. At the sound of a dog, jackal, ass, owl, the *Sāma-Veda*,[75] arrows, and of the oppressed, and near impurity, a corpse, a Śūdra, an outcaste (*antya*), a cremation ground, one who has fallen [from his rights to perform the duties of the twice-born],
149. and when he or the place where he is is impure, when there is repeated lightning and thunder, when his hands are wet after eating, in water, in the middle of the night, when there is a high wind,
150. when dust rains, when the directions of the heavens are aflame, at the junctions [of dawn and of dusk], when there is fog, when in danger, when running, when there is a smell of putrefaction, when a learned person (*śiṣṭe*) comes to the house,
151. when he is upon an ass, a camel, a cart, an elephant, a horse, a ship, a tree, or on barren ground – these thirty-seven are held to be cases in which he does not recite for as long as they last.
152. He should not step on the shadow of [an image of] a god, of a priest (*ṛtvij*), of one who has bathed [after completing his studentship], of a teacher (*ācārya*), of a king, of the wife of another man, nor on blood, excrement, urine, saliva, [used] massage oils,[76] or the like.
153. A Brahmin, a snake, a Kṣatriya and himself he should never treat with contempt. Until death he should strive for good fortune (*śriyam*). He should not touch any man at a vulnerable spot.[77]
154. He should get rid at a distance of left-over food, excrement, urine and water used to wash his feet. He should always rigorously perform what primary and secondary revelation teach (*śrutismṛtyuditam ācāram*).
155. He should not touch a cow, a Brahmin, fire, or food, when he [has not washed his mouth and hands after eating and so] is

standard on the twelfth day of the brightening fortnight of the lunar month of Bhādra (August/September), worship it for four days, and take it down on the first day of the darkening fortnight. Chapter 43 of Varāhamihira's *Bṛhat-Saṃhitā* (ed. and trans. M. Ramakrishna Bhat, Motilal Banarsidass, 1981) gives an account of the festival.

75 Manu (4:124) explains: 'The *Ṛg-Veda* has the gods as its deities, the *Yajur-Veda* is for men, the *Sāma-Veda* is taught to be for the Ancestors. That is why the sound of it is impure.'

76 or possibly 'vomit' (*udvartana*).

77 Vijñāneśvara and Aparārka take this to mean that he should not reveal another man's secret misdeeds.

impure (*ucchiṣṭaḥ*), nor [at any time] with his foot. He should not berate or beat others; [but] a pupil and a son he may beat.
156. With deeds, mind and word he should strive to do his moral duty (*dharmam*). Whatever does not lead to heaven and people hate he should not perform, even if it should be [prescribed by treatises on] moral duty (*dharmyam*).[78]
157–8. If he avoids strife with mother, father, guests, brothers, sisters, relatives by marriage, maternal uncles, the elderly, children, the sick, teachers (*ācārya*), doctors, dependants, [other] relatives, officiating priests (*ṛtvij*), family priests (*purohita*), offspring, wives, servants, blood-relatives (*sanābhi*), then the householder may conquer all worlds.[79]
159. He should not bathe in other people's waters without taking out five lumps [of mud].[80] He should bathe in rivers, natural hollows, lakes and waterfalls.
160. He should avoid the bed, seat, garden, house, vehicles of others, unless they are given him. Except in emergency (*anāpadi*) he should not eat the food of one who does not keep the fires,
161. of misers, of those who are bound, of thieves, of the impotent, of those who appear on stage, of those who live [by making things] from bamboo, of those charged with crimes, of usurers, of courtesans, of priests who perform sacrifices for many people,
162. of doctors, of the sick, of those prone to anger, of adulterous women, of the conceited, of enemies, of the cruel, of the fierce, of those who have fallen [from their rights to perform the duties of the twice-born], of those who have fallen by failing to perform transformative life-rites (*vrātya*), of cheats, of those who eat what others leave,
163. of a woman without a man,[81] of goldsmiths, of men in the thrall of women, of priests who sacrifice on behalf of villages, of

78 As an instance of something so prescribed but objectionable, the commentators mention the slaughter of a cow at a ceremony of welcome called *madhuparka*.

79 Manu (4:182–4) gives a list of worlds which are reached by avoiding strife with the various members of this list.

80 Manu (4:201) gives an explanation of this: '. . . by so bathing he is smeared by a portion of the bad deeds of the man who made the tank.' (Doniger's translation.)

81 reading *avīrastrī-* in 163a.

arms-dealers, of blacksmiths, of weavers, and of those who make their living from dogs,
164. of the ruthless, of kings, of dyers, of the ungrateful, of those who live by killing, of washermen, of those who make a living with liquor, of a man whose wife's lover lives in the same household,
165. of those who pick faults, and of those who lie, of oil-pressers,[82] and of bards – the food of these should not be eaten, nor that of one who sells soma.
166. From among Śūdras he may eat food from servants, cow-herds, family friends, those who till the soil and receive half the produce for wages, and from his barber, and from a man who gives himself as a slave.

[Permitted and Forbidden Food – identifications of the various plants, animals, and food preparations are often uncertain. I have followed the commentators, but sometimes their opinions conflict and they were probably in doubt themselves. This passage closely follows Manu's stipulations in 5:5–26.]

167. Food which is not offered with respect, meat of an animal that has not been killed for a sacrifice, food which has hair or insects on it, which has become sour, which has stood overnight, which is left over by somebody else, which has been touched by a dog, which has been looked at by one who has fallen [from his rights to perform the duties of the twice-born],
168. which has been touched by a menstruating woman, which has been publicly offered, food which is intended for another – such food he should avoid, [also] that which has been smelt by a cow, left by a bird, and that which has been deliberately touched by someone's foot.
169. Food that has been left overnight may be eaten if it is smeared with oil, [even if it has] stood for a long time. Products from wheat, barley and milk [may be eaten when they have been left overnight] even without oil.
170. He should avoid the milk of a cow that is being mated with a bull, one that has given birth within the last ten days, one whose calf has died,[83] that of a camel, that of an animal with a simple

82 or 'potters', or 'wheelwrights' (*cākrika*).
83 Thus Vijñāneśvara; literally 'without a calf'.

[rather than a composite] hoof, that of a woman,[84] that of forest animals, and that of sheep,
171. [also] food intended for oblation for the gods, the Moringa shrub,[85] red [sap] and that which flows from incisions cut in trees [whether red or not], meat, unless it is that of a sacrificial animal (*anupākṛtamāṃsāni*), whatever grows from dung, and mushrooms,
172. carnivorous birds, hawk-cuckoos (*dātyūha*), parakeets, birds that peck [such as pigeons], little finches (*ṭiṭṭibha*), sarus cranes, simple-hooved animals, geese, and all [birds] that live in the village,
173. lapwings, water-fowl that swim (*plava*), ruddy sheldrakes, cranes (*balākā*), herons (*baka*), gallinaceous birds, and, if they have not been made for [religious] purposes (*vṛthā-*), dishes of sesamum; cakes of milk, sugar and clarified butter; milk-rice; and cakes of wheat cooked without and with oil;
174. the sparrow, together with the raven, the osprey, forest doves[86] (*rajjudālaka*), web-footed birds, wagtails, and unknown animals and birds,
175. and blue jays, and red-footed birds, butcher's meat, and dried meat, and fish. If he should deliberately eat these, then he should fast for three days.
176. If he should eat onions, a domestic pig, a mushroom, domestic fowl, garlic, shallots, then he should perform the moon fast.[87]
177–8. The animals with five claws that the twice-born may eat are the hedgehog, iguana, tortoise, porcupine and the hare; among fish the lion-faced (*siṃhatuṇḍa*), the carp (*rohita*), the catfish (*pāṭhīna*), the mullet (*rājīva*) and the scaly fish (*saśalka*).[88] Now listen to the injunction about avoiding eating meat:
179. Whoever eats meat in order to sustain his life, at a ceremony

84 Vijñāneśvara takes this to be a prohibition of the milk of all two-breasted animals except the goat.

85 *Moringa pterygosperma* Gaertn.

86 Thus Viśvarūpa.

87 The faster bathes at sunrise, noon and sunset. He diminishes his food by one mouthful each day during the darkening fortnight and increases it during the brightening fortnight. (See Manu 11:217.)

88 Many of the identifications here are so tentative that there is little point in providing zoological names. Those curious to see how vexed the problems are may see Francis Zimmerman, *The Jungle and the Aroma of Meats* (University of California, 1987) and K. N. Dave, *Birds in Sanskrit Literature* (Delhi: Motilal Banarsidass, 1985).

for the Ancestors, when it has been offered in a Vedic rite (*prokṣite*), at the command of a twice-born [Brahmin], after he has offered it to the gods and the Ancestors, is not at fault.
180. A bad (*durācāraḥ*) man, who kills animals in contravention of the rules, lives in a terrifying hell for as many days as there were hairs on the animals.
181. A Brahmin attains all his desires and the merit of a horse sacrifice[89] by avoiding meat; he is a sage though he lives in a household.

[On the purification of various things. Throughout this section the same vocabulary is used for cleaning and for purification; but, as is clear from certain remarks of Vijñāneśvara and from the nature of the subject, in certain instances one or other is intended.]

182–3. Things of gold, silver, and of substances that come from water,[90] lids and vessels, stones, vegetables, rope, roots, fruits, clothes, wickerwork, animal hide, drinking vessels and soma vessels should be cleaned with water; sacrificial pans (*caru*), ladles (*sruk*), double-spouted ladles (*sruva*) and oily vessels [should be cleaned] with hot water;
184. [so too] the sacrificial spatula (*sphya*), winnowing baskets, the skin of a black buck, grain, pestles, mortars, carts. And much grain and cloth when heaped up together [should be purified by] sprinkling [with water].[91]
185. For wood, horn and bone [is prescribed] shaving; for things made out of fruits, rubbing with cow-hair; for sacrificial vessels during the performance of a sacrifice, rubbing with the hand.
186. Cloth of wool and of silk are cleansed by cow's urine or water mixed with saline earth; cloth of bark[92] (*aṃśupaṭṭam*) with [the same] mixed with Bilva fruit; and a blanket of goats' wool with [the same] mixed with fruits of the soap-berry tree;[93]
187. linen cloth with [the same] mixed with white mustard;

89 An immensely elaborate and expensive sacrifice invested with cosmic significance in *Bṛhadāraṇyaka* I, i; it is proverbial to praise good deeds as being as vastly meritorious as a horse sacrifice.

90 i.e. of pearl, conch shell, mother of pearl etc., according to Vijñāneśvara.

91 Or, according to Vijñāneśvara, 'And solid things, [and] large quantities of grain and cloth [should be purified by] sprinkling [with water].'

92 Thus Vijñāneśvara; 'of flax and bark' according to Mitramiśra.

93 The Bilva is *Aegle marmelos* Correa; the soap-berry tree is *Sapindus detergens* Roxb.

earthenware by firing again. The hand of an artisan is pure,[94] so too wares that are bought, that which is begged, and the mouth of a woman.

188. Earth becomes pure by sweeping, by burning, by time, by a cow walking over it, by sprinkling it [with milk, cow's urine, cowdung and water], by scraping away [the impure portion], by smearing [with cowdung]; the house, by sweeping and smearing.

189. When food has been smelled at by a cow or spoiled by hair, flies, or worms, then water, ash or earth must be thrown [upon it] in order to purify it.

190. Tin, lead and copper are cleaned by water mixed with ash, with acid, and with [plain] water; bell metal and iron, with water mixed with ash; for a liquid [purification is brought about by] filling [its container with more of the same liquid] to overflowing.

191. That which has been smeared with something impure is purified by removing the smell and so forth with earth and water. Whatever is commended by word [as being clean], whatever has been rinsed with water, and whatever one does not know [to be unclean] is always pure.

192. Water is pure that satisfies a cow, is in its natural state, [and] is in the earth; so too meat [of an animal] that has been killed by dogs, untouchables (*caṇḍāla*), carnivorous [animals], and so on.

193. Rays, fire, dust, a shadow, a cow, a horse, the earth, the wind, droplets [of dew], flies, a calf that is sucking are pure when touched.

194. The mouth of a goat and of a horse is pure. That of a cow is not, nor are the impurities that come from humans. Roads become pure through the rays of the sun and moon and through the wind.

195. Droplets [of spittle] from the mouth are pure, so too droplets of sipping water, and the moustache when it gets into the mouth. When he has got rid of [food] stuck between the teeth, then [he becomes] pure.

196. After bathing, drinking, when he has sneezed, slept, eaten, walked on the street, and after changing his clothes, he should twice sip water.

197. Water and mud on the road that have been touched by untouchables (*antya*), dogs, and crows are purified by the wind alone, and so too are buildings of baked brick.

94 This is a most important provision, because dyers, washermen and cooks were of low castes.

[*Giving*]

198. After Brahmā had subjected himself to ascetic self-mortification (*tapas taptvā*), he created Brahmins for protecting the Vedas, for satisfying the gods and the Ancestors, and in order to protect the moral order (*dharma-*).
199. Brahmins practised in Vedic recitation are lords of all, superior to them are those who devote themselves to rituals, and higher still are those excellent ones who know the [supreme] self (*adhyātmavittamāḥ*).
200. Worthiness to receive is not determined just by knowledge or [just] by ascetic self-mortification (*tapasā*); a man who has both these and behaves [in accordance with the prescriptions of the law] is proclaimed to be a worthy recipient.
201. Cows, land, sesamum, gold and the like should be given respectfully (*arcitam*)[95] to worthy recipients. A wise man who wishes his own good should give nothing to an unworthy recipient.
202. A man without knowledge and [who has not subjected himself to] ascetic self-mortification should not accept gifts. If he does accept, then he leads the giver down [to hell] and himself too.
203. Gifts should daily be given to worthy recipients, and especially so on special occasions.[96] And if a man is asked, he should, in accordance with his means, make a donation that is pure because of his faith.
204. A cow rich in milk should be given, one with golden horns, silver hooves, good-natured, equipped with cloths and a vessel of white copper, together with a gift [of gold] (*sadakṣiṇā*).
205. One who gives her attains heaven (*svargam*) for as many years as she has hairs. If she is tawny, then he further rescues [the forebears of] his family up to the seventh generation.
206. The donor of a cow that looks in both directions,[97] if he gives in accordance with the above prescription, attains heaven for as many aeons (*yugāni*) as she and her calf have hairs.
207. While two of the calf's feet and its head are visible when it is [still] in the womb, the cow is to be known to be [deserving of the same respect as] the earth, until she gives birth to the calf.

95 Vijñāneśvara explains that this means they should be given with an appropriate ceremony including the libation of water.

96 Aparārka mentions passages of the sun from one sign of the zodiac to another; Viśvarūpa and the Vijñāneśvara mention eclipses.

97 This is apparently explained by the next verse, which Viśvarūpa's text omits.

208. The donor of a cow that is not sick or weak, in whatever manner he gives her, whether she is a milch-cow or not, is honoured in heaven.
209. Supporting the weary, attending to the sick, worshipping the gods, cleaning the feet [of others of the same or higher status[98]], removing the left-over food of a twice-born are like [in merit to] giving a cow.
210. He who gives land, lamps, food, clothes, water, sesamum, clarified butter, shelter, household goods,[99] gold and a beast of burden is honoured in heaven.
211. He who gives his house, grain, protection, shoes, a parasol, garlands, ointments, a cart, a tree, something he holds dear, a bed, enjoys surpassing happiness.
212. Because the absolute (*brahma*) that consists of all things (*sarvadharmamayam*) is greater than [all other] gifts, he who imparts that [by teaching] attains the world of Brahmā, which never fails.
213. One who does not accept a gift, even though he can accept it, attains the worlds of abundance that are for the generous.
214. Sacrificial grass (*kuśa*), vegetables, milk, fish, perfume, flowers, curds, [fragrant] earth, meat, a bed, a seat, roast barley – these are not to be refused, nor is water.
215. Whatever [of the above] is offered unsought should also be accepted [even] from a wrongdoer; but not from an adulterous woman, an impotent man, one who has fallen [from his rights to perform the duties of the twice-born], nor from an enemy.
216. He may accept gifts from all sources in order to honour gods and guests or for the sake of his preceptor and his dependants, and also in order to sustain himself.

[Ceremonies for the Ancestors. This is a translation of *śrāddha*, a term for a variety of rites in which Brahmins are fed for the benefit of deceased ancestors. They are not funerary rites. As is made clear in 1:269, the Ancestors who benefit are not just the deceased souls of ordinary men, but a class of deities divided into Vasus, Rudras and Ādityas, whom Manu (3:284) calls fathers, grandfathers and great-grandfathers respectively.

There is a huge literature spread over an enormous time span about these ceremonies and there are therefore many inconsistencies

98 Thus Vijñāneśvara.
99 Or 'a virgin bride' (*naiveśikam*).

in details of performance, recommended times, sub-classifications of types of ceremonies and so forth. Manuals of ritual and the interpretations of commentators must be relied upon for resolving such problems.

Yājñavalkya's account takes the *pārvaṇa* rite as the model (*prakṛti*) of which all other ceremonies for the Ancestors are modifications (*vikṛti*). *Pārvaṇa* means '[performed] on the junctions' and is used to refer to the kind of ceremonies intended for the benefit of three deceased Ancestors; the father, grandfather and great-grandfather. Yājñavalkya treats the manner of its performance in some detail from 1:225–49 and thereafter describes the salient deviations of other varieties of ceremony: that performed on the occasion of increase (*vṛddhi*), such as the birth of a son, is treated in 1:250; ceremonies performed for the benefit of only one ancestor (*ekoddiṣṭa*), either recently deceased and so not yet united with the triad of ancestors for whom regular *pārvaṇa* ceremonies are offered, or when the anniversaries of his death occur, are treated in 1:251–2; and the ceremony of 'joining with those who share the same rice balls' (*sapiṇḍīkaraṇa*), by which someone recently deceased is made part of the triad, is treated in 1: 353–4.]

217. The new moon, the eighths (*aṣṭakā*),[100] [when there is] increase, the darkening fortnight, the solstices (*ayanadvayam*), [when there are] provisions, the success [ensured by the presence] of Brahmins [endowed with the good characteristics listed below], the equinoxes, the sun's moving from one sign of the zodiac to the next,

218. at an astrological junction known as *vyatīpāta*,[101] the shadow of the elephant, an eclipse of the sun or moon, and when one is inclined to perform a ceremony for the Ancestors – these are proclaimed to be occasions for ceremonies for the Ancestors.

100 Opinions about what the eighths are differ; Vijñāneśvara espouses the view that they are the eighth lunar day of the darkening fortnights of each of the four months of Mārgaśīrṣa, Pauṣa, Māgha and Phālguna (from November/December to February/March). 'When there is increase' refers, according to Vijñāneśvara, to the birth of a son.

101 *Vyatīpāta* is variously defined; Aparāka cites a verse that explains it to be when the new moon falls on a Sunday and when the moon is in the asterisms of Śravaṇa, Aśvinī, Dhaniṣṭhā, Ārdra, or the first quarter (?) of the asterism Āśleṣā. The 'shadow of the elephant' is again variously understood: Vijñāneśvara espouses the view that it is when the moon is in the mansion of Maghā and the sun in that of Hasta, 'the elephant's trunk'.

219. One who excels in all the Vedas, one who has studied the Veda, or one who knows the absolute (*brahmavit*), a young man, one who knows the meaning of the Veda, one who knows the 'most excellent of chants' (*jyeṣṭhasāmā*), one who knows the *Trimadhu* or the *Trisuparṇa*,[102]
220. a sister's son, a household priest (*ṛtvik*), son-in-law, a man for whom one sacrifices, father-in-law, a maternal uncle, one who knows the triple Naciketas,[103] a daughter's son, a pupil, a relation by marriage, a blood relation,
221. those who are steadfast in performing rituals, those who are steadfast in ascetic self-mortification, those who keep the five fires,[104] those who follow the observances of studentship, and those devoted to their father and mother – these Brahmins are [the ones who ensure] the success of ceremonies for the Ancestors.
222. A sick man, one with too few or too many limbs, a one-eyed man, and the son of a remarried woman, one who has failed to observe chastity [e.g. in studentship], an illegitimate son of a married woman, an illegitimate son of a widow, a man with ugly nails, one with blackened teeth,
223. one who teaches for a fee, an impotent man, a man who has spoiled [by slandering or deflowering] a virgin, a man charged with a crime, one who harms his friends, a man who picks faults, a seller of soma, a man who has married or kindled fire before his elder brother,
224. a man who abandons his parents or preceptor, one who eats the food of an illegitimate son of a married woman, the son of an impious man, the husband of a remarried woman, a thief, those of ill-deeds – these are censured.
225. Self-possessed, pure, he should invite the Brahmins on the

102 The 'most excellent of chants' is *Tāṇḍya-Brāhmaṇa* 21.2.3. The *Trimadhu* and the *Trisuparṇa* are triplets of verses of the *Ṛg-Veda*: I, xc.6–8 and X, cxiv.3–5. According to Aparārka, Brahmins who have followed the observances known by these names and those who have recited these portions of text are to be understood.

103 [1:220] The story of Naciketas is related in the *Kaṭha Upanishad*. The text here may refer to knowing the three answers that Yama gives to Naciketas's three questions. Vijñāneśvara understands also 'one who follows the observance described therein'. (*Kaṭha* I.17–18 speaks of the merit of performing this three times).

104 In addition to the four fires mentioned in 1:97 and the note thereon, a fifth fire, called the *sabhya*, may be kept to warm a large room.

previous day (*pūrvedyuḥ*).[105] They too should be restrained in deeds of thought, words and body.
226. In the afternoon (*aparāhṇe*)[106] he should honour those who have arrived with a welcome and, with a purifying ring of *kuśa* grass on his hand (*pavitrapāṇiḥ*), he should invite them to sit down on seats after they have rinsed their mouths.
227. As far as possible, [he should invite to sit down] an even number for the rite for the gods and an odd number for the rite for the Ancestors in a place that is pure, screened off on all sides,[107] and that inclines to the south.
228. Two [should be seated facing] east for the rite for the gods, three [facing] north for the rite for the Ancestors, or at least one [on each occasion]. A ceremony for maternal grandfathers should also be performed in the same way as [that for paternal ancestors], or the rite for the all-gods [may be performed] once in common (*tantram*) [if both paternal and maternal ancestors are to be invoked in one ceremony].
229. After he has given water for washing the hands [to the Brahmins invited for the all-gods] and sacrificial grass (*kuśān*) for a seat [to be placed on their right side], he should, with the permission [of the assembled Brahmins] invite [the gods] with the verse from the *Ṛg-Veda*, starting 'All gods [come! Hear this call of mine! Sit down here on this grass!]'.[108]
230. After scattering barley he should pour water into a vessel that has [two blades of] purifying [*kuśa* grass] in it with the mantra 'Happiness to us, goddesses',[109] and barley with the mantra 'You are barley'.
231. With the mantra 'These divine [waters]'[110] he should place the guest-offering [of water] (*arghyam*) in their hands, and after giving water [he should offer] fragrance, garlands, incense and a lamp,
232–3. and a garment and water for cleaning the hands. Then

105 *Pūrvedyuḥ* may also mean 'in the morning'. Manu (3:187) allows invitation on the day of the ceremony itself as well as on the previous day.

106 *Aparāhṇe* may also mean 'on the following day', but it is translated as 'afternoon', because that is the preferred time for a ceremony for the Ancestors. *Pavitrapāṇiḥ* may simply mean 'with clean hands'.

107 Reading *pariśrite* in 1:227c. The South is the direction of Yama, the god of death.

108 The mantra starting 'All gods' is *Ṛg-Veda* II, xli.13 and VI, lii.7.

109 The mantra starting 'Happiness to us, goddesses' is *Ṛg-Veda* X, ix.4. The mantra starting 'You are barley' is *Vājasaneyi-Saṃhitā* (White *Yajur-Veda*) 5.26.

110 The mantra starting 'These divine' is *Taittirīya-Brāhmaṇa* II.7.15.4.

[after the rite for the gods] he should place his sacred thread on the right shoulder and give *kuśa* grass folded in two to [the Brahmins invited for] the Ancestors, [to be placed] on their left side [to sit upon] and, summoning the Ancestors with the verse from the *Ṛg-Veda*, 'Joyously [would we put] you', he should, with the permission of those [assembled], recite 'May [the Ancestors] come to us'.[111]

234. [For[112] the Ancestors] the things that are [in the rite for the gods] done with barley should be performed with sesamum. Honouring by giving water (*arghya*) and so forth he should perform as before.

235. After giving the water (*arghyam*) and after collecting what pours down from those [Brahmins' hands] in the prescribed manner in a vessel, he should turn the vessel upside down and put it down with [the mantra] 'You are a place for the Ancestors'.

236–7. When he is about to offer in the fire, he takes cooked rice full of clarified butter (*ghṛtaplutam*) and asks [permission from the assembled Brahmins]. When he has received permission with [the word] 'Do', and when he has offered into the fire as at a sacrifice for the Ancestors (*[piṇḍa]pitṛyajñavat*),[113] he should carefully put what remains over from the oblation into whatever dishes he has got, and preferably silver ones.

238. When he has put the food in, and consecrated the dishes with [the mantra] 'the earth [is your] dish',[114] he should have a Brahmin put his thumb into the rice with [the mantra] 'Viṣṇu [has overstepped] this'.

239. After reciting the Gāyatrī with the utterances and the three verses of the *Ṛg-Veda* starting 'Sweetness the winds',[115] he should say '[Eat] as you wish', and they should eat in silence.

111 The mantra starting 'Joyously' is *Ṛg-Veda* X, xvi.12. Doniger translates: 'Joyously would we put you in place, joyously would we kindle you. Joyously carry the joyous fathers here to eat the oblation.' The mantra starting 'May [the Ancestors] come to us' is *Vājasaneyi-Saṃhitā* 19.58.

112 omitting 234ab, which is probably an interpolation.

113 The *piṇḍapitṛyajña* is a sacrifice of rice-balls for the Ancestors performed on new moon days only by those who keep the Vedic fires.

114 The mantra starting 'the earth [is your] dish' is found in *Hiraṇyakeśi-Gṛhyasūtra* II.11.4. The mantra starting 'Viṣṇu [has overstepped] this' is *Ṛg-Veda* I, xxii.17.

115 For the Gāyatrī and the utterances, see the first item in this anthology and the notes on 1:15 and 1:22. The three verses starting 'Sweetness the winds' are *Ṛg-Veda* I, xc.6–8.

240. Not angry or hurried he should give them food that they like and that is suitable for oblation, reciting sacred [verses] and what he had recited before, until they are satisfied.
241. Taking the food [away, he should ask] 'Are you satisfied?', and [after taking away] also what they have left over, after asking their permission to do so, he should scatter that [left-over] food on the ground, and he should give water to each one.
242. When he has taken away all the food together with the sesamum, he should offer the rice-balls facing south, near where the left-over food was offered, in the same manner as at a sacrifice for the Ancestors (*[piṇḍa]pitṛyajñavat*).
243. For maternal grandparents too [the rites from the summoning of the all-gods up to the giving of rice-balls are] the same. Next he should give [the Brahmins] water for rinsing the mouth. Then he should have the Brahmins say 'It is well' (*svasti*), and also [perform the rite of] 'indestructible water'.[116]
244. After giving a gift of money in remuneration (*dakṣiṇām*) according to his means he should utter the sound *svadhā*. When they have given him leave by saying 'Speak', [he should say] 'Say *svadhā*'[117] to the revered [Ancestors]'.
245. They should say 'Let there be *svadhā*', and when they have spoken, he should then sprinkle water on the ground. When the Brahmins have said 'May the all-gods be pleased', he should recite this:
246. 'May the givers among us increase, and the Vedas, and our lineage, and may our faith not leave us, and may we have much to give.'
247. After saying this and after saying pleasing things he should bow and happily let them leave [with the mantra] 'At every battle',[118] starting with [the dismissal of] the Ancestors [and ending with the all-gods].
248. He should place upright as the vessel of the Ancestors the vessel of the water given to guests, in which he first collected what poured [from off the Brahmins' hands], and then he should let the Brahmins go.
249. After he has accompanied them away, keeping them on his

116 He pours water on their hands and has them say 'May it [i.e. the fruits of the rite] be indestructible'.

117 *Svadhā* might be translated as 'pleasure'. The word accompanies offerings to the Ancestors, and is sometimes used to refer to such offerings.

118 The mantra starting 'At every battle' is *Ṛg-Veda* VII, xxxviii.8.

right, he should eat of the food that has been enjoyed by the Ancestors. That night he should follow the observance [of abstinence from sex] of a student, and so should the Brahmins.
250. [If the rites are those performed] when there is increase [such as on the occasion of the birth of a son], then [what in the model ceremony is performed from right to left] he should do from left to right (*pradakṣiṇāvṛtkaḥ*).[119] He should offer rice-balls mixed with curd and jujube fruit to the Ancestors [called] Nāndīmukha. The rites [should then be performed] with barley.
251. A ceremony performed for one deceased person is without [rites for] the gods, has only one [vessel for the] guest offering [of water], one [blade of] purifying [*kuśa* grass], is without the [rite of the] summoning of the Ancestors, and without oblation into the fire (*agnaukaraṇa*), [and] in it the sacred thread is worn on the right shoulder [as in the model rite].
252. Instead of the rite of the 'indestructible water' [he should say] 'May it reach', [and] when he gives leave for the Brahmins to leave, he should say 'Be pleased'; they should say 'We are pleased'.
253–4. He should fill four vessels with perfume, water and sesamum for guest water; he should pour the vessel of the [recently] deceased into those of the Ancestors with the two [mantras, the first of which starts] 'which together'.[120] The rest he should perform as before. This is the rite of 'joining with those who share the same rice-balls' (*sapiṇḍīkaraṇam*). The ceremony intended for one person [may] also [be performed] for a woman.
255. [Even] for one for whom the ceremony of 'joining with those who share the same rice-balls' occurs before a year has elapsed he should give food with a pitcher of water to a Brahmin for a year.[121]
256. A ceremony for a single deceased should be performed on the day of death each month for the year and thereafter each year

119 Various modifications to the model ceremony are implied by the stipulation that he must act 'from left to right': that circumambulations are performed from left to right, that barley rather than sesamum is used, and that the sacred thread is worn on the left shoulder so that it hangs down under the right arm. This is in fact the way it is worn in everyday life, but in rites for the dead and most kinds of ceremony for the Ancestors (including the kind used as the model of which all others are modifications) this is inverted.

120 The mantra starting 'which together' is *Vājasaneyi-Saṃhitā* 19.45–6.

121 Vijñāneśvara states that this should be done daily or monthly. The rite of 'joining with those who share the same rice-balls' could be performed on the twelfth day after death, after three half-months, on the occasion of increase, or a year after death.

in the same way. The first [such ceremony for just one ancestor] is on the eleventh day [after death].

257. [After they have been offered,] he should give the rice-balls to cows, goats or Brahmins, or he should throw them into fire or water. He should not clear away what the Brahmins have left over while the Brahmins are still there.

258–9. By food suitable for oblation the Ancestors are satisfied for a month, by milk-rice for a year, by the flesh of fish, by the flesh of red deer (*hāriṇa*),[122] ram, bird, goat, of spotted deer (*pārṣata*), of the blackbuck (*aiṇa*), of sambar deer (*raurava*), boar and hare, each for a month longer in the order listed, when these are given in this world.

260–1. The flesh of rhinoceros, crab, honey, or the food of sages, the meat of the red goat, the big vegetable (*mahāśāka*),[123] and the flesh of an old white goat (*vārdhrīṇasasya*), and whatever he gives, if he is at Gayā – all these achieve [satiation for] eternity, so too [do rites performed] on the thirteenth day of the rains and especially under the constellation Maghā.

262. He who always gives ceremonies for the Ancestors on the days [of the darkening fortnight], starting from the first [and] excepting only the fourteenth, attains all his desires – a daughter, sons-in-law, cattle, and good sons, [success in] gambling with dice, agriculture, trade, and animals with simple and cloven hooves,

263–4. sons of divine radiance, gold, silver and copper, supremacy among agnate relatives. But those who have been killed by a weapon should be given [a ceremony] on that [fourteenth] day.

265. Heaven, offspring, vigour, valour, [fertile] land, strength, a son, supremacy, good fortune, prosperity, excellence, goodness,

266. sovereign power, [success in] trade and so forth, freedom from disease, glory, absence of grief, the supreme goal,

267–8. wealth, Vedas, the benefits of medicinal herbs, copper,

122 *Hāriṇa* is used either as a generic term for deer and antelope, or for the female of the blackbuck, *Antilope cervicapra* (Linnaeus). The spotted deer is *Axis axis* (Erxleben) and the sambar is *Cervus unicolor* Kerr.

123 Identifications are problematic: Vijñāneśvara takes the 'food of sages' to mean wild rice and wild plants; *mahāśāka* is glossed with *kālaśāka* 'black vegetable' and the latter is mentioned by Manu (3:272) and translated 'sacred basil' by Doniger. The editor of the *Mitākṣara* comments that the vegetable is well-known in Kashmir. Mitramiśra (of Bundelkhand in central India) says that it is also known as *laḍico*. Vijñāneśvara takes *vārdhrīṇasa* to be an old white goat; but according to Aparārka the word may also mean a bird with a red head, black neck and white wings – probably the black ibis.

cows, goats and sheep, horses and long life – whoever offers a feast for the dead in the manner prescribed starting from [the days marked by the asterism] Kṛttikā to [those marked by] Bharaṇī attains these desires, if he believes and has faith, free of pride and jealousy.

269. The Vasus, the Rudras, and the sons of Aditi are the Ancestors, the deities of the ceremonies. Pleased by the ceremony (*śrāddhena*) they please the ancestors of men.[124]

270. Propitiated, the grandfathers grant men long life, offspring, wealth, knowledge, heaven, liberation and happiness, and sovereignty.

[Sections on the worship of Gaṇapati, propitiating the planets, the behaviour of kings, and the central second chapter on legal proceedings are omitted.]

124 For the Vasus, Rudras, and sons of Aditi see *Bṛhadāraṇyaka* III, ix.2–5. Manu (3:284) identifies these classes of deities respectively with the fathers, grandfathers and great-grandfathers.

THE LAW BOOK OF YĀJÑAVALKYA
CHAPTER 3 (REPARATIONS)

[*Impurity*]

1–2. He should bury a boy of less than two years, and thereafter offer no libation of water. Any other [deceased] should be accompanied up to the cremation ground surrounded by his agnate relatives reciting the hymn to Yama[125] and the songs [to him] (*gāthāḥ*). He should be burnt in ordinary fire. If he was an initiate, then [he should be burnt] by the procedure for one who has set up the fires [but with modifications] according to the purpose.[126]

3. Before the seventh or the tenth [day][127] the agnate relatives should approach water with this [mantra] 'Cleansing our sin away',[128] their faces turned towards [the South,] the direction of the ancestors.

4. In the same way the rite [of pouring a libation] of water [is also to be performed] for maternal grandfathers, and teachers (*ācārya*) who have died, and the optional [libation of] water for friends, married [sisters or daughters], sisters' children, parents-in-law, and priests:

125 The hymn to Yama is *Ṛg-Veda* (X, xiv) and the songs to him are three verses in *Taittirīya-Āraṇyaka* VI.5.2.

126 The commentators make clear that one who kept the household fire (*smārta*) is to be burnt with that, and one who kept the three Vedic sacrificial fires is to be burnt with those. The sacrificial implements of one who kept the Vedic fires must also be disposed of by burning them with him. Hence when the text prescribes that an initiate should be cremated following the procedure laid down for one who has set up the fires, it also adds the clause '[but with modifications] according to the purpose'. This means, as the commentators explain, that libations and other such rites attendant upon the cremation are performed in the same manner for an initiate, but the sacrificial implements need not be disposed of, since an initiate who has not set up Vedic fires has none, and similarly Vedic fires cannot be used to cremate him.

127 Thus Vijñāneśvara; 'agnates up to the seventh or tenth [degree of kinship]' according to Viśvarūpa.

128 The mantra is *Ṛg-Veda* I, xcvii.1.

5. they sprinkle water once, naming the name and the family [named after the sage from whom they descend] (*gotra*) [of the deceased], [but otherwise remain] silent. Those following the observances of studentship, and those who have fallen [from their rights to perform the duties of the twice-born], should not offer water.
6. Those who rejected the authority of the Veda, those who did not adopt the duties of any of the [four sanctioned] walks of life (*anāśrita*),[129] thieves, women who killed their husbands, loose women and the like, women who drank liquor and women who committed suicide are not entitled to [have their relatives observe] a period of impurity [after their death] nor to [receive] a libation of water.
7. When they have performed the libation, have come out bathed, and are seated on a stretch of soft grass, [the elders] should persuade them [from grief] with old sayings.
8. 'Deluded is the man who searches for substance in human life, which is as weak as the trunk of a plantain, like a bubble in water.
9. 'If the body that is composed of the five [elements of earth, water, fire, air and space], because of actions that arose in [the soul's] own [previous] bodies, goes [back] into the five [elements], what is [the need for] lamenting about that?
10. 'The earth will perish, and the ocean, and the gods; how could mortals that are as foam not perish?
11. 'Helpless the deceased consumes the saliva and tears that his relatives let fall; therefore one should not weep; one should perform the rites as one is able.'
12. After listening to this they should go home, the children in front. Controlled, they should chew leaves of the neem tree (*nimba*)[130] at the threshold of the house.
13. After sipping water, after touching fire and so forth,[131] water, cowdung, and white mustard seeds, and after putting a foot on a stone they should slowly enter.
14. The rite of entering and so forth is also for those who [are not relatives and] have touched the corpse. Others [who are not

129 For the four walks of life see note ad 1:1.
130 *Azadirachta indica* A. Juss.
131 According to Vijñāneśvara, 'and so forth' refers to a shoot of panic grass (*dūrva*) and a bull.

relatives and have touched the corpse] become instantly pure, if they should so wish, by bathing and exercising control [over the breath].[132]

15. One who follows observances [e.g. of studentship] continues to follow [those] observances, even if he has carried away his teacher (*ācārya*), father or instructor (*upādhyāya*). He should not eat[133] the food of those associated with the bier (*sakaṭānnam*) nor should he live with them.

16. For three days these should sleep separately on the ground eating what they bought [in advance] or received [unasked, otherwise fasting]. Food should be placed on the ground for the deceased in the manner of the sacrifice of rice-balls.[134]

17. For one day water and milk in earthen vessel[s] should be hung in the air. The sacrifices into the Vedic and domestic fires are [to continue] to be performed according to Vedic prescription (*śruticodanāt*).

18. The impurity caused by the corpse is held to last ten nights or three nights. In the case of a child of less than two years it affects [only] the two [parents]. The impurity caused by a birth affects only the mother.

19. Of the two parents the impurity caused by a birth adheres

132 Thus Vijñāneśvara; following Aparārka one might translate as follows: 'The rite of entering and so forth is for those who voluntarily touched the corpse [as well as for relatives]. Others [i.e. those who handle the corpse, because their profession requires them to do so] are purified instantly by bathing and exercising control [over the breath].' Following Viśvarūpa one might translate thus: 'The rite of entering is also for those who have touched the body voluntarily [or "if they should so wish"]. Others [i.e. non-relatives who did not touch, but merely followed the corpse] become instantly pure after bathing and exercising control [over the breath.]' Following Mitramiśra one might translate thus: 'The rite of entering and so forth is for those who touched the corpse [and] also [for those who followed it]. Others [i.e. non-relatives] who wanted to [take part in order to receive the merit of doing so (such as those who take part in rites for a deceased Brahmin who has no relatives to perform them for him)] become pure immediately after bathing and exercising control [over the breath].' The 'rite of entering and so forth' is interpreted by Vijñāneśvara, Viśvarūpa and Mitramiśra to refer to the prescriptions preceding the entering and by Aparārka to refer to the rites that follow it. Read *snānasaṃyamāt* in 14d.

133 Reading *nāśnīyān* in 15c.

134 The stipulation that he should follow the manner of the sacrifice of rice-balls refers, among other things, to the wearing of the sacred thread over the right shoulder rather than the left and to the form in which food should be offered.

firmly (*dhruvam*) [only] to the mother [for ten days], because her blood is seen. The day of the birth (*tadahaḥ*) is not rendered impure, because it gives birth (*janmakāraṇāt*) to the ancestors.

20. If a birth or death occur in the middle [of a period of impurity occasioned by an earlier event, then the newly occasioned impurity] is cleansed away with the remaining days [with which the first impurity is cleansed away].[135] On the occasion of a miscarriage the same number of nights as [the foetus's age in] months bring about purity.

21. [Purity comes about] instantaneously [for the relatives] of those killed by a king, a cow, or a Brahmin, and for those who kill themselves. When someone [dies] abroad, then [from the time they hear about it] the remainder of the time [of the impurity in ordinary circumstances applies, or,] if that has elapsed, then purity comes about after they have given water.

22. [Impurity following the birth or death of one related by the offering of rice-balls lasts] twelve days for a Kṣatriya, fifteen for a Vaiśya, and thirty days for a Śūdra – a half of that if he behaves obediently.

23. [If a child dies] before the teeth grow, [purity is restored] immediately; if before the tonsure,[136] [then the impurity] is taught to be of one night's duration; if before being instructed in the observances [of studentship] (*vratādeśa*), then it is of three nights; and after that it is for ten nights.[137]

24. Purification takes place in a day in the case of girls not yet promised in marriage and of children,[138] teachers, pupils who

135 Vijñāneśvara does not leave this statement unqualified. He does not allow this to be true in the case of something causing a long period of impurity when it occurs inside a short period of impurity, nor in the case of a death occurring during the impurity after a birth, nor if the father's death occurs during the impurity after the mother's death, nor if the second event that brings impurity occurs very near the end of the impurity caused by the first.

136 Tonsure is to be performed in the first or third year, according to Vijñāneśvara.

137 Instruction in the observances of studentship takes place at initiation. Ten nights are the standard length of impurity for a Brahmin.

138 The mention of children here is in contradiction with the stipulations of the previous verse; but Vijñāneśvara and Mitramiśra obviate the difficulty with the assertion that this applies when children have been cremated in error rather than buried, as taught in 3:1.

live with their teachers,[139] those who teach, an instructor [in works that are necessary auxiliaries to the Veda],[140] maternal uncles, and those learned in the Vedas.

26. In the case of sons that are not his own,[141] adulterous wives, when the king of the country in which he lives dies, then a day brings about purification.

26. A Brahmin should never follow a Śūdra nor [another] twice-born [to the cremation ground]. If he follows one then he becomes pure after bathing in the water, touching fire and consuming clarified butter.

27. Kings are not subject to impurity, nor [are the relatives] of those struck by lightning, nor [of those killed] in a fight for the sake of a cow or a Brahmin, nor one whom the king wishes [not to be subject to impurity].

28. For priests (*ṛtvijām*) and initiates who are performing a sacrificial rite, for those involved in soma sacrifices that are spread over many days (*sattri*),[142] for those following observances, for students, for the generous, and for those who know brahman,

29. on occasions of giving, marriage, sacrifice, battle, a disaster threatening the country, dire emergency, purity is taught [to ensue] immediately.

30. Touched by menstruating women or by those who are impure he should bathe. [Touched] by those [who have been touched by menstruating women or those who are impure] he should sip water and recite the [three] hymns to water[143] and mentally [recite] the Gāyatrī once.

31. Time, fire, ritual action, earth, air, thought (*manaḥ*), knowledge, self-mortification, water, repentance, fasting – all these bring about purity.

32–3. Giving is taught to purify those who do what they should not; speed purifies a river; earth and water [purify] that

139 Viśvarūpa takes the pupils who live with their teachers to be students of crafts, not of the Veda.

140 Thus Vijñāneśvara. For a reminder of what such works are see 1:3.

141 For such sons see, for example, 1:68–9.

142 Because initiates for all sacrifices have already been included, Vijñāneśvara and Aparārka suggest another possible meaning: 'those engaged in continually giving away food'. This, Vijñāneśvara explains, is 'similar [in merit] to the continuous performance [of protracted soma sacrifices]'.

143 For these hymns see note ad 1:22.

which needs [physically] to be cleaned; [renunciation and] internalization [of the fires] (*saṃnyāsaḥ*) [purify] the twice-born; self-mortification [purifies] those who know the Veda; forbearance (*kṣāntiḥ*), the wise; water, the body; recitation, those who do wrong in secret; truth (*satyam*),[144] the mind (*manasaḥ*).

34. Self-mortification and knowledge purify the soul [which mistakenly identifies] with [the body that is derived from] the elements (*bhūtātmanaḥ*),[145] knowledge purifies the intellect. The ultimate purification of the soul is held to come about through knowledge of the Lord.

[*Code of conduct in extremis*]

35. In emergency a Brahmin may live from the work of a Kṣatriya or Vaiśya. If he gets over the emergency (*tām*), then he should purify himself and set himself on the [right] path.

36. Fruits, precious stones, linen cloth, soma, human beings, cakes (*apūpa*), plants, sesamum, cooked rice, juices, caustic substances, curds, milk, clarified butter, water,

37. weapons, spirits, bees' wax, honey, lac, *kuśa* grass, [fragrant] earth, animal hide, flowers, goats' wool blankets, [animal] hair, buttermilk mixed with water, poison, land,

38–9. silk, indigo, salt, meat, simple-hooved animals, lead, vegetables, fresh herbs, asafoetida, [wild] animals and scents he should never sell, even if he is living by the livelihood of the Vaiśya. For religious purposes (*dharmārtham*) he may barter sesamum seed in exchange for an equal amount of corn (*dhānyena*).

40. Lac, salt, and meat, if he sells them, cause him to fall [from the rights to perform the duties of his estate]; milk, curd and liquor make him belong to a lower estate.[146]

41. When in emergency a Brahmin accepts [gifts] or eats [food] from any source indiscriminately, he is not tainted by that wrong, because he is like fire, like the sun.[147]

144 Vijñāneśvara explains this to be 'good resolve'.

145 Thus Vijñāneśvara; according to Aparārka 'the soul enveloped by the elements'.

146 Manu (10:92) is more explicit: 'He falls immediately by [selling] meat, lac and salt. After three days a Brahmin becomes a Śūdra from selling milk.'

147 This verse explains an important and, at first acquaintance, an odd feature of the body of prescriptions about purity. Brahmins are on the one hand

42. Agriculture, crafts, hired labour for wages, [imparting] knowledge, lending money upon interest, [transporting goods in] a cart, [gathering grass, firewood and such from] a mountain, service, [moving to] watered land, [applying to] the king, and begging for alms are the means of livelihood in time of emergency.
43. If he hungers, after waiting three days he may steal grain from a non-Brahmin; if he is caught and charged, he must confess it dutifully (*dharmataḥ*).
44. The king, after finding out about his conduct (*vṛttam*), family, character, knowledge of the Veda, [daily] recitation, acts of self-mortification, and household, should create a livelihood for him that is in accordance with his moral duty (*dharmyām*).

[The remaining sections – on the forest-dweller, the renunciant and on rites of reparation – are omitted.]

---

required to be more fastidious about purity than others (see, for example 1:21), but on the other hand they are intrinsically more resistant to impurity (cf. 3:22–3 and the last note ad loc.).

From the

KIRAṆA-TANTRA

KIRAṆA-TANTRA

Chapter 1

1. After [words of] praise Garuḍa saw Hara, whose diadem is the crescent moon, seated upon a peak of Mount Kailāsa with Umā, and addressed these words to him.
2. Victory, [Lord who were] skilful in splitting the broad knot of the shoulders of Andhaka! Victory, burner of the [triple] city occupied by mighty chiefs among heroes![1]
3. Victory, [Lord who are] terrifying because you cut off a head of Brahmā, the overlord of all the gods! Victory, destroyer of the body of the god of love whose power is spread [everywhere]!
4. Victory, remover of the power of the Kālakūṭa poison which bespattered the body of Viṣṇu! Victory, bearer of the force of the proud and turbulent river [Ganges]!
5. Victory, seducer of the wives of the sages in the grove of the cedar forest![2] Victory, [Lord who are] fearsome because you shake everything in the vigorous playfulness of your dancing!
6. Victory, [Lord] who terrify the gods and the asuras by assuming your fierce form! Victory, [Lord] who showed a stream of blood in the mouths of the prince of the cruel ones![3]
7. Victory, destroyer of the sacrifice of Dakṣa through your minion, Vīra[bhadra]! Victory, [Lord,] proud of your strength

1 As a reward for their self-mortification Brahmā granted three moving cities to three demons, Vidyunmālī, Tāraka and Kamala. From these moving cities they held sway over the triple world, causing distress to the gods, until Śiva was prevailed upon to destroy them.

2 These sages had not conquered their passions. Śiva, in response to Umā's encouraging him to reward them, demonstrated that they were not beyond base emotions when he seduced their wives.

3 The commentators are unanimous in identifying this character with the ten-headed Rāvaṇa who abducted Sītā. According to the most widespread myth of an encounter of his with Śiva, Rāvaṇa shook Mount Kailāsa while Śiva and Umā sat upon it. Śiva stopped Rāvaṇa by crushing him with his big toe.

because of your form as an enormous and astonishing column of fire (*liṅga*)[4]!
8. Victory, [Lord] who, for the sake of Śveta, destroyed the body of cruel Death! Victory, [Lord] who infatuated the daughter of the mountain with love, which is the abode of all pleasures![5]
9. Victory, remover of the darkness of the web of delusion and of the torment of Upamanyu! Victory, burner of the worlds and of super-human [creation] from the base below the subterranean paradises upwards![6]
10. Tell me, a fearful devotee, the supreme knowledge of Śiva, on attaining which all men reach absolute release.[7]
11ab. Addressed in this way, Hara, his moon diadem quivering, replied:
11c–13. Hear the good knowledge you have asked for [that gives] great advancement, the great *tantra* called the Ray (*kiraṇa*), which grants supreme, eternal happiness, bestows compassion on all, is pure and clearly expounds its topics, which sets forth an investigation into knowledge (*jñāna*) of the [three topics, namely] the bound soul, the bonds,[8] and the Lord, and which is accompanied

4 Śiva at one time took the form of an enormous column of fire in order to display his superiority. Brahmā flew up to try to find its top and Viṣṇu dug down to try to find its bottom, but they discovered it to be infinitely long. A column (*liṅga*), in different contexts more or less explicitly phallic, is the aniconic form in which Śiva is most frequently worshipped.

5 Umā in her infatuation underwent intense self-mortification in order to win Śiva as her husband.

6 The Śaiva Siddhānta holds that the material universe, which evolved from primal matter, is periodically resorbed into primal matter, because both matter and souls become weary and need to recuperate. (Cyclical resorption of the universe is an idea common to most Hindu cosmologies.) At this cyclical resorption Śiva causes fire to consume the worlds from the bottom of the universe.

7 Rāmakaṇṭha observes that the qualification 'on attaining which *all* men reach absolute release' shows that Garuḍa is not talking about the Vedas. Not only are these not salvific from a Śaiva perspective, but they also cannot be heard by Śūdras. Śūdras *are* entitled to receive initiation into the Śaiva Siddhānta and thereafter to study the tantras.

8 There are three bonds that bind the soul and occlude its innate omnipotence and omniscience: primal matter, past action and innate impurity. Of these three innate impurity is logically presupposed by the other two and it is the last to be removed. The bond of the evolutes of primal matter is in turn logically presupposed by that of past actions, because actions are only possible when the soul is embodied in evolutes of matter. All three of the bonds are however beginninglessly attached to bound souls, as we shall see in 2:3–5 and 3:7–8

by [disquisitions on] ritual action (*kriyā*) and religious observances (*caryā*) and which brings with it a wealth of the benefits of yoga.[9]
Garuḍa spoke:
14. If that is so, then first of all in order to remove my doubts tell me what sort of entity is this bound soul? how is he[10] bound? and how released?
The Lord spoke:
15. The bound soul is eternal, has no form, is without knowledge, is devoid of activity and of qualities, is impotent and [all-] pervasive. He is situated in the belly of primal matter and he deliberates on means to achieve consumption [of the fruits of his actions].[11]
16–17. The principle that gives limited power to act (*kalā*) joins this impure [soul] from Śiva. The bound soul's strength is empowered by this [limited power], the sphere [of the operation of his senses] is made known by [the principle of impure] knowledge (*vidyā*) and he is also stained by [the principle of] attachment (*rāgeṇa*). And [secondary] matter, which consists of the strands

9 This unit Rāmakaṇṭha calls the root-verse of the tantra that expresses its scope and purpose. He wishes to read into it six topics rather than three, thus bringing the *Kiraṇa-Tantra* into line with another prestigious tantra, the *Mataṅgapārameśvara*. To do this he understands 'investigation' (*vicāra*) and 'knowledge' (*jñāna*) to be the names of two other topics, and the sixth topic he takes to be that of 'means of attainment', which he says will be treated in the sections of the work on ritual, religious observances and yoga. By Rāmakaṇṭha's time it was established that a tantra should be divided into four sections, called *pādas*, dealing with knowledge, ritual, behaviour and yoga. The earliest dated manuscript of the *Kiraṇa-Tantra* (924 AD) does not mark these divisions of the text and, though later manuscripts of the work do divide it, the divisions are unnatural. This verse shows that the categories are nevertheless at least as old as the *Kiraṇa-Tantra*, but at the time of the *Kiraṇa-Tantra*'s composition it was not yet the practice to divide a tantra into sections treating these topics.

10 Masculine pronouns are used to refer to the soul, because this reflects the usage of the tantras of the Śaiva Siddhānta. (See note ad 2:13.)

11 Śiva starts to describe the bound soul at a time when primal matter has resorbed its evolutes (see note ad 1:9). At this stage the soul is called *pralayākala*, 'devoid of limited power to act because of resorption of the material universe' (see 1:22c–23 and note ad loc.). This is a logical starting point, because without an environment and a body in which to dwell, both of which are evolved out of primal matter at Śiva's instigation, the soul would be endlessly entrapped, unable to work off its bonds and to realize its innate omniscience and omnipotence. Śiva then goes on to describe the evolutes of primal matter that are joined to the soul to enable it to function with limited powers, and thus use up by experience the fruits of its past actions.

[that make up the lower material universe] (*guṇa*) [viz. *sattva*, *rajas* and *tamas*] [is joined with the soul]. And the soul is bound through his connection with the intellect and [the principle of self-identity (*ahaṃkāra*) and] (*buddhyādi-*) the army of faculties [of sense and action].[12]

18. Then by the embrace of [the principle of] binding fate (*niyati*) he is also bound to that [body of past action and the fruits entailed thereby] which he has himself accumulated. [He is bound] by [the principle of] time [such that he becomes] deluded in experience among the evolutes [of primal matter] that are divisions of time.

19. Thus bound with these parts [of primal matter] that are the principles (*tattvakalābaddhaḥ*)[13] the soul that is naturally enveloped [by bonds becomes] partially equipped of knowledge, linked to a [gross] body, embraced by experience [generated out] of primal matter and absorbed in that [primal matter] (*tanmayaḥ*).

Then [the soul] experiences his entire experience, composed of happiness and so forth according to his past actions.

20–22b. When action becomes equal [i.e. when two actions block each other by being simultaneously ready to produce fruit and equally urgent] due to the power of [the passing] of intervals of time, [and] when [thereupon], because of an intense descent of grace, the soul is initiated by his guru, he then becomes omniscient like Śiva and devoid of his state of partial knowledge, filled with the unfolding of his [innate] nature of [identicalness to] Śiva and he does not [after death] continue to be involved in the cycle of rebirth.[14]

12 The text appears to describe the principles in the order in which they act upon the bound soul and not in the order of their evolution (for which see 4:22–24ab), and it also seems to collapse the principle of the strands (*guṇa*) together with that of secondary matter.

13 *Tattvakalābaddhaḥ* might also be translated 'thus bound with the powers of the principles'.

14 Rāmakaṇṭha brings all his inventiveness to bear to distort the meaning of the text here, because he must resolve a contradiction within the Śaiva Siddhānta. All sources agree that initiation is performed after the initiand has received Śiva's grace. This one can infer to have taken place by such signs as the initiand's devotion to Śiva. According to some sources, that descent of grace occurs only when the soul's innate impurity is 'ripe' to be removed. Rāmakaṇṭha's difficulty is that the *Kiraṇa-Tantra*'s account makes no mention of the ripeness of impurity; instead its position is that a descent of grace occurs when two actions of equal strength become ripe simultaneously and thus block each other from bearing fruit. This is treated at length in Chapter 5, where Rāmakaṇṭha is forced to explain that there are different kinds of descents of grace and that one such is intended to unblock the flow of experience when such an impasse occurs. The sort of descent

22c–23. Thus [the bound soul is further] bound by a sequence [of evolutes of primal matter and] he is liberated in sequence. The soul is taught to have three conditions; [that of] the one without [at least one of the bonds] (*kevala*),[15] the one with [all three bonds] (*sakala*), and the pure soul. The bound soul has been taught to be of this nature. What else do you ask about?

Chapter 2

Garuḍa spoke:
1. The soul you have taught to have limited powers of knowledge, and Śiva to be omniscient. Tell [me] what is the cause for their [respectively] pure and impure natures.
The Lord spoke:
3–5. Because of the [bound] soul's beginningless connection with impurity I have taught that he has partial knowledge, and because Śiva is beginninglessly free from impurity, he is therefore omniscient. When something is established to have a beginning, then a cause is postulated (*kalpyate*). Such forms, [respectively] pure and impure, are taught (*smṛtam*) truly to belong to these two [viz. to Śiva and to the bound soul]. Why is crystal clear? Why is copper tarnished? Just as there is no cause for this [pair of naturally given facts], so too there is none [for the natures] of Śiva and the [bound] soul.

---

of grace that removes blockages need not, according to Rāmakaṇṭha, be the one that precedes salvific initiation, because the soul's innate impurity may not be ripe. Following Rāmakaṇṭha we might interpret the above as follows: 'When action becomes equal [i.e. when a candidate for initiation demonstrates his readiness by equanimity with regard to all action] because of an intense descent of Śiva's power due to that power of the transformation [by ripening] (*antara*) of his impurity (*kāla*) [and] when [thereupon] he is initiated by his guru, he then becomes omniscient . . . etc.'

15 The souls 'without [at least one of the bonds]' are either souls trapped in a period of resorption of the evolutes of primal matter, and therefore bound only by impurity and action (*pralayakevala*), or souls who 'by wisdom' have attained a state where they are bound only by innate impurity (*vijñānakevala*). The souls bound by all three bonds of impurity, action, and the evolutes of primal matter, are embodied, either with gross physical bodies such as ours or with subtle bodies (also composed of the lower principles that are evolutes of primal matter) which enable transmigration between gross bodies.

Garuḍa spoke:
6–7. For what reason is the [already bound] soul again bound by bond[s] starting with the principle of the limited power to act (*kalā*)? [And for what reason] have you taught, Lord, that he is inside primal matter and that he is all-pervasive? How can he be all-pervasive; and so everywhere, and [yet at the same time] in the belly of primal matter? How can this be, since they exclude each other?
The Lord spoke:
8–9. The soul is bound for the sake of liberation; this [liberation] does not come about for him otherwise. Until he is linked to a body he cannot experience [the fruits of his past actions]. His body is derived from primal matter; if he has no body (*tasya tadabhāvāt*) then he cannot be liberated. Therefore, (*tena*) [though already] dirty through his impotence, he is made [yet more] dirty by [being bound by] that [body] (*tena*).
10. Just as a garment because of being dirty is cleaned when [placed] in dirt,[16] in the same way an unclean soul too [is cleaned] even though situated in the belly of primal matter.
11. The belly of primal matter that has been spoken of consists of the principles (*tattva*) from that of limited power to act (*kalā*) down to the earth, and the absorption into it (*tasmin . . . layaḥ*) that has been taught[17] [was spoken of] with the intention of referring to the subtle body.
Garuḍa spoke:
12. You have taught that impurity is beginningless. Is it derived from primal matter or is it a property also of the soul? or is it something else again? Tell me of what nature impurity is.
The Lord spoke:
13. Impurity is innate, [but] the effects of primal matter are an adventitious impurity (*malaḥ*). Primal matter is not taught to be that which deludes,[18] since (*yataḥ*) she [also] illumines through her effects,

16 Presumably a special dirt with cleansing properties (like Fuller's earth) is intended. (cf. *Yājñavalkya-Smṛti* 1:186ab in this anthology.)

17 The mention of an earlier statement about the absorption of the soul into primal matter must be a reference to 1:19. (For the subtle body see note ad 1:22c–23.)

18 Primal matter does not just delude. This is emphatically stated, in order to underline a fundamental deviation from the doctrine of the Sāṅkhyas, from whom the Śaiva Siddhānta inherits its dualist ontology. According to the Sāṅkhyas, matter (conceived of as feminine) seduces and deludes souls (conceived of as

14. for through the embrace of her effects she illumines the consciousness of the soul. When she has split apart impurity, a partial manifestation of the soul's [innate] consciousness comes about.
15. She is an illuminator through her effects and does not act as a deluder. Illumination [is expressed] by the word 'revelation' (*vyaktiśabdena*) and occlusion, by the word 'impurity' (*malaśabdena*).
16. [But] this revelation [of the powers] of the soul is [also] plainly taught to be an impurity, in the same way as [one speaks of] the distortion produced by a lamp (*dīpāndhakāravat*[19]). Primal matter too [we have therefore also] taught to be a seductress, because of the experience [that the soul has through her] of the taste of external objects.
17–18. Wherever the soul (*asya*) is situated as a result of his own past actions and as a result of impurity, bondage arising from primal matter operates on him [but only] with good cause [viz. the soul's impurity and action]. Would there not [otherwise] be [bondage] for Śiva too who is beginninglessly free of impurity?[20] Therefore impurity is not [the same as] primal matter. It is [demonstrated here] by arguments [to be] distinct.
19–20b. [One might object that] the effects of primal matter should be all [that there is in the way of bondage]. How [can one prove] another innate impurity?[21] That impurity (*tat paśutvam*) must (*syāt*) reside in the soul. And since the bound soul is taught to be situated in the path [of the principles (*tattva*) that are evolutes of primal matter], impurity is therefore held to be different from that [path of principles].

---

masculine) so that they mistakenly identify themselves with their bodies (which are made up of evolutes of matter) and become entrapped in a potentially endless sequence of births in the world.

19 I have followed Rāmakaṇṭha's ingenious interpretation here. This would literally translate 'like the darkness of a lamp'.

20 Alternatively, following Rāmakaṇṭha, '[Otherwise] nothing [in the way of bondage] would arise for the [soul who would be] beginninglessly free from impurity [and thus] also [a] Śiva.'

21 The implication is that there can be no physical impurity outside primal matter and that impurity should therefore, if indeed it exists, be listed as another principle (*tattva*) among the other evolutes of primal matter. The answer explains that the soul's innate impurity does exist, is independent of primal matter, and yet in a sense is inside primal matter inasmuch as it is a part of the bound soul, who is in turn entrapped in the evolutes of primal matter. In some tantras (but not the *Kiraṇa-Tantra*) the category of the bound soul is listed as one of the principles into which the universe is divided.

20c–21. And these are said to be its synonyms: impurity, nescience, bound-soul-ness, that which obscures, darkness, ignorance, envelopment, delusion. It is known in various schools of thought (*mate mate*) by these various synonyms, such as ignorance.
22–23b. Because of its existence the bound soul is held in this system (*iha*) to require being [further] bound, being purified and being enlightened. These various processes [too], such as being bound, which have [just] been proclaimed [to be necessary] for the soul (*tasya*) – and not just the condition of being an experiencer – come into being only when there is impurity.
Garuḍa spoke:
23c–24b. If [the soul is] thus [as above described] and it is settled that he requires being bound, [then] he has (*asya*) impurity, which is linked to the bound soul.[22] Why then is this impurity not posited on the basis of reasoning to be a[n inseparable] property (*dharmaḥ*) of the soul?
The Lord spoke:
24c–25. Because of being beginninglessly connected [with him], [impurity] is referred to figuratively as a property of the [bound] soul. How can [the soul] acquire the property of ignorance, for he is [inseparably] linked to knowledge? Impurity is not a property of the soul (*tasya*). If it were a property then transformation would be apparent [in the soul].
26. [Impurity is] not a natural quality of the soul, whose natural quality is consciousness. If it were, then the soul would be subject to change. [In fact what occurs in bondage by the evolutes of primal matter is that innate] knowledge of one thing is made manifest and [innate] knowledge of another is obscured.
27ab. Transformation is taught [to be possible] of the insentient. It is not possible for what is sentient.
Garuḍa spoke:
27c–28b. Because of their beginningless connection to one another, [and] because they are all-pervasive, they [viz. the soul and its impurity] cannot separate. If it had its innate nature destroyed, would this [impurity] not [itself] be destroyed?[23]

22 The relative clause is redundant in the original.

23 One might also translate 'If the innate [connection between the two] were destroyed, would this [soul] not be destroyed?' or 'If the innate [impurity] were destroyed, would the soul (*tasya*) not be destroyed?' 29–30b and 32c–34 could be taken to support the translation printed in the text; but the examples that Śiva gives in 30c–32b could be taken to support one of the other interpretations. The

The Lord spoke:
29–30b. Though this impurity is all-pervasive, its power is destroyed. By a [certain] means the power in impurity is blocked in a particular way (*kathañcit*): just as the burning power of fire is swiftly blocked by a mantra, so too the power of impurity is blocked, and thereby [the soul] is separated [from impurity]. That is what is taught.
30c–32b. After blocking the power of that [impurity], [the soul] is rendered devoid of all the desires of [this-worldly] existence. Tarnish on copper is innate, and yet by the destruction of that [tarnish] the copper itself is not destroyed. Just as this destruction [of the tarnish] on copper [takes place without destroying the copper], so too the destruction of the impurity of a soul [takes place without destroying the soul].[24] Similarly, even when the husks of rice are destroyed, there is no destruction of that [rice itself].
32c–34. When (*yathā ... tathā*) the power connected with a poison is blocked by mantras, the poison itself is not destroyed. The same is the case when a soul's impurity is destroyed. The nut of the Kataka tree[25] when thrown into dirty water blocks the power [of the dirt]. What does it cast outside the water? [Nothing.] Śiva-knowledge similarly effects the blocking of the power of that [impurity].

Chapter 3

Garuḍa spoke:
1. The condition of being an experiencer has been taught to result from [being bound by] impurity. Does it not arise from desire? Since that [desire] arises from [the principle of] attachment, then attachment should be taught [as the cause of the soul's condition of being an experiencer]. What need is there of [postulating] impurity [as a cause] for this?

---

corollary of the destruction of the soul might be argued to be entailed by the alteration of its innate nature (viz. tht of being bound). If it were to suffer any alteration, then it could not be sentient because of the fundamental principle stated in 27ab.

24 Perhaps this might be translated 'so too the destruction of [the power of] the impurity of a soul [takes place without destroying the impurity itself]'.

25 *Strychnos potatorum* Linn., a nut once commonly used for clearing dirty water.

The Lord spoke:
2. The condition of being an experiencer which we have spoken of is beginningless, [because] it is caused by impurity. Desire [comes about only] when there is a body. And from what cause does the body [come into being]?
3–6b. [From the principle of attachment. And thus desire cannot be the cause, because] attachment itself (*rāgo 'pi*) becomes active for a soul [only] because it is caused by that [condition of being an experiencer]. For just as [the punishment of] binding in fetters depends on theft as its seed, so too the principle of attachment it becomes active depending on impurity. From this [impurity there comes about] the condition of being an experiencer. The body [and] experience result from different causes, for the condition of being an experiencer results from impurity (*paśutvena*); and the bond of primal matter [is the cause] for the body. Experience that a soul has in the form of happiness, unhappiness and the like results from past actions. Not otherwise is the soul's (*asya*) bondage by experience and by the condition of being an experiencer taught [to occur].[26]
Garuḍa spoke:
6c–7b. Lord of the gods, since you have taught that these actions are the cause of experience, and since past actions can only be accumulated when [the soul has] a body, tell me then how [is it possible that the soul has] a body at the time of [the very first] creation?
The Lord spoke:
7c–8b. Just as impurity is beginningless, so too the soul's past actions are beginningless. If it were not established that they are beginningless, how could one account for diversity [of experience]?
8c–9b. Therefore [past actions] are beginningless and so is primal matter and so is worldly existence. So too Śiva, the creator of the entire universe, is established to be (*sthitaḥ*) beginningless.
Garuḍa spoke:
9c–10b. Omnipotent Lord, you have taught earlier that Śiva is the creator; how is he to be known? How is it possible for him to be a creator since he lacks instruments and is not embodied?
The Lord spoke:
10c–11b. [This last objection is invalid,] because just as time, although it is not embodied, is known from experience to bring

26 The text and translation here are uncertain.

about results, so too Śiva, although he is not embodied, produces effects by his will.
11c–12b. Will alone is his instrument, just as [will] is held [to be the instrument] of a true yogin. Although it is devoid of the instruments of sense and action, a magnet is observed to draw out [iron] splinters. And even if the activity [of the creation of the universe] should not be [directly] observed, the effects [are seen and from them the Lord's] will [which is his instrument] is known.
13. [The universe is] gross, diverse, [and therefore] an effect, like a pot. It cannot be otherwise. And so (*ataḥ*) there exists (*asti*) some [instigating] cause. What if it is alleged that it is past actions [that are the cause of the universe]? That is impossible, because [past actions are] insentient.
14. He has been taught to be differentiated according to the division of his activities [into the following three forms]: formless (*niṣkalaḥ*), both gross and formless (*sakalaniṣkalaḥ*), and gross (*sthūlaḥ* [=*sakalaḥ*]) [as] Śānta, Sadāśiva and Īśa [respectively].[27]
Garuḍa spoke:
15. How can the formless [Lord] be known? If He is also gross (*sakalaḥ*)[28] then [He must be merely an ordinary] soul. And the other [Lord], who has two natures is contradictory [because his two natures are] mutually [contradictory].
The Lord spoke:
16. Through the power [gained] from a descent of [divine] power into the soul and from the power of mantras [in initiation] the principle of the formless, [although it is] subtle, is at all times

27 It is difficult to convey with just two words the connotations of the pair of terms *sakala* and *niṣkala* used to describe aspects of Śiva. They mean at the same time gross and subtle, manifest and unmanifest, with and without parts, engaged and disengaged, active and transcendent, aspected and aspectless, qualified and unqualified, embodied and disembodied. The term Śānta literally means 'at peace' and, like *niṣkala*, it is a synonym for the highest principle, that of Śiva. The name Sadāśiva might be translated 'Eternally Śiva'. His ambivalent state is that of being ready and poised to act (*udyukta*), between the latent potency (*śaktatva*) of the highest principle and the state of being engaged in action (*pravṛttatva*) in the next principle, that of Īśa or Īśvara, 'he who rules'.

28 Garuḍa's question makes sense, because the term *sakala*, translated here with 'gross', is not just a label for the Lord when he is engaged in action, but also a technical term of the system (defined in 1:22c–23) for the ordinary soul bound by all three bonds of impurity, past action, and that derived from primal matter.

knowable, just as the effects of poison [can be brought about] through the power [of mantras].[29]

17. Even though he is [called] 'equipped with parts' (*sakalaḥ*), he is not [an ordinary bound] soul, because he is devoid of the parts [that are the evolutes] of primal matter. Because Śiva is pure, those impure parts cannot be posited [to exist] in him (*atra*).

18. He has parts that are made up of mantras. And those mantras are Śiva. With these [mantras] he fashions a gross (*mahat*) body of his own that is presided over by pure senses.

19a–b. Until he acts in this way, there can be no lineage from spiritual preceptor (*guru*) [to pupil]. Embodied he bestows divine favour on all embodied souls.

19c–20. For just as a yogin has power to hold and to release, in exactly the same way the immanent Lord in this [system] must be understood to hold and to release.[30]

21. By ritual gestures (*mudrā*), by ritual diagrams (*maṇḍala*), and by mantras – [all three of] which are employed in order to accomplish [their respective] three aims[31] – by meditation, and by applying [what is taught in] all the scriptures [of the Śaiva Siddhānta] (*sarvajñānapravṛttitaḥ*) the gross [aspect of Śiva] can be known.

22. The other deity, [Sadāśiva,] who has both natures, is not formless (*niṣkalaḥ*) [and yet], compared to the [relatively] coarse body [of Īśa, Śiva's coarse form], He is taught to be formless (*kalāhīnaḥ*).[32]

23. Thus[33] Īśa is directly [perceptible through the prescribed means and is thus] the basis for yoga for [all] practitioners of yoga. Neither yoga, because it would have no target, nor [exercising control over] the channels of the body (*nāḍī*), nor focusing one's thoughts (*dhāraṇā*) [can serve to help one to grasp the formless Lord].

24. But in order to bestow compassion on souls, although He is

29 Thus Rāmakaṇṭha; but following Tryambakaśambhu it might be translated 'just as [one can know that a person has been bitten by a poisonous snake by] the effects [such as swelling that result] from the poison'.

30 Rāmakaṇṭha suggests that what is meant is that yogins can occupy arbitrarily chosen physical objects and use them as if they were their bodies.

31 Rāmakaṇṭha explains that ritual gestures and mantras invite the Lord to come and go and that ritual diagrams are places into which the Lord can be invited for the purposes of external worship.

32 The second half of the verse might also translate 'compared to [Īśa] whose body is [relatively] gross, He is taught to be formless'.

33 According to Rāmakaṇṭha 'by being joined to a body on which one can meditate'.

transcendent (*paro 'pi*), He has lowered Himself (*aparatāṃ gataḥ*). He is in primal, unvoiced sound (*nāda*), in almost gross sound (*bindu*), in [the sound of] ether, in [the gross sound of] mantras [that express Śiva Himself], in [the coarser mantra-souls called] *aṇus*, in the power [which controls those], in the seed[-syllables such as *oṃ* that precede the enunciation of mantras] (*bīja*), in the sound units [of the seeds] (*kalā*), and in the end[-sounds such as the final nasalization of the seed syllable *oṃ*].[34]

25. Like a yogin, He is conscious of service done to Him, because He is omniscient, [and] He bestows boons [accordingly]. Because by His own will He bestows compassion, He has [three aspects: these are] resorption (*laya*), enjoyment (*bhoga*) and office (*adhikāra*).[35]

26. He is represented as threefold with different names according to the different activities [He performs in those aspects]. The Lord (*īśvaraḥ*) urges the Lords of the lower mantras to act.

27. Once they have been urged, and no more, by Him, they create the lower universe. In the pure path Śiva is the creator. Ananta[36] is taught to be the lord in the impure [path].

28. Just as a ruler of a kingdom in this world employs another man, powerful like himself [to do his business], so too this [Ananta] does everything [after being] awakened by Śiva's power (*tacchakti-*). He is omniscient, his body is pure, and he reveals all the scriptures (*sarvajñānaprakāśakaḥ*).

Chapter 4

Garuḍa spoke:

1–2. And it is said that Ananta awakens by the might of Śiva's power. And that awakening power is taught to be all pervasive: why does it not awaken others [than those that it does awaken]

34 These interpretative translations are based on Rāmakaṇṭha's commentary.

35 'Enjoyment' is the phase in which Śiva knows the world; and 'office' is that in which Śiva governs the world. The three phases tally with the three aspects of 3:14.

36 Ananta is a *vijñānakevala*, that is to say a soul bound only by impurity (see note ad 1:22c–23). At the beginning of each cycle of creation Śiva selects such souls to hold offices. He arrests their further development and employs them to create or rule parts of the impure universe, which are derived from primal matter. (Śiva is himself too pure to have any direct contact with primal matter and its evolutes.) Ananta is the name of whichever soul Śiva invests with the highest of these offices.

who are also [equally] near it? If He helps only those that are 'suitable' then Śiva must be [partial and therefore] possessed of attachment (*rāgavān*).

The Lord spoke:

3–4. [No,] because just as the awakening of lotuses from the contact of the rays of the sun is not consistent – some awaken and others never do – and yet the sun has neither hatred nor affection, so too the Lord does not have either [hatred or affection].

4c–5b. Because of his [suitability to hold] office (*adhikārāt*[37]) Ananta (*asya*) is employed. He would not have a body (*sthitiḥ*) if he were not [thus] employed. Through the Lord's power (*tatsāmarthyāt*) Ananta has omniscience, O Garuḍa.

Garuḍa spoke:

5c–7b. If he has a body then Ananta cannot be omniscient, because the faculties of the senses are limited and [can only] grasp limited [objects]. That body [must be] made up of primal matter and born of the causes that are [past] actions; [the fruits of] which remain [to be consumed]. If there is indeed a difference [between his faculties and those of other embodied souls, then it must be that] he can hear and [see and] so on from a great distance.

The Lord spoke:

7c–8b. His body is taught to consist of pure matter[38] [and is] not born of past action. Because he is freed of [impure] bonds, what can stop him from being omniscient?

8c–9b. Just as a snake's poison that is in the snake does not destroy that [snake] in which it resides, so too that which is connected with him that causes his [continued] existence [in the material world][39] does not destroy Ananta.

9c–10b. Just as a Guḍūcī plant (*chinnodbhavā*),[40] when it is cut off, comes back from the strength [left] in the place in which it grew (*sthānāśrayavaśāt*), so too the overlord of mantras (*mantreśe*)[, Ananta,] must necessarily bear a body by virtue of his position.

10c–11b. Just as a body sustained by the power of mantras can

37 Rāmakaṇṭha glosses this with 'ripeness of impurity' (*malasya pakvatvam*).

38 Rāmakaṇṭha tells us that Ananta's body is made up of 'pure knowledge' (*śuddhavidyā*), the first principle above that of primal matter.

39 i.e. his body of 'pure knowledge' and the impurity entailed by holding an office (*adhikāramala*).

40 *Tinospora cordifolius* Miers, a plant that grows from a bulb.

remain for some time and through [that] power can reach some desired place, even if it has been bitten by death,[41]
11c–12b. so too through the might of Śiva's power (*tacchakti-*) his body remains. For this reason his body is to be understood to be utterly pure like a lotus-leaf.[42]
12c–13b. And just as the healthy nutrient fluid (*kalyaḥ . . . rasaḥ*) of the body remains in this [human] body by means of [its] channels (*tantraiḥ*), so too the mighty power of knowledge [remains in Ananta in spite of him having a body].
13c–14. Just as great strength [can be attained] by weak people through the power of medicine, so too Ananta has great strength through the might of Śiva's power (*tacchakti-*), and, because he has this might, he immediately stimulates the matrix [of primal matter to generate from herself all that is material].
Garuḍa spoke:
15–16 He is the one who stimulates in the lower realm [i.e. in primal matter and the principles that evolve from her]. Why must there be one who stimulates primal matter? She is of herself prone to transformation by [the very fact of her] transformation [of herself] into this world, since she is taught to be the matrix of the universe and her evolutes [are the principles that] start from that of limited power to act (*kalādayaḥ*). As a result of [that] transformation [must there not follow] the destruction of everything?[43] [And yet if there is] no transformation, how can the universe [come about]?
The Lord spoke:
17. She is insentient and that is why she has to be stimulated [to transform herself] for the sake of the good of souls. Of herself she does not transform and therefore there must be an Ananta who impels her to act.
18. Just as the ocean changes on the surface alone from the force of the wind, so too primal matter, since she is unshakeable, is

41 Or, as Rāmakaṇṭha inteprets, 'bitten [by a snake] at [the very moment of] death'.

42 Because it is through Śiva's power and not through the evolutes of primal matter that Ananta bears a body, his body is as pure as a lotus leaf. Water cannot for a moment remain on a lotus leaf and grows in mud, just as Ananta lives in the realm of impure matter.

43 What is implied is that matter herself is destroyed by her own transformation into the effects that are the universe, and so all will be irrevocably destroyed at the time of the supposedly cyclical destruction of the universe. What the Śaiva Siddhānta in fact teaches is the cyclical resorption of the effects that are the universe back into primal matter, their source.

subject to change [only superficially] through [her evolutes,] the principles of limited power to act and so on.

19. Someone may point out that (*cet*) she cannot produce her effects if she is not shaken up, that she must be shaken, be impelled by Ananta (*tadīraṇam*). Once stimulated by him this power produces her effects incessantly.

20. [This is true, but] as the [material] cause of the [material] universe, she is [nevertheless] taught to be 'unshakeable', because she pervades everything. The body of her effects in the universe are not, as primal matter [herself] is, pervasive [and yet] transcendent. [Since] she pervades all things from the principle of limited power to act downwards (*bhāvān kalādikān*), it is therefore taught that she is unshakeable.

21. The power which produces her effects is called 'action' (*kriyā*), and [as such] her form is subtle. Although she is subtle [she transforms herself] into gross effects like the seed of a banyan tree.

22. Therefore she should be understood to be the cause of this entire (*samantataḥ*) gross [universe]. From this [cause are produced] the principles of limited power to act (*kalā*), time, binding fate (*saṃsthā* = *niyatiḥ*), [impure] knowledge (*bodhinī* = *aśuddhavidyā*), attachment (*abhilāṣakṛt* = *rāgaḥ*),[44]

23. and [secondary] matter (*sūkṣmam* = *prakṛtiḥ*). From that [last-mentioned evolve] the strands of material existence (*guṇāḥ*), and from those the principle of the intellect (*buddhiḥ*); from the intellect the principle of the sense of self-identity (*ahaṃkāra*); and from that the eleven faculties[45] [of the mind, ears, skin, eyes, tongue, nose, mouth, hand, anus, reproductive organs and feet,] and the five subtle elements [viz. sound, touch, form, taste and smell].

24ab. From these [subtle elements the five] gross elements [viz. ether, air, fire, water and earth] come into being. All [this] below the Lord [Ananta] generates.

44 The mature post-scriptural doctrine is that knowledge and attachment evolve from the principle of limited power to act (*kalā*) and not directly from primal matter.

45 It is not clear whether the 'eleven faculties' refers to the organs themselves or the faculties of those organs, as Abhinavagupta understands (*Tantrasāra*, edited by Mukunda Ram Sastri (Srinagar, 1918) p. 88). Furthermore it is not clear whether the eleven faculties and the five subtle elements are principles (*tattva*) in this tantra. (See the discussion of the principles of the system of the Sāṅkhyas and the Śaiva Siddhānta in the Introduction pp. xviii and xxxv–xxxvii.)

24B. The Lord, the ruler [Ananta], equipped of the powers of Śiva, created the whole body of effects that are [composed] of primal matter in which the [relatively] pure and impure are mixed, and the various states of mind of all creatures born of wombs. If [all] that is one [i.e. from a single source], how can it be of two kinds [pure and impure]? [The answer is that] in cases [such as that] of fireflies [that emit light] and other such [insects which do not] we experience one phenomenon and its opposite where both are effects of the same cause.[46]

24cd. Thus this [universe] is of varied composition and has [relatively] pure and impure parts.

25. You must know that it [i.e. the universe] is the effect that arises from the power of the [primal] cause and that it results from the seed [viz. from impurity and past action].[47] Thus these effects of that [primal matter] which – because they make up the transmigratory body – reside in the gross body, have been explained.

26–27b. Although this body of effects consisting of primal matter (*asitātmakam*) is [full of] mutually contradictory [effects], nevertheless, [since its contradictory parts are] totally integrated in one entity,[48] it clearly accomplishes the various requirements of the soul, just as the various [disparate] parts of a man's chariot [accomplish what he requires].

27c–28b. Thus Ananta created this means of bondage to a [gross] body (*dehanibandhanam*). Without a [gross] body there can be no liberation, [because there can be no] consumption [of the fruits of past actions], [no powers of] knowledge and action, and no teacher (*guruḥ*).

28c–29. This Śiva also[49] (*ca*) does, because He acts entirely as He wishes, since He is omnipotent. He is at peace, [and] bestows grace on all. Through His power [the suppliant may attain] all desires.

46 All insects are born of one cause: warm moisture.

47 See *Kiraṇa-Tantra* 3:3–4.

48 Rāmakaṇṭha takes this one entity to be the soul's subtle transmigratory body. As we have seen above (1:15–23), the various constituents of the subtle body endow a soul with limited faculties of knowledge and action whereby he can use up the fruits of accumulated past action and work towards liberation. It is through the subtle body that the soul is linked to the various gross bodies.

49 This interpretation is Rāmakaṇṭha's. Ananta is a minion performing what the supreme Lord commands. Thus they are both in different senses authors of creation.

Chapter 5

Garuḍa spoke:

1. Initiation should take place after a descent of Śiva's power; [but there can be] no descent, because [Śiva's power is] all-pervasive. Since [all is] pervaded by Śiva, his power must at all times be in the bound soul.

2. Should not all [material] existence have been extirpated, if [Śiva's] power had always been [in the soul]? And (*vā*) what is this 'time' [that you have] taught? If it is time [that brings about the right conditions for initiation] then what need is there of Śiva?

The Lord spoke:

4. Words are used figuratively here: just as the soul is said to move, though all-pervasive, and is said to be perishable, though it is eternal; just as a 'cutting' of bonds is spoken of; just as Lord Śiva is said to be 'King of mantras', so too in the Śaiva tradition a descent of power is spoken of in a secondary sense.

5–6b. Just as the sudden falling of a thing instils fear, so too the descent of power is said to instil fear of worldly existence. In the same way in other contexts than these [we say that] the soul also (*tathā*) 'goes' to its teacher.[50]

6–7. Just as a teacher awakens pupils that have fallen asleep in front of him with a stick, so too Śiva awakens those asleep in the slumber of delusion with His power. When [a soul attains] realization of his own nature, then it is said that [Śiva's power has] fallen.

8ab. Therefore 'descent' is used in a secondary sense. [To have received] a 'descent' means [to have] the signs [of enlightenment].

8cd. And[51] the time of the descent of this [power] is [that of] the equal balance of [two simultaneously maturing] actions.

50 The problematic half-verse 6ab is not commented upon by Rāmakaṇṭha. If we read with Vivanti, we might translate 'and similarly this [sort of metaphorical usage of words of movement is found] elsewhere than here: so [it is with] the soul [going] towards its teacher.' Alternatively 'Therefore (?) elsewhere too this [power falls] in the same way, as [when] the soul goes to his teacher'.

51 Resorting to a widespread commentarial device Rāmakaṇṭha maintains that with the word 'and' an oblique reference to the ripeness of impurity is made, which is, according to him and to other exegetes of this school, a prerequisite for the descent of power (cf. 1:20–22b and note ad loc.). The *Kiraṇa-Tantra* teaches that the moment of the blocking of experience by the fruits of actions that are simultaneously ready to be experienced and equally powerful is the moment when Śiva intervenes. It is almost certainly the position of the *Kiraṇa-Tantra* that that

8ef. The equal balance of [simultaneously mature] actions is the time [of the descent of power]. It is either destroyed or [made] unequal [by the descent of power].[52]
9ab. How can this equal balance of past actions be reached? [In answer to this objection one might ask the equally unanswerable question] how [is it ordinarily possible that fruition sometimes requires relatively] little or lots of time?
9c–10b. At the very time when this equal balance [of actions] that is beyond our senses (*sūkṣmam*) occurs, this [power of Śiva] straight away illuminates the [soul's] own nature, [and this is discernible] by means of the marks characteristic of enlightenment (*bodhacihnabalena vai*).[53]
10cd. [Ordinarily] a more powerful past action [gives its fruit] first; another one will give its fruit later.
11. When there is equal balance, how can the soul's (*tasya*) experience arise? It is mixed action[54] that generates [experience], for if it is equal, then there can be no experience.
12. And it should be explained that one past action has to be more powerful [than the others], otherwise there can be no

moment of blockage is the only moment when liberation through Śiva's power is possible; but, because it is not explicitly denied that liberation occurs in any other way, Rāmakaṇṭha interprets the text to mean that some descent of Śiva's power is indeed essential to deal with blockages of experience, but that such a descent of power is not necessarily the one that must be followed by initiation and then liberation, since a salvific descent must invariably be preceded by ripening of the soul's innate impurity. On two other occasions (1:20c and 5:30b) Rāmakaṇṭha has to interpret what is intended to mean 'balance of actions' to mean 'equanimity with regard to actions'.

52 Rāmakaṇṭha explains that a descent of power at this moment either destroys all remaining actions together with the principles that make up the transmigratory body thereby rendering the soul free of all the bonds except impurity, or it renders one of the two opposing actions unequal to the other, so that experience is again made possible.

53 i.e. by signs such as devotion to Śiva and detachment from worldly pleasure and pain. Following Rāmakaṇṭha this might be translated as follows: 'this [power] illumines [the soul's] nature by means of the force [which is the ripeness of impurity] whose characteristic mark is enlightenment'.

54 'mixed' appears to mean 'of mixed strength'; but Rāmakaṇṭha, perhaps anxious to fight off possible criticism that the text here is repetitious, interprets this to refer to a widespread threefold division of action: that which causes birth, that which causes long life, and that which causes worldly experience. Consumption of the fruits of action is possible only when they are all mixed together.

happiness or unhappiness. When [actions] are powerful and weak [relative to each other], no confusion [i.e. blockage] occurs.
13. When actions are not more powerful or weaker than each other, then the soul resorts to [Śiva's] power. That is to be known as a 'descent'. Devotion [to Śiva] is a sign by which it can be recognized [to have taken place].
14. The time of [the descent of] power is [figuratively called] skilful, [because] it is that in which the soul receives the Lord's grace. Because [the soul is] beginninglessly connected to its past actions, Śiva waits for the time.
15–17b. It is called the hole of time. The Lord Śiva knows it. Just as someone [firing at] a moving target waits for a particular moment and also knows that [moment], so too Śiva waits for the time when there is equality [of actions], since otherwise, if there were no equality of actions, liberation would be simultaneous [for all]. If this sequence is denied, then there should be no need of paths and means by which to achieve [liberation].
17c–18b. It is Śiva who must be understood to be the governing power (*prabhuḥ*) in this; how could time be thought to be the governing power? He is the governing power, because his nature is omniscience. Time is not, because it is insentient.
18c–20. Just as the sun is the governing power in the matter of the awakening of lotuses – even though time is also present and blossoming does not occur in this [process of awakening] without time, nevertheless it is the sun that is referred to in this world as the awakener of lotuses – so too here, although that time alone when there is a balance of [the fruits of past] actions [is when a descent of power occurs], nevertheless it is God who is the governing power over the descent of His power.
21. You may question (*cet*) how it is that this [power] awakens many although she is one. There is no logical fault although [she awakens] many: it is not impossible, because she is all-pervading.
22ab. Thus this linking [of the soul] to power – [a linking] which is imperceptible to our senses – has been taught in this scripture.
Garuḍa spoke:
21c–25. And if initiation occurs after [the soul's] being thus linked to the Lord's power, [then why is it that] even after initiation we see [that souls suffer] occlusion?[55] If this power causes occlusion,

55 What Garuḍa refers to by 'occlusion' is a lapsing from observances. Initiates can lapse only if the right knowledge in them is occluded.

then the soul (*tasya*) does not attain the bliss [of liberation]. Let the Lord arrange it so that the soul (*asau*) does not deviate.
The Lord spoke:
21c–25. This [power that descends before initiation operates] at Śiva's will among souls who are in darkness. It is not this [power] that is called 'the occluding power', because she creates darkness, [but another facet of Śiva's power].[56] This [salvific] power does not descend in order to occlude, because its nature is to bestow grace.
26. When the time approaches, this power that awakens souls illuminates the [soul's] self. After illuminating it she departs like lightning.
27. If a particular soul (*ayam*) is in darkness even though completely initiated, occasionally (*kvacit*) he reaches a station [of office in a subterranean paradise (*pātāla*) or the like, where he is] also in a twofold darkness [occluding his powers of knowledge and action].[57]
28. According to the Śaiva Siddhānta (*iha*) there arises in a soul situated there the same mental conditioning [from initiation]. When he has that, the soul attains unqualified liberation.
29. [A soul] may become occluded [though initiated] by this sequence;[58] [but] it would entail the utter pointlessness [of the sequence], if the same (*sā*) liberation did not [eventually] come about.
30–1. [Śiva's] power is [said to be] slow or very slow; this is said with the intention of referring to the [speed of the attainment of] equal balance of actions.[59] It is not however the case that such a power is subject to transformation, as milk is, because the power of Śiva is differentiated [only nominally] by the nature of its

56 Thus Rāmakaṇṭha.

57 Rāmakaṇṭha explains that an initiate can infringe the rules of conduct for initiates (this infringement being a clear sign that he is in darkness although completely initiated) and thereby be reborn as an office-bearer in a world of flesh-eating demons.

58 viz. by the sequence described above of simultaneously maturing actions blocking the soul's experience followed by a descent of Śiva's power and then by initiation.

59 Rāmakaṇṭha is at variance with the intention of the text here, for he takes this to mean 'with the intention of referring to its balancing the activity [of the maturing of the soul's innate impurity]'.

functions. It is a ladder for the estates starting with the Brahmins and it clearly liberates.

Chapter 6

Garuḍa spoke:
1. You have taught that Śiva bestows compassion on all, that he is the supreme cause. Now the estates, starting with the Brahmins, are [hierarchically ranked relative to each other as] inferiors and superiors.
2. If the purificatory rite [of Śaiva initiation] were also thus [i.e. unequal], then would the result not be similarly [unequal]? And if the purificatory rite is the same for them [all], then how is the status of some inferior and of some superior?
The Lord spoke:
3. [Initiation] is held to be not a rite of purification of caste, nor a purification of the body, [but] of the soul. If [it purified] one's caste (*jāteḥ*), then, as soon as a single individual is initiated, all [individuals of that caste] should be initiated.
4a–d. Therefore it cannot be said to be [a purification] of the caste, nor is it taught to be [a purification] of the body, since that is insentient. We have taught that the all-compassionate Śiva bestows grace on the sentient [i.e. on souls alone] (*cidrūpānugrahaḥ*).
Garuḍa spoke:
4e–6b. Because [the Lord is] the agent of grace to all, he must bestow grace [even] on children, the foolish, and on those who live for enjoyment (*bhoginām*). And that grace is dependent on the purificatory rite [of initiation]. Since it is taught in the tantra that liberation is only possible through the purificatory rite [of initiation], then [the enjoined] methods of approach, such as rituals, knowledge, and religious observances (*kriyājñānavratādīnām*), must be useless.
The Lord spoke:
6c–8b. The Lord bestows grace on people, O Garuḍa, exactly to suit the way they are; for some people in this world are suited to ritual and they attain liberation accordingly; others are suited to knowledge; and others again to religious observances (*caryāyogyāḥ*). Thus for each of these the Lord (*tena*) has taught a [means of] liberation [and they are to follow it] accordingly, after they have been joined [through initiation] to the Lord (*īśayojanāt*).

8c–9b. Initiation is held to be a prerequisite for the [further] means [to liberation], which are knowledge [ritual, observances] and [yoga] (*jñānādīnām*). By initiation alone there need not be liberation.[60] It is the [subsequent] means which determines that.
9c–f. Because He is compassionate to all, [the Lord] taught those means. Why did He not teach [just] the one means? Because [scripture elsewhere teaches[61]] otherwise.
10. [The initiating teacher] should cleanse away the obligations [to perform what is enjoined for ordinary initiates] (*samayān*)[62] from women and other such, because they are incapable [of fulfilling those obligations]. That is no fault, because they are ignorant; but for those who are not ignorant it would be a great sin.
11. Therefore these [ignorant ones] attain liberation [just] through initiation, because they have devotion [to the Lord]. Those who are capable [of performing what is enjoined for ordinary initiates] are not to have their obligations cleansed away [in initiation]. To them [the initiating teacher] should reveal [those obligations].
12. Thus he should reveal all [the means of] knowledge, [ritual, religious observances] and [yoga] to those capable of them. Otherwise there would be a break in continuity, and continuity is what is taught in the Śaiva tradition.
13. If there were no continuity, there would be nothing. And so this injunction exists because of the [Lord's] desire to teach means to maintain continuity (*sthityupāyavivakṣayā*), since He is compassionate to all.
Garuḍa spoke:
14. Now it is said that it is for the sake of removing bonds that initiation is performed. And yet no removal is seen. Since it is not seen, tell me how [it happens].
The Lord spoke:
15. The destruction of the bonds is brought about by stunning them, and that is achieved by well-known mantras (*śambaraiḥ*),

60 The text is not making the heretical assertion that initiation is not salvific, but is stressing that initiation entitles and binds normal initiates to certain religious practices. Initiation followed by the performance of enjoined observances is salvific. Only those incapable of following those observations have their obligations to do so ritually removed in initiation.

61 Thus Rāmakaṇṭha.

62 These obligations are held to be a further bond (*samayapāśa*) that, for ordinary initiates, can only be removed by observing them.

for [the powers of] mantras are unthinkable, as [we commonly experience when they effect such supernatural things as] the destruction of physical poison.

16. Just as some distant person is made to appear simply by the calling of his name, so too the destruction of [the fruits of] actions [is brought about] in the Śaiva Siddhānta (*iha*) by the principal mantras.

Garuḍa spoke:

17. If, Lord, all the bonds are removed by initiation, then, once the accomplishment of that object is attained, how can the body remain?

The Lord spoke:

18. Just as the potter's wheel still turns, sustained by its momentum, when the making of the pot has been achieved, so too this body remains.

19a–d. The action of many existences has its seeds burnt, so to speak (*iva*), by mantras [in initiation]. Future [action] is also blocked; [but] that by which this [body is sustained can be destroyed only] by experience.

19e–h. [Only] when the body collapses, [does the soul attain] liberation. Otherwise [initiation] which gives immediate liberation (*sadyonirvāṇadā*) may also be effected by mantra-souls (*aṇubhiḥ*) that are eternally established, and therefore they link [souls] to Śiva.

Garuḍa spoke:

20–21b. Why does one not see the slightest sign of [the fact that] someone [has been] released from bonds? [You may say that it can be recognized] when there is the sign of devotion [to the Lord] (*bhakticihne*). That is wrong (*na*),[63] and [in any case] that sign [of devotion] is sometimes not unambiguous, and where it is unambiguously seen, there too it is not constant.

21c–22. That union of the soul (*tasya*) [with the Lord] which has been spoken of above [in 6:8b] is necessarily dependent on grasping.[64] Grasping hold of the soul (*tasya*) is impossible, because it is all-pervasive and also incorporeal. There is a great inconsistency on this point. How can this be? Tell me.

63 It is wrong, because it has been taught to be a sign of the descent of Śiva's power that must precede initiation, not necessarily of initiation itself.

64 The initiating priest, with the help of mantras, ritually removes the soul from the body of the initiand in order to purify it.

The Lord spoke:
23–25b. The sign of those [released from bonds] is the firmness of their mental conditioning [by initiation] (*vāsanāniṣṭhā*)[65] and their absence of doubt about the ritual [enjoined] for [accomplishing] that. How could this not be inferred by some [evidence], however slight, to be present in one involved in those [Śaiva] rituals? If that sign is intense from beginning to end [of a person's life after initiation] then how can [one speak of] inconstancy in that person, whose thoughts are thoroughly conditioned [by the initiation] (*vāsanāhitacetasaḥ*)? And the conditioning is brought about by the ritual (*kriyāmūla*) and that depends on the mantras (*mantrānugā*).
25c–26b. Just as ether, though it is all-pervading, can be grasped through sound, [which is the quality peculiar to that element,] just as [the power of] poison [though] incorporeal is grasped[66] by the power of mantras, so too [the soul] whose power is consciousness (*cicchaktiḥ*) [can] definitely [be grasped] through their power.

Chapter 7

Garuḍa spoke:
1. In mantras is it Śiva that is expressed? or His power? or individual souls? Or is it all three that are expressed in one? That would be in contradiction with other tantras.
The Lord spoke:
2. Śiva is the instigating cause (*nimittabhūtaḥ*), He impels the individual mantra-souls by His power. All three are expressed here, for if one is missing, the rest do not [function].
3–4. Just as when one person commands another: 'Cook the rice!', that other performs the cooking, and he in turn is equipped

65 The same compound Rāmakaṇṭha interprets to mean 'the end of traces [of impurity and past action]'. Rāmakaṇṭha's interpretation of 23cd has been ignored; he reads the text differently and appears to have moved it to between 25b and 25c. From here to the end of Chapter 6 the text of the tantra and of Rāmakaṇṭha's commentary appear to be irreparably corrupt. Following Tryambakaśambhu we might translate 23 thus: 'The distinguishing mark of those [released from bonds] is being firm in [devotion to Śiva, which is one of] the traces [left by initiation], and the absence of doubt about ritual [enjoined] for [accomplishing] that [firmness]. How could this [sign] not be in one who is there [in the preceptor's presence]? Even a fool can infer it.'

66 It is grasped perhaps in the sense that it is taken hold of and then 'expressed' by them in such a way that their utterance can produce its effect.

with instruments such as firewood, so too Śiva is the agent of instigation (*hetukartṛtvam*), the mantra-souls are the instruments, and His power is the immediate agent (*kāraṇatvam*) – this is how these are in the Śaiva Siddhānta (*iha*).

5. Just as a human composition is made vividly manifest [by another] on a stringed instrument,[67] similarly Śiva's power, taking residence in [the mantras that are] individual souls, makes manifest [the results of] all [ritual] action.

Garuḍa spoke:

6. If the individual mantra-soul is as you have described, then it is Śiva who is expressed [in mantras] and His power too, because the one does not exist without the other (*avinābhāvāt*). Why bother with hypothetical individual souls [as mantras] as well?

The Lord spoke:

7–8b. [The functions] of mantras are taught [to be] cutting, binding, pinning down, destroying, beating, splitting, pleasing, drying, and fettering and bolting, and others of this kind. . . . [68]

8c–9c. [His] power [merely] controls these; she is the awakener of souls. That is why, O Garuḍa, individual souls must also be posited [as mantras] apart from Śiva and his consort [power] (*muktvā śivaparigraham*).[69]

Garuḍa spoke:

9c–10b. All these mantras that have been taught, whatever function they perform here, are they dependent on the past actions (*karma*) [of the individuals whom they affect] when they act, or not? Tell me clearly.

The Lord spoke:

10c–11b. They do not have [past action that is the cause of all else in men's lives as their] cause. The mantra-souls are held [to

67 Or perhaps 'Just as the song of a stringed instrument [performed] by a person [through that person's power] becomes clearly manifest . . .'

68 8b is corrupt and perhaps irreparable, for the commentary of Tryambakaśambhu is lost after Chapter 6 and Rāmakaṇṭha's is lacunose and corrupt here. The intended sense appears to be: 'Must all these various functions not be the preserves of separate individual mantra souls?' The following attempt at a translation follows my interpretation of Siṃharāja's (very badly transmitted) commentary: 'and so is it possible that (*kim*) [the functions] of [all of] these are in [Śiva's] self?' Rāmakaṇṭha cites 2:27a, the principle that something sentient cannot be subject to transformation, and this might be adduced in defence of the interpretation I have suggested.

69 Thus Siṃharāja; alternatively 'must be posited [as mantras] and are not part of Śiva's equipment'.

act] independently. They are to be known to be such from a teaching of [this] tantra (*jñānoktyāpi*) [viz.] from their supporting [i.e. reanimating] a body that has been bitten [by death or by a snake].[70]

11–12d. They have been taught to cut through [what is entailed by past] action at the time of initiation and they produce effects such as [those of] poison and so they are independent [of past action]. They depend on auspicious ritual action alone, complete in all its parts.[71]

Garuḍa spoke:

13. One person is seen to be raised to life [by mantras], but the same thing is not [necessarily] seen to happen to another person who has been bitten [by a snake or by death]. And because of this irregularity [it can be shown that] action is [a factor that affects the functioning] of mantras. How can that not be so? [13]

The Lord spoke:

14. The power of [certain] mantras is limited, because their application is limited. [Sometimes even] those [mantras taught] in this system (*atra*) which can perform all tasks do not produce their results, because of some deficiency [in the circumstances of their application].

15. [But in other cases] mantras do indeed manifest their innate power, even when an adept (*sādhakaḥ*)[72] [successfully] performs a ritual without having all the [prescribed] circumstances (*sāmagrīvikalaḥ*).

16. That is why these mantras are acknowledged to be [of] unthinkable [power] even by disputatious quibblers (*tarkaparair api*). They are omniscient, eternal (*nityarūpāḥ*), and they assume [any] form at will.

70 This is a reference to 4:10–11.

71 Rāmakaṇṭha interprets this to mean that they produce fruits only for the man who honours them. Honouring them consists in using them as scripture prescribes.

72 An adept is a particular type of initiate who devotes his life to acquiring supernatural powers and pleasures rather than aiming just for liberation. Rāmakaṇṭha appears to adduce, as an example, Kaula practitioners and the like, who lack all the prescribed circumstances, because they involve sexual congress and other transgressive elements in their ritual, and yet they can achieve the intended results of their rites. It is commonly asserted that it is for power-mongering rites aimed at attaining supernatural pleasures that all the circumstances must be exactly as prescribed, but that this is not essential for salvific rites.

Garuḍa spoke:
17. If mantras are eternal, how can they assume a variety of forms, because a variety of forms entails their impermanence.
The Lord spoke:
18–19. They are granters of desires [and] are referred to as such, [because] they produce [effects] in conformity with our desires. Whatever an adept should desire, they transform themselves accordingly. And their power of knowledge does not transmute. It is the external nature of mantras that we experience [transforming itself] like [that of] an actor, O Garuḍa.
20. Just like a large chameleon that is seen in this [world] to wear many colours for some reason, so too [mantras assume many forms]. And the power [of the mantras to change] is not destructible.
21. Through [this] teaching of [Śiva, who is the one] competent authority, you must understand mantras to be as I have told you. They move about impelled by Śiva's will throughout the path [to identity to Śiva].
Garuḍa spoke:
22. A path is said to be a road. Literally this is impossible (*na*), because Śiva is all-pervasive. If we must suppose there really to be a road, then Śiva's all-pervasiveness must be unreal.
The Lord spoke:
23. The transformation of the source [i.e. of primal matter] is the cause of the bondage of souls. This seductive abundance should be left behind, since Śiva is beyond that.
24. Although he is all-pervasive, he is to be understood in this system to be just like a fire that stands above a scorched tree [though it pervades the tree as well]. He is said to be above [it], because He is pure.
25ab. Because He is superior [to all others], He is taught [using a spatial metaphor] to be higher (*paraḥ*). Even though He is all-pervasive, [the expression 'path' is used, but] it is used figuratively.
25c–27b. The principles starting from earth, [all] the places where experience is [possible] for embodied souls, together with [all] the worlds [therein] are to be purified in sequence. Thus [the soul progresses] from this place to a higher one, and from that to another, and from [that] higher one to one [still] higher, until [the soul] is absorbed into the place of Śiva (*śivasthānam*). This is dissolution into [the principle of] Śiva.
27c–28b. The soul's 'going' into dissolution is said to be imposs-

ible, because the soul (*tasya*) is all-pervasive; [but] just as copper is said to enter a state of being golden, correspondingly the soul might be said to go into a state of being Śiva, even though he is [already] there.[73]

[The rest of the sixty-four chapters of the text are omitted. They deal with the structure of the cosmos, the descent of knowledge to this earth, the performance of Śaiva rites, architecture, the behaviour and observances enjoined for different kinds of initiates, and yoga.]

Modifications to the printed text of the Kiraṇa-Tantra

Chapter 1

7a *-pariskanda-*, 8c *-sukhāvāsa-*, 14d *-vinivṛttaye*, 16c *tayodbalitasāmarthyo*, 17b as A, 18b *svārjite viniyamyate*, 23cd omit.

Chapter 2

2 omit, 3b *kiñcijjño 'sau mayoditaḥ*, 3d *sarvajño 'sau tataḥ śivaḥ*, 5b *sakālikam*, 10c *pudgalo 'py evaṃ*, 12d as A, 13a *sahajaḥ syān malo*, 14cd as B, 17c *māyotthaṃ*, 26c as A, 28a as B, 28b as B, 29c *dāhikā*, 29d *mantreṇāśu*, 30c *kṛtvā tacchaktisaṃrodhaṃ*, 33d as B, 35 omit.

Chapter 3

1c as C, 3d as C, 4a as C, 5b *tanau sthitaḥ*, 5c as C, 7b *tanuḥ kutaḥ*, 8d as C, 12cd as C, 15b *pumāṃs tadā*, 15c as C, 16c *niṣkalaṃ*, 16d as BC, 18b as BC, 18d *-dhyāsitaṃ*, 22b *devaḥ*, 22d *kalāhīna iti smṛtaḥ*, 23d *dhāraṇā*, 25c *icchānugraha-*, 26c as B, 28b *svasamaprabhuḥ*.

Chapter 4

1c as C, 6d *-nimittajam*, 8d as B, 9b as BC, 10d as C, 12ab as B, 12c *tantraiś copacitaḥ*, 14d *prerayate kṣaṇāt*, 15cd *svata eva vikāreṇa jagaty asmin vikāriṇī*, 16b *tadvikārāḥ*, 18d *savikārā kalādibhiḥ*, between 20b and 20c *yathā māyādhikā vyāpya na*

73 Any verb of motion with a noun in the accusative expressing 'the state of being X' in Sanskrit means 'to become X'. Thus 'to go to instability' would be an idiomatic way of saying 'to become unstable'. This common idiom is what is referred to in this verse justifying statements to the effect that the all-pervasive soul moves.

tatkāryagaṇo 'dhvani, 20d *sthitākṣobhyā*, between 24b and 24c *so 'sṛjad bhagavān īśaḥ śivaśaktisamanvitaḥ/ kṛtsnam māyātmakaṃ kāryaṃ śuddhāśuddhavimiśritam/ yonijām buddhibhedāṃś ca tad ekaṃ ced dvidhā katham/ dṛṣṭaṃ khadyotakādes tad viruddhaṃ caikahetukam*, 25c *samādiṣṭaṃ*, 27b *śakaṭāṅgavat*, 27c *evam etad*, 28b *cit kriyā*, 28d *prabhutvataḥ*, 29 *śāntas tadvaśād akhilam phalam*.

Chapter 5

4a *pāśacchedo*, 6a *anyatra yāty eva*, 8ab *tasmād bhākto nipātaḥ syān nipātaś cihnavācakaḥ*, between 8d and 9a *tulyatvaṃ karmaṇaḥ kālaḥ kṣīṇaṃ vā yadi vāsamam*, 9c as C, 10a *svarūpaṃ dyotayaty āśu*, 14b as AC, 15a *kālacchidram iti proktaṃ*, 18cd *yatpadmabodhe*, 20d as B, 22b *proktaḥ sūkṣmo 'tra śāsane*, 25c as A, 26a *yenāsannatamaḥ*, 30a *mandā mandatarā śaktiḥ*.

Chapter 6

1c *-kāraṇam*, 2b *phalam evaṃ*, between 4b and 4c *cidrūpānugrahaḥ proktaḥ sarvānugrāhakaḥ śivaḥ*, 9a *dīkṣayaiva na mokṣaḥ syāt*, between 9b and 9c *sarvānugrahakartṛtvād upāyās te prakīrtitāḥ*, 9c *upāyo na*, 10a *samayāṃś*, 10d *jñatvād doṣo*, 11b *dīkṣayā bhaktiyogataḥ*, 14a *pāśaviśleṣaṇārthaṃ tu*, 14d *adṛṣṭatvāt*, 16c *dūrastho mantra-*, 19b as B, between 19d and 20a *dehapāte vimokṣaḥ syāt sadyonirvāṇadāpi vā/ kāryāṇubhiḥ sadā siddhais tena te śivayojakāḥ*, 20c *bhakticihne na*, 22d *katham etad bravīhi me*, 23a *taccihnaṃ*, 23b *-vikalpanā*, 23cd *tatrasthasya kathaṃ naitat svalpenāpy anumīyate*, 25c *vibhutve khaṃ*, 26b *cicchaktis tadvaśād dhruvam*, 26cd omit.

Chapter 7

2c as BC, 2d *vinetarat*, 3b *eva tu*, 5c as AC, 6c *śaktir apy*, 8a as BC, 8d as C, 9a *tasmāt kalpyā 'ṇavas tārkṣya*, 14d *tatphalam*, 16a *tenācintyās*, 16b *mantrās tarkaparair api*, 20b as C, 20cd *tadvan na ca śakter*, 21a as A, 22cd *athādhvā kalpyate tathyaṃ vyāpakatvaṃ tadā gatam*, 24ab *vṛkṣāc chuṣkād ūrdhvaṃ*, 24c *jñeyo 'tra tadvad*, 24d as C, 26c as C, 27a *tāvad yāvac*, 28c *tadvat puṃ vyapadiśyeta*, 28d *tatstho 'pi*.

From the

BHĀGAVATA-PURĀṆA

BHĀGAVATA-PURĀṆA BOOK X

Chapter 29

Śuka spoke:

1. When He saw that on those nights the jasmine had reached its full autumn bloom, even the Lord made up His mind to take pleasure in love with the help of the mirific power of His yoga (*yogamāyām upāśritaḥ*).[1]

2. Then the lord of the stars arose, soothing the distresses of men and painting red the face of the East with his balm-giving beams, just as a [returning] lover seen from afar soothes the cares of his beloved and rubs her face with vermilion [powder] with his balm-giving hands.[2]

3. Seeing [the moon,] under whom white waterlilies thrive, reddish like fresh saffron, full-orbed, and radiant as the face of Lakṣmī, and [seeing] the forest coloured by his gentle rays, [Kṛṣṇa] sang sweetly, catching the hearts of lovely-eyed women.

4. Hearing this music that made their love grow, their minds captivated by Kṛṣṇa, the women of Vraja came to where their beloved was, their earrings swinging in their haste, unmindful of each other's exertions.

5. Some were milking and came leaving the milk in their eagerness. [Some] had set milk on [to boil] and others came without taking off the wheat cakes from the fire.

6. [Some were] serving [food] and left that. [Some were] suckling infants. Some were waiting on their husbands. Those who were eating put aside their food.

7. Some were oiling and rubbing themselves. Some were putting collyrium on their eyes. Some came to Kṛṣṇa's presence with their jewellery and clothing awry.

1 Śrīdhara uses the fact that the Lord resorts to this miracle-working power to explain away the moral awkwardness that Kṛṣṇa is described as making love to other men's wives.

2 'just as a [returning] lover soothes . . . hands' retranslates the preceding words to render the pun in the original.

8. These infatuated ones, their hearts stolen by Govinda, were not turned back [though] restrained by husbands, fathers, brothers, relatives.
9. Some Gopīs could not get out and, absorbed in their devotion to Him, with closed eyes, they meditated in their inner quarters on Kṛṣṇa.
10. [The fruits of] their evil past deeds were shaken off by the unbearable intensity of the pain of separation from their lover; [the fruits of] their good past deeds wasted away because of their bliss in the embrace of Acyuta attained in meditation.[3]
11. All their bonds were destroyed in a moment and they left their bodies made up of the [three] constitutive strands of the material world (*guṇamayam*)[4] and they reached Him, the Supreme Soul, even by thinking of [Him as] their Lover.
King Parīkṣit spoke:
12. Sage, they knew Kṛṣṇa as their greatest love, but not as brahman. How then could the continuity of the strands [of material existence] (*guṇapravāha*) cease for these women, whose minds were upon those [very] strands alone.
Śuka spoke:
13. I have told you before how [Śiśupāla], the king of Cedi attained the [ultimate] goal although he hated Kṛṣṇa (*hṛṣīkeśam*). How much more then [must it be plain that] they who love Kṛṣṇa (*adhokṣajapriyāḥ*) [attain it].
14. It was for the highest good of men, O king, that the Lord, who is unchanging, immeasurable, devoid of the strands that constitute the material world (*nirguṇasya*), and [yet] the soul of the constitutive strands (*guṇātmanaḥ*),[5] manifested himself.
15. For those who constantly direct towards Hari [feelings of] love, anger, fear, affection, oneness or devotion become absorbed in him.[6]

3 The using up of the results of *all* past action, both good and bad, is regarded as a prerequisite for liberation from mundane existence.

4 The three *guṇas* of light/goodness (*sattva*), redness/passion (*rajas*), and darkness/delusion (*tamas*) pervade the material world. They are categories adopted from the philosophical school of Sāṅkhya.

5 There are frequent such pointers to the monism in the *Bhāgavata-Purāṇa*; but they can almost invariably be explained away by commentators of other persuasions. This Vīrarāghava glosses as 'the abode of infinite wondrous qualities'.

6 The phrase *yānti tanmayatām* to a monist commentator means 'they become one with him'; but Vīrarāghava offers two other possibilities: 'They become like Him, or they become filled with knowledge of Him and are thereby released.'

16. You should not be so amazed at Kṛṣṇa, the unborn Lord, the overlord of yogīs, through whom this [universe of creatures] is released.

17. The Lord saw that these women of Vraja had come into His presence and he, the best of skilful speakers, spoke to them, confusing them with clever words.

Lord Kṛṣṇa spoke:

18. Welcome to you, fortunate ladies! What favour can I do for you? Is all well at Vraja? Tell me the reason for your coming.

19. This is the night and it is frightening, and fearsome creatures roam about in it. Go back to Vraja. Women shouldn't stay here, you slender-waisted ones.[7]

This night is mild, inhabited by gentle creatures. Don't go back to Vraja, slender-waisted ones. Women should stay here.

20. For your mothers, fathers, sons, brothers and husbands will be searching when they don't see you. Don't give your relatives cause for anxiety.

Don't worry about your relatives, for your mothers, fathers, sons, brothers and husbands will be searching without finding you.

21. You have seen the forest in flower, tinged with the rays of the full moon and made lovely by the buds on the trees, playfully quivering in the breeze from the Yamunā.

22. So go back home. Don't delay. Obey your husbands, good wives. The calves and the children are calling out. Go and milk and suckle them.

Don't go back straight away and attend to your husbands, you good wives. The calves and the children are calling out [so someone else will attend to them]. Don't go [straight off] to milk and suckle them.

23. Or perhaps you are come out of affection for me, your minds beyond your own control. If that is so, then it is natural, for all creatures delight in me.

24. Virtuous ladies, it is the supreme duty (*dharmaḥ*) of women to attend their husbands[8] without deceit and [to obey] their relatives and to feed their offspring.

7 As verse 17 implies, many of the verses that Kṛṣṇa speaks are deliberately ambiguous. I have translated some of them twice to convey this and have put each second interpretation in italics after the more obvious translation.

8 Vallabhācārya observes that 'by nature the Lord himself is the husband of all creatures', and so this verse is also ambiguous; but the *Toṣaṇīsāra* suggests that 'without deceit' (*amāyayā*) is added so that the Gopīs cannot use this sophistic argument.

25. Even if he has his vices, is unlucky and old, stupid, diseased or indigent, women who look to [future lives in better] worlds should not abandon a husband unless he is guilty of some crime that makes him forfeit caste (*apātakī*).
26. For a well-born woman adultery is an obstacle in the way of heaven; it brings scandal, is wicked, low, dangerous, and universally regarded with loathing.
27. [You should show your] devotion to me by listening [to my praises], by bringing [me] before your eyes, by meditating [on me], by proclaiming [my praises], not by being near me like this; so go back to your homes.
Śuka spoke:
28. Hearing this unwelcome speech from Govinda the Gopīs were despondent, their desires frustrated, and they fell prey to anxious care that they could not dispel.
29. They turned their faces to the ground, their full lips drying up under their sighs of pain, and stood scratching the ground with their feet, washing the saffron from their breasts with their collyrium-stained tears, burdened with a heavy sorrow, silent.
30. The impassioned Gopīs, wiping their eyes that were so full of tears that they could not see, spoke with voices choking a little with anger to their beloved Kṛṣṇa, [Kṛṣṇa] who now talked to them as though he were an enemy, [Kṛṣṇa] for whose sake they had renounced all [other] desires.
The Gopīs spoke:
31. You shouldn't say such cruel things, Lord. We have renounced all the objects of the senses and are come to your feet. Take us, don't reject us, unfathomable [Lord], just as God, the primaeval soul (*devo yathādipuruṣaḥ*), accepts those who seek liberation.
32. You know what is right (*dharma*) and you have said that it is the natural duty (*svadharmaḥ*) of women to attend on their husbands, offspring and dear ones. Let that be so for you, who are the Lord and the subject of all teaching [i.e. let our obligations to serve be directed towards you].[9] You are, as is well-known, the dearest love of all creatures, their kinsman, their [very] soul.
33. For the wise devote their love to you, O my own soul, who

9 The commentators offer various interpretations for *astv evam etad upadeśapade tvayīśe*: 'Let that be so, for you are the Lord, the basis of all teaching' or, 'That would be so if you, the Lord, were our instructor [and if we were come to hear about *dharma*].'

are at all times dear. Why bother with husbands and sons and the others, who cause [nothing but] suffering. So be pleased to favour us, bestower of favours.[10] Don't cut off our yearnings fixed so long on you, lotus-eyed Lord.

34. Our hearts, which were settled in our homes, you stole easily away, and our hands too, which were busy with housework. Our feet don't move a step from your feet. How are we to go to Vraja? And what are we to do when we get there?

35. Ah, shower a stream of the nectar of your lips upon the fire of our love, set alight by your sweet song and laughing looks. If you do not, then, our bodies consumed with the fire of the pain of separation from you, we will tread the path that your feet tread, through meditation, dear friend.

36. Lotus-eyed Lord, who are fond of the people of the forest, from the moment we touched your feet – a happiness granted rarely [even] to Lakṣmī – we have been enchanted by you and cannot bear to stand before other men.

37. Though Śrī has attained a place on your chest,[11] she, together with Tulasī, covets the dust, worshipped by your servants, of your lotus feet – [Śrī,] for the sake of a glance from whom the other gods strive. Like her we have sought the dust beneath your feet.

38. Be gracious then, destroyer of pain, to us, who have left our homes and reached your feet (*aṅghrimūlam*) eager to wait on you. Ornament among men, bestow on those whose souls are scorched with an intense passion [set ablaze] by your lovely smiles and glances [the honour of] being your slaves.

39. We have seen your face framed by the locks of your hair with the glimmer of your earrings on your cheeks and the nectar of your lips and your laughing glances and we have seen your staff-like arms that assure freedom from danger and your chest that is Lakṣmī's only true delight. Let us become your slaves.

40. Once entranced by the soft-syllabled song of your flute that is as nectar,[12] and after seeing this beauty that is the glory of the three worlds, when [even] the cows, birds, trees and [wild] beasts bristle with pleasure [at this sight and sound], what woman in all the three worlds would not stray from the path laid down by the righteous?

10 Reading *varadeśvarā in 33c.*

11 Kṛṣṇa is said to have a curl of white hair on his breast called the *śrīvatsa*. This is sometimes represented as a cruciform flower.

12 Reading *kalapadāmṛtaveṇugīta-* in 40a.

41. Plainly you were born into the world to remove the suffering of the people of Vraja[13] just as God, the primaeval soul (*devo yathādipuruṣaḥ*), [was born] to be the protector of the gods. Friend of the troubled, lay then your lotus-hand on the heated breasts and heads of these your servants.

Śuka spoke:

42. Hearing their agitated talk, the Lord among lords of *yoga* smiled compassionately and, though He delights in Himself, He delighted the Gopīs.

43. His jasmine teeth sent out bright rays with each lovely smile and, with the Gopīs gathered around Him, whose every gesture is noble, their faces blossoming under the eyes of their lover, Acyuta shone like the moon in the midst of the stars.

44. While He was being praised in song, He sang out, the leader of a throng of a hundred women, and went wandering about gracing the forest wearing His Vaijayantī garland.

45. He reached the bank of the river, where the sands were cool and made love (*reme*) to the Gopīs in the breeze fragrant with the lotuses that thrilled in the waves of the river.

46. By stretching out His arms and embracing them, playfully grabbing at their hands, locks of hair, thighs, the fastenings of their clothes at their waists, and at their breasts, by digging His nails into them, and by looks, laughter, and teasings He aroused love (*ratipatiṃ*) in the beauties of Vraja and delighted them.

47. Receiving such honour from the magnanimous Lord Kṛṣṇa the proud creatures reckoned themselves the best of all women on earth.

48. When He saw their intoxication in their great good fortune and their pride, in order to calm them, to show His divine grace to them, on that very spot Kṛṣṇa disappeared.

Thus [ends] the twenty-ninth chapter in the tenth book of the glorious *Bhāgavata-Purāṇa*.

Chapter 30

Śuka spoke:

1. When the Lord suddenly disappeared, the women of Vraja were mortified, like she-elephants not seeing the leader of the herd.

2. Their hearts had been drawn by His gait, His smiles of love

13 Reading *vrajajanārtihara-* in 41a.

and capricious glances, by His pleasing chatter and diverting games. Absorbed in Him (*tadātmikāḥ*), intoxicated, they imitated now these and now others (*tās tāḥ*) of the Lord of Lakṣmī's gestures.
3. With His gait, smiles, glances and speech the lovers took on the appearance of their beloved; they identified with Him (*tadātmikāḥ*), their playful games [were] those of Kṛṣṇa, and the women proclaimed [to each other] 'But *I* am He'.
4. Loudly singing only His praises they went in a troupe searching for Him from one [part of the] forest to another, as if they had lost their senses; and they asked the trees about a person (*puruṣam*) who, like space, is in all creatures, inside and out.
5. 'Peepal (*aśvattha*), Plakṣa, Banyan (*nyagrodha*),[14] have you perhaps seen the son of Nanda go by, stealing our hearts with His smiles of love and sidelong glances?
6. 'Perhaps you, red amaranth (*kurabaka*), Aśoka, Nāga, Punnāga, Campaka,[15] saw [Bala]rāma's younger brother go past, whose smile crushes the pride of spirited women.
7. 'Perhaps you, Tulasī, fortunate one who are favoured by the feet of Govinda? Did you see Acyuta, most dear to you, who wears [a sprig of] you thronged with bees?
8. 'Mālatī, perhaps you saw Him? Mallikā, Jātī, Yūthikā,[16] did Mādhava pass by, gladdening you with the touch of His hand?
9. 'Mango (*cūta*), Priyāla, Bread-fruit-tree (*panasa*), Asana, Kovidāra, Jambu, Arka, Bilva, Bakula, Mango (*āmra*),[17] Kadamba,

14 *Ficus religiosa* Linn., *Ficus infectoria* Roxb., and *Ficus benghalensis* Linn. These are unproblematic; but many of the botanical identifications given are by no means beyond doubt. I have drawn on Appendix 4 of G. J. Meulenbeld's *The Mādhavanidāna and its chief commentary. Chapters 1–10.* (Leiden: Brill, 1974) and his appendix to Peter Rahul Das's *Die Wissen von der Lebensspanne der Bäume – Surapālas Vṛkṣāyurveda.* (Stuttgart: Franz Steiner Verlag, 1988).

15 These are all known primarily for their blossom: *Barleria cristata* Linn., *Saraca asoka* Roxb., *Mesua ferrea* Linn., *Calophyllum inophyllum* Linn., and *Michelia campaka* Linn.

16 These are probably all varieties of jasmine: *Jasminum augustifolium* Vahl, *Jasminum zambac* (Linn.) Ait., *Jasminum grandiflorum* Linn., and *Jasminum auriculatum* Vahl.

17 According to Vallabhācārya the difference between *cūta* and *āmra* mangoes might be that the former is sweet and the latter sour, or simply that they fruit at different times. Both are generally identified with *Mangifera indica* Linn. Kadamba and Nīpa often refer to the same plant: *Anthocephalus indicus* A.Rich. The other trees from Priyāla onwards are probably: *Buchanania latifolia* Roxb., *Artocarpus integrifolia* Linn., *Pterocarpus marsupium* Roxb., *Bauhinia variegata* Linn., *Syzy-*

Nīpa and all you others who [by providing fruit] live for others and grow on the banks of the Yamunā! Tell us, who are without our soul, the way that Kṛṣṇa took.
10. 'Ah! what self-mortification did you perform, O Earth, that you are now so radiant, with all that grows on your body bristling with pleasure as it revels in the touch of Keśava's heel? [Are you radiant] because His heel touched you [just now] or because of His broad stride as Trivikrama? or is it from His embrace when He wore the form of Varāha, the boar?
11. 'Friend doe, did Acyuta come here with a lover, delighting your eyes with [the sight of] His body? The scent wafts past here of the garland of Kunda blossom[18] that the Lord of Gokula wears, tinged with saffron from the breasts of a lover He has been embracing.
12. 'Perhaps Balarāma's younger brother acknowledged your bowing, O trees, with loving looks, as He passed by over here, pursued by clouds of bees, blind with nectar-drunkenness, that cling to His Tulasī – His hand holding a lotus and resting on the shoulder of a lover?
13. 'Ask those creepers, for although they embrace the arms of a tree, surely their shoots stand on end, touched by His fingernails.'
14. Raving in this way the Gopīs became discouraged in their pursuit of Kṛṣṇa and began to imitate now these and now others (*tās tāḥ*) of the Lord's playful deeds, their minds absorbed in Him (*tadātmikāḥ*).
15. One of them, playing the part of Kṛṣṇa, sucked at the breast of another pretending to be Pūtanā. One cried, acting the part of the baby [Kṛṣṇa] and kicked over another [Gopī], who was pretending to be the cart.[19]
16. One, acting like the demon [Tṛṇāvarta] carried away another, who was acting the part of Kṛṣṇa in His childhood.

gium cuminii Linn., *Calotropis gigantia* (Linn.) R. Br. ex Ait., *Aegle marmelos* Correa and *Mimusops elengi* Linn.

18 Kunda is *Jasminum multiflorum* Andrews. The doe's eyes appear hugely distended, as though they had just seen Kṛṣṇa and had been eager to drink in as much as possible of the intoxicating sight.

19 As a baby Kṛṣṇa revealed his enormous strength by overturning a heavily laden cart when kicking his feet in his impatience to be breast-fed. The story is told in *Bhāgavata-Purāṇa* X.7:4–10.

Another crawled about on all fours dragging her feet behind her with the tinkling of anklets.
17. Two of them took the parts of Kṛṣṇa and Balarāma and others acted being cowherd boys. Another [acting the part of Kṛṣṇa] slew [in pretence] one who was playing the part of Vatsa. One among them slew one who was playing the part of Baka.
18. Just as Kṛṣṇa would call back those [cows] who had strayed far afield, one of them, imitating Him, sounded the flute and played about while others applauded her, shouting 'Well done! Well done!'
19. One [Gopī] placed her arm on another and with Kṛṣṇa in her mind (*tanmanāḥ*) said: 'Look at this graceful gait! It is I who am Kṛṣṇa.'
20. 'Don't be afraid; I am protecting you from the wind and the rain' said another, stretching out one hand and holding up her garment.[20]
21. One climbed and stood on another Gopī's head, O king, and said to her: 'Evil serpent, get away, for I have been born wielding a rod of punishment for the wicked.'[21]
22. One of them said: 'Look cowherds, there is a violent forest fire. Quickly close your eyes and I will straightaway see you to safety.'[22]
23. One Gopī bound another with a garland to a mortar,[23] and that timorous Gopī with lovely eyes closed her mouth and took her part in the acting out of [Kṛṣṇa's] fear.
24. While they had been thus asking the trees and shrubs of Vṛndāvana about Kṛṣṇa, as was described above, in one part of the forest they caught sight of the footprints of the Supreme Lord (*paramātmanaḥ*).[24]

20 In order to protect the inhabitants of Vraja from the terrible storm raised by Indra to punish them for failing to worship Him, Kṛṣṇa lifted up Mount Govardhana and held it above them. This is related in *Bhāgavata-Purāṇa* X.25.

21 This refers to the expulsion of the serpent Kāliya from a pool in the Yamunā river.

22 This refers to Kṛṣṇa's rescue of the cattle and cowherds described in *Bhāgavata-Purāṇa* X.19.

23 *Bhāgavata-Purāṇa* X.9 describes how Yaśodā tied Kṛṣṇa to a mortar to keep him out of mischief after he had broken her pot of curd and been found secretly eating butter.

24 Hardy (*Viraha-Bhakti: The early history of Kṛṣṇa devotion in South India* (Oxford University Press, 1983, p. 502, fn. 69) suggests that verses 14–23 of this chapter may have been interpolated to accord more closely with the version of the story found in the *Viṣṇu Purāṇa*. Verse 24 would indeed follow more naturally

25. 'Clearly these are the footprints of the Great Soul (*mahātmanaḥ*), the son of Nanda, for they are distinguished by the emblem of His flag, a lotus, the thunderbolt, an elephant-goad, a barley grain and the rest [of His insignia].'
26. By these footprints the women traced His path onwards step by step (*tais taiḥ*), and when they saw, closely mixed up with His prints, those of a woman, they were upset and started to talk together:
27. 'Whose footprints are these? Who walked with the son of Nanda, His forearm resting on her shoulder, like a she-elephant with a bull, [his trunk resting on her back]?
28. 'Surely Lord Hari, the Supreme Ruler, must have been propitiated by this woman (*anayā ārādhitaḥ*[25]), since Govinda did not abandon her, but was pleased with her and has led her off in secret.
29. 'Blessed is the dust, friends, from Govinda's lotus feet. Brahmā, Śiva and the goddess Lakṣmī wear it on their heads for dispelling all wrongs.
30. 'These footprints of hers drive us to distraction, since she alone is now enjoying Acyuta's lower lip in secret, after stealing it from [us] Gopīs.
31. 'Her footprints can't be seen here. The soles of her tender feet must have been sore from the grass and shoots, and her lover [must have] lifted His dearest up.

['These prints are especially deep. They were pressed down, look Gopīs! with a heavy load where Kṛṣṇa went forward[26] carrying the woman. And here he set His love down to get some flowers.]

---

upon verse 13, and the intervening verses are in a simple narrative metre (*anuṣṭubh*). Hardy's suggestion is further supported by the fact that they are not commented upon by Vijayadhvaja. See note ad 30:35.

25 The *Toṣaṇīsāra* and commentators of Eastern India claim that the use of the form *ārādhitaḥ*), 'propitiated', is intended, by allusively suggesting her name, to make plain that this special Gopī is Rādhā. Hardy (op. cit., p.503) speculates that this is possible, and that the text may avoid using the name Rādhā because neither the *Viṣṇu Purāṇa* nor Tamil poetry (which Hardy argues are sources used in the redaction of the *Bhāgavata-Purāṇa*) mention her. Rādhā and Kṛṣṇa subsequently became a joint focus of devotion for many Vaiṣṇavas. An example of fine poetry about them is the *Gītagovinda*, translated in Lee Siegel's *Sacred and profane dimensions of love in Indian traditions as exemplified in the Gītagovinda of Jayadeva* (Oxford University Press, 1978).

26 Reading *gāminaḥ* with Vīrarāghava. This verse is bracketed because it is not in the text commented on by Vallabhācārya or by Śrīdhara.

32. 'And here the lover (*preyasā*) gathered flowers for His beloved. Look at these two half-prints where He stood on tip-toe.
33. 'Now here the lover (*kāminā*) adorned His love's hair. Here He must have sat down by His dearest, weaving the flowers into her braid (*cūḍayatā*).'
34. The Lord delights in Himself, is blissful in Himself, and yet He relished the pleasures of love with her, unaffected (*akhaṇḍitaḥ*), thus showing up the poverty of lovers and the mean-heartedness of women.
Śuka spoke:
35–36. While they were thus acting out these [games of Kṛṣṇa], the Gopīs took to wandering about disconsolately.[27]

But the Gopī whom Kṛṣṇa had led off, abandoning the other women in the forest, then thought herself the best of all women. 'Leaving the pining Gopīs my love honours (*bhajate*) me.'
37. And so when they got to a [certain] part of the wood, inflated with pride she said to Keśava: 'I can't walk any further. [Pick me up and] take me wherever you wish.'
38. In reply Kṛṣṇa said to His lover (*priyām*): 'Climb on my shoulder',[28] and thereupon he disappeared and the woman was full of remorse (*anvatapyata*).
39. 'Ah! my Lord, my pleasure, my dearest, where are you? Where are you, strong-armed [Lord]? Show that you are near, friend, to me, your miserable servant.'
40. As the dejected Gopīs were tracing the path of the Lord they caught sight of their unhappy friend, distracted in her separation from her lover.
41. They heard what she related, of the honour she had received from Mādhava, and then contempt because of her mean-heartedness, and they were supremely astonished.
42. Then they went into the forest as far as the moonlight penetrated, and when they saw darkness encroaching, Hari's Gopīs drew back again.
43. Their minds His, their chatter His, their gestures His, their

27 The bracketed half-verse is commented upon by Vallabhācārya and Vijayadhaja but not by Vīrarāghava or by Śrīdhara (though it is sometimes printed in editions with his commentary). Like verse 24, it does not fit the immediately preceding context, and may be evidence of other deliberate interference made to the text.

28 As Vallabhācārya points out, this can also mean 'Climb up on your own shoulder'.

selves His (*tadātmikāḥ*), they sang only of His qualities (*tadguṇān eva*), not giving a thought to themselves or their homes.
44. Once again they came to the bank of the Yamunā, absorbed in Kṛṣṇa, and together sang of Kṛṣṇa and yearned for Him to come.

Thus [ends] the thirtieth chapter in the tenth book of the glorious *Bhāgavata-Purāṇa*.

Chapter 31

The Gopīs spoke:
1. By[29] your birth here Vraja thrives, for Lakṣmī[30] (*Indirā*) resides here uninterruptedly. Beloved [Lord, we], your [hand-maidens], are searching for you everywhere; our [very] life-breath depends on you. Look upon us![31]
2. With that look that steals the loveliness from inside a perfect lotus in full bloom on an autumn lake you are killing your slave girls that you got for free.[32] Lord of love, granter of requests, is this not murder?
3. From death by poisoned water,[33] from the snake-demon [Agha,],[34] from wind and rain and the fire of lightning,[35] from the bull[-demon Ariṣṭa], and from Vyomāsura (*vṛṣamayātmajāt*)[36] and from dangers from all quarters, bull among men, you have been our saviour time and again.

29 In this chapter the poet has striven to make the second consonant in each quarter of each Sanskrit verse the same. Within most quarter verses the initial consonant of the first and seventh syllables is also the same. This sort of rhyming is reminiscent of poetry in Tamil and other South Indian languages.

30 Lakṣmī is goddess of prosperity as well as Viṣṇu's spouse. According to Vallabhācārya, she now resides uninterruptedly in Vraja, because with so many beauties there in the company of Kṛṣṇa she is anxious lest she may not have her chance.

31 This last imperative is ambiguous and may mean 'Let us see you!'.

32 By separating the words differently Vallabhācārya interprets *te śulkadāsikāḥ* to mean 'hired for a price' and says that they were given to Kṛṣṇa by Brahmā or by Kāma, the god of love, for the introduction of love into the world.

33 This refers again to Kṛṣṇa's expulsion of the serpent Kāliya (see 30:21).

34 Thus Śrīdhara and Vīrarāghava; Vallabhācārya assumes that several demons are referred to.

35 This refers to Kṛṣṇa's lifting of Mount Govardhana.

36 Thus Śrīdhara; but this is problematic, if the narration of events is held to be chronological, because Kṛṣṇa's destruction of both these demons is not related until later in the text.

4. Indeed you are plainly not the son of the Gopī [Yaśodā]; [for] you see into the souls of all creatures. [Assuredly] Brahmā asked you, O friend, to protect all beings and you took birth in the clan of the Sātvatas.
5. Leader of the Vṛṣṇis, we have come to your feet, which provide refuge from the dangers of repeated rebirth (*saṃsāra*). Place on our heads, dearest, your lotus-hand, which grants [every] desire (*kāmadam*[37]) – [your hand,] which has taken the hand of Śrī in marriage.
6. Destroyer of the afflictions of the people of Vraja! Hero whose smile crushes the pride of your devotees! Favour us, friend, your servants. Show your lovely lotus-face to us, your women.
7. Your lotus-foot, that abode [of beauty and] of Śrī (*śrīniketanam*), that follows the cows, draws out the [fruits of] evil actions from those who prostrate themselves before you. Place it on our breasts, as you placed it on the hoods of the serpent [Kāliya,] and crush the god of love.
8. Revive us, these your swooning servants, Lord (*vīra*), with the nectar of your lips – your sweet voice that delights the wise [and] whose [every] utterance is lovely, O Lord of lotus-eyes.
9. The nectar of the stories about you is life to the weary, lauded by seers (*kavibhiḥ*), it drives out [all moral] blemishes. It is glorious, to hear it is auspicious; those people who proclaim it widely here on earth bestow great wealth.[38]
10. Your laughter, dearest, your looks of love, and your games, [just] thinking of which brings good fortune, and your secret promises, which touched our hearts, deceitful [Lord], confound our wits.
11. When you go out of Vraja, driving out the cattle, our minds, beloved, reel at the thought that your feet, Lord, lovely as lotuses, are being chafed on shoots, grass and stones.
12. And when at the close of the day you show your face, framed with dark locks, like a forest lotus, covered with the dust from the cattle, again and again, Lord (*vīra*), you reach [out and put] passion into our hearts.
13. Lord of delight (*ramaṇa*) who remove our cares, place on our breasts your peace-giving lotus-foot that grants the wishes of

37 Or, 'which instils passion'.

38 *bhūridāḥ*, 'bestowing great wealth', could, as Śrīdhara also suggests, be interpreted to mean that they must in previous births have been beneficent with their wealth to have merited the reward of being able now to celebrate the stories about Kṛṣṇa.

suppliants, that is revered by Brahmā, that ornaments the earth, and which is to be [turned to and] meditated on in times of distress.

14. Bestow on us, Lord (*vīra*), the love-enhancing, grief-destroying nectar of your lower-lip, which your sounding flute sweetly kisses – [the nectar] that makes men forget all other desires.

15. Each second seems an aeon, when you wander the forest by day and we do not see you, and when [in the evening at your return] our eyes look up at your beauteous face with its curling locks, how stupid [the creator seems,] who gave us lids over our eyes.

16. Entranced by your song, we have neglected our husbands, children, members of the household (*anvaya*), brothers and relatives, and have come, Acyuta, to you, who knew [all along] of our coming. O deceiver! Who would abandon women at night?

17. We have seen your secret signals that give rise to heartache, your laughing face, your looks of love, and your broad chest where Śrī resides. Again and again our minds reel with boundless desire.

18. Your manifestation [in the world], Kṛṣṇa (*aṅga*), should [be to] destroy completely (*alam*) the wrongs of those who live in Vraja and its forests. It is auspicious for the whole universe. Release a little of that [medicine] which destroys the ills of the hearts of us, your devotees, who yearn for you.

19. With that tender lotus foot of yours which we anxiously place gently, dearest, on our rough breasts, you go wandering about the jungle. Is it not sore from the gravel and such? Our minds, whose life you are, reel in perturbation.

Thus [ends] the thirty-first chapter in the tenth book of the glorious *Bhāgavata-Purāṇa*.

Chapter 32

Śuka spoke:

1. Thus the Gopīs loudly lamented, singing and babbling in various ways, yearning for a sight of Kṛṣṇa.

2. And Śauri (Kṛṣṇa) appeared to them, a love god for the god of love himself, incarnate[39] before their very eyes, garlanded, clothed in yellow, and with a smile on His lotus-face.

39 The god of Love is himself without a body, because it was burnt by Śiva when enraged at being struck by one of Love's arrows.

3. When they saw their love had come, the women's eyes grew large with delight, and all stood up in the same instant like the limbs of the body when the breath of life enters them.
4. One [Gopī] joyfully took Śauri's lotus-hand in her clasped hands. Another lifted on her shoulder His arm smeared with sandal.
5. Another slender [Gopī] took the chewed remains of His betel nut in her clasped hands. One, feverish [with love], pressed His lotus foot (*aṅghri*) to her breasts.
6. One, distracted with the violence of her love, knitted her brow, bit her lips, and stared at Him as though she would kill Him by onslaughts of sidelong glares.
7. Another could not be satisfied, though she drank in the nectar of the lotus of His [very] face and savoured it with unblinking eyes, like the sages (*santaḥ*) [who contemplate merely] His feet.
8. One took Him into her heart through the orifices of her eyes, shut them, and remained (*āste*) embracing Him there, all the hairs of her body on end, immersed in bliss like a yogin.
9. All were enraptured at the sight of Him, a feast for the eyes, and shook off the pain [they had suffered] from separation from Him, like people who reach the All-knowing one (*prājñam*[40]).
10. Their grief cast off, they surrounded Acyuta, and the Lord shone brightly like the [Supreme] Soul (*puruṣa*) surrounded by His powers.[41]
11–12. The immanent Lord came with them to the banks of the Yamunā (*kālindī*), where there were bees and a breeze fragrant with blossoming white jasmine (*kunda*) and coral-tree flowers – [banks that were] kindly, because the darkness of the dusk was dispelled by the clusters of rays of the autumn moon, [and] whose gentle sands had been smoothed out by the hands of waves of the dark river.

40 *prājñam* could refer to God, or to a person of wisdom, or to a state of wisdom.

41 The comparison can be variously interpreted: Śrīdhara suggests the supreme soul (*paramātmā*) surrounded by the three constituent strands of the material world (*guṇa*); a devotee equipped with knowledge (*jñāna*), vigour (*vīrya*), and strength (*bala*); or a devotee enveloped by primal matter (*prakṛti*) and other such conditions that beset the soul. Vijayadhvaja interprets the phrase to refer to Viṣṇu attended by various forms of Lakṣmī (*lakṣmīvibhūtibhiḥ*). A comparison of Kṛṣṇa with himself as the supreme godhead is perhaps most likely, because the conceit is then that he is comparable only to himself. We have seen other comparisons (e.g. X.29:41) which are probably to be interpreted as such.

13. The pain in the [Gopīs'] hearts was shaken off in the bliss of beholding Him, and they attained the summation of all their desires, just as the Vedas.[42] With their upper garments that were flecked with sandal-paste from their breasts they prepared a place for the soul's friend (*ātmabandhave*) to sit.
14. There the Lord God, who has a seat made for Him in the hearts of masters of yoga, sat down, and in this assembly of Gopīs He shone in His form that is the one focus of [true] beauty in all the three worlds.[43]
15. They honoured Him who inflamed them with love by caressing His hands and feet on their laps; they laughed, shot playful glances at Him, and their brows flickered and they praised Him, and said, a little reproachfully:
The Gopīs spoke:
16. 'Some people love in return [only] those who love them, and some, the opposite. Others love neither [those who love them nor those who do not]. Tell us truly, sir, [why is this?]'
The Lord spoke:
17. 'My friends, those who love in reciprocation are striving only for their own ends. There is no [loving] friendship (*sauhṛdam*), no moral behaviour (*dharma*) in that, merely serving one's own ends and nothing else.
18. 'People who, like parents, love those who do not [necessarily or at first] love them are full of compassion. In this there is moral behaviour (*dharma*) beyond reproach and loving friendship, my lovely-waisted ones.
19. '[Now] some people, who do not love even those who love them and still less those who do not, are people [sufficient in themselves] who delight in themselves, [or] they are people who have obtained all that they require, [or] they are ungrateful, [or] they wrong their elders.
20. 'But I do not [always visibly] love [in return] creatures even when they love me, in order that they may continue to follow me

42 Vallabhācārya says that the Vedas are intended solely to describe the qualities of the Lord and thereby they attain him. Śrīdhara's interpretation is that the scriptures in the portion pertaining to the performance of rituals are unsatisfied, because they 'do not see the Lord', but in the portion pertaining to knowledge (*jñānakāṇḍe*) – that is to say in the Upanishads, the last phase of Vedic literature – they attain their end, knowledge of God, and are thus fulfilled.

43 *trailokalakṣmyekapadam* might also be translated: 'His body which alone in all the three worlds is the place [enjoyed by] Lakṣmī.'

(*anuvṛttivṛttaye*), just as a poor man who gains wealth and loses it is then aware of nothing else, sunk in anxious thought about that [lost wealth].

21. In the same way I loved you, my women, and concealed [the fact, so that it was] beyond your knowing – [you,] who for my sake gave up this world, your traditions (*veda*) and your relatives in order to follow me. My loves, you should not be angry with me, your lover.

22. I cannot, even in the life-span of Brahmā, make return to you, whose devotion (*saṃyuj*) to me is irreproachable, for you have sundered the unwearing fetters [that bound you] to your homes. May that be your reward.

Thus [ends] the thirty-second chapter in the tenth book of the glorious *Bhāgavata-Purāṇa*.

Chapter 33

Śuka spoke:

1. The Gopīs heard these delightful words of the Lord and forgot the pain of their separation [from Him], their desires increasing at [the touch of] His body.

2. There Govinda began the game of the Rāsa dance with those jewels of women, who linked their arms together, devoted and joyful.

3–4. Kṛṣṇa set in motion the festival of the Rāsa that was made beautiful by the circles of Gopīs. The Lord of yoga entered between each pair among them and put an arm about each one's neck, [so that] each woman thought Him next to herself.[44] The sky was crowded with the hundreds of celestial chariots of the gods and their wives, who were filled with curiosity.[45]

5. Then the kettle drums sounded, showers of blossoms fell and the greatest of the celestial musicians (*gandharvapatayaḥ*) and their women sang of His spotless glory.

44 Vallabhācārya points out that Kṛṣṇa does not at this point multiply himself so that there are as many of him as there are Gopīs, but only so that there are half as many – one Kṛṣṇa in the middle of every pair. Hence, according to Vallabhācārya, it is stated that each woman knew herself to be next to Kṛṣṇa and imagined that the others were not. Furthermore, it is only in verse 20 that it is stated that Kṛṣṇa makes himself as many as the Gopīs, and it is clear that he cannot have done so before.

45 Reading *autsukyanibhṛtātmanām* in 4d.

6. A confused noise of the bangles, anklets and girdles of the women and their lovers arose in the circle of the Rāsa game.[46]
7. The Lord, the son of Devakī, shone with intense brightness among them, like a great emerald amidst golden jewels.
8. With the movements of their feet, the shaking of their arms, their smiles and flickering brows, their flexing waists, fluttering stoles, and earrings that swung at their cheeks, the women of Kṛṣṇa shone out as they sang, like streaks of lightning in a mass of cloud,[47] their faces glowing and the knots of their girdles worked loose.
9. They sang out loud with impassioned voices as they danced, thrilled at Kṛṣṇa's caresses, in love with love, so that this [whole world] was filled with their song.
10. One [Gopī] with Mukunda sang out (*unninye*) an unmixed range of notes,[48] and He was pleased and honoured her, [saying,] 'Well done! well done!' [Then] she sang out the same [in] the [rhythmic cycle called] *dhruva* and [then] too he honoured her.[49]
11. Another, exhausted by the Rāsa, put her arm around the shoulder of the Kṛṣṇa (*gadābhṛtaḥ*) who stood to her side, as her [loose] bracelets and jasmine flowers slipped down.
12. She smelt Kṛṣṇa's arm, placed across one of her shoulders, fragrant as a lotus and smeared with sandal paste, and, as the hairs of her body stood on end, ah! she kissed it.
13. [One Kṛṣṇa] gave His chewed betel nut to another, as she pressed her cheek to His – [her cheek] which was adorned with

46 Vallabhācārya says that this is music to those inside the circle and a confused noise only to those who are not devotees. They are not entitled to hear and should refrain from reading this description of the Rāsa dance.

47 Kṛṣṇa's bodies, because he is so dark, are compared to rain clouds.

48 It is not clear to me what this means. Tagare's translation (1978:1459), following a possible interpretation of Śrīdhara's commentary, has her sing out of tune with Kṛṣṇa. Vallabhācārya appears to explain that a range of notes is unmixed when produced in sequence in a way appropriate to the revealing of an aesthetic mood. Because music varies from region to region and changes fast, technical descriptions of it can quickly become unintelligible. This in part accounts for the range of interpretations offered by the commentators, none of which is satisfactory.

49 This translation follows Śrīdhara's gloss 'a rhythmic cycle called *dhruva*' (*dhruvākhyaṃ tālaviśeṣam*); but Vallabhācārya rejects this interpretation, offering no further justification than that it is not worthy of consideration. Following his commentary we should rather translate '[Another Gopī] sang out the same (*tad eva*) [singing it as] the fixed ground, and the Lord honoured her [too].'

the [reflected] glimmer of her earrings as they were tossed about in the dance.

14. One weary [Gopī] pressed to her breasts the soothing lotus-hand of the Kṛṣṇa (*Acyuta*) who stood at her side, [all the while] singing and dancing with jingling anklet and girdle[-bells].

15. The Gopīs [each] attained Acyuta, Lakṣmī's only beloved, as their lover, and they played, singing His praises with His arms around their necks.

16. The Gopīs, their garlands slipping from their hair, their faces glowing with perspiration, their cheeks [adorned] with the tips of curls of their hair and with lotus-blooms hung at their ears, danced with the Lord in the Rāsa gathering – [a gathering] in which bees were the singers accompanied by the sounds of their bangles and anklets as instruments.

17. Thus the Lord of Lakṣmī (*rameśaḥ*) played with the beauties of Vraja like a child confused with His own reflections [in a mirror], with laughter, unrestrained love-games, fond looks, caresses and embraces.

18. Their senses were in turmoil at the intense pleasure [they felt] from the touch of His body [and] the women of Vraja, whose garlands and ornaments had [already] slipped off, became incapable of setting straight their hair, their veils or their breast-cloths, O great Kuru.

19. The women [of the gods] in their chariots in the sky swooned at the sight of Kṛṣṇa's games, pained with love, and the moon with all His attendants marvelled.

20. He multiplied Himself so that there were as many of Him as of the women, and, even though He [is sufficient in and] delights in Himself, the Lord took pleasure among them in sport.

21. Compassionate, He lovingly stroked their faces with His balm-giving hand, O king (*aṅga*), when they were exhausted with this intense love-making (*ativihāreṇa*).

22. With nectarous, laughing looks, [brilliant] with the bright beauty of their cheeks, adorned with locks of their hair and their quivering golden earrings, the Gopīs honoured Him, [that] bull [among men], as they thrilled to the touch of His nails, singing of His blessed (*puṇyāṇi*) deeds.

23. In order to dispel their tiredness, He went into the water with them, pursued by the lords of celestial musicians, the bees, [that hovered] about His garland [that was now] crushed in embraces with the bodies [of the Gopīs] and tinged with [the smell of] sandal

from [the Gopīs'] breasts, just as a weary elephant bull that bursts dams[50] [plunges into the water] with his she-elephants.
24. Being thoroughly (*alam*) splashed by the laughing women in the water, and looked upon, O king, from all sides with love, and honoured by those in the celestial chariots showering blossoms, He took His pleasure [with them] here as He wished (*svayam*), playing about like an elephant bull, [though] He delights in Himself.
25. Then [after these water-games], like a rutting bull with his she-elephants, thronged by bees[51] and infatuated [Gopīs], He wandered about in the forest by the Yamunā, every corner of which savoured breezes fragrant with blossoms of the land or of the water.
26. In this way Kṛṣṇa spent all the nights that are glorious with the rays of the moon [and] in which resides the mood [of love], which is appropriate to tales told in autumn poetry – surrounded by infatuated women, true in His desires, His semen held within Himself.
The King spoke:
27. The Lord, the master of the universe, descended [merely] with a part [of himself] (*aṃśena*)[52] in order to establish moral order (*dharmasya*) and to quell the reverse.
28. How could He, the teacher, the creator, the protector of moral boundaries (*dharmasetūnām*), do this contrary thing, O Brahmin, and touch the wives of other men?
29. Why did the Lord of the Yadus, whose every desire is accomplished, do something repugnant. Cut away this doubt of mine, [O sage,] who strictly follow your observances (*suvrata*).
The venerable Śuka spoke:
30. This transgression of what is right that we learn of, and the intemperance [characteristic] of gods, does not damage those who are fiery, just [as it would not damage] an all-consuming fire.
31. Whoever is not a god should never, even in thought, do what

50 Śrīdhara takes this phrase to refer also to Kṛṣṇa because he has transgressed worldly moral laws.

51 The bees pursue Kṛṣṇa for his garland and pursue male elephants for their rutting juice.

52 The doctrine of the *Bhāgavata-Purāṇa* appears to be that Kṛṣṇa is only a partial incarnation of Viṣṇu, the supreme Godhead. Some commentators denied this, holding Kṛṣṇa to be God in his most complete and perfect form. Passages such as this formed but a small problem for these exegetes: thus Vallabhācārya explains that the Lord, when He became incarnate as Kṛṣṇa, 'descended together with a part of Himself (*aṃśena*)', i.e. with Balarāma, Kṛṣṇa's elder brother.

He did. One who does so perishes from his folly, just as anyone except Rudra [would, should he consume] the poison [churned] from the ocean [of milk].[53]
32. What gods teach is right and sometimes also what they do. A wise man should do what concords with what they teach.
33. O king, those without selfishness (*nirahaṅkāriṇām*) can gain nothing from moral conduct in this world, nor does any ill result from the reverse.
34. How much less can He who rules over all creatures, animal, human and divine, have any connection with the [results] of the good and bad [actions] of His subjects?
35. Those who delight in worshipping the dust of His lotus-feet, and sages too, who have shaken off the bondage of all past actions through the power of their yoga, can act as they please without being fettered. How [then] can the Lord (*tasya*) [Himself] suffer bondage as a result of [actions performed in] a body that He has assumed at His own wish?
36. He who dwells in the Gopīs, in their husbands, and in all creatures (*dehinām*), is the Lord that oversees (*adhyakṣa*), who assumed a body in this world [just] in play (*krīḍanena*).
37. He resorted to a human body and played these sorts of games in order to bestow grace on [all] creatures. When one hears them, one becomes devoted to Him (*tatparo bhavet*).
38. The men of Vraja were not angry with Kṛṣṇa; deluded by His mirific power (*māyā*), each supposed his wife to be by his side.
39. When dawn came, the unwilling Gopīs were given leave by Vāsudeva and went back to their homes, loved by and in love with[54] the Lord.
40. Whoever listens to or relates this [account of the] sport of the women of Vraja and of Viṣṇu with faith, attains supreme devotion to the Lord, quickly throws off passion, the disease of the heart, and soon becomes steadfast.

Thus [ends] the thirty-third chapter in the tenth book of the glorious *Bhāgavata-Purāṇa*.

53 For this myth see under Kālakūṭa in the Glossary.
54 This is a double translation of the ambiguous *-priyāḥ*.

GLOSSARY

This is not an exhaustive list of characters mentioned in the book. About some, particularly those in the Upanishads, very little or no extra information can be offered.

Acyuta A name of Viṣṇu (and therefore also of Kṛṣṇa) meaning 'not fallen, imperishable'.

Āditya A class of deities identified with the great-grandfathers that receive what is offered in the ceremonies for the Ancestors. See *Bṛhadāraṇyaka* III, ix.2–5 and *Yājñavalkya-Smṛti* 1:269.

Agha/Aghāsura Baka's and Pūtanā's younger brother, a demon who took the form of an enormous serpent. The cowherds with their cows walked into its open mouth, supposing it to be a cave, but Kṛṣṇa rescued them by entering and then stretching himself so that all the passages of its life-breath were choked. This is related in *Bhāgavata-Purāṇa* X.12.

Agni The god of fire, to whom more hymns of the *Ṛg-Veda* were addressed than to any other deity except Indra. (The name is cognate with the Latin *ignis*.)

Ajātaśatru The king of Benares in *Bṛhadāraṇyaka* II, i.

Ananta 1) A name of Viṣṇu meaning 'infinite'.

2) In the Śaiva Siddhānta the name of the chief soul to whom Śiva deputes the task of creating the lower universe (*Kiraṇa-Tantra* 3:27 and 4:1).

3) The serpent on whom Viṣṇu is said to recline at the time of resorption (*Bhagavad-Gītā* X.29).

Andhaka A demon whose name means 'blindness' and 'darkness'. He was difficult to overpower not just because of his one thousand arms but because each drop of his blood that fell to the ground sprung up into a demon. Śiva slew Andhaka after producing a fierce form of the Goddess from his right ear, called Karṇāmoṭā, who drank up Andhaka's blood.

Aṅgiras The name of a sage who composed some hymns of the *Ṛg-Veda* and of his descendants. He is also credited with authorship of a work of law (*Yājñavalkya-Smṛti* 1:4). The name is also used to refer to hymns of the *Atharva-Veda* and to a group of minor deities.

Aparārka A king of the Konkan (on the west coast, around what is today Goa) credited with a commentary on the *Yājñavalkya-Smṛti*. The commentary, which was written in the first half of the twelfth century AD,[1] quotes extensively from a huge number of other authorities. It has been suggested that it is in fact the work of a team of pundits under the king.

Ariṣṭa A bull demon which terrified Vraja and was killed by Kṛṣṇa with one of its own horns. This is related in *Bhāgavata-Purāṇa* X.36:1–16.

Arjuna Son of Indra and Kuntī. The third of the five Pāṇḍava brothers and the man with whom Kṛṣṇa converses and to whom he reveals his godhead in *Bhagavad-Gītā* XI.

Aryaman An Āditya who is the chief of the Ancestors (*Bhagavad-Gītā* X.29).

Asita Asita and Devala occur in lists of sages who were pupils of Vyāsa. Asita is sometimes said to be the father of Devala, elsewhere they appear as one person called Asitadevala (*Bhagavad-Gītā* X.13).

Aśvatthāman The son of Droṇa and a warrior who fought for the Kauravas (*Bhagavad-Gītā* I.8).

Aśvin The celestial twins. They are horsemen and the physicians of heaven, and are perhaps to be connected with Castor and Pollux.

Baka/Bakāsura A demon who assumed the form of a crane (*baka*) and swallowed Kṛṣṇa; he was finally torn apart by him. The tale is related in *Bhāgavata-Purāṇa* X.11:46–53.

Baka Dālbhya Also called Glāva Maitreya. An odd episode is related about this man's Veda recitation being interrupted by dogs in *Chāndogya* I, xii.

Balarāma Kṛṣṇa's elder brother and an incarnation of Viṣṇu.

Bharata A legendary emperor after whom India is called Bhārata. The epic *Mahābhārata* is so called because it deals with his descendants (*Bhagavad-Gītā* II.18).

Bhaṭṭa Rāmakaṇṭha See Rāmakaṇṭha.

Bhīma Son of Vāyu, the wind god, and Kuntī. The second and physically the strongest of the five Pāṇḍava brothers.

Bhīṣma Commander of the Kaurava army (*Bhagavad-Gītā* I.8).

1 Thus P. V. Kane, *History of Dharmaśāstra* (Volume I, Part II of the revised and enlarged second edition; Poona: Bhandarkar Oriental Research Institute, 1975), pp. 721–3.

Brahmā Frequently described as the lord of the gods – though so are Śiva and Viṣṇu in other contexts. His fifth head was cut off by Śiva (see *Kiraṇa-Tantra* 1:3). It is to atone for this injury to a Brahmin that Śiva smears himself with ashes from the cremation ground and wears ornaments of human bone. (The nominative (Brahmā) of the noun *brahman* is used to refer to the god, in order to distinguish him from the neuter entity brahman.)

brahman The one, self-existent, impersonal, eternal, universal soul. Variously identified, according to context, with Viṣṇu, Śiva and Brahmā.

Bṛhaspati The teacher of the gods. His name (a synonym of Brahmaṇaspati) means 'lord of brahman' (*Bhagavad-Gītā* X.24).

Cedi The region (perhaps modern Bundelkhand) over which Śiśupāla ruled.

Cekitāna An ally of the Pāṇḍavas (*Bhagavad-Gītā* I.5).

Citraratha The king of the *gandharvas*, semi-divine musicians (*Bhagavad-Gītā* X.26).

Dakṣa The father of Śiva's wife, Satī. He held a sacrifice to which he failed to invite Śiva. Śiva sent henchmen to destroy the sacrifice and Satī killed herself in shame. She was reborn as Umā, the daughter of the mountain Himālaya and again became Śiva's wife (*Kiraṇa-Tantra* 1:7).

Devakī Kṛṣṇa's mother.

Devala See Asita.

Dhṛṣṭaketu The son of Śiśupāla. He fought on the side of the Pāṇḍavas (*Bhagavad-Gītā* I.5).

Dhṛtarāṣṭra The blind king, brother of Pāṇḍu, but father to the Kauravas, the enemies of the Pāṇḍavas. His minister, Sañjaya, relates the *Bhagavad-Gītā* to him.

Draupadī Daughter of Drupada and wife of all five Pāṇḍava brothers (also called Kṛṣṇā).

Droṇa A warrior hero and teacher of both the Pāṇḍava and Kaurava princes.

Dṛptabālāki A man arrogant (*dṛpta*) about his learning, who offered to teach King Ajātaśatru, and who, realising his own ignorance, then became the king's pupil (*Bṛhadāraṇyaka* II, i.1).

Drupada Father of Dhṛṣṭadyumna, Śikhaṇḍin, and Draupadī (wife of the five Pāṇḍava brothers). Dhṛṣṭadyumna was the commander-in-chief of the Pāṇḍava forces.

Duryodhana The eldest son of Dhṛtarāṣṭra and the leader of the Kauravas against the Pāṇḍavas.

Gandharva A class of minor deities associated at first with marriage and later with music. (*Bṛhadāraṇyaka* III, vi; *Bhāgavata-Purāṇa* X.33:5.)

Gārgī Vācaknavī A woman who questioned Yājñavalkya in the *Bṛhadāraṇyaka* (III, vi and viii).

Gārgya A patronymic used to refer to Dṛptabālāki.

Garuḍa The bird on whom Viṣṇu rides (*Bhagavad-Gītā* X.30) and the questioner who learns the Śaiva Siddhānta from Śiva in the *Kiraṇa-Tantra*.

Gautama A patronymic used of Uddālaka Āruṇi (q.v.).

Gayā A city of pilgrimage in modern Bihar, north-east India.

Glāva Maitreya See Baka Dālbhya.

Gopī A cowherd woman. The term has been left untranslated, because no English rendering is satisfactory.

Govardhana A mountain in Vraja which Kṛṣṇa lifted up to protect the inhabitants from Indra's rage (*Bhāgavata-Purāṇa* X.30:20).

Govinda One of Kṛṣṇa's many names. It probably means 'chief herdsman'.

Hara One of Śiva's many names.

Hāridrumata Gautama The teacher of Satyakāma Jābāla.

Ikṣvāku The son of Manu Vaivasvata and the first king of the solar dynasty at the city of Āyodhya.

Indra The god of rain and at one time overlord of the other deities. He was superseded by Viṣṇu and Śiva after the Vedic age.

Jabālā A serving maid and the mother of Satyakāma Jābāla.

Jaivali Pravāhaṇa The man who unsettles Śvetaketu, previously confident of his education (*Bṛhadāraṇyaka* VI, ii and *Chāndogya* V, iii), and is approached as a teacher by Śvetaketu's father in *Bṛhadāraṇyaka* VI, ii.

Janaka A king of Videha, renowned for his generosity, whom Yājñavalkya instructed in Books 3 and 4 of the *Bṛhadāraṇyaka*.

Kailāsa The name of the mountain on which Śiva sits (*Kiraṇa-Tantra* 1:1). It is sometimes said to be a peak of Mount Meru, the enormous mythical mountain that stands in the middle of the earth, sometimes an independent mountain to the south of Meru. Sometimes it is identified with a site in Kashmir called Haramakuṭa, sometimes with a mountain in western Tibet.

Kālakūṭa A virulent poison that came out of the milk ocean, when the gods churned it in order to obtain ambrosia. Śiva swallowed it to save the world from destruction and it left a dark stain on his throat (*Bhāgavata-Purāṇa* X.33:31 and *Kiraṇa-Tantra* 1:4).

Kāliya A serpent demon whom Kṛṣṇa subdued, danced upon and expelled from a pool of poisoned water in the Yamunā river which he had inhabited. The tale is recounted in *Bhāgavata-Purāṇa* X.16.

Kāma The god of love, whose body Śiva burned in rage after he discovered himself struck by one of his arrows.

Kaṃsa A cousin of Kṛṣṇa's mother, Devakī, and – as it was prophesied to Kaṃsa that he would be killed by the eighth child of Devakī – Kṛṣṇa's implacable enemy.

Kapila The sage credited with having founded the philosophical school of the Sāṅkhyas (*Bhagavad-Gītā* X.26).

Karṇa The son of the sun god and Kuntī before her marriage to Pāṇḍu. He was adopted by a charioteer called Adhiratha and his wife, Rādhā. He fought on the side of the Kauravas (*Bhagavad-Gītā* I.8 and XI.26).

Kāśī The city of Vārāṇasī (Benares).

Kātyāyanī The less favoured of Yājñavalkya's wives (*Bṛhadāraṇyaka* IV, v).

Kaurava A name (derived from Kuru) for the enemies of the Pāṇḍavas.

Keśava A name of Kṛṣṇa meaning 'having abundant hair'.

Kṛpa A master of archery who fought for the Kauravas (*Bhagavad-Gītā* I.8).

Kṛṣṇa Cowherd, lover of the Gopīs, Arjuna's charioteer and interlocutor in the *Bhagavad Gītā*, and incarnation of Viṣṇu. The name means 'dark', and Kṛṣṇa is usually blue when depicted in Indian art.

Kuntī The first wife of Pāṇḍu; mother of the eldest three Pāṇḍavas and sister of Kṛṣṇa's father, Vasudeva. She is also called Pṛthā, whence is derived the matronymic Pārtha.

Kuntibhoja Foster father of Kuntī and a king on the side of the Pāṇḍavas. He had a son also named Kuntibhoja (*Bhagavad-Gītā* I.5).

Kuru The name of a tribe of north central India. Used also of the sons of Dhṛtarāṣṭra, enemies of the Pāṇḍavas.

Lakṣmī A name for the spouse of Viṣṇu, meaning 'beauty' and 'prosperity'.

Mādhava A name of Kṛṣṇa, meaning 'descendant of Madhu'.

Madhu 1) A descendant of Yadu, from whom Kṛṣṇa is in turn descended.
2) A demon born from Viṣṇu's ear-wax.

Maitreyī Yājñavalkya's favourite wife (*Bṛhadāraṇyaka* II, iv and IV, v).

Manu The name given to (four, seven, or fourteen) mythical progenitors and rulers of the human race. The first, Manu Svāyambhuva, is said to be the author of the law book of Manu, referred to in 1:4 of the 'Law Book of Yājñavalkya'. Manu Vaivasvata (the seventh Manu, according to the law book of Manu), is the progenitor of the solar dynasty of Āyodhya (*Bhagavad-Gītā* IV.1).

Marīci One of the mind-born sons of Brahmā. It is not clear why he is classed among the Maruts in *Bhagavad-Gītā* X.21.

Marut A group of storm gods closely associated with lightning (*Ṛg-Veda* II, xxxiii).

Mātariśvan In the *Ṛg-Veda* he is said to have brought fire to earth. He later became identified with the wind god (*Atharva-Veda* X, vii.4).

Mithilā The capital of King Janaka of Videha in north-eastern India.

Naciketas The man who conversed with Yama, the god of death, in the *Kaṭha Upanishad*.

Nakula The fourth of the Pāṇḍava brothers and twin brother to Sahadeva. Both were born of Mādrī, Pāṇḍu's second wife, and the celestial twins, the Aśvins.

Nanda Kṛṣṇa's father by adoption.

Nārada A sage who often serves as a messenger between gods and men and who is credited with the invention of the stringed instrument called the vīṇā (*Bhagavad-Gītā* X.13).

Pañcāla The name of a people and of their country in north India.

Pāṇḍava A patronymic used of the five 'brothers' Yudhiṣṭhira, Arjuna, Bhīma, Nakula and Sahadeva. (See Pāṇḍu.)

Pāṇḍu The brother of Dhṛtarāṣṭra and referred to as the father of the five Pāṇḍavas, because he was the husband of their mothers, Kuntī and Mādrī.

Parīkṣit The son of Abhimanyu and father of Janamejaya and the king who, in the frame story of the *Bhāgavata-Purāṇa*, withdraws from the world to prepare for death and meets and questions the sage Śuka.

Prahlāda The king of the demons and son of the demon Hiraṇyakaśyipu whom Viṣṇu killed (*Bhagavad-Gītā* X.30).

Prajāpati A creator god in the late Vedic hymns (*Ṛg-Veda* X, cxxi). Later the name (which means 'lord of offspring') came to be used as an epithet of Viṣṇu, Śiva and other progenitors.

Pravāhaṇa Jaivali See Jaivali Pravāhaṇa.

Pṛthā See Kuntī.

Purujit Son of Kuntibhoja (and brother of another Kuntibhoja) and a warrior on the side of the Pāṇḍavas (*Bhagavad-Gītā* I.5).

Pūṣan A god associated with paths; he guides men and flocks and bestows prosperity (*Īśā Upanishad* 18).

Pūtanā A demoness employed by Kaṃsa to kill Kṛṣṇa. She killed many babies by suckling them with poisoned milk, but the infant

Kṛṣṇa sucked her to death. The tale is recounted in *Bhāgavata-Purāṇa* X.6.

Rādhā Kṛṣṇa's favourite Gopī in some later devotional literature. It is conceivable that an allusion is made to her name in *Bhāgavata-Purāṇa* X.30.28, where the other Gopīs speculate about a woman whose footprints are mixed up with those of Kṛṣṇa. (The name is also sometimes used to refer to Lakṣmī.)

Rāma The hero of the second Sanskrit epic, the *Rāmāyaṇa*, and regarded as an incarnation of Viṣṇu.

Rāmakaṇṭha (*c.* 1050–1100 AD.) The author of the earliest extant commentary on the *Kiraṇa-Tantra* and of other influential commentaries on tantras of the Śaiva Siddhānta.

Rāvaṇa A ten-headed demon who was crushed under Śiva's big toe because he shook Mount Kailāsa while Śiva and Umā were sitting on it. (*Kiraṇa-Tantra* 1:6).

Rudra 1) The Vedic name for Śiva, commonly derived from the root *rud* ('to weep').
2) A class of deities identified with the grandfathers that receive offerings in the ceremonies for the Ancestors (*Bṛhadāraṇyaka* III, ix.2–5 and *Yājñavalkya-Smṛti* 1:269).

Sādhya A class of minor Vedic deities (*Bhagavad-Gītā* XI.22).

Sahadeva The fifth of the Pāṇḍava brothers and twin to Nakula (q.v.).

Sanatkumāra One of the mind-born sons of Brahmā. He is sometimes identified with Skanda (*Chāndogya* VII, xxvi).

Sañjaya The minister of the blind king of the Kauravas, Dhṛtarāṣṭra. Sañjaya narrated the war between the Kauravas and the Pāṇḍavas to the king.

Śaṅkara (fl. 700 AD) The best-known exponent of Advaita Vedānta, the orthodox school of exegesis which grounded its monist view of the world as identical with the one brahman upon the Upanishads. It considered the diversity of the empirical world to be a cosmic illusion.

Sātvata A descendant of Yadu, from whom Kṛṣṇa is in turn descended. The name is therefore applied to Kṛṣṇa, to those of his lineage, and to his devotees.

Satyakāma Jābāla The son of a serving maid called Jabālā. He did not know who his father was, but, because he admitted this honestly, Hāridrumata Gautama accepted him as a student (*Chāndogya* IV, iv). He became the teacher of Upakosala Kāmalāyana (*Chāndogya* IV, x). His opinion is mentioned in *Bṛhadāraṇyaka* IV, i.6.

Sātyaki A patronymic used to refer to the warrior Yuyudhāna (*Bhagavad-Gītā* I.17).

Śauri A name of Kṛṣṇa meaning 'grandson of Śūra'. Śūra was the father of Vasudeva, Kṛṣṇa's natural father.

Savitṛ A Vedic solar deity (*Ṛg-Veda* III, lxii.10, *Atharva-Veda* X, viii.5).

Śibi The name of a kingdom, its people, and of its kings (*Bhagavad-Gītā* I.5).

Śikhaṇḍin Born as a female child to Drupada, she was changed into a man and fought for the Pāṇḍavas (*Bhagavad-Gītā* I.17).

Siṃharāja Author of a poorly transmitted, undated commentary on the *Kiraṇa-Tantra*.

Śiśupāla The king of Cedi, who insulted Kṛṣṇa on the occasion of the Rājasūya sacrifice of Yudhiṣṭhira and was decapitated by Kṛṣṇa's discus (*Bhāgavata-Purāṇa* X.74).

Śiva Originally a euphemistic epithet, 'mild' (*Śvetāśvatara* IV. 14–18), and later the most common name for the marginal Vedic deity, Rudra, who became the focal deity both of certain monotheistic cults such as the Śaiva Siddhānta and of devotion outside them.

Skanda Second son of Śiva and the god of war (*Bhagavad-Gītā* X.24, *Chāndogya* VII, xxvi).

Somadatta Father of Bhūriśravas, a prince who fought for the Kauravas (*Bhagavad-Gītā* I.8).

Śrī A name for the spouse of Viṣṇu meaning 'beauty'.

Śrīdhara (fourteenth century AD.) The author of the *Bhāvārthadīpikā*, the most celebrated of the commentaries on the *Bhāgavata-Purāṇa*. He was a monist, but his commentary primarily discusses the literal meaning of the verses and – unlike that of Vallabhācārya – lacks lengthy theological discussion.

Subhadrā Kṛṣṇa's sister and a wife of Arjuna (*Bhagavad-Gītā* I.6).

Śuka A son of Vyāsa and the sage who related the bulk of the *Bhāgavata-Purāṇa* to King Parīkṣit.

Śveta A sage and devotee of Śiva who died and was restored to life. *Kiraṇa-Tantra* 1:8 implies that this was by the grace of Śiva.

Śvetaketu Āruṇeya A seeker of knowledge and the son of Uddālaka Āruṇi (*Bṛhadāraṇyaka* VI, ii, *Chāndogya* VI).

Trivikrama A name for Viṣṇu in his incarnation as a dwarf; he appeared before the overweening demon, Bali, and asked to be given as much land as he could cover in three strides. He expanded with each step and thus covered the entire universe.

Tṛṇāvarta A demon, sent by Kaṃsa, who took the form of a whirlwind and carried the infant Kṛṣṇa off into the sky to kill him. Kṛṣṇa made himself as heavy as a mountain and throttled Tṛṇāvarta (*Bhāgavata-Purāṇa* X.7:20–32).

Tryambakaśambhu The author of an undated commentary on the *Kiraṇa-Tantra*.

Tulasī The plant *Ocimum sanctum* Linn., sacred to Viṣṇu.

Uddālaka Āruṇi The son of Aruṇa of the family of Gautama. One of Yājñavalkya's questioners in the *Bṛhadāraṇyaka* (III, vii) and the father of Śvetaketu Āruṇeya.

Umā Śiva's spouse and the daughter of the mountain Himālaya.

Upakosala Kāmalāyana A pupil of Satyakāma Jābāla (*Chāndogya* IV, x–xv).

Upamanyu An ascetic who stood on tiptoe for 1,000 years, ate only fruit for 100 years, then only fallen leaves, then only water, and, for a further 100 years, only wind. After this he received a theophany from Śiva. (*Kiraṇa-Tantra* 1:9).

Uśan The father of Naciketas (*Kaṭha* I.1).

Uśanas A sage credited with the authorship of a treatise on moral duty (*Bhagavad-Gītā* X.37 and *Yājñavalkya-Smṛti* 1:4).

Uṣasti Cākrāyaṇa A beggar and one of Yājñavalkya's questioners in *Bṛhadāraṇyaka* III, iv.

Vallabhācārya (1479–1531 AD) The founder of the devotional Vallabha Sampradāya and author of the *Subodhinī* 'that which makes easy to understand', one of the fullest, sweetest, most inventive of the commentaries on the *Bhāgavata-Purāṇa*, and therefore also one of the most distortive.

Varāha Viṣṇu's incarnation as a boar, in whose bristles sages took refuge, he raised up the goddess Earth on his tusks to rescue her when she was submerged in the ocean (*Bhāgavata-Purāṇa* X.30:10).

Varuṇa (cognate with Greek *ouranos*) The god of the ocean, associated in Vedic times with the sky and with truth and moral order (*ṛta*). (*Ṛg-Veda* I, xxiv, *Bhagavad-Gītā* X.29.)

Vasu A class of deities identified with the fathers who receive ceremonial offerings for the Ancestors (*Bṛhadāraṇyaka* III, ix.2–5, *Yājñavalkya-Smṛti* 1:269).

Vasudeva Kṛṣṇa's real, rather than adoptive, father and the brother of Kuntī. Kṛṣṇa is often called by the patronymic Vāsudeva.

Vāsuki When the gods and the asuras churned the ocean of milk (see Kālakūṭa) they used a mountain as a churning stick; they twisted the serpent Vāsuki around the mountain, pulling him back and forth to make the mountain turn (*Bhagavad-Gītā* X.28).

Vatsa/Vatsāsura A demon who took the form of a calf (*vatsa*) and was killed by Kṛṣṇa. (*Bhāgavata-Purāṇa* X.11:41–5).

Vāyu The god of wind.

Videha The name of a place and people ruled by King Janaka.

Vijayadhvaja The author of the *Padaratnāvalī*, a fifteenth-century dualist commentary on the *Bhāgavata-Purāṇa*.

Vijñāneśvara (early twelfth century AD) The author of a commentary on the 'Law Book of Yājñavalkya' called the *Mitākṣarā* ('of measured syllables'). This succinct commentary was an important legal textbook throughout most of India.

Vikarṇa A son of Dhṛtarāṣṭra (*Bhagavad-Gītā* I.8).

Vīrabhadra One of the henchmen whom Śiva sent to destroy the sacrifice of Dakṣa (*Kiraṇa-Tantra* 1:7).

Virāj The first emanation from primal man (*Ṛg-Veda* X, xc.5). The word came to be a name for primal matter.

Vīrarāghavan Author of the *Bhāgavatacandrikā* ('moonlight upon the *Bhāgavata-Purāṇa*'), a fourteenth-century commentary on the *Bhāgavata-Purāṇa* of the theological school of Viśiṣṭādvaita, which holds that souls have qualified identity with the one God. Like Śrīdhara, he sticks to brief exegesis of the literal meaning of verses. Occasional glosses reveal his theological perspective.

Virāṭa A warrior who fought for the Pāṇḍavas (*Bhagavad-Gītā* I.4 and I.17).

Viṣṇu The Vedic deity with whom Rāma and Kṛṣṇa became identified. Like Śiva he became the focal deity of certain monotheistic religious systems. He was originally one of a number of solar gods, and his pacing through the universe (*Ṛg-Veda* I, civ) probably refers to the passage of the sun through the sky. The three steps of this passage were subsequently reclothed in another myth (see Trivikrama).

Viśvarūpa (perhaps early ninth century AD.)[2] The author of the *Bālakrīḍā*, ('child's play') the earliest extant commentary on the 'Law Book of Yājñavalkya'.

Vivasvat A name for the sun, the father of Manu Vaivasvata (*Bhagavad-Gītā* IV.1).

Vraja The district around Āgra and Mathurā in which Kṛṣṇa grew up.

Vṛndāvana The forest on the banks of the Yamunā, near the town of Gokula in Vraja, where Kṛṣṇa made love to the Gopīs.

2 Thus P. V. Kane, *History of Dharmaśāstra* Volume I, Part I (of the revised and enlarged second edition; Poona: Bhandarkar Oriental Research Institute, 1968), pp. 562–4.

Vṛṣṇi A descendant of Yadu, from whom Kṛṣṇa in turn is descended, hence a name for Kṛṣṇa.

Vyāsa The sage credited with compiling and arranging the Vedas, the *Mahābhārata*, the Purāṇas, etc. (*Bhagavad-Gītā* X.13).

Vyoma/Vyomāsura A demon who kidnapped many of the cowherd boys while they were playing and shut them up in a mountain cave until he was recognized and slaughtered by Kṛṣṇa. (*Bhāgavata-Purāṇa* X.37:26–33).

Yādava The descendants of Yadu, a clan to which Kṛṣṇa belonged.

Yadu The name of a king of Vraja from whom Kṛṣṇa is descended and hence used as a name for inhabitants of Vraja and for Kṛṣṇa.

Yājñavalkya The sage who, in *Bṛhadāraṇyaka* III, carried off the thousand cows offered by King Janaka as a gift to the most learned Brahmin. He is alleged to have learnt the so-called 'white' recension of the *Yajur-Veda* from the sun after he fell out with his own teacher. He is also credited with authorship of the *Yājñavalkya-Smṛti.*

Yama The god of death, with whom Naciketas conversed in the *Kaṭha Upanishad.*

Yamunā The river that flows through Vraja and through Delhi.

Yaśodā Kṛṣṇa's mother by adoption.

Yudhāmanyu A warrior on the side of the Pāṇḍavas (*Bhagavad-Gītā* I.6).

Yudhiṣṭhira The son of Dharma (a name of Yama) and Kuntī. The eldest of the five Pāṇḍava brothers.

Yuyudhāna A warrior who fought for the Pāṇḍavaṣ (*Bhagavad-Gītā* I.4).

SUGGESTIONS FOR FURTHER READING

General

A. L. Basham, *The Wonder that was India: a Survey of the Indian Subcontinent before the Coming of the Muslims* (London: Sidgwick and Jackson, 1954)

J. L. Brockington, *The Sacred Thread: Hinduism in its Continuity and Diversity* (Edinburgh University Press, 1981)

Thomas J. Hopkins, *The Hindu Religious Tradition* (California: Wadsworth, 1971)

The Vedic hymns

The most up-to-date complete translation (into German) of the hymns of the *Ṛg-Veda* remains:

Karl Friedrich Geldner, *Der Rig-veda*, 3 vols. (Harvard University Press, 1951)

An anthology of hymns translated into English is:

Wendy Doniger O'Flaherty, *The Rig Veda* (Penguin, 1982)

An anthology in Sanskrit, but with translations and informative introductions and commentaries for every hymn is:

Arthur A. Macdonell, *A Vedic Reader for Students* (Oxford University Press, 1917)

The only complete translation of the hymns of the *Atharva-Veda* remains:

W. D. Whitney and C. R. Lanman, *Atharva-Veda Saṃhitā* (Harvard University Press, 1905)

A survey of early Vedic literature is provided by:

Jan Gonda, *Vedic Literature* (Wiesbaden: Harassowitz, 1975)

The Upanishads

Other translations include:

Robert Ernest Hume, *The Thirteen Principal Upanishads translated from the Sanskrit with an Outline of the Philosophy of the Upanishads and an annotated Bibliography* (Oxford University Press, 1934)

and, with three extra Upanishads,

S. Radhakrishnan, *The Principal Upanishads edited with Introduction, Text, Translation and Notes* (London, 1953)

The following translations into French (with Sanskrit text) are to be recommended; they come with useful summaries:

Émile Senart, *Bṛhad-Āraṇyaka-Upaniṣad. Traduite et annotée* (Paris: Les Belles Lettres, 1934); and *Chāndogya-Upaniṣad. Traduite et annotée* (Paris: Les Belles Lettres, 1930)

On the Bhagavad-Gītā

There is a huge literature on this popular work. The following three translations contain substantial commentary:

Franklin Edgerton, *The Bhagavad Gītā*, 2 vols. (Harvard University Press, 1952; reprinted in one volume, Harvard University Press, 1972)
R. C. Zaehner, *The Bhagavad-Gītā with a Commentary based on the Original Sources* (Oxford University Press, 1969)
J. A. van Buitenen, *The Bhagavadgītā in the Mahābhārata* (University of Chicago Press, 1981)

The last of these contains a translation of chapters of the *Mahabharata* that precede the *Gītā* in order to set it in context.

The Law Book of Yājñavalkya

The best complete translation (with Sanskrit text and useful cross-references to the law book of Manu) is one into German:

Adolf Friedrich Stenzler, *Yājñavalkyas Gesetzbuch* (Breslau, 1849; reprinted, Osnabrück: Biblio Verlag, 1970)

There is a translation of the first section of the work with the commentary of Vijñāneśvara:

Śriśa Chandra Vidyârṇava, *Yajnavalkya Smriti with the Commentary of Vijnaneśvara called the Mitaksara and notes from the gloss of Bâlambhaṭṭa. Book 1. The Âchâra Adhyâya* (sic) (Allahabad: The Pâninî Office, 1918; reprinted, New York: AMS Press, 1974)

The following translation has other commentaries; but these are not all translated in full:

J. R. Gharpure, *Yâjñavalkya Smṛti with Mitâkṣarâ, Vîramitrodaya and* [from the legal section onwards] *Dîpakalikâ* (Bombay: The Collection of Hindu Law Texts, 1936–1942)

There are two complete translations (the first of which gives many useful references to the commentaries) of the law book of Manu, on which Yājñavalkya drew:

Georg Bühler, *The Laws of Manu* (Oxford, 1886; reprinted, New York: Dover Press, 1969)
Wendy Doniger, with Brian K. Smith, *The Laws of Manu* (Penguin, 1991)

An invaluable reference work for Hindu law is:

Pandurang Vaman Kane, *History of Dharmaśāstra*, 5 vols (Poona: Bhandarkar Oriental Research Institute, 1930–1962; parts I and II of Volume 1 were revised and republished in 1968 and 1975 respectively.

Interesting shorter surveys include:

J. Duncan M. Derrett, *Dharmaśāstra and Juridical Literature* (Wiesbaden: Harassowitz, 1973)
Robert Lingat, *The Classical Law of India. Translated from the French with Additions by J. Duncan M. Derrett* (University of California Press, 1973)

The Kiraṇa-Tantra

There are no other translations into English of this or of any other tantra of the Śaiva Siddhānta; but one has been translated into French with two commentaries:

Michel Hulin, *Mṛgendrāgama, Sections de la Doctrine et du Yoga, avec la vṛtti de Bhaṭṭanārāyaṇakaṇṭha et la dīpikā d'Aghoraśiva* (Pondicherry: Institut Français d'Indologie, 1980)
Hélène Brunner-Lachaux, *Mṛgendrāgama, Section des Rites et Section*

du Comportement avec la vṛtti de Bhaṭṭanārāyaṇakaṇṭha (Pondicherry: Institut Français d'Indologie, 1985)

For a presentation of the main tenets of Śaiva Siddhānta doctrine see the introduction to the third volume of the text and translation of this Śaiva manual of ritual:

Hélène Brunner-Lachaux, *Somaśambhupaddhati, vol. 3* (Pondicherry: Institut Français d'Indologie, 1977)

For a summary of the topics covered by those parts of the *Kiraṇa-Tantra* not translated here see:

Hélène Brunner-Lachaux, 'Analyse du Kiraṇāgama' in *Journal Asiatique* 253 (Paris, 1965) pp. 309–28.

For an analysis of ritual in the Śaiva Siddhānta see:

Richard H. Davis, *Ritual in an Oscillating Universe: Worshipping Śiva in Medieval India* (Princeton University Press, 1991)

The following article locates the Śaiva Siddhānta among other Śaiva traditions:

Alexis Sanderson, 'Śaivism and the Tantric Traditions' in Stewart Sutherland, Leslie Houlden, Peter Clarke and Friedhelm Hardy (eds) *The World's Religions* (Routledge, 1988)

The Bhāgavata-Purāṇa

The best complete translation in English is:

Ganesh Vasudeo Tagare, *The Bhāgavata Purāṇa*, 5 parts (Delhi: Motilal Banarsidass, 1976 and 1978)

The commentary of Vallabhācārya on the chapters in this anthology has been translated:

James D. Redington, *The Love Games of Kṛṣṇa* (Delhi: Motilal Banarsidass, 1983)

An account of the development of devotional literature on Kṛṣṇa including discussion of the same chapters, appears in:

Friedhelm Hardy, *Viraha Bhakti (The early history of Kṛṣṇa devotion in South India)* (Oxford University Press, 1983)

A survey of the literature of the genre of the Purāṇa is:

Ludo Rocher, *The Purāṇas* (Wiesbaden: Harassowitz, 1986)

Anthologies of translations of myths from other Purāṇas include:

Cornelia Dimmitt and J. A. B. van Buitenen, *Classical Hindu Mythology, a Reader in the Sanskrit Purāṇas* (Philadelphia: Temple University Press, 1978)

Wendy Doniger O'Flaherty, *Hindu Myths. A Sourcebook translated from the Sanskrit* (Penguin, 1975)

An eccentric but delightful and invaluable guide to who's who is:

Vettam Mani, *Purāṇic Encyclopaedia* (Delhi: Motilal Banarsidass, 1975)

Other Anthologies

An insightful, illuminating, and eminently readable anthology is:

Franklin Edgerton, *The Beginnings of Indian Philosophy: Selections from the Ṛig Veda, Atharva Veda, Upaniṣads, and Mahābhārata* (Allen and Unwin, 1965)

Of much wider scope is:

Wm. Theodore de Bary, *Sources of Indian Tradition* (Columbia University Press, 1958)

ACKNOWLEDGEMENTS

It would be impossible to construct a full list of all the people who have provided assistance in the production of this book or apportion thanks to them. But amongst those to whom I am most indebted are Jürgen Hanneder, Harunaga Isaacson and Professor Alexis Sanderson, whose thoughts, advice and criticism have been invaluable. I should also like to thank Dr Elizabeth Tucker, Professor Richard Gombrich and Dr James Benson for their support, and Professor Wezler of the University of Hamburg and Dr François Grimal of the French Institute in Pondicherry for their generosity and help in acquiring manuscripts of the *Kiraṇa-Tantra*. Jörg Gengnagel, Shunil Roy-Chaudhuri and Isabelle Onians have been especially helpful in reading, criticizing and suggesting improvements to portions of the work. Several other people have also read parts of the book or have helped in other ways. These include the Goodall family, Mr P. Anantha Krishnan, Dr Mary Heimann, Dr Godabarisha Mishra, Dr Sue Hamilton, Kate Crosby, Gerard Wales, Alex Watson, Susmita Mallick, Dr Heeraman Tiwari, Dr Paul Newton, Girindre Beeharry, Bronwen Riley, Somdev Vasudeva and Isabelle Phan.

The editor and publishers wish to thank the following for permission to use copyright material:

HarperCollins Publishers for material from Franklin Edgerton, *The Beginnings of Indian Philosophy*, George Allen & Unwin, 1965; Oxford University Press, India for material from Robert Ernest Hume, trans., *The Thirteen Principal Upanishads*, 1934; Penguin UK for material from Wendy Doniger O'Flaherty, trans., *The Rig Veda*, Penguin Classics, 1981.